# INTERNATIONAL TELECOMMUNICATIONS AND INFORMATION POLICY

EDITED BY
CHRISTOPHER H. STERLING

COMMUNICATIONS PRESS, INC.
WASHINGTON, D.C.

Grateful acknowledgment is made to International Communication Projects, Inc., for permission to reprint the series of articles by Roland S. Homet, Jr., in the *Chronicle of International Communication*, III:3 (April 1982), III:4 (May 1982), III:5 (June 1982), and III:7 (September 1982), copyright © 1982 by International Communication Projects, Inc.

ISBN 0-89461-040-6

Published by Communications Press, Inc.

Printed in the United States of America

*Library of Congress Cataloging in Publication Data:*

Main entry under title:

International telecommunications and information policy.

Consists of papers from a symposium held at George Washington University, May 1983; and, "Long-range goals in international telecommunications and information," a report of the National Telecommunications Administration published in 1983.
   1. Telecommunication  policy—United States—Congresses. 2. Telecommunication—United States—Congresses. 3. Telecommunication—International cooperation—Congresses. I. Sterling, Christopher H., 1943-    . II. Long-range goals in international telecommunications and information. 1984.
HE7781.I59 1984  384'.068  84-4306
ISBN 0-89461-040-6

# Contents

**Part Two: LONG-RANGE GOALS IN INTERNATIONAL
TELECOMMUNICATIONS AND INFORMATION: AN
OUTLINE FOR UNITED STATES POLICY (NTIA report)**

# Preface

On May 6, 1983, the Center for Telecommunications Studies of The George Washington University held a day-long symposium on issues in international telecommunications and information policy. The symposium was based on a government report issued four months earlier which outlined some of the policy options facing the United States. This book consists of proceedings of that symposium, completely edited for publication, followed by a facsimile reprint of the government report.

No symposium or published book of proceedings is the work of any single person. Our thanks, first of all, to each of the speakers represented here, both for their initial efforts at the symposium and for subsequent revisions undertaken on tight deadlines. The Center is grateful to the several providers of financial support which made the symposium possible. An initial unsolicited grant from the International Communications Association provided the all-important first step to conference preparation. It was followed by generous grants from the Tobin Foundation, the Armed Forces Communications and Electronics Association, the Benton Foundation, and the American Telephone and Telegraph Co. Without these supporters, this book would not exist.

Thanks are due as well to those crucial behind-the-scenes members of the Center's staff and others who helped us in the planning and execution of the symposium. Brent Weingardt did much of the initial symposium planning and logistical support. Stephen Thompson aided the planning and provided considerable help in preparation of the final proceedings. Veronica Ahern and Wilson Dizard, among others, provided very useful suggestions on participants. Center Associate Director Jill Kasle provided invaluable editing—as did Mary Louise Hollowell and David Dietz of Communications Press. Tamlyn Nagle and Shelley Winograd assisted in mountains of typing and registration chores, all with considerable good cheer. Numerous others in the University's Division of Continuing Education, of which the Center for Telecommunications Studies is a part, also assisted us.

Christopher H. Sterling
Director
Center for Telecommunications Studies

*Note: The brief author biography at the beginning of each presentation in Part One of the book provides data current as of the May 1983 symposium.*

*vii*

Introduction

# The United States in International Communications

Christopher H. Sterling and Stephen G. Thompson

*Christopher H. Sterling directs The George Washington University's Center for Telecommunications Studies, an interdisciplinary research facility. From 1980 to 1982 he served as a Special Assistant to FCC Commissioner Anne P. Jones. From 1970 to 1980 he was a member of Temple University's communications faculty. He is author or co-author of six previous books, and edits the monthly* Communication Booknotes.

*Stephen G. Thompson is an attorney with the FCC's Common Carrier Bureau. He holds a J.D. degree from Ohio State University and is an LL.M. candidate at The George Washington University's National Law Center. Prior to his FCC service, he served as conference assistant for the symposium on which this book is based.*

*". . . it is necessary in the interests of the United States that a national and an international policy of the United States with respect to international communications should be determined and declared . . ."*
—S. Res. 187, 78th Cong., 1st Sess. (1944)

*". . . The Government should adopt the policy of maintaining the strength of the private competitive international communications system [and] there should be a government agency charged with the responsibility for implementing this policy."*
—President's Communications Policy Board *Report* (1951), p.181

*"Substantial modifications in the present [defective] international communications industry structure and regulatory scheme may not be feasible except in the context of a consolidation that create[s] a single transmission entity."*
—President's Task Force on Communications Policy, *Final Report* (1968), p. II-49.

Early in 1983, the National Telecommunications and Information Administration (NTIA), a part of the U.S. Department of Commerce, released a report entitled *Long-Range Goals in International Telecommunications and Information: An Outline for United States Policy.* As the preceding quotes show, the issue of international telecommunications policy is not new, having been debated even before World War II, and in some detail since then. Questions about the impact of U.S.

domestic policy on international carriers, about organization of the agencies of U.S. government for regulation of international telecommunications services, about trade balance and technology flow, about matters of national security and communications—all of these have long been discussed.

Expression of the most recent congressional concern with international telecommunications is recorded in the Communications Amendments Act of 1982,[1] which contains the congressional directive to the NTIA for its *Long-Range Goals* study. In response to the congressional mandate, the head of NTIA, Bernard J. Wunder, assembled a study group of eighteen staff members and two consultants under the direction of economist Kenneth Leeson, acting chief of the Office of International Affairs.[2] The group issued a notice of inquiry, published in the *Federal Register* in November of 1982,[3] to solicit industry and other comments on questions relevant to international telecommunications policy. Forty-four respondents filed comments by January of 1983 (these comments, while not published in the report, are on file at the agency's Public Affairs office). The Leeson group completed a draft report in late January; after final changes by the NTIA's head office, the report was sent to the Hill in February of 1983. It was released in committee print form in March, but was available for only a short time before the supply was exhausted.

In the meantime, two other developments added to the group of options under consideration. The General Accounting Office (GAO), an arm of Congress, issued in March of 1983 a report entitled *FCC Needs to Monitor a Changing International Telecommunications Market.* This report examined the ability of the FCC to measure the impact of its decisions on the international telecommunications market. The report concluded that the FCC has neither the resources nor the structure to monitor the competitive impact of its decisions on the market.

The second major development was the introduction in the Senate in April of 1983 of a bill (S. 999) containing a host of provisions for reforming the regulation of international telecommunications. Two of these provisions are especially relevant: (1) deregulation of all international services except those where the commission specifically finds a need for continued regulation; and (2) creation of an Office of the Special Representative for Telecommunications and Information in the Executive Office of the President, to coordinate the formulation and implementation of international telecommunications policy. The bill, which has triggered much comment, was still in committee as this book went to press.

The NTIA effort, the GAO report, and S. 999, in conjunction with six years of intense congressional effort to rewrite parts of the baseline 1934 Communications Act, have helped to crystallize current discussion on United States needs in facing an increasingly complex international scene. To promote debate on the report and the issues it raised, The George Washington University Center for Telecommunications Studies held a symposium on May 6, 1983. This book consists of papers presented at that symposium, some of the resulting discussion, and the NTIA report.

## International Telecommunications in Modern Society

The increasing pace of technological advance in electronic communications has revolutionized both domestic and international telecommunication in the past two decades. Driven by continuing improvements in computers—especially the microelectronic or "chip" revolution—and in means of transmission, the entire scope of telecommunication is expanding at an unprecedented rate. The many resultant new uses and markets place substantial pressure on existing government and corporate structures and policies; this has brought the most recent debate about U.S. international telecommunications policy to a head. The revolution in domestic telecommunications and electronic media is not happening in a vaccuum; given the importance of American communications in the world scene, what happens here has substantial impact in the international arena. Accordingly, the NTIA report and the Symposium were designed to create a forum for debating the issues, increasing the available information, and developing policy options.

The importance of international telecommunications and information can be measured in at least three ways.[4] First, U.S. providers of telecommunications equipment and services gain by aggressive participation in world markets. Some estimates have projected an international telecommunications market of $85 billion by 1987. If U.S. providers can compete in this market, their success translates into profits and fortifies the domestic economy.

Second, international services are important for telecommunication users, especially those heavily dependent upon information. As the United States moves further into a service economy, many businesses will be increasingly dependent upon rapid, efficient worldwide information networks. The banking and finance business, for example, is dependent on current information from money markets around the world. Minor delays or disruptions in service can translate into substantial losses. In addition, as overseas operations of U.S. banks face increased competition from local foreign banks and third-country banks, efficient and economic communications becomes a competitive necessity.

Third, advances in the development of international telecommunications and information systems are related to social progress, producing improvements both in the standard of living and in the quality of life. An effective international telecommunications network can increase access to education, entertainment, and public health and safety, while helping to safeguard national security.

United States participation in international telecommunications is rooted in a domestic free-market economy and is increasingly characterized by a regulatory regime with government intervention only as a last resort in the face of market failure. Not only does the U.S. lack comprehensive telecommunications policy; we also lack unified, cohesive structure capable of generating such a policy. The existing policies have been created by default from the usually uncoordinated actions of a number of federal agencies, departments, courts, and private firms. At best, there is a loosely informal attempt at cooperation; more often than not, policy results from adversarial proceedings. As the NTIA report (see Part Two of this book) concludes, the present system is "clearly inadequate" to meet current needs. The only way to ensure consistent and effective policy is to establish a proper organizational scheme with clear responsibility for policy formulation and implementation on an ongoing basis. (See Part One, Chapters 3 and 4 of this book.)

## U.S. Policymaking Agencies and Participants

Of the domestic[5] players in this scene, certainly the best known and most visible is the Federal Communications Commission (FCC). Established by the Communications Act of 1934, the Commission is an independent regulatory agency with five commissioners appointed by the President and confirmed by the Senate. Of the eight offices and bureaus of the FCC, three account for most international activities: the Common Carrier Bureau, responsible for overseeing domestic and international telecommunication carriers; the Mass Media Bureau, responsible for electronic media; and the Office of Science and Technology, which includes a core of international technical expertise.

The statutory mission of the FCC is to make available "a rapid, efficient, nationwide, and worldwide wire and radio communication service with adequate facilities at reasonable charges . . ." In the international market, the FCC performs this role in two ways: (1) authorization of facilities and services by U.S. carriers,[6] and (2) participation in international telecommunications policymaking, although only in a "consultative" capacity. Thus, the Commission serves in a liaison role for the World Administrative Radio Conferences (WARCs) and Regional Administrative Radio Conferences (RARCs), and is represented on the consultative committees for radio (CCIR) and wireline communications (CCITT) of the International Telecommunication Union (ITU).[7] (See Part One, Chapter 2.)

The Commission's statutory mandate limits its international role. The FCC does not officially represent the United States but acts as expert support at international conferences. It is here that a significant difference arises between the United States and most foreign ministries of post, telephone and telegraph (PTTs). The PTTs are generally governmental carrier monopolies and as such can formulate policies to protect their own interests as national systems. A PTT can employ discriminatory tariffs to benefit its own network at the expense of foreign competitors and in general act to promote its national economic and social interests. The FCC, on the other hand, regulates but does not operate U.S. facilities and services—many of which are represented in U.S. delegations on their own. While the FCC has in the past considered reciprocity as a factor in denying foreign carriers operating permission in the United States, it has done so only on a limited case-by-case basis as part of its review process and could not establish such a policy as a part of international diplomatic relations.

The official U.S. representative in all international negotiations is the Department of State. In international telecommunications matters, the Department is responsible for coordinating selection of U.S. delegates to international meetings, and for establishing the U.S. objectives to be pursued at these meetings. Actual substantive preparation for any conferences, and recruitment of most conference personnel, generally comes from other entities, both public (FCC and NTIA, chiefly) and private (carriers, consultants, and users).

Of these, NTIA plays the pivotal role in coordinating administrative policymaking. As a branch of the Commerce Department, NTIA has several functions, all of which have an impact upon international telecommunications. The NTIA serves as the chief advisor to the President on telecommunications policies and helps to develop and coordinate U.S. participation in international conferences and negotiations. NTIA is directly responsible for overseeing telecommunications spectrum needs of the federal government; it also assigns radio frequencies to meet such federal needs as marine, aviation, and defense communications, and engages in planning and development of communication systems for federal agencies. Although United States participation in the WARC is formally under the jurisdiction of the State Department, participation of various government and private entities in the WARC delegation is in fact largely coordinated by the NTIA. This complex arrangement serves to diffuse actual decisionmaking even further.

Among other government players are two support arms of Congress— the Office of Technology Assessment[8] and the aforementioned GAO.

The "private" actors consist primarily of the several U.S. international carriers. Their policymaking role takes place in the various advisory committees to the CCITT and CCIR, and usually involves formulation of technical standards. AT&T participates in the CCITT and CCIR as a recognized private operating agency; at present, AT&T representatives chair three of the CCITT working groups. Other U.S. private entities include ITT World Communications, RCA Corporation, Western Union Telegraph Co., Western Union International, and Communications Satellite Corporation (COMSAT).

COMSAT's role in international telecommunications is unique, for it is a private corporation statutorily created by the Communications Satellite Act of 1962, and regulated by the FCC. In addition to participating in study groups, COMSAT's primary international responsibility is to represent the United States in the International Telecommunications Satellite Organization (INTELSAT) and the International Maritime Satellite Organization (INMARSAT).

### Telecommunications and Information Policy in Other Countries

It is from the interaction of these various governmental and private players that U.S. international telecommunications and information decisionmaking, if not actual policy, emerges. While such a system of dispersed and diffused decisionmaking may work effectively in competitive markets, it does not function nearly as effectively in the complex international arena. Since almost every other country controls its telecommunications through a PTT monopoly, the PTTs have internal structures to coordinate activities toward a predetermined goal. In addition, some countries, recognizing that a comprehensive policy towards information needs to be established, have adopted policies that attempt to integrate these concerns with telecommunications. Examples include France (which coined the term *telematique* or "telematics" to describe the new computer interface with telecommunications), Japan, and Canada, as well as collective activities by such associations as the European Community (EC).

France developed its telematique policy to control information flow. This policy emerged from two reports commissioned by the

French government. In 1978, the Nora-Minc report[9] emphasized the impact of information policy on the future of French economic, political, and social progress. In 1980, a commission on transborder data flow, chaired by Alain Madec, produced a report entitled "Economic and Legal Aspects of Transborder Data Flows."[10] Both of these reports urged a policy that would treat information as a finite commodity, enabling the state to evaluate its economic worth and thus tax its accumulation, license its storage, and regulate its transport.

While French policy focused primarily on the concept of information as a scarce vital resource, Canadian policy expressed concern about cultural sovereignty. Fearful of the erosion of its cultural autonomy, and concerned lest failure to maintain economic development of telecommunications should cause it to lose control over the lifelines of its economy, the Clyne Committee in 1979 issued a series of twenty-six specific recommendations.[11] These included provisions encouraging Canadian businesses to use Canadian broadcast and data-processing firms for their advertising and business needs as well as provisions encouraging Canadian-produced television programming. Japanese policy, as expressed by the Ministry of International Trade and Industry (MITI), has involved identifying the specific "knowledge intensive" industries and then targeting these for development.[12] Rather than starting with a given social or economic condition as a goal and then establishing criteria to reach that goal, the Japanese policy assumes that growth in these knowledge-intensive industries will act as the foundation for a strong future economy. Specific targeted sectors have included semiconductors, telecommunications equipment, computer hardware and software, and fiber optics, as well as other high-technology industries.

In addition to the policies of individual countries, telecommunications and information policy has been affected by regional groups of nations such as the EC and the OECD. The establishment of Euronet, a data communications network serving all EC members, is one example of such a consortium. In addition, the EC has been active in considering unified policies for such social issues as the protection of privacy of information in data banks and the formulation of basic economic policy.[13]

## The Need for Telecommunications Policy

As these various nations and communities implement their telecommunications policies, private U.S. telecommunications and information providers are confronted with two broad categories of problems:

(1) *barriers* to competition erected by countries seeking to discourage external (including U.S.) activity within their borders, and (2) *disincentives* to competition created by countries that place U.S. and other multinational firms at a competitive disadvantages by encouraging sheltered development of their own industries.

Barriers to competition can be of two types, either economic or noneconomic, the latter generally to further some social, political, or cultural objective. The most common economic barrier facing U.S. firms consists of tariff and pricing discrimination. Most PTTs discourage use of private leased lines for international telecommunications by tariffing them at higher rates on a usage-sensitive basis. The purpose is to increase PTT revenues and at some point encourage a switch to the PTT public network. The consequence is international service which is more expensive, less efficient, and less reliable. Technical interconnection standards may impose such an additional burden that users end up relying on the public network instead of leased lines, thus incurring the same disadvantages in cost, speed, and reliability. (See Part One, Chapter 5.)

A second economic barrier involves direct restrictions on, or denial of, participation in a nation's markets. For example, Brazil requires that its computers and communications equipment be of domestic manufacture, and Germany requires data processing to be done within the host country. These barriers can also involve limitations or denial of permission to do business. Mexico will not allow U.S. computer firms to have a controlling interest in a Mexican subsidiary, and France has in the past denied attempts by U.S. data processing and telecommunications firms to incorporate locally. Finally, a country can effectively bar a service provider by simply refusing to grant it an operating agreement, thus denying interconnection; it can also delay market entry by long and protracted procedures for obtaining such an agreement.

Perhaps the dominant *noneconomic* barriers of concern in the last twenty years have been privacy laws, particularly those protecting the privacy of information in data banks. Most European countries have enacted some form of privacy legislation and assigned some agency responsibility for enforcement of it; violations may subject the offender to fines or even imprisonment. Such laws traditionally include licensing of data banks, the imposition of time limits on storage, and controls on the manner in which the information can be disseminated. Sweden, for example, has placed limits or restrictions on the transfer of data across national boundaries without prior approval.

The United States recognizes that privacy and confidentiality of personal information in data banks is a legitimate concern and has passed legislation to protect against abuses.[14] However, while the U.S. has recognized a distinction between real and legal persons, most other countries have not. Thus, European privacy laws apply to information which concerns corporations as well as human beings; the result often creates an impediment to transborder business with the host country.

Noneconomic barriers may also be imposed for the protection of national sovereignty or the preservation of cultural autonomy. In some instances these may overlap with economic justifications, as when Japan determines that strong "knowledge intensive" industries are necessary for the future ability of the country to participate in international political affairs and economic markets of the future. In addition, some countries control information vital to the running of the country; Canada, for example, has expressed concern that processing its data abroad leaves it vulnerable to technical failures or political sabotage beyond its control. Further, some countries are concerned about erosion of their cultures through broadcasting of foreign news and entertainment. These concerns have been fueled by the development of direct broadcast satellites (DBS) which can relay information directly to an audience without any supervision or control by intermediaries.[15] While many perceive the problem of cultural autonomy as one mainly for lesser developed countries, many developed countries share this concern as well. The Clyne report, for example, expressed concern about the inability of Canadian children to identify Canadian political leaders, public figures, and folk heroes.

Some noneconomic barriers involve the flow of information which a country does not want to go beyond its borders. This may pertain to news information that depicts a country in a bad light or that conveys false impressions or even inaccuracies. It may include classified information or proprietary industrial information which a nation sees as vital to its security. (See Part One, Chapter 9.) Or it may even involve information about the resources of the country itself; many countries have objected to the remote sensing of natural resources without prior approval.

All of these various barriers create obstacles to the free flow of information, to the detriment of the U.S. While these problems may be solved through international political negotiation, there are the additional problems of *foreign* policy, involving actions of specific governments in their own countries, which create competitive disincentives for American firms. (See Part One, Chapter 1.) These have involved subsidies to their own firms, relaxation of their antitrust laws and other regulations, and tax policies favorable to innovation and the expansion of their own targeted industries. All of these place U.S. firms in a comparatively disadvantageous position in world markets.

Perhaps the best illustration of this competitive disadvantage involves foreign trade in manufactured goods. (See Part One, Chapter 7.) In 1980, the U.S. exported $3.45 billion in telecommunications equipment; by 1981 this had risen to $3.85 billion. During this same period, however, U.S. imports of telecommunications equipment rose from $6.72 billion to $8.91 billion, with virtually all of the imports coming from the Far East. Perhaps more significantly, U.S. world export share in telecommunications equipment has been continuing to decline; in the ten-year period between 1970 and 1980 the U.S. international market share dropped from 22 to 18 percent, while that of Japan rose from 12 to 23 percent.

These statistics result in part from economic barriers to market entry, such as those already mentioned. However, they also reflect a difference in the manner in which Japan and the U.S. treat their own firms. Japan has, through MITI, "targeted" the telecommunications equipment sector, through a coordinated government policy of loans, subsidies, and permissive legislation. The result has been to stimulate industrial research and development, and to unify and strengthen domestic Japanese telecommunications equipment providers. On the other hand, there has been no unified U.S. domestic policy toward U.S. telecommunications firms, and a number of uncoordinated laws and regulations concerning taxes, antitrust, and trade regulation have actually served to discourage R&D, marketing, and trade innovations. U.S. firms are thus committed to safer short-term R&D and to more conservative policies, and find themselves with decreasing shares in international telecommunications markets. (See Part One, Chapter 8.)

The lack of any clear, coordinated policy contributes to the erosion of the competitive position of U.S. firms in international telecommunications and related markets. Such foreign problems need to be pursued through domestic solutions, as well as through international bodies; in addition, bilateral negotiations may be necessary to deal with some of these problems. Approaching the solution in this manner, however, requires appropriate policymaking structures as well as substantive and comprehensive goals, both presently absent. (See Part One, Chapter 4.)

## What's Next?

This brief overview of barriers and impediments facing the U.S. demonstrates the need for change. The NTIA report is not the first to signal such a need, and indeed it may be too narrow in its examination of the problem. The report assumes, for example, that the free flow of information and free market competition are foundations of U.S. international policy; that all U.S. effort must be directed toward furthering these goals in international telecommunications and information activities. It very well may be the case that this is a legitimate premise for the formulation of substantive policy; the First Amendment, for example, is a very strong statement of U.S. dedication to the free flow of information and its aversion to censorship. (See Part I, Chapter Six.) Nonetheless, by not examining other possible foundations (e.g., enhanced regulation of U.S. international activities), the report leaves itself open to some criticism.

Nevertheless, even assuming such principles as a foundation, the report makes clear that both structural and substantive reform is imperative. Perhaps the greatest danger lies in the inaction which is so characteristic of limited government involvement in a free market economy. The present stakes are too high to accept delays and patchwork approaches; the NTIA report makes it clear that a perpetuation of the present system is clearly an unacceptable alternative. Regrettably, no solution appears imminent; although congressional hearings on S. 999 were held in May of 1983, the bill remains in committee, and the spectre of piecemeal solutions may well continue to haunt us. Thus, while the NTIA report outlines the problems much as prior reports have done, the critical question remains: "what's next?" We hope that this volume will stimulate some answers.

## NOTES

1. 97 Stat. 1087, 1099 (September 3, 1982).
2. A list of the individuals comprising the staff has been included with the report in Part II of this book.
3. 47 Fed. Reg. 49694 (November 2, 1982).
4. A useful overview of the international telecommunications environment can be found in O. Ganley & G. Ganley, *To Inform or To Control? The New Communications Networks* (New York: McGraw Hill Book Co., 1982).
5. A guide to most international players is found in Appendix C of the NTIA report, at pp. 242-265.
6. Under provision of Section 214 of the 1934 Act.
7. On the ITU and its component agencies, see G. Codding, Jr. & A. Rutkowski, *The International Telecommunication Union in a Changing World* (Dedham, Mass.: Artech House, Inc., 1982).
8. See, e.g., Office of Technology Assessment, *Radiofrequency Use and Management—Impacts from the World Administrative Radio Conference of 1979* (G.P.O. 1982).

9. S. Nora & A. Minc, *The Computerization of Society: A Report to the President of France* (Cambridge, Mass.: MIT Press, 1980).

10. Commission on Transborder Data Flows (French Government Interdepartmental Working Party), *Economic and Legal Aspects of Transborder Data Flows* (OECD Doc. DSTI/ICCP/80.26, September 1980).

11. Consultative Committee on the Implications of Telecommunications for Canadian Sovereignty, *Telecommunications and Canada* (Hull, Quebec: Canadian Government Publishing Centre, 1979).

12. See generally Ministry of Post and Telecommunications (Japan), *Report on Present State of Communications in Japan—Fiscal 1982* (The Japan Times, Ltd. 1982).

13. See, e.g., OECD, *Telecommunications—Pressures and Policies for Change* (Paris: OECD, 1983).

14. A useful synthesis of United States privacy legislation is found in NTIA, *Privacy Protection Law in the United States*, NTIA Report 82-98 (G.P.O. May, 1982); see also Privacy Protection Study Commission, *Personal Privacy in an Information Society* (G.P.O. July, 1977).

15. For a discussion of the impact of direct broadcast satellites on international telecommunications, see K. Queeney, *Direct Broadcast Satellites and the United Nations* (The Netherlands: Sijthoff & Noordhoff International Publishers, 1978).

# Part One

# International Telecommunications and Information Policy

Chapter One

# International Telecommunications in Perspective

# Veronica M. Ahern

*Veronica M. Ahern is Washington Counsel, Chadbourne, Parke, Whiteside and Wolfe. Ms. Ahern received her B.A. from Rosemont College and a law degree from Georgetown University Law Center. She was Director of the Office of International Affairs of NTIA, U.S. Department of Commerce, and represented the United States at many international organizations. Before joining NTIA, Ms. Ahern was Chief of the International and Satellite Branch of the FCC's Common Carrier Bureau.*

When I joined the FCC, the Common Carrier Bureau was called affectionately "Mystery Land." The most mysterious, arcane, and difficult corner of Mystery Land was the International Division. I am flabbergasted at how easy it was then compared to how it is now.

## Historical Perspective

First of all, at that time, in the early 1970s, you could count on one hand the number of firms providing international services. AT&T was providing voice service; there were a number of international record carriers (IRCs), three of them primary: ITT, RCA, and Western Union International; plus COMSAT.

COMSAT's role had been dictated by the Communications Satellite Act of 1962 and subsequent regulatory policy as a carrier's carrier; that is, it was not permitted to provide service directly to the public. COMSAT provided services to the carriers, which, in turn, provided service to the public. These, then, were the five: AT&T and three primary IRCs were the carriers; COMSAT was the carrier's carrier for satellite service.

Certain identifiable services were offered: (1) voice service, which was a fairly well understood and clear-cut category of service; and (2) record services, such as telex and telegram, and other services which had as their product a "hard" copy. These were provided by the international record carriers; voice service was provided by AT&T, and the distinction was fairly clearly made. It was, incidentally, a facility-based distinction and not necessarily one of regulatory policy. When we look at it now, it sometimes appears a little bit antithetical to common sense to have these restrictions rigidly enforced, but they did stem from fairly good bases at the time.

There was in that long-ago time, a relatively clearly understood reason for the Commission's activities. That reason, of course, was rate-based regulation. Under the theory of rate-base regulation, carriers made an investment and earned a return on that investment. The tariffs which they filed with the FCC were structured so as to allow them to recoup their costs and a return on investment. The FCC determined the rate of return and the rate base, that is, the total amount of investment involved.

Problems with COMSAT led to further FCC concern and action. The precise nature of COMSAT at the time was limited, as I said, to being a carrier's carrier. Because of that, they were not able to directly market their services to the public and, therefore, maintained that they needed special protection by the FCC against the service carriers which might have incentives to use submarine cables rather than satellites. It was impossible for them to increase or control satellite usage without relying on the carriers or, as it turned out, relying upon the FCC, in some way, to guarantee that the satellite system which was offered by INTELSAT would be used.

This resulted, in the early 1970s, in a facilities planning exercise and in various kinds of formulae to determine the appropriate usage between cables and satellites. Those were the two major regulatory themes that went through the FCC's International Division at the time: rate-based regulation and some type of formula to determine cable versus satellite usage.

In addition to these clear-cut themes, services, and carriers, several international institutions have long played important roles. The International Telecommunication Union (ITU) was created in order to assure that telecommunication services could be provided without undue harmful interference among the services and between the parties. As I'm sure the other speakers will mention, it is important to recognize that the ITU does not affect the sovereign rights of any nation which is a member. In reality the ITU is a group of nations voluntarily getting together, recognizing that for the common good they have to make some adjustments in their methods of operation. From a legal and political standpoint, however, they do not give up their right to operate their telecommunication systems in their national environments. Therefore, it is important to understand that the authority of the ITU is moral, not regulatory, authority.

Another institution which existed in the early 1970s and remains today is INTELSAT. INTELSAT was created in 1964 as a result of a U.S. effort, in combination with other, principally European, countries. It is a commercial organization, the purpose of which is to provide global communication satellite systems. In the early 1970s the formal agreements establishing the organization had not yet come into force.

The other important institution, which existed long before the 1970s, is the other "half of the circuit." In international telecommunications it is essential to remember that there is a *partner* on the other side with whom we share facilities and with whom the service is provided. It is infeasible to consider that a phone call between New York and London could be made without connecting in London. At least it used to be infeasible to consider that.

The providers of telecommunication services in most other countries are government-owned and -operated monopolies. They do not typically have a competitive environment. They provide all services and for the most part the philosophy upon which they are based is a philosophy of public service; that is, there are few private networks in non-U.S. countries.

It is also important to remember that it is probably true in most cases, that the revenues derived from telecommunication services in other countries are applied not only to recouping investment on telecommunication facilities, but also to other things. In many countries telecommunications revenues subsidize other public services, especially the post office.

Now, something else which was true in the 1970s is that there were specific policies at work here. The first and most obvious was *telecommunications policy*. Telecommunications policy stemmed from the 1934 Act. It was rather simple. Its purpose was to make available, insofar as possible, to all the people of the United States, a worldwide/nationwide wire and radio communication service at reasonable rates with adequate facilities. That is telecommunications policy. That is what it is all about. The FCC is, of course, the arbiter of that policy and is responsible for its implementation.

There was, of course, an additional concern—*foreign policy*. It was quite clear that if one dealt with foreign correspondents there were going to be some aspects of foreign policy involved. In addition, the fact that the provider of telecommunication services on the other side of the pond was a government agency added another layer of foreign-policy consideration.

In addition, in the early 1970s we were very much interested in the success of INTELSAT. After all, the United States was the mother of INTELSAT, and it was important for the organization to be a success and to accomplish the goals which were set in the Communications Satellite Act.

Therefore, we had two areas of foreign policy concern: the success of INTELSAT and our relations with foreign governments dealing with telecommunications. Obviously, we also had foreign policy concerns involved in the ITU, but these were not as strong as the concerns for technical compatibility.

## International Telecommunications Today

Clearly a great deal has changed in the last decade. No one really knows how many companies are now providing international telecommunication services. We know that the big five continue to exist, but others, including Western Union, are now in the marketplace.

Section 222 of the Communications Act required Western Union to divest itself of its international operations. For almost 20 years Western Union operated only domestically. [Western Union International has no corporate relationship to Western Union.] That Section has now been repealed and Western Union is once again free to provide international services.

We also know that the FCC has authorized additional carriers—or maybe they are not carriers anymore. For example, TELENET is a provider, at least in the initial authorization, of a form of international data base service; however, I don't know whether TELENET is an international carrier, because I don't know whether TELENET's international services fall under the FCC's Computer II decision. I imagine that the courts may ultimately decide whether the FCC properly extended its basic-enhanced dichotomy to the international arena.

In addition to those carriers which have been authorized and which we are aware of, of course, I am convinced there are a number of other companies in the environment which are providing international services without being authorized by the FCC, and I am not suggesting that authorization is necessary. I am not taking a legal position on it. I am simply saying it is a fact of life.

One of the ways in which they are doing it is very simple. Back in the early 1970s when everything was pretty clearly defined, AT&T, the voice carrier, was not permitted to provide record services. That distinction began to erode in the mid-1970s and has almost completely eroded now, and AT&T is able to provide a service known as "Overseas Dataphone Service."

It works like this: I hook a piece of equipment on one end of my telephone and I can hook a piece of equipment on the other end of my telephone, assuming they are technically compatible, and I can then provide a hard-copy record service using voice lines.

I once was in an office building in New York and noticed a sign on a door which said, "If you need to send anything to London, let me know." I asked what that was all about. Some people had set up a data-phone system in their office. They were connected at one end in New York and at the other in London. They were distributing, for a fee, I assume, the hard-copy record that was going over their phone line.

I found that very amusing. I wouldn't be surprised if there were other people who were providing that kind of service. I'm not sure it is a communication service. I'm not sure whether the provider is a common carrier. All I'm sure of is that things have certainly changed in the last ten years.

Nowhere have those changes been more difficult than in the case of COMSAT. COMSAT is now, according to the Authorized User decision of August 1982, pending a court-ordered stay, permitted to provide service to the public. That is, the corporation is permitted to provide basic transmission capacity. A "retail" subsidiary is permitted to provide end-to-end service. COMSAT, therefore, becomes a competitor in the direct public market.

These are major changes, when you begin to think about the impact of the introduction of ten new companies in the field. I'm sure I haven't mentioned them all.

What kinds of services are being provided? Well, in the early 1970s we had a pretty fair recognition and knowledge of what the services were. Now I'm afraid I can't tell you. I don't know what people are providing anymore. I don't know how sophisticated it is. It has become difficult even to say whether a particular service is a "communication" service.

Domestically, of course, we have pretty much figured out that enhanced services are not communication services and thus are not regulated under Title II of the 1934 Act. Enhanced services are clearly being provided internationally and, therefore, does that mean we have a new service category which we can't define? Probably yes. Do we also have value-added services? Of course.

In addition, I should point out that the Commission recently overturned its relatively ancient TAT-4 decision, now permitting the record carriers to provide voice services and AT&T to provide record services. So, again, these clear-cut definitions of service providers and the services they can provide are no longer so clear-cut.

## Coming of Competition

Everything that I've been talking about up to this point stems from the regulatory theme of common carriage. The FCC has presently an application before it from the Orion group which would propose to offer private communication satellite facilities internationally. This, too, represents a fundamental change.

Okay, where do we stand on regulation? Well, again, who knows? Insofar as the FCC is concerned, the international regulatory philosophy has been spelled out in the course of the last several years in a series of very interesting decisions. That philosophy is, "Well, competition is a better arbiter than we are. Let's leave it, insofar as we possibly can, to the marketplace."

I should add that the FCC has tried very hard to recognize that in the international arena we can't simply mandate "competition," because one can't interconnect for most services without the agreement of the foreign—usually monopoly—correspondent. So, we cannot control the degree or kind of competition which is permissible or which can be accomplished in the international environment.

The philosophy of competition also means, naturally, a diminishing of the rate-base type of regulation. In other words, competition goes hand in hand with deregulation. There has always been a suspicion that rate-base regulation might not work terribly well in the international environment, and I will tell you a story about that.

Back in the early 1970s there was a major facility acquisition for which AT&T and the carriers had applied. I was responsible for analyzing it and for determining whether it should be granted or not, and then making a recommendation to the higher-ups in the Common Carrier Bureau. I looked at the application and I came to the conclusion that it probably shouldn't be granted. I made that recommendation, and was immediately reversed. When I asked why, the answer was, "Because we'll get a rate reduction out of this."

Clearly, adding to the investment didn't mean a rate reduction. If anything, it could well have meant a rate increase, so how was it that a rate reduction was going to come from the grant of this application? Well, the answer was, "We will put a condition on the grant that rates be reduced." While it was not logical, it worked and it made sense. I have subsequently come to believe that sometimes in the international environment, the illogical turns out to be the best way of approaching things.

Another example of the problems of rate-base regulation in the international environment occurred about two or three years ago. The

FCC threw up its hands and said, "Okay. We can't decide what rate of return the international record carriers are earning. We really just cannot figure the whole thing out, so any question with regard to rates earned by international record carriers is more or less on the back burner at this point." In other words, it is very difficult to achieve and enforce rate-base regulation in the international environment (and I'm not suggesting that it is easy to do in the domestic environment). I am also reminded at this point of a speech that was made by a former common-carrier chief shortly after he left office, in which he said, "Regulation was impossible anyway."

What institutions exist now and how have they changed? Well, we have an additional international satellite provider known as INMARSAT which is structured in a manner very similar to INTELSAT and which provides maritime communication satellite services. We also have a changed INTELSAT, that is, an INTELSAT which is an almost mature international organization that provides excellent services and high quality at reasonable rates, and which has passed its period of adolescence and nurturing.

We have a changed ITU. The ITU has many more members than it did ten or fifteen years ago. Those members are interested in different things. They are interested in their national development as well as in the international provision of services. I would point out, however, that if we say that the ITU has changed, we should also remember that we have changed.

Of course, we have a changed foreign correspondent environment. Whereas it was fairly simple to say in the early 1970s that correspondents were government monopolies, we know that is not necessarily the case any longer. In almost all of our major communications partners we can see trends towards liberalization, that is, permitting some degree of competition. Clearly the U.K. is an example of a changed structure in international telecommunications. Those changes may mean something very important to us. Then again they may not. I don't know.

### Balancing Policies

We still have a telecommunications policy. It still has the same principle behind it. It still has the same arbiter, that is, the FCC. We still have foreign policy. The goal and concern of foreign policy, obviously, is to harmonize international relations and to avoid discord among nations. This goal must be achieved within the context of United States objectives. The principal arbiter of foreign policy remains the State Department, and that is a very important point to remember.

Now, it has always been true that there is some tension inherent in looking at those two policies. I will give you an example. There was a decision made by the FCC, in December of 1977 (Docket 18875) which postponed the construction of a major North Atlantic cable facility. The Commission made its decision based upon what it perceived to be telecommunications policy. The Commission retreated from that decision eight months later. It did not change its telecommunications policy findings. It did, however, consider foreign policy issues and, in fact, its decision in that matter was based upon a desire to achieve a mutually-agreed-upon plan. In other words, "let us avoid discord in this."

I would also point out that in the early 1970s facilities authorizations were used for purposes other than the acquisition of the facilities. So, too, in today's environment, facilities authorizations have been used for other purposes. Underlying much of the North Atlantic cable versus satellite controversy in 1977 and 1978 was a desire on the part of the FCC to convince foreign correspondents to interconnect with new carriers. In fact, cable was being held hostage in an attempt to force the foreign correspondents to interconnect. One of the Commissioners was very specific about this at the meeting and said, "It is tit for tat." (That's a pun.)

Now, we've had telecommunications policy at least since 1934. We have had foreign policy since 1789, and we continue to have to balance the concerns of both. I am not suggesting that one is preeminent over another, or should be at any given point in time; we simply have to consider the balance. But now something has changed, and it is very critical. There is another policy which we now have to consider: that is *industrial policy.*

Of course I was a very low-level person in the Common Carrier Bureau in the early 1970s, but I do not recall a great number of industrial policy concerns being mentioned. Today, however, such concerns are being considered, and I point to the NTIA report as evidence of that.

I can give you an example of an occasion in which the FCC undertook to make an industrial policy decision. That was in the case of the Northeast Corridor Fibre Optic Cable acquisition. In Phase II of that case, the Commission determined that acquisition of that cable should be open to the general trade, that is, the procurement would be for open bidding.

The presumption was that the lowest bidder would win the procurement. Apparently, however, the lowest bidder was not a United States company and, consequently, the FCC permitted the next-lowest bidder, a U.S. company, to win the procurement. The application went forward on those terms. Now, this is clearly an industrial policy issue and it was balanced against the telecommunications policy issue, that is, acquisition of the facility from the lowest bidder. (I am amused that the *Fortune* cover story on this particular issue was entitled "Japan Runs Into America, Inc.")

Industrial policy is something which we haven't really considered openly very much, at least up until the last couple of years. We now have to. Industrial policy is what the NTIA report is all about. It was at least in part what the recent *Washington Post* series on high tech has been about. It is what numerous white papers are all about.

* * *

In conclusion, there are two points I would like to make. First, it is clear that international telecommunications is in the midst of a transition. I don't think anyone has a good enough crystal ball to be able to tell you where it will wind up. I don't think anybody should. It is kind of fun to be in flux. In any case, since we have no choice, we must learn to discard the comfort of certainty and to enjoy not knowing what will happen next.

Secondly, I want to make the point that the three policy areas which we have identified—telecommunications policy, foreign policy, and industrial policy—are each important, and I would prefer that we consider those policy areas as substantive matters rather than as matters of turf. In other words, if one decides that international telecommunications should have as its lead agency the State Department or the Commerce Department within the executive branch, we should remember that in doing so we may be selecting the kind of policy which will be preeminent in the field.

Chapter Two

# The International Telecommunication Union and the United States: Partners or Rivals?

# Anthony Rutkowski

*Anthony Rutkowski is Staff Advisor for International Communications Issues and Technology Assessment, Office of the Chief Scientist, Office of Science and Technology, Federal Communications Commission. He is an Adjunct Professor in the Master's Program in Media Law at the New York Law School in New York City, and co-author of* The International Telecommunication Union in a Changing World.

"I think what we have here is a failure to communicate." Remember that famous line from *Cool Hand Luke?* I believe it describes a situation we have today with respect to the International Telecommunication Union and U.S. participation in its activities. The public, the press, even many of those in the Washington telecommunications community have only seen small fragments, unfortunately the most contentious and anomalous fragments. The situation is exacerbated by limited access to the meetings, which are predominantly held in Geneva, and the materials, which are only partially available at a few Advisory Committee meetings. Usually these meetings are of such an esoteric nature that much of the discussion is a little bewildering.

With a little luck, I hope to rectify some of those problems without imparting a bewildered glaze over all of your eyes. My message today is a positive one. I don't want to stray into a metaphysical argument over what is political or not. My intention is to present facts—largely a heretofore unseen overview of ITU activities and the United States' participatory process—and some possible conclusions.

I want to echo Ronnie Ahern's opening comment regarding the ITU [see Chapter One]. The Union provides an opportunity for nations' system operators and manufacturers to gather, exchange views, and agree on an extremely broad range of multilateral arrangements. That is primarily what the ITU does.

Secondarily, it also consists of a Geneva-based staff that provides a variety of useful administrative services at low cost. The great preponderance of these activities are highly regarded by all nations, including the United States. Such activities are also a key part of the global mechanisms for promoting new equipment and services and improving foreign trade opportunities.

United States participation in these activities is proficiently provided largely by the private sector. In those matters involving the government, the existing flexible mechanisms for gathering, distilling, and advocating U.S. points of view have either been very effective, or as effective as they can be in a multinational forum given the intrinsic contentiousness of a few issues. There are very few activities which can produce truly deleterious obligations, and those which may arise can be effectively avoided by the U.S.

A positive approach to the ITU seems not only warranted but necessary to future effective U.S. participation. The pro-private-sector, flexible approach needs augmentation through better information resources and the employment of permanent, analytical, and participatory staff with multidisciplinary backgrounds.

### The Scope of ITU Activities

In Figure 1 you may notice that 63 percent of all the major meeting days—the total is 712—are of the CCITT dealing with telecommunication services; 22 percent, of the CCIR dealing with radio matters, as are the 10 percent representing Administrative Radio Conferences; and only 3 percent are the Plenipotentiary and the Administrative Council. The others are almost inconsequential.

The ITU today is very different from what it was even 10 years ago. There has been a lot of focus on the changing composition of its members. There has been an even more significant evolution going on regarding the nature of its forums and, if you browse through the FCC printout that lists the infrastructure of the ITU, you may note the rather rich number of forums provided within the CCITT. It goes on for page after page after page, and these are not small forums.

Typically, the United States will send a delegation of 30 people or more composed largely, if not wholly, of private-sector people on some occasions. The product of all these forums is 10,000 pages of ITU arrangements. You may also notice that better than 50 percent of them deal with telecommunication services; 34 percent are the output of CCIR; 9 percent of them are radio regulations; and the others are the Convention and Administrative Council resolutions and telecommunication services regulations.

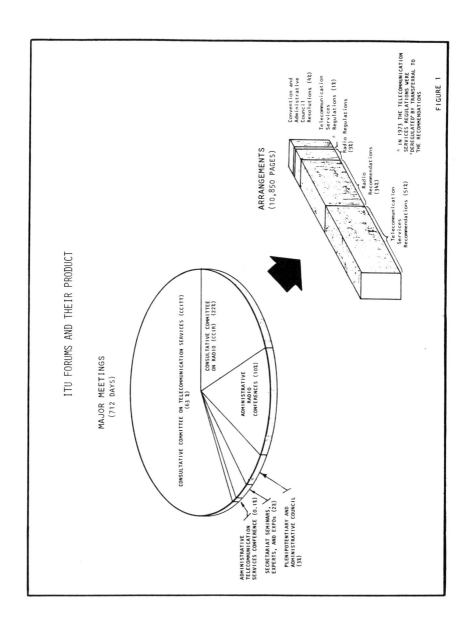

ITU FORUMS AND THEIR PRODUCT

MAJOR MEETINGS
(712 DAYS)

CONSULTATIVE COMMITTEE ON TELECOMMUNICATION SERVICES (CCITT) (63 %)

CONSULTATIVE COMMITTEE ON RADIO (CCIR) (22%)

ADMINISTRATIVE RADIO CONFERENCES (10%)

ADMINISTRATIVE TELECOMMUNICATION SERVICES CONFERENCE (0.1%)

SECRETARIAT SEMINARS, EXPERTS, AND EXPOs (2%)

PLENIPOTENTIARY AND ADMINISTRATIVE COUNCIL (3%)

ARRANGEMENTS
(10,850 PAGES)

Convention and Administrative Council Resolutions (4%)

Telecommunication Services Regulations (1%)

Radio Regulations (9%)

Radio Recommendations (34%)

Telecommunication Services Recommendations (51%)

* IN 1973 THE TELECOMMUNICATION SERVICES REGULATIONS WERE 'DEREGULATED' BY TRANSFERRAL TO THE RECOMMENDATIONS

FIGURE 1

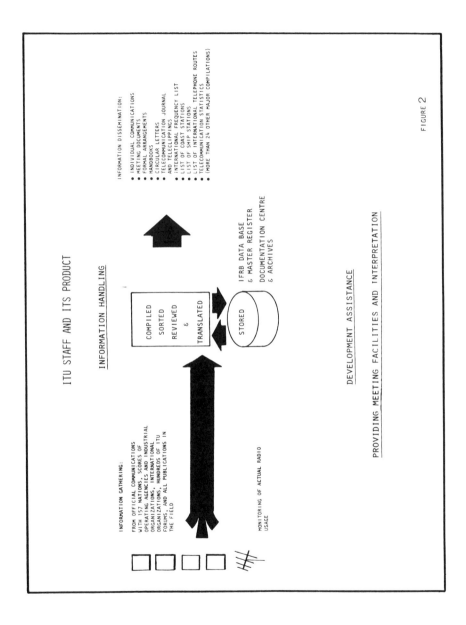

ITU STAFF AND ITS PRODUCT

INFORMATION HANDLING

INFORMATION GATHERING:

FROM OFFICIAL COMMUNICATIONS
WITH 157 NATIONS, SCORES OF
OPERATING AGENCIES AND INDUSTRIAL
ORGANIZATIONS, INTERNATIONAL
ORGANIZATIONS, HUNDREDS OF ITU
FORUMS, AND ALL PUBLICATIONS IN
THE FIELD

MONITORING OF ACTUAL RADIO
USAGE

COMPILED
SORTED
REVIEWED
&
TRANSLATED

STORED

IFRB DATA BASE
& MASTER REGISTER

DOCUMENTATION CENTRE
& ARCHIVES

INFORMATION DISSEMINATION:

• INDIVIDUAL COMMUNICATIONS
• MEETING DOCUMENTS
• FORMAL ARRANGEMENTS
• HANDBOOKS
• CIRCULAR LETTERS
• TELECOMMUNICATION JOURNAL
  AND TELECLIPPINGS
• INTERNATIONAL FREQUENCY LIST
• LIST OF COAST STATIONS
• LIST OF SHIP STATIONS
• LIST OF INTERNATIONAL TELEPHONE ROUTES
• TELECOMMUNICATION STATISTICS
• (MORE THAN 24 OTHER MAJOR COMPILATIONS)

DEVELOPMENT ASSISTANCE

PROVIDING MEETING FACILITIES AND INTERPRETATION

FIGURE 2

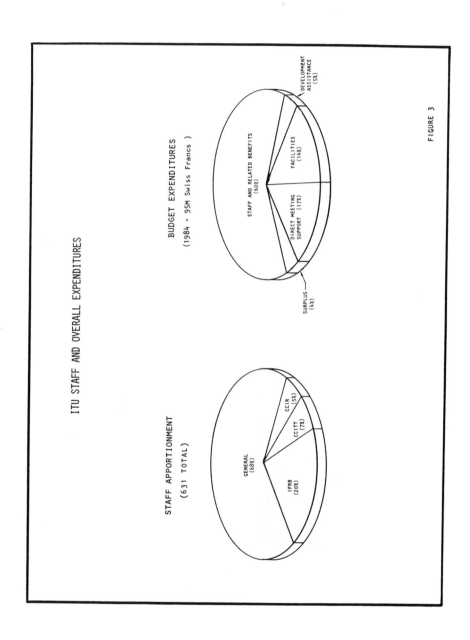

ITU STAFF AND OVERALL EXPENDITURES

STAFF APPORTIONMENT
(631 TOTAL)

GENERAL
(68%)

IFRB
(20%)

CCITT
(7%)

CCIR
(5%)

BUDGET EXPENDITURES
(1984 - 95M Swiss Francs )

STAFF AND RELATED BENEFITS
(60%)

FACILITIES
(14%)

DIRECT MEETING
SUPPORT (17%)

SURPLUS
(4%)

DEVELOPMENT
ASSISTANCE
(5%)

FIGURE 3

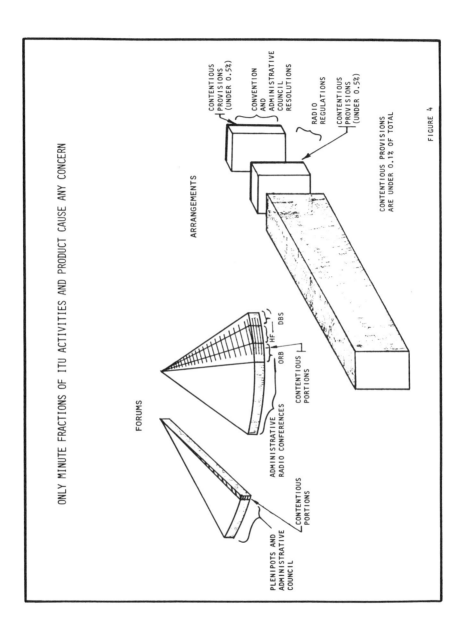

ONLY MINUTE FRACTIONS OF ITU ACTIVITIES AND PRODUCT CAUSE ANY CONCERN

FORUMS

ARRANGEMENTS

PLENIPOTS AND
ADMINISTRATIVE
COUNCIL

CONTENTIOUS
PORTIONS

ADMINISTRATIVE
RADIO CONFERENCES

CONTENTIOUS
PORTIONS

ORB

HF

DBS

CONTENTIOUS
PROVISIONS
(UNDER 0.5%)

CONVENTION
AND
ADMINISTRATIVE
COUNCIL
RESOLUTIONS

RADIO
REGULATIONS

CONTENTIOUS
PROVISIONS
(UNDER 0.5%)

CONTENTIOUS PROVISIONS
ARE UNDER 0.1% OF TOTAL

FIGURE 4

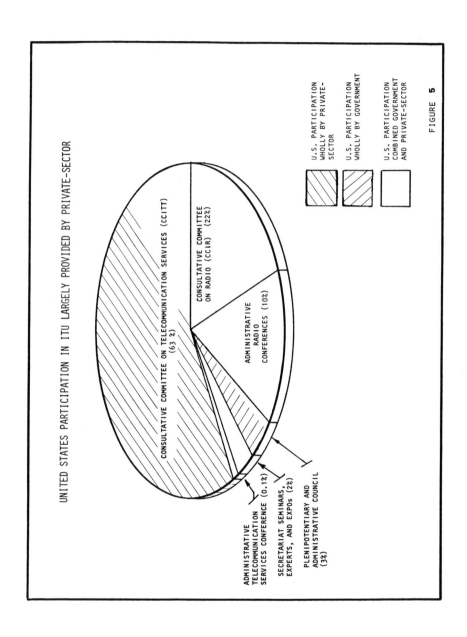

UNITED STATES PARTICIPATION IN ITU LARGELY PROVIDED BY PRIVATE-SECTOR

CONSULTATIVE COMMITTEE ON TELECOMMUNICATION SERVICES (CCITT) (63 %)

CONSULTATIVE COMMITTEE ON RADIO (CCIR) (22%)

ADMINISTRATIVE RADIO CONFERENCES (10%)

ADMINISTRATIVE TELECOMMUNICATION SERVICES CONFERENCE (0.1%)

SECRETARIAT SEMINARS, EXPERTS, AND EXPOs (2%)

PLENIPOTENTIARY AND ADMINISTRATIVE COUNCIL (3%)

U.S. PARTICIPATION WHOLLY BY PRIVATE-SECTOR

U.S. PARTICIPATION WHOLLY BY GOVERNMENT

U.S. PARTICIPATION COMBINED GOVERNMENT AND PRIVATE-SECTOR

FIGURE 5

You may note a little footnote at the bottom of Figure 1. A fundamental decision was made in 1973 by the whole telecommunication services side of the ITU house that administrative conferences were not a very good way to make international arrangements, that technology was changing too quickly. So they decided essentially to deregulate. They moved the whole body of their regulations relating to telecommunication services into their "recommendations." They exist there today and are dealt with in those forums today.

The ITU staff can largely be viewed as one big information function, and that's what Figure 2 shows. It is really rather illuminating to look at it from that perspective. By the way, ITU membership is now up to 158. It grows almost daily. I think Andorra just asked to join, so it may soon jump to 159.

The ITU Secretariat gathers a tremendous amount of information from all member nations, all national organizations, and all publications in the field, and even monitors actual radio usage (in large part, actually, with the assistance of the U.S.)

All of this goes into various kinds of data bases within the ITU where it is compiled, sorted, reviewed, and translated—all of these one big function—and regurgitated in the form of a large number of lists, bulletins, individual communications, and telexes that are extremely important to the continuing operation of telecommunication systems around the world.

They also provide some developmental assistance activities and assistance for meetings such as interpretation services, but this is a relatively minor function.

Figure 3 is an attempt to depict how the staff of 631 is apportioned. Most of those are in the General Secretariat, with a few sprinkled in the IFRB, CCITT, and CCIR Secretariats. The 1984 budget is based on a proposal of 95 million Swiss francs (about $45,100,000), and you can see most of it goes for staff purposes.

A relatively small amount, 5 percent, is proposed to go directly to development assistance. It's also worth noting, on the staff apportionment side of Figure 3, the CCITT and CCIR Secretariats. Previously the heads of those staffs, the directors, were elected by the CCITT and CCIR plenary assemblies. In the future, they will be elected by the plenipotentiary conference. This was a matter of some controversy at the recent Nairobi conference, but it can be viewed relatively benignly in the context of long-term institutional developments. Indeed, the United States made a similar proposal in 1947 and lost because of the intransigence of European PTTs.

In Figure 4, adapted from the first chart, the message is that only minute fractions of ITU activities and product cause any significant concern on the part of the U.S. or, for that matter, anyone else. What I have done is excised the Plenipotentiary and Administrative Council and the Administrative Radio Conferences portions of the pie, and note that only these are contentious. Indeed, it is only the plenary sessions of plenipotentiary conferences that give rise to some concern.

But those portions have typically, for years, been the subject of significant political controversies which go back as far as 1927, or even before. It is illuminating to read the actual source documentation from those early conferences. There was endless bickering, taking as much as the first week of some of these conferences, over such things as who would have control over what colonies and territories, because in the early days the number of votes a nation had in the ITU was a function of the number of colonies and territories that nation controlled, and they would haggle endlessly over their sovereignty over different pieces of territory.

In 1927 the USSR was not allowed to attend the Washington conference, largely for political purposes. In 1947, under a resolution by the UN General Assembly at that time, the Franco regime of Spain wasn't allowed to attend. There are a fair number of those kinds of examples occurring throughout the history of ITU Plenipotentiary Conferences.

While the situation is getting somewhat more disconcerting, the point is that it is still only a minute fragment of what's going on within the ITU. The same may be said as to what is happening in the Administrative Radio Conference area. Only a few of these conferences give rise to concern, and I think Wilson Dizard may want to amplify some of that.

Again, looking at those 10,000-some pages of arrangements, those that give rise to concern on the part of the U.S. probably occupy no more than 10 or 20 pages, so I think when one talks about difficulties with the ITU, one has to look at it from this kind of perspective.

ITU activities provide for satisfactory operation of telecommunication services, both international and domestic. They allow networks to interconnect and interoperate; they establish international routing of telecommunications, set international tariff and billing arrangements, and prevent harmful interference among radio stations in scientific research.

On the domestic side, I determined the extent to which foreign telecommunication and information services may be provided domestically. This is where it is critical to American technology to participate effectively in the ITU.

Most ITU activities this year, for example, are concerned with the integrated services digital network (ISDN) and the ability to create the most flexible kinds of telecommunication/information service arrangements in other countries through the liberalization of the specifications that are being drawn up. ISDN is critically important.

These arrangements also serve as a model for the detailed design and implementation of domestic systems, a very new role for the ITU in just the last few years. Many of the arrangements are adopted as domestic law. Such ITU activities also promote new business opportunities; they provide sufficient certainty of a common approach to induce manufacturers to produce equipment, and operators and users to buy and build systems.

Through the preponderance of these developing telecommunication/information service arrangements along with small changes in specifications in the way such things are developed, potential future opportunities for U.S. entrepreneurs will be dramatically affected. On the trade side they promote business relationships through informal interchanges at meetings. Many governments use ITU provisions to specify purchase of equipment, and development assistance activities produce large new markets for U.S. hardware and software providers, facts which are largely, it seems, ignored.

Figure 5 is also rather interesting and goes back to the original pie. United States participation in the ITU is largely provided by the private sector, although I suspect most people think it is the government. If you look at the list of U.S. delegates and others at all the major meetings of the ITU, and study the relative proportions, you will find the private sector constitutes probably 80 to 90 percent of the total U.S. participation. In the CCITT as well, most representation is provided by the private sector. It is only in the smaller shaded area on Figure 5 that U.S. participation is wholly by the government.

While typically one only sees a few U.S. preparatory mechanisms, there are actually many. These include delegation meetings, particularly widely used in the context of all the CCITT activities in which everything is moving so fast. Final policies are often made within delegations that are actually over there on site.

There are constant interagency committee meetings, private-sector organization meetings (becoming increasingly important) such as ANSI and a lot of the ISDN, and data communications forums.

There are numerous public advisory committee meetings. This has been a tool increasingly used, particularly by the FCC, in the last ten years. At one point prior to WARC 1979 there were literally dozens of advisory committee meetings to bring the private sector into the policymaking process. The FCC conducts various kinds of agency proceedings; there are several ongoing at the moment. In addition, there are all sorts of other communications that occur amongst the staff who are regularly working on all these issues. There are contractor reports and individual initiatives. Individual initiatives, I point out, are particularly important. A large number of rapporteurs and private-sector U.S. chairmen of various groups play a very important role in shaping the output of these meetings.

### Costs and Benefits

What are the attributes of this system, both favorable and unfavorable? It promotes private-sector participation; it minimizes government involvement; it fosters diversity; it promotes leadership and concensus among parties most affected or most expert; it is flexible and pragmatic; it minimizes expenditures on rhetoric. This is particularly true for the private-sector gatherings, and it mirrors U.S. values and domestic arrangements in the field.

Unfavorable attributes result from occasional inconsistencies and occasional dominance by private entities, and give an appearance of uncoordinated or unorganized activity; government dominance of some activities tends to exaggerate their importance; and the assistance of the private sector in bilateral matters gets low priority.

United States participation is generally effective in an overwhelming preponderance of ITU activities, though it has limited effectiveness in a few that traditionally are contentious.

Regarding the question of deleterious obligations, I point out that ITU obligations are avoidable through various kinds of reservation, and allotment plans do not prevent implementation of facilities where no harmful interference can occur. On the other hand, there are an awful lot of economic and operational constraints with respect to the recommendations that come out.

I suggest, in conclusion, a positive approach, that prevents loss of ITU jurisdiction to less desirable forums. The UN, IBI, UNESCO, and a number of other organizations are interested in getting into this field and promoting the ITU. I think we should foster our most favorable forum for these matters. This approach promotes the perception that the U.S. is interested in cooperating to devise multilateral arrangements, prevents unilateral retributions (particularly in the leased line area), and enhances U.S. ability to shape multilateral arrangements; thus it is, on balance, objectively warranted.

Lastly, I think the field needs more permanent, experienced, multidisciplinary participants in both private and public sectors; the field needs better organization and availability of relevant information; the private sector needs more government assistance in bilateral meetings with foreign governments, ever growing in importance as Ronnie Ahern pointed out; and the field needs some additional public- and private-sector active coordination.

Along those lines I think Diana Dougan's new role coordinating international communication policy within the State Department is one that is just the right touch for this field.

# Wilson P. Dizard

*Wilson Dizard is Vice President (Washington), Kalba Bowen Associates, a communications, information policy, and management consulting firm. Mr. Dizard, a graduate of Fordham University, is a lecturer in communications at the Massachusetts Institute of Technology and a professorial lecturer in communications in the School of Foreign Service at Georgetown University. He was Executive Director and Vice Chairman of the U.S. delegation to the World Administrative Radio Conference, 1978-1980, and served for many years as a State Department and U.S. Information Agency foreign service officer.*

The genesis of this conference was the publication of the NTIA report, which is a very useful compilation of policy issues now and in the future—and which gives us an agenda to work with.

There are some troubling aspects to the report, specifically the issue that we are focusing on here—the U.S./ITU relationship. The report tries to be fair on this issue but it shows its bias when it says, on page 36: "the extraordinary degree of politization characterizing the 1982 Nairobi Plenipotentiary Conference has raised anew U.S. concerns about continued participation in the ITU and has provoked an examination of alternatives."

This strikes me as hyperbole stemming from what I regard as insufficient evidence. It is based on assumptions that the ITU has suddenly become politicized. In fact, it has been political from the start.

The United States had refused to join it for the first 30 years or so. When we did join, we insisted on having six votes, matching the Russians and others. Moreover, we insisted over the years on refusing ITU membership to countries we didn't like for political, not technical, reasons. In the 1950s and 1960s the Communist Chinese could legitimately make noises about the "internal politicization" of the ITU because they were denied entry.

There may have been good reasons for this, but it was basically the politicizing by us of a technical organization. We could do this because it was an "old boys' club" that we ran with the Europeans, Russians, and Japanese. Now times have changed. We and the other "old boys" are a minority in a one country–one vote organization.

We've lost some influence. One result is that U.S. discussion has turned to alternatives, such as scaling back our participation or even leaving. It would be naive to eliminate these options altogether. We could be pushed one day into an unenviable situation where either pulling out or reducing our activities are viable options. This almost happened in Nairobi on the Israeli issue.* We were right to do what we did. Hopefully we made our point. I doubt it, but I think we're getting closer.

### ITU Issues

However, having said this, let's get down to the "pure" ITU issues. For instance, there is the technical assistance issue, which has been defined more precisely in the new charter as an ITU function.

There is nothing new about this. The ITU has had modest technical assistance programs for a long time. Moreover, the U.S. supported the concept of expansion of ITU technical assistance in several resolutions at the 1979 WARC.

There's no chance for a vast expansion of this program given the constraints of the ITU budget. However, a good case can be made that a properly managed technical assistance program in the ITU can benefit us. Our international spectrum problem comes from poor frequency management and sloppy engineering, particularly in Third World countries—not keeping the transmitters tuned properly, that kind of thing.

Mention also has been made of the new form of elections in the CCITT/CCIR organizations. Presumably, this stems from a fear of takeover by Third World technical incompetents. Our big problem in the CCIs, I would argue, is not this, but the Europeans and Japanese who try to snooker us on technical standards so they can get an industrial jump, the kind of thing that Ronnie Ahern talked about [see Chapter One]. It is to our advantage to get competent Third World specialists into the system. In practice, there would be a better geographical distribution of responsibilities. I don't think it would be a gang up by Third World nations.

*To the surprise of the American and many other delegations, at the Nairobi Plenipotentiary Conference, a concerted effort was made by some Third World countries to oust the Israelis from active membership in the ITU. The emotional debate took up much of the first three weeks of the conference, preventing consideration of the serious policy and technical matters on the agenda.

Another issue is the size of the Administrative Council. In Nairobi it was increased to over 40 members. But is there a magic number? A smaller number on the Administrative Council is more manageable, but ITU is not a haven for efficiency experts, and, in fact, the new number represents a more equitable ratio of member interests.

Finally, there was a whole series of changes of words and phrases in the charter, and they do have a certain importance. They tilt towards interests of the Third World majority; they are lawyers' words, and the legal profession is one area where we outproduce, on a per capita basis, the rest of the world.

In sum, it doesn't add up to an apocalyptic scenario, certainly not to the extent of picking up our marbles and leaving.

### Recommended Approach for the U.S.

We should stay and we should fight the good fight as Tony Rutkowski has stated. We should fight this battle inside the organization. We have important assets on our side as a leader in telecommunications. We have a record of influencing decisions on straight technical grounds, and, moreover, there are hopeful indications that the transition period of the past dozen years in the ITU is coming to a close.

There are more competent Third World representatives—technically competent, that is—and there seems to be more willingness to listen, particularly on the part of more moderate Third World members. Also, in Nairobi there were signs of moderation on administrative issues, such as dues assessments. They could have voted us down but they didn't.

One reason is that there is no such thing as a Third World bloc. There is a spectrum of interests and some of their ideas impact on us negatively, but they also impact on each other in similar ways. By and large, once the rhetorical exercises are finished, the developing countries are interested in orderly telecommunications development.

What should we do? I suggest some self-discipline in exercising our influence in the ITU. Setting up a confrontational environment is not warranted by the facts and is not particularly useful as an intimidation tactic. The alternative of pulling out is weak as far as I am concerned. Where would we go? At one point some mention was made of the OECD. Who would follow us? Despite some vague suggestions, probably no one.

The best approach is pragmatic. The ITU is an imperfect instrument because we and the Europeans shaped it that way a long time ago. Our interests in the ITU are limited and concerned primarily with

North America. Here we have such a large land mass that we can handle most of our frequency problems ourselves or in coordination with the Mexicans and the Canadians. Our best bet is to work inside the ITU to defend specific interests, not vague ideological principles.

First we should sharpen our negotiating skills with trained people and other resources. Secondly, when decisions go against our interests, we should take discreet countermeasures—using "footnoting" and reservations to decisions where we give ourselves some flexibility.

In summary, leaving the ITU is an option but, given the present situations, it should be treated in a very low-level fashion. It is significant to my mind that the NTIA report acknowledges, "Rather than alternatives to the ITU, most respondents"—that is, people who responded to draft copies of the report—"called for increasing U.S. effectiveness and influence in the organization and trying to make the ITU work." To that I say amen.

# Chapter Two Discussion

*QUESTION: Would you view the 1982 Plenipotentiary as strengthening the General Secretariat of the ITU, the Office of the Secretariat, and why?*

MR. DIZARD: Well, I think that it didn't strengthen the General Secretariat. If you're talking simply about the Office of the Secretary General, the answer is no. However, Dick Butler's election as Secretary General was a plus in terms of overall leadership. The ITU, as you know, is a collection of organizational bases, and I think that there was some ganging up. The Third Worlders were involved in this weakening of the very top of the organization, so that they could wield more influence within the IFRB (the International Frequency Registration Board) and the other organs of the ITU. I think that's a fact. It doesn't necessarily help us.

MR. RUTKOWSKI: I would only say that the General Secretariat was strengthened by the Butler election. I think he was clearly the best of the field. The man possesses remarkable background and familiarity with the whole field of communications. One has only to read his speeches over the last ten years, which, by and large, he personally wrote, to realize that. And he is dedicated to making ITU a more representative and, in fact, a more technically oriented organization.

I think in that sense we have a better General Secretariat today, but, bear in mind, the ITU is not just its staff. Indeed, prior to 1947 the staff was the Swiss Government. The ITU is the bodies that are comprised of member states, RPOAs, and SIOs; and I think that's an important distinction one has to keep in mind.

*[The following remarks relating to this discussion were offered by Donald Jansky at the beginning of his presentation on satellite communications policy (see Chapter 3).]*

Before I talk about geostationary orbit, or GSO, let me add a few comments about what has been said here. I want to make two points about the ITU because I really can't resist, as one who has been toiling in these vineyards for some 16 years. The first one is to reemphasize a point that Tony Rutkowski was trying to make, which is, the ITU is really only as powerful as the individual countries who are its members make it.

The real manifestation of that ties into the World Administrative Conferences and Plenipotentiary Conferences. It is an organization where the real power lies still with the Administrations. I think it is very important to understand that.

In that respect, I think it is also important to understand that in the present, on a yearly basis, the most important body, in my view, is one that did not get touched on too much, and that is the Administrative Council. It is a combination of what in this country would be OMB (Office of Management and Budget) and a policymaking organization, and it is made up of some 43 member countries. It meets for two to three weeks. It always has an extensive agenda.

I think it is important for the United States to spend a little bit more time coordinating its participation in this yearly event with friends—otherwise known as WEOGS (Western Europeans and Other Governments)—who are to some extent the counterpoints to the "Group of 77" in the U.N.

I think the other point that should be mentioned here is the role played in this ITU debate by the United States private sector, which is larger than all other private sectors of all the other countries in the world put together. I mention this only because unless you understand it, you cannot imagine how different the United States is from the rest of the world, and how the United States looks to other countries.

So what does that mean? To my mind, what it means is sort of where we are starting out this morning—that is that the U.S. private sector has got to be more effectively integrated into governmental policymaking mechanisms.

I don't mean to sound self-serving here, but I really believe it is true; there are too many barriers and suspicions surrounding the inter-action of government and industry. We have got to develop some better mechanisms, because there is a terrific amount of resources in the private sector that must be effectively coupled with the governmental process if we are going to have better participation, generally speaking, in the ITU.

Chapter Three

# Satellite Communications Policy:
# Due for a Change?

# Donald Jansky

*Donald Jansky is President, Jansky Telecommunications Inc., Washington, D.C. Until recently, Mr. Jansky was the Associate Administrator for NTIA, U.S. Department of Commerce. He received his M.S.E. degree from The Johns Hopkins University and is the coauthor of* Communication Satellites in the Geostationary Orbit: Technical and Policy Considerations *and* Spectrum Management Techniques.

The geostationary orbit (GSO) was conceptualized by Arthur Clarke in 1945. What I thought I would do is cover three points: first, give a perspective of what has happened in the last twenty years and do that by comparison of what has gone on in the international arena with the U.S., or North American orbit; second, to comment on some of the forums that have been the foci for debate on what is going on with regard to access to geostationary orbit; and, finally, to discuss where we are going, where we should be going, where we should be coming from and how we should be getting our act together.

Well, for those of you who are not familiar with this, there is a very simple representation of the geostationary orbit: it is a unique gravitationally-based place where you can put a satellite 22,300 miles directly over the equator, and the satellite therefore has the appearance of being relatively stationary, relative, that is, to the earth. The satellite rotates around the earth at the same rate at which the earth is rotating on its axis. It is not crowded up there, at least in physical terms.

The problem is electrical. The World Administrative Radio Conference on Space Telecommunications in 1971 defined approximately fifteen space telecommunication services, and subsequently allocated a great number of frequency bands that could be used by satellites, particularly those in the GSO.

The largest growth in the use of this orbit by satellites has taken place in what we have come to call the "Fixed Satellite Service" as defined by the ITU, which many of you probably think of as communication satellites, though it has also been used by a number of other services.

This year [1983] marks the twentieth anniversary of the time when this ability was first demonstrated technologically, through the launch and operation of a GSO satellite called Syncom II, built by Hughes Aircraft.

Its successful launch demonstrated the feasibility of putting and maintaining a satellite in this orbit in 1963. Since that time we have seen development of satellites both domestically and internationally.

First, I want to deal with the domestic situation. ABC and Hughes Aircraft petitioned the FCC for a license to operate a domestic satellite in 1965. But the real origination of U.S. domestic GSO policy did not occur until 1970, with what has been referred to as the "Flannigan Memorandum" from the White House to the FCC, which advocated, on behalf of the Nixon Administration, a policy of "Open Skies" access to the geostationary orbit.

That policy came to fruition in a 1973 Memorandum Opinion and Order of the FCC. Subsequently, in 1976 and 1978, the earth stations that were used with commercial satellites in the United States went through several stages of deregulation which, in fact, even more than the Open Skies policy itself, probably precipitated the terrific growth in use of communication satellites in the United States.

There has been a burgeoning of the number of satellites in the North American arc. The FCC is talking about some 38 satellites over a range of orbital arc from approximately 143 degrees west down to about 67 degrees west longitude.

So you have seen a terrific growth during the past decade in terms of the numbers of satellites. All of these satellites are operating in only four frequency bands: the 4 and 6 GHz bands and the 12 and 14 GHz bands.

I think this testifies to our institutional processes in the United States, both policymaking and regulatory, which have allowed us to do this. I give an awful lot of credit to the FCC for the way in which it has managed the development of this orbit thus far. Sometimes people tend to criticize, but I think in this case the Commission has done an outstanding job.

## INTELSAT

I want to move to INTELSAT which, of course, started its satellite development in 1965 with Early Bird, or INTELSAT I. There has been a progressive growth in the capacity and number of satellites and membership since then.

I suppose if you wanted to find alternatives to the ITU, the United States might use INTELSAT as a vehicle. INTELSAT is, of course, a quasi-corporate entity, with the degree of participation by members more or less in accordance with the amount of their actual use. Using this approach, the U.S. has been a large participant. I am certain Joel Alper will tell you a lot about that.

INTELSAT has been vastly successful. Like the ITU, it seems to add new members every year and now totals 109. Do you think it will catch up with the ITU? We hope so.

In any event, it has operated in an essentially noncompetitive environment until recently; whereas, the U.S. domestic environment has seen, because of the Open Skies approach, a burgeoning of access to the GSO. You've seen new services developed. You've seen a terrific amount of investment in earth station technologies. You've seen progress made as a result of this competition.

Now, INTELSAT is entering into a period where it is beginning to deal with a kind of competitive environment in the international arena. First of all, coming on fairly strongly are several regional satellite systems. I know "regional" is a dirty word, but the fact is there are a number of regional arenas in which groups of countries have decided to put up satellites of their own, notably, EUTELSAT, ARABSAT, and PALAPA II; and there are other ideas being bandied about.

On the other hand, INTELSAT also is responding with development of policy for domestic leases; that is to say, it is providing a vehicle whereby many developing countries can utilize this umbrella organization to get into the satellite business to provide their own domestic services in an affordable fashion.

I think you are going to see more rather than less of that. However, I think you will also be seeing a push from INTERSPUTNIK, a Soviet-based geostationary satellite system which is coming on, and which could conceivably serve as a basis for competition. In fact, there are some members of INTELSAT who are also members of INTERSPUT-NIK. I would be interested to know from Joel Alper how they get away with it.

Anyway, there is developing competition in the international area, and what you may see is a breaking down of the differentiation between international and domestic over a period of time.

**Progress in Satellite Communication**

Let me next give you a kind of tour of the biggest and best satellite; that's INTELSAT VI, which again is doubling capacity. I think it is important to understand that the geostationary satellite has virtually revolutionized the way we do business in telecommunications, particularly internationally. Previously, high frequency radio communication and cable were the only forms of international electrical communication.

I remember when I first got into the business of working in the ITU, and I would go to my hotel room and try to place a call back home. I would have to place it with the operator, and would then have to wait until early morning and be woken up—and then pay an arm and a leg for the privilege. Today I can make a direct-dial call to my wife and have her call me right back because it is about half the cost. It's now a very easy thing to do—just the way we are used to placing a direct-dial domestic call. It has become a part of our lifestyle, and I think great credit should be given for what INTELSAT has been able to accomplish during these past ten years.

But there is nothing like success to breed controversy, and indeed in the last few years we've had a terrific amount of controversy.

It really goes back to WARC 79 (World Administrative Radio Conference, 1979), which was sort of the opening salvo in a worldwide debate regarding access to geostationary orbit. At WARC 79 there was a resolution passed that said essentially, "In the very near future we are going to have some planning conferences to guarantee in practice access to the geostationary orbit." This was Resolution 3. It, and some of its language, has recently been considered in the Administrative Council of the ITU. It is being debated right now because the Administrative Council is the body designated to establish agendas for World Administrative Radio Conferences.

## Institutions for Satellite Policymaking

Let me just briefly mention several of the forums that have been the basis for debate. First, we had a debate at Unispace 82. The language which was adopted there was very balanced. Unfortunately not all of that language was transferred by my colleagues at the recent Nairobi conference. Instead, they only took part of it. So, now we have language in the ITU Rules and Regulations that says you have to take into account special geographic considerations of certain countries, without the balancing language relating to effective use of technology, that we had worked hard to obtain.

I expect that the present ITU Administrative Council meeting will adopt the agenda for what's now going to be called ORB 85, which is a World Administrative Space Radio and Planning Conference. As its first objective, ORB 85 will have to choose (I emphasize the word "choose" because a lot of people seem to think we are going to plan—we are *not* going to plan at that conference; we are going to *choose*) which of these fifteen or so space services, and which of the frequency bands associated with them, are actually going to be planned, and perhaps the basis upon which they are going to be planned, but the Conference is not actually going to plan. In addition, there is an Interim Working Party of the CCIR whose tenth meeting coming up in Australia will continue to establish the technical basis for efficient use of the geostationary orbit.

We are now entering a new round of these various planning groups leading up to major meetings. Typically, the technical part of an Administrative Radio Conference provides a vehicle for introducing the technical sharing conditions under which any plan must take place.

In the U.S. government, there is a committee called Ad Hoc 178. It is a subcommittee made up of governmental officials only, of the Interdepartment Radio Advisory Committee (IRAC), which advises the National Telecommunications and Information Administration (NTIA) on executive branch spectrum authorization matters. In addition to all this, a recent FCC docket sets forth new orbit spacing policy. Whereas previously we had two- and four-degree orbit separation, we now have about nine separation rules which reflect agreements between Canada, the United States, and Mexico in the two sets of frequency bands for communication satellites in North America, e.g., 4 and 6 GHz, and 12 and 14 GHz.

### How the U.S. Should Proceed

Where does this all lead? I think what we should be doing is leading from strength. I think the U.S. experience is a valid laboratory for the rest of the world. By looking at one of the key characteristics of orbit use, namely, earth station characteristics, the FCC was able to push back the frontiers of access to the geostationary orbit. Studies by the IWP 41 and others indicate that we may be able to double the present capacity of GSO satellites in the North American arc.

The fact of it is, there is a lot of capacity available. Our experience in the United States is documented and ought to be pointed out to the rest of the world in terms of how in fact that was accomplished. For example, compare WARC 77, the World Administrative Radio Conference on Broadcasting Satellites in 1977, to what is going on in WARC 83. I think you could come to the conclusion as you look at countries trying to implement a detailed plan, such as they did for Regions 1 and 3, that such plans don't work. We can use that as a vehicle for trying again to explain to the rest of the world how and why they don't work. We ought to be able to adopt proposals that indicate how we can incorporate flexibility into space planning. I think that has to be the keynote of where the United States is coming from.

Competition is good domestically, and might not be so bad internationally. I just throw that out because competition does speed technological change; it does force people to reexamine how best to get enhanced capacity from the geostationary orbit.

I think U.S. institutions have been flexible—remarkably so—far in excess of those institutions that we have to deal with in other parts of the world. I think that we have to try to sell that institutional flexibility both in the ITU and in the World Administrative Radio Conferences.

I guess, to paraphrase Franklin Roosevelt, there is nothing to fear about change except change itself.

# Joel Alper

*Joel Alper is Vice President, Communications Services, COMSAT World Systems Division. Mr. Alper who has a B.S. degree in Engineering from the Cooper Union, an M.S. in Engineering from the Massachusetts Institute of Technology, and an M.B.A. from Boston University, represents COMSAT on the Board of the International Telecommunications Satellite Organization (INTELSAT). Prior to joining COMSAT, he worked with TRW Systems and the Jet Propulsion Laboratory.*

The topic of this panel ends with a question mark. Given the FCC's actions this year and the introduction of S. 999 in the Senate, it seems clear that U.S. policymakers have determined that it is time for a change. Yet there have been surprisingly few public discussions and little examination of the ramifications of the proposed changes on the United States.

The NTIA study, which is the basis for this conference, and the GAO report, "FCC Needs to Monitor a Changing International Telecommunications Market," appear to be the main efforts examining the possible effects of deregulation in the international environment.

Recalling the extensive inquiries and hearings conducted to gain an understanding of the domestic telecommunications industry and the possible impact of deregulation in that industry, one cannot help but be perplexed at the absence of such analyses regarding international communications. In that regard this symposium provides a needed forum to examine certain of these issues.

A recent observation made by Congressman Glenn English in commenting on the GAO report is worth quoting: "The FCC cannot afford to act on blind faith and assume that the goal of increased competition will automatically be achieved by actions taken by the United States. Clearly, the issues confronting international telecommunications need to be fully explored."

I hope this panel will provide some of this needed exploration. In my own remarks, I would like to make a general observation about the policies and goals raised in the NTIA report as they relate to this symposium, and then I would like to touch on a few specific changes that INTELSAT and COMSAT will have to make to adjust to the new environment.

### Policy Goals in Satellite Communications

The NTIA study denotes several goals and policies in specific areas that we feel are potentially inconsistent with full reliance on the marketplace. One such goal is efficient allocation of spectrum and geostationary orbit resources.

Don Jansky just elaborated on the explosion of satellites in the domestic orbit. There is an interest in using the rest of the orbital arc by virtually all the countries of the world. Presently, with the exception of the arc over the United States and to some extent over western Europe, INTELSAT is satisfying not only international traffic requirements but also the domestic communications needs of several countries, and it is doing it in a very efficient manner.

Don discussed INTELSAT's satellites from INTELSAT I through INTELSAT VI. It is worth noting that the growth and capacity of the INTELSAT satellites have increased over 12,000 percent since 1965. That initial Early Bird Satellite could handle only 240 voice circuits and one TV channel; INTELSAT VI, which will be in orbit in 1986, will have a capacity of 30,000 voice circuits and several TV channels. This concern for the efficient use of the geostationary orbit was emphasized during a lengthy discussion at the April INTELSAT Meeting of Signatories in Bangkok. The discussion was summarized in INTELSAT's press release as follows: "The geostationary orbital arc and the radio frequencies available for satellite communications are limited natural resources and their use by additional unnecessary systems would make an already difficult situation far worse."

Another goal stated in the NTIA report is the importance of communications with developing nations and of assisting these nations in providing necessary communication services. These are very noble goals and they are goals which are being pursued by a number of organizations, particularly INTELSAT. There are 109 members and 169 users of INTELSAT. Over 80 percent are developing countries. For most of these developing countries INTELSAT provides the only system not only for communications outside their country, but for some 27 of them it is the only system for communications inside their country.

Now, what happens with a purely competitive policy? Any competing system would clearly focus on the high density routes which would divert the most remunerative traffic from INTELSAT. If this were allowed to occur, two related consequences would follow.

In the first instance, if INTELSAT were to continue its policy of global rate averaging for its services, the decrease in revenues resulting from traffic diversion would cause rates for *all users* to go up. On the other hand, if INTELSAT were to depart from global rate averaging and move to something which might be more conveniently characterized as cost based, then, of course, the cost of INTELSAT services to smaller users—those who are primarily communicating over smaller volume routes—would go up dramatically. This would have a negative impact on underdeveloped areas. Currently, INTELSAT's plans call for spending roughly $2 billion over the remainder of this decade for satellite communications and facilities which will be in use well into the 1990s: of those $2 billion, $1.2 billion are presently committed.

Another objective raised in the NTIA report is maintaining and increasing U.S. leadership in telecommunications. It is worth emphasizing that while U.S. leadership in communications may be decreasing in some areas, the U.S. has demonstrated a very strong leadership role in establishing INTELSAT; in fact, there is evidence that INTELSAT has been the major foreign policy success in telecommunications for the United States.

Aside from these policy aspects, INTELSAT also has been and continues to be a major commercial success for the United States. The U.S. has been the main provider of spacecraft, launch service, and of research and development. The prime contractors for all six INTELSAT spacecraft series have been American companies. Of the close to $1 billion spent to date on satellites, 83 percent (over $778 million) has been spent in this country. This is significant since we have only a 24 percent ownership investment in INTELSAT. In addition, all the satellites launched to date have been launched by NASA launch vehicles amounting to an expenditure of about $706 million; another $164 million has been committed for future launches.

In raising the potential inconsistencies between these goals—efficient spectrum and orbital use, encouraging communications with developing nations, and maintaining and enhancing U.S. leadership—and the overriding policy of relying on marketplace competition, I don't want to leave the impression that I am advocating that procompetitive policies be abandoned. I do want to make clear, however, that if all of these goals are important, policymakers need to carefully implement competitive policies so as not to undermine the success that has already been achieved in meeting these goals.

I would like to try to suggest ways this might be achieved as I discuss some of the specific issues raised in the NTIA report. The first of these issues I was asked to address is facilities planning.

The report reviews briefly some problems with international facilities planning, poses options and alternatives to the current process, and gives as its "recommendation" that it would be "troubling to maintain the status quo." Regrettably, the pros and cons of the options proposed are not discussed.

I think it is important, whether talking about facilities planning, facilities competition, or facilities deregulation, to have a clear idea of the distinction between the domestic and international arenas. The two cannot be treated in the same way. The following distinctions must be made. Please excuse me if this sounds like an acute perception of the obvious, but it needs to be said.

The other end, the distant end in the international arena, is a foreign entity over which U.S. policymakers have no control. International facilities cannot be implemented without the cooperation of foreign entities, and since the ownership and operation of communication systems in other nations is generally in government hands the establishment of competing facilities really means that the foreign government, which would own the other half of the competing facility, would go into competition with itself. For most foreign governments this isn't a very interesting prospect. They really have no incentive to interconnect with a number of competing systems and the U.S. has no authority to force this. There are other problems associated with facilities competition internationally: problems of whipsawing—foreign entities negotiating between competing carriers for most favorable rates and anticompetitive practices such as the exclusive bidding proposition which was put forward by the Benelux and the Nordic countries earlier this year. These aren't hypothetical. These are real problems.

Another key difference between the domestic and international arenas is the greater amount of investment required for international facilities. It would just not be feasible from a cost standpoint to attempt to duplicate a global international telecommunication system either by satellite or state-of-the-art undersea cables. I mentioned the $1.2 billion committed out of a $2 billion planned investment for this decade for the global satellite system. Our latest information indicates an estimated cost of a minimum of $250 million for the TAT-8 cable planned for deployment across the ocean in 1988.

Any proposals regarding facilities planning, deregulation, or competition in the provision of international facilities have to take these factors into account. If they don't, the consequences could be a considerable waste of resources, whipsawing by foreign monopolies, or other difficulties or barriers over which the U.S. has no control. We don't believe such consequences are in the United States' interest.

### Policy Options

Given the costs involved and the fact that overseas communications is a joint undertaking, some FCC or other government involvement in facilities planning is essential. This could take the form of a joint government/industry task force which is one of the options offered by NTIA. The FCC also should retain its role in authorizing facilities. I would like to note that GAO reached the same conclusion in its report.

Again, this does not mean there should not be competition. We believe that a great deal of technological competition currently exists between submarine cable and satellite systems; without a doubt the technological improvements represented by the fibre optic cable system certainly light a fire under any of those in the satellite field.

Nor does this mean that other satellites should never be used for international services. We believe that this is appropriate as long as certain conditions are satisfied.

The latest U.S. policy pronouncement on this issue occurred in conjunction with the Commission's Transborder decision and in a letter to the FCC from James Buckley, then Under Secretary of State for Security Assistance, Science and Technology. The Buckley letter began by affirming that the foundation of U.S. international communication satellite policy includes the concept of a single global system. However, in recognizing that there might be conditions under which other systems might be used for international services, Buckley elaborated on the conditions as follows:

- Use of other systems would be appropriate where a global system could not provide the service required or where it would be uneconomical or impractical to use the INTELSAT system for the service planned; and
- Any such use must be authorized only pursuant to Article XIV(d) of the INTELSAT Agreements. The Commission adhered to these policies in its Transborder decision, and we support these policies.

We were very pleased to see the NTIA study conclude that INTELSAT has become "an unqualified, outstanding success, on institutional, financial and operational grounds and must be considered a triumph of U.S. foreign policy."

We believe it just doesn't make any sense—politically or economically—for the U.S. to undermine this system. However, while COMSAT remains very supportive of the global system, we do acknowledge that there are changing forces in the marketplace and a changing policy environment. We recognize that we will need to make major adjustments in the way we conduct our jurisdictional business, and we also recognize that INTELSAT can and should behave in a more market-oriented manner.

I am very confident that under the leadership of a dynamic, creative, market-oriented new Director General who will take office at the end of this year and who will hopefully be the U.S. candidate, Richard Colino, these changes will be made and INTELSAT will more aggressively respond to market demands.

There are changes underway within INTELSAT. It is utilizing new technology to develop a new totally integrated digital service, including voice, data, and teleconferencing. In 1984, INTELSAT will implement an integrated digital services network through the use of the TDMA/DSI (time division multiple access with digital speech interpolation) which will provide an even wider range of services to customers.

COMSAT also has undertaken major efforts to adapt to the new environment. On behalf of ESOC, we recently filed plans with the FCC to expand access to U.S. international earth stations by enabling U.S. domestic users or carriers to locate facilities at or near international earth stations and to obtain international interconnection.

During the past year we have spent considerable time and effort studying the prospects and the means by which COMSAT could respond to the changes in the policy environment and in the marketplace for international communications. As a result, COMSAT has developed a proposal making major adjustments in its jurisdictional business practices. We have begun preliminary discussions with a number of government officials and expect to make known further details of the proposal in the very near future. COMSAT—and I believe I could speak on behalf of INTELSAT as well—recognizes that the environment is changing and that adjustments must be made.

It is the job of those of us in the international communications industry to make sure that policymakers are well-informed and aware of the practical effects of their decisions, and I would like to say that this forum has provided an opportunity to do that.

# Chapter Three Discussion

*QUESTION: I understand INTELSAT opposes the Orion proposal, but I'm wondering how far the organization would be willing to go with respect to deregulating the international communications market. Can you set any limits on how far regional systems can go or how far INTELSAT is willing to let them go?*

MR. ALPER: INTELSAT has had occasion over the last several years to coordinate several regional systems under Article XIV (d) of the Agreements. Article XIV (d) states that INTELSAT members can use separate systems under two conditions: the first is that the systems are not technically incompatible with INTELSAT, and the second is that they do not cause significant economic harm. The wording I think was a very difficult compromise between government representatives of the major INTELSAT signatories, with the United States really coming down as hard as it could on the side of a single global system. It might be noted that INTELSAT has no teeth as an organization. The only suasion it has is moral. If the INTELSAT Assembly were to find that a separate system proposed for use by one of its members was in fact contrary to the conditions of Article XIV (d), all it could do is issue that finding. Thus far INTELSAT has agreed to specific uses of ECS, the European regional system; the Arab System; the Palapa system; certain U.S. transborder applications; and INTERSPUTNIK on a very limited basis.

None of these systems indicated a level of traffic which, on a percentage basis, would even approach the percent of INTELSAT's revenues. The cross-border systems that were coordinated by the United States last year potentially represent more in terms of revenue loss than the European system, and yet even that is very small.

As to how far INTELSAT would be prepared to go, this really depends on the views of the Director General and the Board. Again, there are no teeth in the agreements. There is no enforcing power.

*QUESTION: Same question to Mr. Jansky: how far could they go and still keep INTELSAT?*

MR. JANSKY: Well, I'll give you a personal opinion. What I hear Joel saying is that so far, at least, there seems to be a lot of flexibility on the part of INTELSAT, that there have been a number of systems that have been proposed or thought of as potential competitors, and yet some way or another there has always been a way found to accommodate them. I guess I think there will always be an INTELSAT. It has already demonstrated the viability of what it set out to do almost twenty years ago, so it has been a success. We've all acknowledged that, and the question is, what happens next? INTELSAT is up for a change in leadership soon which may be a very significant change in its history. It may change direction. Obviously, there is a lot of ferment in the satellite arena at the moment, and there is a lot of policy reexamination going on now.

*QUESTION: Just one clarification. Mr. Alper, you draw the line at the major routes such as the one across the Atlantic, which are the primary money-makers for INTELSAT. That's definitely not an over-accomplishment.*

MR. ALPER: I certainly believe that once you begin to plan and implement competing systems on the major routes, the door is open wide enough to drive a truck through it. The Atlantic traffic of INTEL-SAT represents something over 25 percent of all the traffic in INTEL-SAT. Other significant traffic streams are those from the United States to Latin America, and from the United States across the Pacific. U.S. traffic in INTELSAT represents 48 percent of INTELSAT. The question is, what is INTELSAT without the United States, and that is the concern that was reflected at the April Meeting of Signatories.

There really isn't an INTELSAT unless the United States supports it.

*QUESTION: Actually I just wanted to make a clarification of something that Joel said of INTELSAT. At the Meeting of Signatories there was a unanimous resolution adopted which made it perfectly clear, lest there be any doubt, that what were characterized as trans-oceanic or heavy-route satellite systems would be considered a fundamental attack on the principles of INTELSAT. Article XIV (d) coordinations have been carried out on a unanimous basis thus far, which I think reflects the INTELSAT approach to things.*

*I do believe that some of the comments that Don was making earlier about competition, or lack of competition, don't reflect the situation. I have a friend who is a market economist, and he says, "I just don't understand it. You people [at INTELSAT] are antithetical to what economic theory says is supposed to happen. You have consistently reduced your rates since you started 18 years ago. How is this possible when there is no competition? You are destroying all of my theories!" So I was able to reassure him, "it is because we now have submarine cable and fiber optics—and thus technological competition—to spur INTELSAT ahead."*

*Obviously, at the deregulatory level within the United States, there will be other things that will perhaps push INTELSAT ahead in those regards, but there is that fundamental misunderstanding.*

*There have been several allegations made that somehow there is a difference between "private" and "public" services. There has also been the suggestion that INTELSAT cannot carry video services, cannot respond to video or other types of specialized needs. There has also been the suggestion that just by passing an act in Congress and signing a bill, U.S. commitments to INTELSAT, under the INTELSAT agreements, can somehow be changed. I would like both of the panelists to comment on how realistic or accurate are those allegations.*

MR. ALPER: I think that I addressed some of the questions that Joe [Pelton, of INTELSAT] is raising in my talk. Our own view of the concept of a private system was clearly expressed in our comments in opposition to the Orion application, in which we indicated that INTELSAT's agreements do not make any distinction between "private" and "public" communications. They make a distinction between "public" and "specialized" services and the categories are very clearly defined in both of those areas. It is not a question of who the user is; it is a question of the type of services involved.

INTELSAT is providing a wide range of digital services and will increase that range with the new INTELSAT business services. It has also introduced a new service for international TV leases which is the fastest growing service on INTELSAT. There are currently five international TV leases on a full-time basis. There is no evidence to support a contention that INTELSAT can or cannot provide those kinds of services in this system.

MR. JANSKY: I would say largely the same thing, except that like any common carrier's common carrier, INTELSAT is subject to what its users want to put over it, and as a general fact, I think proportionately television has been rather small.

Chapter Four

# Reshaping the U.S. Government
for the Information Age

# Henry Geller

*Henry Geller is Director, Washington Center for Public Policy Research, Duke University, Institute of Policy Sciences and Public Affairs. Mr. Geller received his B.S. from the University of Michigan and a J.D. from Northwestern University School of Law. Until January 1981, he was Assistant Secretary for Communications and Information and Administrator of the National Telecommunications and Information Administration (NTIA), U.S. Department of Commerce. He was appointed General Counsel at the FCC in 1964, and in 1970 became Special Assistant to the Chairman.*

On the subject of governmental structure, I thought I would begin by addressing the optimum, and then retreat to the feasible, the more pragmatic. I think it is important to talk about the optimum because it sets the goal. It thus tells you whether the small steps you can take are in the right direction.

I have not changed my views in this area from those I held previously. What is needed is a centralized agency in the executive branch. I am not talking here about just international communications. I don't see any way you can split domestic from international. No one would sensibly propose such a split.

You will hear a panel describing how domestic events have an enormous and profound impact on the international: the domestic resale decision, Computer II, all these spill over into international. [See Chapter 5.] Of course, there are differences, as the panel will elaborate, but there is no way anybody sensibly would say they wanted to have policymaking segregated into domestic and international.

I think the 1934 Communications Act was right to create centralization but it just didn't go far enough. There remains a split here between government and non-government, and it does not work well. Take the most important aspect in telecommunications policy, the allocation of the spectrum: there shouldn't be government and non-government allocation by two separate entities; one body should allocate for both.

Thus, land mobile frequencies should be allocated for the government and for the non-government user by one body, because you get much greater efficiencies, as we found out at NTIA when we looked into this one aspect. You also conserve staff resources and get greater responsibility—more "sunshine" and scrutiny of whether government or non-governmental allocations are being efficiently utilized. There are, of course, some military impediments to public scrutiny of defense allocations, but even with this limitation the change should be beneficial.

As to where I would place the responsibility for centralized policy-making, it seems to me that the executive branch—an EPA-type administration—is most desirable. First, you get much more accountability. Notice what recently happened with EPA. The President was responsible for EPA since it is part of his Administration. He therefore had to step in and do something to clean up the mess.

In the case of the FCC, the President is not responsible. He simply appoints and, because it is an independent agency, washes his hands. As a Senate study shows,* the quality of appointments is not consistently high. On all too frequent occasions, the FCC is used as a dumping ground to pay off political debts. Why not? The President has no responsibility for the agency. And as for congressional oversight, I don't think that it has worked very well at all: just fits and starts.

What I am urging is not new. The idea of a single administrator in the executive branch serving at the will of the President has been pushed by Elman, by Louis Hector, by Minow, by the Ash Committee, and by many others.

The Ash Committee did find that the approach didn't fit the FCC because its sphere of regulation is so sensitive—licensing, rate making, equal opportunities, fairness, and so forth. But that simply means that these sensitive areas should be entrusted to a board of senior employees (10 years or more experience at the agency), which serves not at the will of the administrator but is removable only for good cause shown to the Office of Personnel Management.

The board would act to implement policies laid down by the administrator. That would be a plus because today there is a lack of specific overall policy guidelines. Under the approach I have urged, the administrator has to lay down policies because somebody else—in this case the senior employee board—is going to implement them in *ad hoc* situations. That forces them to focus on what the overall policies

*Appointments to the Regulatory Agencies (the FCC and FTC—1949-1974), Senate Committee on Commerce, 94th Congress, 2nd Session, April, 1976.

should be. Further in the present deregulatory trend, there should be less need for adjudication and rate making.

I won't go on further about this approach. As I say, it is the optimum. NTIA tried for some portion of it during the "rewrite" days and did not do too well. As a matter of fact, our proposal on centralized spectrum allocation sank very quickly. Nevertheless, I think it is the goal towards which we should aim.

Stepping away from the optimum, and looking just at the international arena—and that is a tremendous retreat because, as I told you, you cannot sensibly separate international policymaking from the domestic—there is still a need for centralization. There is a need to bring together all policymaking in one entity in the executive branch.

A lawyer would use the word *a fortiori* to describe this need in international as compared to domestic policymaking. For, as Ronnie Ahern said this morning [see Chapter One], the considerations that are applicable are not just technical and those stemming from domestic facets; there are also foreign policy considerations, and those of trade and industrial policy. And these considerations lend themselves to treatment by the executive branch far more than an independent agency.

### Problems With the Current Approach

Let's review some concrete examples, some of which have already been touched on. In the facilities areas you have heard about the 1977-78 TAT-7 decision [see Chapter One]. The FCC approached it initially as an economic and technical matter and didn't do a bad job on that score. The problem, as you heard, is that the decision also involved large foreign policy considerations. The Commission therefore had to retreat from its high economic ground. In a face-saving decision, it said that, for reasons of comity, it would authorize TAT-7 with a slight delay.

Another example is the ITU. As you heard [see Chapter Two], there certainly are foreign policy considerations, such as increased politicization, the Israeli question at Nairobi, and so on.

An example of trade issues arose recently with regard to the effort by Control Data to end some inappropriate restrictions placed on KDD [Japan's international telegraph and telephone company]. Control Data sought to use as leverage opposition to a filing at the FCC involving KDD and activation of the U.S. end of its Venus packet-switched data transfer service.

It is not a bad idea to use such leverage. But it doesn't work well at the administrative agency level, because the FCC has to proceed on a record and makes decisions that are appealable on that record. The agency is supposed to stay within the record and not exert "leverage" for a wholly different purpose. This need for leverage will continue to arise.

Ronnie Ahern and other speakers mentioned that we are moving toward competition in the international arena, but that presents difficulties because it is so different from the domestic arena. Therefore, you have to negotiate, have "give and take" discussions, use rough tactics. Again, the Commission is not good for that kind of negotiation. That is not the agency's fault. As I say, the agency is accustomed to proceeding on the record, and to defending itself in court—activities quite different from the "tit for tat" negotiations that are necessary to resolve such cases as the TAT-7 controversy. Such "trading" negotiations are much better suited to the executive branch.

They are, for example, done all the time with foreign aviation routes. I think Walter Bolter [Chapter Five] is right; international communications is a subset of all kinds of trade offerings that will take place between the executive branch and its foreign partners.

A final example involves the Orion Satellite application already mentioned. This application raises large foreign policy issues. The INTELSAT treaty is involved, as are foreign policy aspects of the Communications Act and the Satellite Act of 1962. The executive branch is not only more appropriate for resolution of these aspects, but the FCC gets in more and more difficulties when it proceeds in this sensitive area.

In the mid-1970s, the Commission commendably decided to engage in "consultative practices" with the Conference of European Postal and Telecommunications Administrations (CEPT) countries in order to end the confrontational situation that had arisen as a result of cases like TAT-7. One of the record carriers, ITT, understandably wanted in on those processes because they could affect future decisions involving facilities for the carriers. It filed a complaint using, among other things, the Sunshine Act, and it just recently won in a decision issued by the Court of Appeals for the District of Columbia Circuit.* The Sunshine Act is applicable, the Court held, because three Commissioners were participating and later were going on to decisional matters.

As you can see, FCC process just doesn't fit the rough realities of foreign negotiations. These are sensitive liaison meetings and you really don't want to conduct them in a "sunshine" fashion. If a single administrator in the executive branch were conducting this process, the Sunshine Act would be inapplicable.

*ITT* v. *FCC*, 699 F. 2nd 1219 (D.C. Cir. 1983).

To give one final example concerning INTELSAT and the authorization of international satellites, the arena is the INTELSAT Board of Governors meeting. We have our representative, COMSAT. COMSAT is to vote under instructions from the State Department, with participation by the FCC and NTIA. It is a 24 percent voter in that setup. After INTELSAT has voted, at that point all COMSAT can do is salute and carry out the Board's decision by filing the requisite applications with the FCC if they involve U.S. frequencies. If ITT or some other record carrier follows the Communications Act and petitions to deny under Section 309, the resulting situation makes no practical sense. The decision is gone, done. So far as the FCC is concerned, it's really ministerial at this point.

The only time that ITT or some interested person could have participated was during the instructional process, and yet again, that is a sensitive, closed procedure. So here also, the present Act is simply out of step with reality, I believe.

Looking at the present status, then, one finds an unfortunate split between the Administration (the executive branch) and an independent agency (FCC), and also an executive branch that does not have its house in order. The governing document here is Executive Order 12046 [see NTIA report, page 72]. I was present at the creation, or maybe it is better to say, at the commission of the crime. It simply was a turf fight, and I can tell you the Department of Commerce does not have strong cards in a fight with Defense, State, or OMB. We therefore did not come out too well in that turf fight.

Under that executive order, State has—and no one disputes this— the overall foreign policy control, and also does coordination. But NTIA was expressly created to do most, if not all the coordination here, because it was to have the expert staff—in engineering and economics—and thus was to be the principal advisor to the President on telecommunications policy. What has happened is that NTIA has not received adequate staff to carry out its role, and has run into severe turf battles in the trade area and lost them. There may be recent improvement.

We mentioned Ambassador Dougan's efforts, but State does not have adequate staffing. In that connection, I don't think it is sound to put rotating foreign service officers in the telecommunications field. Their careers don't really depend on this field; rather they are usually there two to four years and then go on to other things. Also, when one examines the organizational chart as set out in the NTIA report, the only conclusion is a bureaucratic horror.

There is a communications official reporting to the Under Secretary for Security, Science and Technology. But there are other officials involved with matters like transborder data flows and economic issues reporting to the Under Secretary for Economic Affairs. And officials concerned with UNESCO or International Organizations, report to still another, the Under Secretary for Political Affairs. It is really a hodgepodge. I also think that it is wrong that Ambassador Dougan is based in the office of one of these under secretaries, for Security, Science and Technology. I believe she ought to be in the Deputy Secretary's Office if she is to be effective. In sum, responsibility for telecommunications foreign policy lies with State, but it cannot carry through. It lacks resources and it is not properly organized.

In the NTIA you also have inadequate resources. Further, it lacks clout and is not doing too well, as I say, in a number of areas—for example, trade and industrial policy. There clearly needs to be a strong focal point with adequate resources and with clout, with the power to act. I am not saying that you want to cut out the State Department, Defense, NASA, and the others. Their input is necessary and, indeed, invaluable. There must be coordination with these agencies and on some issues they will carry the day. If this strong focal point acted against their recommendation, they can carry the matter to the President through the National Security Council. But those situations would entail extraordinary circumstances.

**Proposed Reforms**

Let's look now at the proposed remedies set out in the NTIA report. The report is excellent, I believe, in prescribing what is needed here. It is set out on page 24 of the report, and refers to high-level attention and responsibility; central locus of coordination and decision with the authority to implement the policy; adequate and expert staff; well trained negotiators in this field; prompt decisions that reflect domestic, foreign, national security, trade, and industrial policy; and private sector input that is taken into account. No one would argue with all that. It's motherhood. The question is how to do it.

Judging the proposals against these criteria, I think the best one is the fourth proposal where all executive branch policymaking is consolidated in one entity in the executive branch and the FCC would be left simply to carry out policies in a few appropriate areas, such as rate making. The main policy work would be done by the executive branch.

As to where in the executive branch, I think Ronnie Ahern makes a good point: don't put this responsibility in State or Commerce or a similar agency. For that would skew the orientation to foreign policy or to trade or whatever. I believe, therefore, that the responsibility should be put in the Executive Office of the President (EOP)—an international OTP, if you could get around the fact that presidents don't like to see additions to EOP staff.

If that ruled out the EOP approach, then there should be an EPA-type, with the administrator doubling as the special assistant to the President in this area. That would constitute half a loaf. It would not involve the entire domestic/international area but it could be regarded as a way station. As I say, it is illogical to separate the domestic and international areas but, if regarded as a way station, it seems to me it is the best of the proposals today, flawed as it is.

The NTIA report says that in view of all the congressional, private sector, and governmental players, the "transactional costs" of these major changes is high. That is a euphemism for saying it would be a very bloody turf war and probably unsuccessful.

The second-best approach in the report is the Presidential veto. Once again it is very flawed. It did not work well in the CAB area. There is no reason to think it would work very well here. But everything in life is compared to what, and it would be an improvement over the present situation. As I say, I believe the executive branch has a very important role to play here, and I believe there would be greater attention to the threat of an executive branch veto.

The FCC would have to focus more on executive branch positions because the President could set aside its action. He couldn't make his own policy, but he could probably force the FCC along lines he thought sound because of foreign policy, national security, or trade considerations.

The third alternative listed in the report is to better coordinate executive branch activities in this field. For reasons I have already explained in connection with both NTIA and State, that is clearly a step forward and is thus desirable.

At this point I should touch on S. 999, as it seeks to accomplish the same goal of better coordination. The bill establishes a Special Representative for International Telecommunications in the Office of the President. That Special Representative would have a small staff and would be head of a temporary task force for three years, which could be extended for three more years.

State would undoubtedly oppose this. But the idea is to put the focal point in the Office of the President for coordination and clout and to avoid the parochial interests of Commerce or State. It is, in a sense, an OTP but just restricted to one field, international (which, as I say, is illogical).

You still would have the split with the FCC. The task force could not set aside any policy determination of an independent agency, such as is the FCC. The argument again in favor of doing this would be that, at least compared to the present, it affords greater focus and is a step forward.

The argument against it is that it is still very flawed, for the reasons I've given. There is an old adage, "If you strike at kings, strike at the throat." In other words, rather than going for this flawed half-measure, it might be wiser to attempt something a lot better, because you may not have many cracks at this policy ring.

The fourth approach in the report is the status quo. I think that's the worst. As to some of the steps to be taken, I think Robin Homet has written an excellent series of articles in the *Chronicle* [they follow his remarks in this book], and I will not preempt his discussion of them. As a realistic matter, I think that any improvement will come through some pragmatic small steps.

In sum, the international communications area is clearly one of great importance. It is in transition. We face great strains. Our present process for policy formulation is flawed. I believe we should keep in mind an ultimate goal: the consolidation of policymaking in one executive branch agency, and take whatever small steps we can now to get there.

# Roland Homet

*Roland Homet is a Principal, Communications Law and Policy Counseling, Washington, D.C. Mr. Homet is a graduate of Harvard College and Harvard Law School and is the author of* Politics, Cultures and Communication. *He was the Director of International Communications Policy for the U.S. International Communication Agency from 1978-1981, and the Assistant Director for Domestic Policy, White House Office of Telecommunications Policy, 1975-1976.*

The basic difference between Henry Geller and me, as we were discussing it beforehand, is that he thinks the proposed solutions set out in S. 999 (and implicit, I would say, in the NTIA report) *cannot* be adopted, to which I would add they *should not* be adopted, and that will take a little longer to explicate.

In reviewing the NTIA report and S. 999, as I was asked to do, I asked myself, and I would like to invite you to ask with me, three questions: First, what is the problem? Second, what solutions will not work? Third, what does that leave? That's the way I've approached it. It does seem to me that it is very important to get hold of the problem properly because otherwise we are unlikely to come out with the right solutions. I would like to take as my starting point a really marvelous book written during the Ford Administration called *Remaking Foreign Policy* by Allison and Szanton, Graham Allison being the dean of the Kennedy School at Harvard. A review, by Richard Neustadt, Sr., said in brief that this is a remarkable book, the most searching analysis of foreign policymaking we've had in a generation.

So let me just read to you from the passage where the authors draw their general conclusions because, for me, it is a useful starting point. This comes after a review of the totality of foreign policymaking across all sectors and interests.

"In our view," it says, "current organization or arrangements embody three principal defects: First, they are out of balance. They favor immediate results over long-range objectives, maintenance of the status quo over management of change, and narrow military and economic concerns over broader foreign policy considerations.

"Second, they bring too little competence to bear on complex issues. Likely foreign developments are poorly assessed, obstacles and implementation are neglected, and insufficient technical expertise is devoted to the advancement of general foreign policy perspectives.

"Perhaps most fatally, current arrangements make almost inevitable the disintegration of policy. They neglect the many-sidedness of issues like oil or nuclear energy (to which we today would add, and have been adding, communications)."

### Defining the Problem

So to summarize the three defects, they are incompetence, imbalance, and disintegration; and my opening observation is that NTIA and S. 999 do not address the first two. That seems to me rather basically important because poor people with poor policies will not be much improved by sitting in nice boxes.

As to the incompetence problem, which Henry Geller touched upon, there is a statement by CBEMA in the NTIA report pointing out that the people that deal with this area have insufficient experiential background in the issues. I will recall to you the letter by Representative Dante Fascell, dated October 3, 1980, to then Secretary of State Muskie in which he pointed out: "We need to focus on training, recruiting and career development in communications diplomacy"; and that, I would suggest, is an important part of the problem.

As for imbalance, again, the NTIA report cites and quotes the 1951 Truman Review which found that there were no long-range studies and no comprehensive policy development underway, and we all know that that is still the case.

The OTA report, which many of you must have read, on radio frequency use and management says that: "We need strategies not yet developed and tested." And I might add, from my own somewhat dispiriting experience sitting in on a few Space/WARC Advisory Committee meetings last summer and fall, I found them focused entirely on maintenance of the status quo with no imaginative addressing of the serious equity problems we face *vis-a-vis* the Third World. That whole exercise, in my judgment, is courting disaster.

The policy framework, to be balanced, must be comprehensive and not jammed into one basket as S. 999 suggests. There are problems with using trade as a framework. You have heard that trade is just one element of a broad range of U.S. policy concerns. Yet trade negotiations do not reach tax and regulatory measures taken by other governments or by international organizations, which is a very large part of the problem.

Trade policy also carries with it the risk of treating all information as a commodity and, so, of casting aside the First Amendment protections that we would wish to attach to many of our information flows. I think the NTIA report on that particular subject is much sounder.

To sum up on the imbalance point, I think what all this suggests is that we do need an institutionalized arrangement for sustained policy research and development. There is no effective agency for that in the government at the present time.

To continue with this question of the scope of the problem, the institutional dimensions surely extend beyond the executive branch to Congress and to industry. Again, the OTA report puts it as the information industries exhibiting no top-level appreciation of the issues; therefore, there is no effective constituency for international communications policy. That's fundamental.

Furthermore, Congress has not been substantively engaged in this area. I would like to read just one portion of what I wrote last summer about my first experience at a UNESCO conference in 1978 where the United States achieved all of its objectives, and I said: "That was the achievement of unsupported diplomacy. Congressional committee staffs, meeting," with me, as it was, "after the event to review what the *International Herald Tribune* had termed 'a diplomatic triumph for the West,' professed astonishment that no commitments had been made upon the Congress. This was because our legislature has never shown any willingness, either then or since, to authorize real resources in support of communications diplomacy. In part it has not been asked to by the Executive, and in part it has not been told to by industry constituents. The string on such unsupported diplomacy is running out."

Now, therefore, we have incompetence, imbalance, and disintegration; in Congress, industry, and the Executive. These materials in front of us [the NTIA report and S. 999] deal with only the last entry in each of those sets.

Executive disintegration: what is the problem there? The first and most basic point I would make is that it is not just coordination, since coordination gives you the lowest common denominator, and the NTIA report, to its credit, recognizes that. (As you will have observed, there *is* an organizational problem within the Department of State, set out in the NTIA charts at pages 79 and 80, a problem of fragmentation and inadequate resources; curiously, the NTIA report notes but does not deal with it.) Interagency coordination and information exchange are fine, and they are obviously needed, but they are going to happen anyway under any dispensation; and if that is all we are after, I would have to tell you from my experience that we have too much coordination already. An amazing amount of time and paper is devoted to interagency coordination which is too often a device for identifying and avoiding all risks.

A basic flaw, in my judgment, of S. 999 as expressed in its sections 202 and 204 is its exclusive emphasis on "coordination." That just is not the problem. If you think it is the problem, you are going to come up with the wrong solution. The key words are rather "leadership," "decisiveness," and "accountability." NTIA calls for an "ultimate arbiter," and a "focal point." I think I would add a "chief spokesman." CBEMA uses active verbs—"articulating," "negotiating," "dealing." Those are in the right direction. For this purpose we need something that's a lot more than just a conference preparation staff as described in the NTIA report. That is in-basket work—necessary but by no means sufficient.

The other major objective is to summon resources in support of policy. For example, funds must be made available to the State Department upon its request, to support the U.S. policy initiatives for communications development throughout the world which are intended to advance our First Amendment interests. Congress must become receptive to the new leader's requests, whoever this new leader may be.

Finally—and I say this with deference to the sponsors of our gathering—the focus cannot be limited to telecommunications but must cover all of communications and information policy, all of which is interdependent. Thus UN and UNESCO issues of concern to the U.S. press community are discussed later [see Chapter Six]. That is all part of the same ball of wax. We are dealing with a single political, economic, cultural, and social impulse which I call "information sovereignty" and which exerts itself as against both print and electronic forms of information distribution.

## Unacceptable Options

Now then, given that raised, and I think strengthened, definition of the executive disintegration problem, what solutions seem to me *not* to work? What should be avoided? Of the NTIA options, the first one to avoid is the status quo. It equips the U.S. to be reactive only, at best. Likewise, in my judgment, we should not spend any time formalizing an interagency group. That would simply entrench the erroneous "coordination" premise.

I think it would also be a fundamental mistake—and here is where I start to diverge from Henry Geller—to put a governing agency in the Executive Office of the President or to give the lead responsibility to the Department of Commerce or to a new Department of International Trade.

In this connection, I would like to read again from what I wrote in the article that follows these remarks. It says: "International communications policy—engaging as it does relations with our allies, with the Third World, and with the Soviet bloc—inescapably forms a part of our foreign policy which neither a White House body nor any other agency is competent to manage." I have found nothing in the papers before us that would cause me to change my mind about that.

Finally, like Henry Geller, I would certainly agree, since the two of us looked carefully into this in 1976, that there is no point in pursuing the creation of a Department of Communications. It would be a source of mischief, not of assistance.

Now, I have not been asked to testify on S. 999 and I gather there are not likely to be many congressional staff people here, but I still will try to give you a very short critique of the main points that trouble me in S. 999. I have to be candid with you. I find this to be an ill-considered and ill-drafted piece of legislation. Just picking the high points, it gives the Executive Office of the President authority over international, not domestic, telecommunications policy, and for the reasons you have heard you just cannot separate them.

Further, without any declared reason or finding, it puts *operational* responsibility in the Executive Office of the President. Here, if I may, I'll quote from a document that I drafted two years ago and sent over to the Baker triumvirate [at the White House], where it seemed to strike a responsive chord. That was on H.R. 1957, which is the spiritual predecessor of this document. The memorandum argued that it is "unsound management practice to divorce policy from operations, communications policy from foreign policy, or to place operational responsibilities in the White House." Again, I see no present reason to change that view.

There are some drafting peculiarities in S. 999 that I won't get into in any detail. Suffice it to say that one section of the bill has the Special Trade Representative directing telecommunications and information policy; another has the Special Telecommunications and Information Representative directing the trade agreements program. Other provisions have a Deputy Assistant Secretary in one bureau appointing an Assistant Secretary in another bureau as his deputy. Presumably the various drafters will get together at some point.

Section 306(a) bears some mention because it would create—with no staff or any resources to begin with—an Assistant Secretary of State for Telecommunications Affairs, with the rank of Ambassador. There is the germ of something here if it can be rooted out. I would have to say first, however, that "telecommunications" is still too narrow. The jurisdiction has to be Communications and Information. And it should not be limited, as it is in the bill, to economic matters. (This Assistant Secretary would not even be in the Economic Bureau.) As many of us have said, there are economic, political, cultural, and security considerations, all intertwined, so a step like this would contribute to a greater fragmentation. Now, if this were to become the only State Department bureau dealing with communications and information policy, that would be a different matter. Such a bureau would aggregate unto itself all of the bits and pieces that are set out on that chart in the NTIA report; but in that case, clearly, the jurisdiction would not be limited to economic matters. Finally, I would point out within the scheme of this statute that this Assistant Secretary would also be an ambassador, rivaling the ambassador who was in the Executive Office of the President, and I would have thought that for substantive as opposed to geographic responsibilities we would want to avoid that.

Turning now to the interagency task force set out in the bill, it is, in my judgment, much too elaborate procedurally; it's overstuffed, and there is no need for legislation to create a gathering of the clan. It is going to happen as a matter of course. If you create, for the first time, a center of real power and responsibility, everybody is going to want to be involved with it. There will be plenty of meetings, and there is no need for Congress to concern itself with that.

Now to a serious problem: the advisory committee for industry is, in my judgment, a very bad idea. It will eat up enormous amounts of staff and time which are badly needed for other things. A policy cannot be developed through a group of people who meet once a quarter. I mean, a real-world policy statement or negotiating position is ready only within the week before delivery. This whole business just will not work.

I might say, on the general subject of advisory committees, it is fine to have them, but these involve Washington representatives who, if you take them aside, will tell you their problem is that they don't have sufficient clout within their own companies. If we want to create a constituency that will promote a sensible structure and a dynamic for international communications policies, we have got to find a way to engage senior people in industry. That is something I will come back to at the end of my presentation.

The basic question is the governance of communications and information policy internationally. There are two choices: to put it in the Executive Office of the President or to place it in an augmented Department of State. S. 999 seems to give us both choices. We must take one, and I'll take the State Department. Again, I will come back to that.

I don't have time to go into the FCC-related proposals in any depth. Just very quickly, they are all answered in and fully developed by the 1981 report that was carefully considered over many months by an NTIA-chaired task force. That should be exhumed and read, and you will find the following points:

1. Yes to executive branch views being taken into account by the FCC.

2. No to a Presidential veto of the FCC. There was no consensus for that. The State Department and ICA and industry were all opposed to it. Industry found it cumbersome and feared it would interfere with business planning; further, it is unnecessary. The NTIA report says part of the problem is that there is now no focus in the executive branch for policy positions. That is going to be corrected. Then, we have this new provision for the FCC being required to take executive branch views into account. We ought at least to try that before moving to the radical further step of a veto. It didn't work well in the CAB international route decisions. There were suspicions, at least, of corruption. Ask Edward C. Schmults, who is now the Deputy Attorney General and who, in the Ford White House, insisted that process be changed.

3. As for integrating some of the FCC's international functions into the executive branch, it may be a decent idea but, for me at least, more careful assessment would be needed. It is not adequately explained or supported in the NTIA report.

**The Best Solution**

Finally, then, what is the answer? In the executive branch we need leadership, responsibility, accountability, balance and competence. They all have to come together; and they must come together—because of the foreign policy considerations—at the Department of State. We don't have those qualities grouped there now. How would we get them? I think there are two choices: either we create an Assistant Secretary and consolidate all the authorities currently fragmented around the Department in this one bureau; or (as I suggested in my paper) we create a Special Ambassador with the ability to direct all these people—and, as the paper says, he or she would have to be located in the Deputy Secretary's office, which is what was done with WARC and the Law of the Sea.

The choice has to do with the creation of a new bureau, whether Congress wants to wait and see as it did with Human Rights or is ready to move right now. If it wants to wait and see, State can move now to create the Special Ambassador. There is no need for authorizing legislation. There is need for some appropriations, though. I'll get back to that. The mandate of this office, whatever we call it, should include the following:

1. International communications and information policy.
2. Power to choose and approve all delegations, speeches, and testimony and policy statements.
3. The first choice to chair international delegations. The Senate bill has the head of the office chairing all of them. If you count them, that's physically impossible, but the choice should be there.
4. Chairmanship of interagency and interdepartmental meetings.

A coherent voice and vision is what we would be aiming for. Very important to this is the staff. That has to be addressed; otherwise, we are not in the real world.

I count eight necessary positions or, if it is an Assistant Secretary, it might be eight desks. First is an administrative assistant, an executive secretary to knock down bureaucratic barriers and establish training and career paths in communications and diplomacy. Then the others would have subject matter scope as follows: communications development policy; space communications policy; data communications policy; facilities planning; free flow of information; spectrum and standards policy; and, finally, policy development. Now, these would either consolidate or, in the case of the Special Ambassador, monitor and work with the various bureaus and offices of the Department. But the last of these, policy research and development, would be new. It would have the authority and budget to contract for policy studies in this country or abroad and to finance and participate in policy conferences anywhere in the world. I would say, too, we do need a fresh start. For myself, I would like to see half of these new positions recruited from the private sector for the first two or three years while career training paths unfold.

Interagency coordination is something we don't need to specify. That will take care of itself. I would have no massive industry advisory process. But I would say that the White House can have an important role here if it wishes. A Special Assistant to the President for Communications and Information Policy would be justified for both domestic and international issues. (The Special Assistant could have two aides: one domestic and one international. With two secretaries, it would not be a large office.) There are, after all, some presidential issues. I think the Bell breakup is one. Perhaps the new world information order is another. This would also provide accountability and reassurance to industry, which has not had a happy history of dealing with the line departments. Further, it would be a way to pressure AID, USIA, and others to put together the resources we need for policy.

Congress, as I said, does not need to adopt a statutory charter now; but if it accepts the Special Ambassador route, it would need to enact appropriations including a research and travel budget. There is need to bring continuing pressure on the White House and on State to get things done, and it must be substantive pressure.

I think Congress must start getting familiar with the long-range and comprehensive interests and opportunities of the United States. This has nothing to do with the short-term policies such as "pick-up-your-satellites-and-go-home," or the Beard Amendment for UNESCO. These are essentially frivolous and have nothing to do with the long-range interests of the United States. It is a complex but beckoning world. We can kick away our advantages through ignorance or incompetence, or we can harness our advantages to promote fundamental and continuing U.S. interests.

I think with appropriate informational hearings and by bringing in all the agencies to testify, Congress can play a very helpful shaping role. Indeed, it can exercise its policy guidance much better that way than through formal legislation. Ask the agencies: what risks does the OPEC oil precedent represent for orbit/spectrum allocations? What does the Law of the Sea process suggest for an eventual Law of Information Conference? Nobody in the executive branch is now addressing these questions.

As for industry, if you look at my paper you will find that I recommend—and this is a subject that has been the product of quite a lot of consultations with industry, in Congress and the executive branch—a freestanding Council on International Communications and Information Policy comprised of chief executive officers from each of the four major sectors of the information industries. They would not be engaged in issue lobbying. They already have staffs to do that. Their job would be to elevate the priority and the quality of attention that is given to problems in this area. I think that is fundamental.

My judgment is that there may be no effective reform, no matter what Congress or anybody in this room or in this town wants to do, unless we get that kind of magnetizing or catalyzing impulse. You know, if could be done so simply. To dramatize this, one conversation between Secretary of State George Shultz and Citibank's chairman Walter B. Wriston would do it. Everything would fall into place after that. Maybe some of us can carry the word in that direction.

Without that sort of thing happening, I fear that we may not be accomplishing very much. At the least, however, I think we should try to avoid some of the mistakes that I've tried to point out in the proposals before us.

INTERNATIONAL COMMUNICATION POLICY

# U.S. Policy and International Information Flows: Some Keys to an Integrating Perspective

*By Roland S. Homet, Jr.*

In the field of U.S. international communication policy, the bits of the puzzle are reasonably well understood, but the inter-relationships and broad dimensions are perceived only fitfully. We in the United States have been addressing these matters issue by issue, medium by medium, forum by forum.

Some of us with government experience have had the opportunity to work on mass media issues in the United Nations Educational, Scientific and Cultural Organization (UNESCO); on data transmission controversies at the Organization for Economic Cooperation and Development (OECD) and Intergovernmental Bureau for Informatics (IBI); on spectrum allocation questions at the International Telecommunications Union (ITU); and on direct broadcasting or remote sensing arguments in the UN. The more usual pattern, however, is for these issues and others to be dealt with by entirely different sets of people. They rarely have occasion to compare notes and never to reconcile differences, except at the highest level of generality such as "the free flow of information" — an inert principle that by itself can settle nothing. There is an inescapable tendency to

*This paper originally appeared as a series of articles in* Chronicle of International Communication, *as follows: Part I in III:3 (April 1982); Part II in III:4 (May 1982); Part III in III:5 (June 1982); and Part IV in III:7 (September 1982). Copyright © 1982 by International Communication Projects, Inc. Reprinted with permission.*

deal with each challenge only as it enters the in-box in the form of the next conference at Geneva or Paris or New York. This does not make for an integrating or forward-looking policy perspective.

The fragmentation of decision-making in government is, however, an accurate reflection of the constituencies that underlie it. Editors, publishers, broadcasters, and advertisers congregate once a year at high level to impress on the Secretary of State the importance they attach to UNESCO debates, but they never stay around to hear what is happening on computer-communications policy. Yet news and entertainment increasingly pass through the same conduits as business and banking data, and therefore are subject to the same constraints. Even without that — even when the forum varies, or the applicable regulations differ — the underlying political impulse (information sovereignty) is the same and feeds on its own triumphs. When spectrum is squeezed, therefore, or data transmission curtailed, press freedom is threatened and also the other way around. Still, publishers continue to go to one set of meetings while traffic managers go to a second and engineers (sometimes from the same companies) go to a third.

It is no wonder, then, that specialized enclaves have developed in the government to service these separate con-stituencies. It is also perhaps no wonder that the defense of information freedom as a vital, generic principle has failed to ignite any genuine sense of importance, either among business organizations or the U.S. government. When the specialists are in charge, the generalists look elsewhere. This may explain why the specialists themselves are under-manned, undertrained, and ill-supported: Resources flow to support priorities, and international communications policies at present command no priority in business or in government.

So, thought is fragmented and action irresolute. There is for example no systematic, cross-disciplinary policy research now being conducted into the causes or cures of the information sovereignty we confront abroad. Movements to restrict information flow are labeled ''political'' or

"protectionist" with little inquiry into motivation.
Sometimes, as with the wish to promote indigenous communications development, we detect a "legitimate" need
and move to meet it; but we do not take this as a sign to
search for parallels in other communication fields. There is,
again, no constituency for it.

The object of any policy review in this field must
therefore be to strengthen both thought and action,
knitting together constituencies and resources into a
unified, purposive sense of the whole. It should aim (1) to
promote integrated, comprehensive, and forward-looking
policy formulation; and (2) to spawn effective instruments
of execution.

One thing that is needed is to de-mystify the field, to
make it readily accessible to generalists as well as specialists.
As we look at the corrrespondences among international
communications issues, we should also examine the
similarities they bear with familiar domestic communications
issues. Foreign policy, it has been justly observed, is the
management of contradictions. We need to do a far better
job of recognizing that in the communications field. But
domestic policy is also and more visibly the management of
contradictions, and as an open information society we have
learned much to guide our hand in foreign dealings.

We should use the experience with our own internal
contradictions to help reconcile the kindred pluralisms of
the world. This would help gain broadened domestic
understanding and support for needed efforts, and would
allow us to contribute to international debates from our
own strength. The global communications tensions to be
canvassed in the next of these articles — freedom vs.
fairness, cultural intercourse or domination, efficiency vs.
security, monopolies and marketing, the parsing of
intellectual property — all have their vital domestic counterparts. We should draw on them far more persuasively than
we have.

This is not to suggest that we can lecture to, or in any
way patronize, foreign interlocutors. We have done too
much of that in the past, with talismanic invocation of the

First Amendment. That will not suffice domestically — as against competing claims of fair trial, national security, personal privacy — and we should not expect it to suffice internationally. A sensitive grounding in the national experience should sharpen the persuasiveness of our international posture.

Of course the world is not the United States and the issues are not all similar. Some new policy scales for balancing interests may eventually be needed. But the essential correspondence between the two political contexts remains: Policies that work and stick are those that serve a perceived mutuality of interests.


## II


Policy is the management of contradictions—in communications no less than agriculture, in international transactions no less than domestic. The American experience with domestic communications policy tensions may indeed provide some lessons for U.S. international communications policy. Let us consider five examples.

***Freedom vs. Fairness:*** In the course of American constitutional history, neither of these fundamental values has automatically eclipsed the other. There has been an accommodation. Today's Supreme Court and public opinion are still concerned to protect values such as personal privacy and a fair trial (often on behalf of the "little guy") against undue intrusions by a largely corporate press. The answers are elusive and may not always be correct. But as a society, we have been aiming to locate a balance that preserves *both* freedom of expression and fair dealing.

Our foreign policy seems in its formulations to forget or lose that balance. We proclaim the "free flow of information" as if it were the only value meriting recognition. In fact, the tension between freedom and fairness is the root tension internationally, affecting not just the mass media, but also data movements and spectrum allocations and the rest. It springs from the resistance of have-nots against haves, the objects of information transfer against the subjects. Very often the reaction is overdone. But the strength and legitimacy of the underlying sentiment can be ignored only at peril, both to our foreign policy and to our foreign information enterprises. The tension must be recognized and managed.

***Cultural Intercourse or Domination:*** At issue here is the potential homogenization of world cultures by societies (primarily the U.S.) whose dominance is seen as merely technological. The Swedes speak of "vulnerability," a concept that is difficult for Americans to grasp; less than one percent of our broadcast programming, and virtually none of our processed data, comes from abroad. (No other nation, not Russia or China, is so information insular.) It is, of course, possible to overplay "vulnerability." In a fair debate, any speaker is vulnerable to counter argument; indeed, he should be; and so should Sweden. But the terms of discourse are not always even, and cultural domination can be a real concern. That is what we have learned domestically from the protests of blacks and women and Chicanos who have historically been under-represented or misrepresented in the American instruments of mass culture.

In non-media fields, the cultural concern about U.S. data processing hegemony may be more subtle, but is nevertheless real. Computers order data relationships along principles such as cause-and-effect or affinity. These are logical constructs, and there is no one universal system of logic. If, therefore, Americans dominate data processing, it is U.S. economic and social modeling—a cultural bound way of perceiving the world—that prevails over all others. A recognition of our own self interest in preserving cultural diversity should help us learn over time to manage the resulting tension.

*Efficiency vs. Security:* U.S. policy understandably favors free trade in information goods and services. That is where our comparative advantage lies, in banking and computing and telecommunications. And as the progress of technology brings about an erosion of "natural monopoly" in these fields, we can properly assert the economic efficiency of allowing maximum freedom for competitive entry. That is one value. Another is the preservation of job and investment security, of market diversity, and of reasonable service stability. That this is not a trivial contradiction is illustrated by the massive and continuing domestic policy struggle over the future role of AT&T. It might surely be "efficient" to open all video and data services to the surviving Bell System. Newspaper and cable television companies have, however, viewed this prospect with alarm and have exacted restraining legislation from Congressional committees. Here is a search for balance between competing values, not essentially different from what our information industries encounter abroad. Neither story is yet concluded.

The introduction of new, high capacity information products or services almost always threatens existing jobs and investments. When the source of the disruptions is local, governments can take temporizing or transitional measures. Not so when its origin is foreign. The proponents of such innovations, or of the removal of barriers to trade, should take care not to press for an all-or-nothing answer. An argument for phased entry, buttressed by a show of accumulating benefits to the host economy, will usually do better than a ritual incantation of marketplace efficiencies. Those who resist this suggestion may be those who prefer the argument to the trade.

*Monopolies and Marketing:* U.S. cultural and political history—a nation of immigrants escaping authoritarian rule elsewhere—conditions us to see state control of information enterprises as evil. That perception, however, is atypical. In most other countries, including our OECD partners, the villain to be avoided is big business — hence the British Broadcasting Corporation, Radio Television Francaise, Sveriges Radio and Nihon Hoso Kyodai, for example, and the many foreign post and telegraph administrations. Most have safeguards to prevent narrow political misuse of the channels of communication, and these offer models to soften the media grip of the governments in emerging nations. It is also reasonable to suggest (once again) that rigid state monopolies tend to retard the introduction of innovative services, to the likely detriment of the host society.

But in international commerce, particularly as regards the Third World, it is the perceived inequality of bargaining power between the transnational corporation and the local government that underlies a great many restrictions on freedom of operation. This is understandable when the country in question disposes of no countervailing industry power. To its eyes, the alien company is an "AT&T" that alone possesses the data by which its own operations might be evaluated. We in the U.S., baffled by AT&T's autonomy despite decades of professed subjection to regulation, should appreciate the situation. Indeed, it was in large part to deal with this source of tension—to reduce monopoly power and open up new markets—that the International Program for the Development of Communications (IPDC) was created and awaits fulfillment. (The next of these articles will have more on that subject.)

*The Parsing of Intellectual Property:* Economists argue about whether information is a conventional commodity that can be valued for tax and customs purposes. The practical implications are momentous, not just in fiscal terms, but also as regards forced disclosure of proprietary information (what is on the tape) and beyond that, the whole regime of freedom for information transactions. The question affects media products, computer products, and new products like videotex and video discs.

Here again, the definitions and their consequences are every bit as important for domestic legal treatment as for

French value-added taxes. At present, apart from a scattering of court decisions, there are no settled answers in this country and none that is obvious. As with other transactions, information is probably a commodity for some purposes and not for others—or it can be made so, depending on the perceived balance of interests. The matter can be arbitrated by Congress and the answer exported with greater or lesser success. Perhaps an expert commission would be a place to start; or, given the delicacy and uncertainty of the issue, an exploratory essay by a thoughtful group of students.

We should not ask for answers internationally that escape us at home. When we do have answers—settlements among competing values—we should not hesitate to advance them for all they are worth. Often we may find a reception more congenial than we are currently experiencing.

## III

The relative ineffectiveness of U.S. international communication policy—relative, that is, to the scale of U.S. interests—arises in fair measure from its paucity of resources. The instruments by which to discern and pursue attainable national objectives are not in place. And that is because those who might forge such instruments are not persuaded of their importance. Policy refinement and constituency building are both prerequisites for an effective U.S. communications diplomacy.

To take the first one first, "free flow" is too blunt a policy instrument to be persuasive. It would of course be unwise to abandon this standard without securing some other dependable bulwark against information restrictions, and unrealistic to commit the search for an alternative to any imaginable set of global negotiations. But it would be quite appropriate for the U.S. unilaterally, drawing on its domestic experience, to designate "free flow" not as an absolute but as a preferred value, one with presumptive validity. This would maintain our position that, in case of inescapable collision with other values, information freedom should prevail; but it would also commit us to seeking avoidance of such collisions where possible. We would aim by this means to do what our Supreme Court does, which is to find room for competing values within a framework of information freedom.

Making room for other peoples' needs, interests, and values will typically cost very little, but may return a great deal. In the 1978 UNESCO negotiations over a New World Information Order (NWIO), there was only one paragraph that survived without a single change. Drafted by the U.S. delegation, it recognized "the benefits that might accrue to the peoples of the developed countries, and of the world, from an expanded opportunity to hear the authentic voice of differing societies and cultures in a dialogue made progressively more equal." Mood music, perhaps, but the long-range self-interest to which it paid court is unmistakeable. Even in the short run, the inclusion of such language helped turn the drafting of the NWIO resolution, and the companion Mass Media Declaration, in our direction.

That was an achievement of unsupported diplomacy. Congressional committee staffs, meeting after the event to review what the *International Herald Tribune* had termed a "diplomatic triumph for the West," professed astonishment that no commitments had been made upon the Congress. This was because our legislature has never shown any willingness, either then or since, to authorize real resources in support of communications diplomacy. In part it has not been asked to by the Executive, and in part it has not been told to by industry constituents. The string on such unsupported diplomacy is running out.

To begin with, what is at stake? In domestic political terms we are dealing with jobs, investment, and trade. Electronics and information exports, if grouped together—something present statistical formats do not permit—may very well constitute the largest positive contribution to the American balance of trade and payments. (Banking, insurance, technology, and other "invisibles" would be included in this grouping.) One would expect to find information industry leaders regularly voicing the litany of jobs, investment, trade—a language members of Congress understand—in support of an effective communications diplomacy. Apart from a narrow focus on trade negotiations, however, this does not occur, and no industry grouping has yet documented the effects on the domestic economy of actual or anticipated foreign restrictions on information movement. If industry hopes to gain serious policy attention and a focused response, it will have to do a far better job of quantifying what is at stake.

The fastest growing segment of U.S. trade is with the developing countries. These are also the countries that are making up their minds how to structure their own information sectors and how to cast their votes (the majority) on information-related issues in UN bodies. The outcome is not foreordained even for these countries that currently exhibit a clear preference for government control of information transactions; they are at least open to practical arguments about the benefits to them of a more open system. U.S. diplomacy can and should ceaselessly remind its Third World interlocutors that in the 18th and early 19th centuries, America was very much a developing nation, also non-aligned, and that we found information freedom a spur to our development. This is what has led, we can responsibly assert, to America's current emergence as the world's first "information society."

But this suggestive seed will take root only if accompanied by aid and development for the fragile communications infrastructures of the developing countries. The U.S. has taken a rhetorical lead in this direction by proposing and shaping the International Program for Development of Communications (IPDC). This means telecommunications, computers, and postal service to support economic growth and to integrate rural communities into the national structure. It also means, and in UNESCO it tends to mean primarily, expansion of the mass media of radio and television and films and newspapers. This is something that European and Japanese governments are equipped to provide, but in the U.S.

Government at present there is not one agency with a program to equip or train people working in the media. There is a communications program in the Agency for International Development (AID), but it is regularly starved for funds and it is subject to the over-riding statutory requirement that it contribute to "basic human needs." Those needs are defined as health care, education, population control, agricultural improvement. Information as such is not considered a basic human need. Nor does AID, or the World Bank for that matter, regard communications investments as causally connected to economic growth. The result is that communications and information are not admitted to the aid pantheon, and without legislative change there is little the U.S. can do to back up its commitment to the IPDC.

The IPDC has now held two meetings and can fairly be said to be in business. U.S. government and industry pledges are, however, so paltry as to be insignificant (less than Indonesia, much less than France or the Soviet Union). Clearly, a change to a more expansive and realistic course can come only at the instance of the private sector. But that sector has thus far shown no recognition of the IPDC's potential to open up growing markets for U.S. information products and services, or to lessen the information disparities that contribute to the promulgation of restrictive regulations by host countries. This indifference, whether studied or not, is a prescription for maintaining governmental controls and for handing over markets to more enterprising nations. It is also an invitation to future demands for spectrum fees or taxes as an alternative way of financing communications development.

It may be that industry is put off by the lack of evident priority or coherence in the conduct of U.S. communications diplomacy. For reasons earlier suggested, industry has itself in part to blame for the fragmentation **of the policy structure; and the industry-promoted legislation to shift decisions to the White House (H.R. 1957, et** al.) could detract still further from the necessary joinder of communications policy with foreign policy. But certain frustration with present arrangements is inescapable. As Congressman Dante Fascell has pointed out, there is in the foreign service no career path or specialized training or recognition for communications diplomacy, hence no attraction for the most capable people. (Economic diplomacy was in the same condition up until a few years ago, when Congress intervened.) The departmental bureaus do not reinforce each other on related issues, and even single offices—the UNESCO office comes to mind— are so egregiously understaffed that they find it difficult to sustain a focus on the same issue. As a kind of political coup de grace, the White House regularly intervenes to name senior diplomatic and delegation heads without any regard to their substantive competence in communications diplomacy. A field that is treated like a dumping ground begins to look like one.

If the Department of State needs intelligent internal restructuring, as it surely does, comparable attention must also be paid to other related agencies. The International Communication Agency (USICA) has a mandate by statute to help develop and execute a comprehensive national policy on international communications, but no resources are being devoted to the second half of that responsibility. There is need to review the pertinent struc- ture and functioning of AID, and also to refresh the supportive potential—now sadly diminshed—of the Commerce Department's National Telecommunications and Information Administration.

None of this is likely to happen until and unless sufficient importance is attached to the enterprise by the Secretary of State and the relevant committees of Congress. They in turn will be moved in the direction only if industry leaders tell them it is necessary. If such initiatives can be brought into being, it should be possible for the first time to begin to mount an effective U.S. communications diplomacy. It will then become apparent that the orchestration of all this potential—its diminuendo no less than its crescendo—should be guided by a single, integrating hand at the State Department.

## IV

America disposes willy-nilly of an awesome information power. That power is recognized and resisted by other nations resentful of its perceived economic, political, social and cultural effect. The bulwark of "information sovereignty" that the rest of the world erects—in the form of actual or threatened laws, regulations, decrees, and declarations—impairs to a very real if still unmeasured extent the realization of the comparative advantages U.S. industries happen to hold in this field.

It is therefore a matter of the highest national interest that the United States should find ways of civilizing and ingratiating its global information power—to hold and attain markets, to project the idea of freedom, to safeguard national and collective security.

There is much that U.S.-based information industries can do and in certain cases have done on their own to allay reactive tensions from abroad. Because of their regulated status, banking and insurance affiliates in foreign lands have long operated as good citizens of their host countries; so too, with an eye on sales, have leading computer and data-processing firms. The American mass media, with their constitutionally rooted adversary stance towards all governments, have until recently been more abrasive. But there is reason to suppose that they too may be gaining a new sophistication without sacrifice of mission—drawing perhaps on the illuminating exercises in self-criticism that marked the 1982 annual conventions of the newspaper publishers and editors. (In effect, these gatherings were told that the possession of a right or power does not invariably require its exercise: Information gatherers and publishers can engage in their own, unsupervised, balancing of transactional values.) Some such humanizing of the information enterprise, on a strong plateau of professionalism, seems essential to gaining the acquiescence of important constituencies both here and abroad.

### An Industry Council

But industry cannot carry the work burden of communications diplomacy by itself. The duty to respond to information-flow curtailments proposed by other governments or by international organizations falls by definition on the U.S. Government. It is the Secretary of State or his representatives who must address the Canadian Banking Act, French taxing measures, Brazilian import restriction, Organization for Economic Cooperation and Development (OECD) codes, and declarations by the United Nations Educational, Scientific and Cultural Organization (UNESCO). If, then, the enlightened leaders of American industry wish to promote an effective defense of their own long-range interests, they will have to organize a suitable political constituency for that purpose. Nothing that is sufficiently high-level or comprehensive now exists.

One instrument that I have suggested elsewhere is a free-standing Council on International Communications and Information. Composed of chief executive officers from the four pertinent industry sectors—mass media, telecommunications, computers and data processing, and major information users—the council would take as its chief objective the strengthening of the U.S. policymaking process. It would communicate to Congress, to the President, and to the American public its reasoned conviction of the priority, the resources, the coherence, and the far-sightedness that this presently under-attended field of public policy should enjoy. It would draw on academics and on experienced government officials, and would presumably employ a small staff, but its judgments would remain those of industry leaders committed to an intelligent deployment of America's information capacities.

### A Policy Structure

That development, if it takes place, should be enough to propel into being the other long-overdue reform: a restructuring of the U.S. Government. This has now been an active topic for some time, among Congressional committees and elsewhere, and there are doubtless as many plans as there may be authors; nothing, however, has happened. In the interest of simplicity and ease of execution, I have suggested a starting point that ought to initiate some degree of consensus. It focuses on the Department of State, because international communications policy—engaging as it does relations with our allies, with the Third World, and with the Soviet bloc—inescapably forms a part of our foreign policy which neither a White House body nor any other agency is competent to manage. The proposal leaves room for concomitant structural reforms at sister agencies like the Agency for International Development (AID), U.S. Information Agency (USIA), and the National Telecommunications and Information Administration (NTIA), once a responsible leader at State has been invested with the requisite authority and standing to intitiate such reforms.

### Leadership vs. Coordination

The need is for leadership, for direction—not merely for "coordination" as is sometimes suggested. There are if anything far too many inter-agency groups in existence now, "coordinating" everything down to the lowest ineffectual denominator. I would begin, then, with the creation of a Special Ambassador-at-Large for Information and Communications Policy. This worthy would be located administratively in the Deputy Secretary's office, as was done with the World Administrative Radio Conference and with the Law of the Sea Conference. The Ambassador would have a senior administrative assistant to knock down bureaucratic barriers and start establishing communications diplomacy as a recognized career path within the Department. In addition, there would be (by my count) seven special assistants each dedicated to a substantive area (space communications, spectrum resources, data transfers, mass media, etc.) which would be monitored for the Special Ambassador. All policy papers, delegations, speeches and the like would be cleared by the Ambassador, who would serve as the principal spokesperson for the Administration on relevant matters. The special Ambassador would of course be subject to confirmation by the Senate and questioning by Congress.

This beginning structure could in time evolve into a bureau headed by a regular Assistant Secretary. That would evoke opposition from established and rival bureaucracies, and there is no need to decide on successor arrangements at this time. There is a need to make a decisive start, and the Special Ambassador route appears in my private soundings to elicit less opposition and more support from decision-making quarters than any other. It would get the necessary policy process rolling.

What remains then is only for the enlightened industry leaders we all wish to meet, to see their opportunity for policy leadership and to take it.

Chapter Five

# Domestic Deregulation of Telecommunication Services: Can It Coexist with a Regulated International Environment?

# Walter Bolter

*Walter Bolter is a Partner, Bolter and Nilsson Consultants, Washington, D.C. Dr. Bolter received a Bachelor of Mechanical Engineering degree and an M.S. in Industrial Management from the Georgia Institute of Technology and an M.A. and Ph.D. in Economics from the University of Maryland. He was formerly Chief Economist for the House of Representatives' Subcommittee on Telecommunications, Consumer Protection and Finance. He has also served as Chief of the Economic Division of the FCC's Common Carrier Bureau and worked as Senior Economist with the Department of Commerce's Office of Telecommunications.*

I hope to examine four or five major subjects. First, in order to get everyone started off with the same knowledge, I will compare the development of public policy in domestic and international telecommunications markets, taking special notice of policies dealing with competition, resale, and deregulation.

Second, I will delve into a few revealing statistics, as well as institutional differences between the domestic and international arenas. My major institutional concerns relate to the limitations of the FCC's authority and differing goals and objectives between international institutions.

Finally, it would be appropriate to deal with the functioning of these markets. Whipsawing effects that seem evident in international markets are important, as are foreign entry into U.S. markets, and discrimination.

With that introduction, let's talk about the FCC's policies in the domestic arena and compare those to its international policies.

## Domestic and International Regulation

For domestic private-line markets, entry policies of the FCC evolved from an initial approach of gradually introducing competition, starting with the MCI and Specialized Common Carrier decisions.

However, the Commission's policy of "gradualism" did not deal with switched offerings. Competition there actually had to be initiated by external forces, namely the 1978 Court of Appeals *Execunet* decision, which permitted the entrance of the plethora of new competitors so evident today.

Another market-entry phenomenon relates to "bypass," a term much more in common use today than when bypass first became a practical possibility back in 1959. At that time, noncarrier based or private microwave systems, particularly for large telecommunications users, were authorized under the FCC's Above 890 decision.

Since then "bypass" has gone through 23 years of evolution. Today, many options are emerging such as cable television, fiber optics, digital termination, private microwave systems, and even the sale of satellite transponders. While not a serious threat as a substitute for the facilities of franchised carriers as yet, eventually these alternatives may present large users with some viable options for many of their telecommunications needs.

Resale and sharing is another important development in domestic telecommunications markets. The first major breakthrough in this area occurred in 1976, with an FCC decision affecting only private-line services. At that time, the Commission required that tariff prohibitions against resale be removed. Similar decisions for switched services followed, so that now full resale of MTS (regular long-distance service) and WATS is permissible.

During this period, there were important changes in the FCC's historical approach toward regulation. These included a movement toward a "dominant firm" theory of regulation, under which AT&T and Western Union were treated differently from all other firms. In particular, only AT&T and Western Union were to be subjected to full regulation, whereas other firms would not need to supply cost support materials for their tariffs, delay implementation of tariffs until a review process was completed, and otherwise submit to substantive regulatory oversight or surveillance.

Finally, the Commission's domestic deregulatory policies should be noted. Computer Inquiry I (CI 1) in the 1960s resulted in the removal of data processing as an area in which the FCC would exercise regulatory oversight. In Computer Inquiry II (CI 2), the FCC extended deregulation to the areas of enhanced services and provision of customer-premises terminal equipment.

Let us now review these domestic policy initiatives for application to international communications, starting initially with those dealing with market entry and industry structure.

Within the ambit of its authority, Commission interference in international markets historically has been intensive. For example, the FCC has attempted to structure these markets through the facilities authorization process, whereby the Commission would "condition" facilities applications to suit its policy objectives.

An important illustration of this interference was establishment of the voice/record market division or dichotomy under the FCC's 1964 TAT-4 decision. That decision separated provision of voice and record services between AT&T and the international record carriers (IRCs), respectively. This division remained in effect for nearly twenty years.

In recent years, the Commission has removed these divisions and permitted AT&T to provide record services. Similarly, it permitted the IRCs to offer voice services, along with any other firm that could reach an operating agreement with foreign administrations at the overseas or "other end" of the communications path.

Although the FCC has been the major catalyst in promoting changes in international markets, Congress has also "gotten into the act." The most recent congressional initiative was the Record Carrier Competition Act (RCCA) of 1981. That legislation permitted Western Union to re-enter overseas markets, and also allowed the IRCs to offer domestic services. In addition, it contained requirements for nondiscriminatory interconnection among the IRCs and the unbundling of their domestic and international transmission offerings.

Access to INTELSAT is another important area of international market policy. In August 1982, the FCC permitted noncarrier access to INTELSAT, but, as a balancing measure, permitted COMSAT, with some restrictions, to enter the end-user market service area.

Bypass has international overtones as well. To date, bypass is not truly a *problem*, in the sense that actual evidence of this phenomenon is miniscule. In the future, however, bypass may present important policy concerns. For example, the Brazilians and other countries have given indications that national or regional systems may be in the offing, apart from INTELSAT. And Orion or others' applications for private systems would result in bypass of INTELSAT. These applications may be favorably acted upon by the Commission.

Resale and sharing, as well as deregulation, in international telecommunications have created a storm of controversy. The CCITT has recommended prohibitions against resale, largely following the policy position of foreign administrations. In April 1980, the FCC issued a Notice of Proposed Rulemaking (NPRM), noting the benefits of resale to small users and the increases in traffic that it might spur, and requested comments.

Positions of the parties commenting on the NPRM have followed predictable lines. The IRCs oppose resale, while AT&T notes the usefulness of resale—on terms suitable to the company. Large users basically support resale if implemented in such a way as to avoid foreign retaliation or loss of flat-rate pricing for private-line services. Foreign administrations seem to fear resale might cause revenue losses and thus generally oppose the concept.

Unilateral action of the Commission in this area, while possible, would cause significant problems in that the FCC does not control the "other end." Retaliation might be severe. Foreign administrations might even eliminate private-line services, which are so important to large users, in addition to putting "meters" on private-line services.

Clearly, the Department of Defense, large data processing firms, banks, and many other large users would face crushing price increases in such an adversative environment. Indeed small users would hardly benefit either if private-line services were metered. What will actually happen is anybody's guess.

In the area of deregulation, CI 1 and CI 2 have both been found to apply to international communications. The FCC will continue to regulate basic common carrier transmission capacity, and will require the unbundling of basic and enhanced services.

A current area of controversy is whether deregulatory FCC policies will prejudge Commission determinations in the area of international resale. Some argue that the FCC's August 1982 decision affirming the enhanced/basic service dichotomy precludes any Commission determination against resale.

The FCC's position is that there are no necessary connections between deregulation of enhanced services and resale. And, there are no findings concerning third-party use of tariffed common carrier facilities in the August 1982 decision. In short, resale policy determinations are still "open."

The Commission's reasoning has satisfied nearly no one. For instance, the position of the Director of the CCITT seems to be that resale issues are prejudged. The IRCs agree. And Western Union International (WUI) feels that basic services, Telex/leased channels, and message telephone are going to be seriously affected by deregulation of enhanced services. These will be resold no matter what the FCC proclaims.

### Domestic and International Markets

Let us now turn to a few market statistics and remaining issues. In particular, what is the split of revenues between voice and record services and between carriers? About 81 percent of international traffic relates to voice services with the remainder split between record and alternative voice/data offerings. This market does not fit classical definitions of "competitive."

AT&T still retains control of voice offerings, while RCA, ITT, WUI, TRT, and FTCC still supply most record services. However, record carriers, as a group, do not compare in size with AT&T, even though these firms are now in a position of competing "head-to-head" with that company. Taken together, the IRCs amount to only about one percent of Bell System revenues, or fifty percent of AT&T's overseas sales. With the removal of TAT-4 restrictions, each of these firms' revenues are now subject to competitive erosion by a very large entrenched supplier having no important restrictions placed upon it.

Domestic market policies have also been subject to a degree of change in other countries that is reminiscent of the directions taken by the FCC. The United Kingdom, Australia, and Canada are among those nations that have made attempts to make their domestic telecommunications industries more competitive. These have been limited largely to special areas, such as the Mercury System in the U.K. Even Japan may attempt to restructure its domestic long distance markets along more competitive norms.

Nevertheless, on balance, foreign administrations have not wholly embraced competition and particularly the FCC's policy initiatives. Indeed, some European observers predict that there will be requirements imposed so that new U.S. carriers will have to bid for operating agreements among themselves. In this way, European administrations will still have to deal with only a few U.S. companies.

Because of the sovereign foreign operator at the "other end," international policymaking presents special problems not usually encountered in domestic markets. For example, since foreign administrations have the power to choose which U.S. firm they will operate with and to control traffic distributions between competing firms, these entities can "whipsaw" U.S. carriers against one another.

Foreign administrations can affect the accounting or settlements rate on intercountry traffic and, in turn, carrier revenues. If the accounting rate falls (for the U.S.), U.S. carrier revenues will fall. In turn, if resultant losses are passed on to U.S. users, these users would pay rates higher than foreign service users. Implications for this nation's balance of payments would be negative.

Reliance on a "market approach" as some advocate as a norm for U.S. telecommunications policy would not work to alleviate the effects of whipsawing. Indeed, recognizing this problem in the past, the FCC has intervened to protect U.S. interests. But the issue remains in the new deregulatory environment for enhanced services. What role will the Commission play?

The traditional trade problem of dumping has also called for market intervention. In services, unlike products or equipment, there is little precedent for dealing with this issue. Entry of foreign firms into U.S. markets could cause serious problems in this area, problems that our institutional system is poorly suited to deal with.

In addition, there is the issue of U.S telecommunications firms gaining access to foreign markets. Reciprocal provisions contained in recent legislative efforts are one approach toward dealing with this discrimination. However, this approach has the serious failing of not viewing trade issues as a "package" and may remove needed flexibility in trade negotiations concerned with much broader issues than those that just affect telecommunications.

And it is unlikely that legislation can be fine-tuned sufficiently to deal with the particular circumstances of a given situation involving discrimination. For instance, the prices paid for transiting traffic across a nation between the U.S. and some third nation might involve disparities, or distribution of traffic might involve a foreign entrant into U.S. markets being allocated a greater share of inbound U.S. traffic than a similarly situated U.S. firm. It is inconceivable that legislation could deal with the myriad of such situations that may arise better than a properly motivated agency charged with protecting U.S. interests.

## Conclusions

What conclusions can one draw from the current international telecommunications institutional and market situation? Well, it seems certain that no simple transfer of U.S. domestic market policies, whether laissez-faire or fully interventionist, can be made to international telecommunications markets.

International telecommunications is concerned with more concentrated market conditions, presents situations vital to national interests, and involves entities that U.S. policymakers simply do not control. Moreover, for basic services that remain regulated, regulatory "tools" for control differ from those used domestically, and there are a multitude of U.S. agencies involved.

Special problems like whipsawing, foreign entry, and discrimination may even require the Commission to rethink entirely its free-market approach for these issues. Indeed, the FCC, and the nation, may be much better off if the Commission acts as a quasi cartel manager in certain instances and an advocate of market determinations in others.

Other alternatives appear infeasible. Legislative based "general solutions" are simply too cumbersome to deal with all international issues. Antitrust protections may fail for want of needed data and complications related to the need to consider telecommunications issues in a much broader national trade context.

If anything seems clear, it is that there are no easy answers. The FCC in its traditional role as interpreter of societal interests in the telecommunications arena, after all, still seems to be a proper administrative vehicle. If the FCC can avoid employing a doctrinaire competition or deregulation set of solutions for whatever ails the industry, particularly in international telecommunications, it can go a long way toward protecting vital interests of U.S. consumers.

# Alan Pearce

*Alan Pearce is an economic consultant on telecommunications policy. Dr. Pearce received his B.S. and M.S. degrees in Economics from the London School of Economics and a Ph.D. from Indiana University. He has served as Chief Economist for the House Subcommittee on Telecommunications, as Special Assistant and Advisor to the FCC Chairman, and as a consultant to the Executive Office of the President. He is editor of* Telecom Insider *and President of Information Age Economics.*

The seven issues that I plan to address are as follows:

1. TAT-4 revisited, which Walter Bolter mentioned;

2. The Authorized User decision revisited;

3. COMSAT restructuring, which is still under active FCC consideration, and which may arouse the interest of the Congress;

4. Direct access to INTELSAT which is also still under FCC consideration;

5. Ownership of U.S. international earth stations which, again, is still under FCC consideration;

6. The NORDTEL and the Benelux proposals: a case study of the so-called whipsawing effect, and certainly an excellent case study of potential international competitive problems; and

7. A European Common Market case, known as the Telespeed case, which was Europe's first international telecommunications competitive conflict, and which pitted the Bundespost, not the most enlightened national monopoly, against British TELECOM, which is just a little bit more enlightened than the Bundepost, though not by much. British TELECOM, like all companies, wants to exploit any competitive advantage that it may have. It does not want to promote full and fair competition. Make no mistake about that.

## TAT-4 Revisited

In 1964, the Federal Communications Commission, in authorizing the construction of transatlantic cable number four, decided to codify its policy regarding the dichotomy between voice and record (or non-voice) traffic. Although this voice-record dichotomy confuses many people in this industry, it shouldn't be confusing at all. The dichotomy has to do with the fact that technocrats who develop a technology have a right—even under the law—to exploit their unfair or fair competitive advantage in the marketplace.

The invention of the telegraph and the formation of Western Union in 1848 resulted in what became known as record traffic. The invention of the telephone by that great Scot Alexander Graham Bell resulted in the development of voice traffic. Therefore, there was an obvious technical dichotomy which became embodied in FCC policy. For many years, no one questioned its wisdom.

The policy was recently reviewed in Docket 81-432 with the goal of providing more competition between the IRCs who, as you know, collectively control record traffic in a very neat cartel, and AT&T, which has had and will continue to have, I believe, the monopoly in voice traffic. The FCC assumed that by reviewing this policy and by abolishing this rather bizarre distinction, effective international competition would result.

Many Americans have a rather simplistic view of competition. We don't understand it. We have a faith in it without knowing what competition is, or how it really works. Consequently, there is a simplistic faith in full and fair competition internationally, merely because the FCC has abolished the voice-record dichotomy.

## The Authorized User Decision Revisited

The FCC decision made in August 1982 enables COMSAT to provide end-to-end service to its customers. The original Authorized User decisions made by the FCC in the late 1960s restricted COMSAT's business activities to those of a carrier's carrier. In other words, COMSAT would only deal with certain authorized users, namely, AT&T, the international record carriers, and the Department of Defense. Other potential customers could not approach COMSAT directly but had to go through one of the authorized users. The Department of Defense was included as an authorized user for obvious reasons—chief among them being the importance of communications to our national and international security.

## COMSAT Restructuring

The restructuring of COMSAT is an extremely controversial inquiry at the FCC. It is also likely to involve some congressional hearings. The issue of concern here is whether COMSAT's competitive joint ventures and subsidiaries, the most important being Satellite Business Systems (SBS) and Satellite Television Corporation (STC), are being cross-subsidized by revenues from the COMSAT rate-base regulated international service offerings.

The FCC has required COMSAT to restructure itself in a way that will prevent cross-subsidies of any kind flowing from one company to another or one subsidiary or joint venture to another.

COMSAT has already submitted its own plan for restructuring. The FCC is considering this plan, and one of the reasons that Congress might get involved concerns the fact that Congress, rightly or wrongly, believes that it created COMSAT in 1962 under the Communications Satellite Act. COMSAT began operations in March of 1963, and Congress still regards COMSAT as a creature of the Congress and, therefore, wants to keep an eye on it.

## Direct Access to INTELSAT

Western Union initiated this FCC inquiry. The international carriers, now including Western Union, want to gain direct access to INTELSAT rather than pay a fee to COMSAT for access. This is a manifestation of a competitive war breaking out in the marketplace. Western Union and the IRCs saw that COMSAT was getting some competitive breaks from the FCC, so they decided to strike back at COMSAT.

This is under active consideration at the FCC, although both COMSAT and INTELSAT, which have always been very closely related to each other, clearly oppose any change in the current relationship.

## Ownership of International Earth Stations

This is another anti-COMSAT move on the part of COMSAT's competitors. Under a 1966 FCC policy, COMSAT owns 50 percent of an earth station consortium, ESOC, which simply means Earth Station Consortium. AT&T Long Lines owns 35 percent; RCA Globcom owns 10 percent; some of the smaller carriers, TRT, for example, 2.5 percent.

This particular FCC inquiry is a competitive response to the changes in the Authorized User decision. The IRCs are currently attempting to get existing FCC policy changed in order to allow them to own their own earth station facilities so they can end run COMSAT, and more effectively compete.

The IRCs are afraid that COMSAT's dominance in international earth station ownership might hurt them competitively, especially if the Circuit Court of Appeals upholds the changes in the Authorized User decision. The objective here is that the IRCs and AT&T Long Lines want to become independent international earth station owners so they can create "more competition" internationally.

### The NORDTEL/Benelux Proposal

This is referred to in the NTIA report and caused enormous controversy when it was first announced. Because the FCC's Computer II decision was applied internationally, some foreign PTTs saw that they could play the U.S. international service providers off against each other. They saw that the service providers of enhanced telecommunications services would perhaps be stupid enough to bid against each other in order to strike exclusive deals with foreign administrations (PTTs—Ministries or Departments of Post, Telegraph and Telecommunications).

NORDTEL, which is an association of PTTs in Scandinavia—Norway, Sweden, Finland, Denmark, and Iceland—approached some of the U.S. international service providers and asked them to submit proposals regarding service offerings and prices of those offerings.

When the FCC heard about this, Chairman Mark Fowler, an avowed unregulator and a free-marketeer, suddenly had a great concern about the international application of procompetitive deregulatory policies. The FCC believed that NORDTEL's approach to the American carriers might be in contravention of the Uniform Settlements Policy which was updated and codified by the FCC in 1980. This policy sets rules for the international accounting of rates.

What the FCC thought was happening here was that NORDTEL was attempting to get perhaps a 60/40 or even an 80/20 split by negotiating an exclusive contract with a particular U.S. provider of enhanced services, which Walter Bolter referred to as whipsawing the American carriers, a very good policy if you are sitting over in Europe.

The FCC and the State Department almost went berserk. An Interagency Task Force was formed consisting of representatives from the Office of Management and Budget, National Telecommunications and Information Administration, the Department of State, the FCC, and the Foreign Trade Representative's Office. It was a high-caliber task force because, for the first time in the Reagan Administration, high administration officials saw that competition doesn't work quite the way some supply-siders think it does.

No sooner had the original NORDTEL proposal been made than the Benelux countries—Belgium, the Netherlands, and Luxembourg—made an almost identical proposal. In fact, it was almost word-for-word the same proposal.

The NORDTEL and Benelux administrations said, "We weren't going to do anything unfair. You are misinterpreting our real intentions!" The issue was of such importance that it was raised in Paris in December 1982 and January 1983 by FCC Chairman Fowler and the State Department at the OECD meeting. Both NORDTEL and Benelux capitulated—at least for time being. Letters of understanding have been sent from the State Department to the PTTs saying rather bluntly, "Don't mess about with U.S. international carriers." For its part, the FCC has told the American carriers that they can deal with the Scandinavian and Benelux PTTs as long as the International Settlements Policy is observed. So we averted what could have been an international competitive tragedy.

**The Telespeed Case**

This concerns the arbitraging of international Telex rates and poses serious pricing problems for all PTTs and in particular for the members of the European Community, formerly the European Common Market.

The Telex collection rate from the Federal Republic of Germany to Great Britain is 15p.—that's about 25 U.S. cents. From Great Britain to the United States it is 40p., which is about 60 cents. From Germany to the United States, however, it is £2.25—about $3.40.

What does this mean? It means the rate from Germany to the United States, via Britain, is less than $1.00 and from Germany to the United States directly it's approximately $3.40. Capitalists in Western Europe are just as smart as we capitalists in North America, so this pricing situation presented significant arbitrage opportunities for companies setting up the machine in London, to collect Telex messages from Germany and then transmit them to the United States of America. A good business idea!

The Bundespost, Germany's telecommunication as well as postal monopolist, got very edgy about this, as you can expect, and complained to British TELECOM (BT). BT was disinclined to do anything about the problem because it had a distinct competitive advantage here, largely because traffic volume between Britain and the U.S. is very high and presumably profitable. The facilities between Britain and the U.S. are more effectively and heavily used.

Because BT was unflinching, the Bundespost took BT to the European Community, saying that this pricing difference was a violation of Articles 85 and 86 of the European Community, which relate to antitrust and the abuse of a dominant position.

Britain is believed to have a dominant position because of the greater traffic that flows from the United Kingdom to the United States and vice versa. The European Community came down very heavily on the side of the Bundespost. But BT has not given up yet. They decided to appeal the case to the EC Court of Justice at the Hague and a decision is pending. The original EC decision was made in December 1982.

### Conclusion

The bottom line seems to be that there is lots of confusion in this business and that's partly because we do not understand the way other nations behave. This is caused in part, by our simplistic view of competition and the presumed benefits that it is bound to bestow upon us all. Many other nations simply do not accept that notion.

So the only thing that I can suggest to you is to try to develop the greatest possible sensitivity to other political institutions, other beliefs, and other economic systems. After all, we do believe in the rights of others. We have laws making it illegal to discriminate against our own minorities. We are a very unusual and unique nation, but so are the other nations of the world. We really need to try to understand them. We need to talk with them, not to intimidate them.

Other nations are intimidated because we are powerful. We are bright. We are the best-educated nation in the world. That may come as some surprise to you, given all of the reports recently that our educational system is falling apart. In higher education this country is second to none, and technologically we are second to none. Consequently, we are an intimidating force—educationally, economically, politically, and culturally.

We've got to understand that competition is not simple to understand. Some people simply don't like competition and we are not going to persuade some other nations that it is good. We might persuade the Chinese that competition in some areas is good, or that private ownership might be good in certain circumstances, but we are not going to de-Communize the Communist bloc, and we are not going to desocialize the Western European countries. That's simply not going to happen. We are not going to convince them that we are right about competition in the free market, because they think the free market has inherent problems associated with it, and the sooner we understand that, the better.

# Chapter Five Discussion

QUESTION: *I recently read COMSAT's annual report and they are very glib and very up-front about their regulated service being their cash cow; if you look at their listing, they are a deficit company without that regulated service. Alan, apart from tinkering with COM-SAT's structure, can they survive without that cash cow, and are we really making a business mistake going down the slippery slope?*

MR. PEARCE: I'll answer the first part of your question. No, they can't survive.

MR. BOLTER: I have questions about a corporation that has a domestic satellite system and has no satellites, and that has a direct broadcast company which doesn't have any programming and created its own competition in the form of SBS.

QUESTION: *Since the U.S. did write to the Nordics and to the U.S. carriers withdrawing its opposition to proceeding with the bidding for exclusive franchises, why do you think we haven't heard about any bids entered or considered?*

MR. PEARCE: The letter from Gary Epstein [then Chief, FCC Common Carrier Bureau] to the American carriers went out at the end of February 1983, I think, so obviously this particular case study has sensitized the international record carriers or any carriers that are interested in entering the international service market, and I think they are quite wisely waiting to assess the situation. I think it has been something of a cultural shock. The letter, as I say, has only recently gone out, so I'm not surprised that there is a lack of urgency to respond to the NORDTEL and Benelux proposals as reformed at the meetings in Paris, so I would expect some of our carriers to be interested in making deals. Several of them are really assessing the situation and developing the smarter approach, and that's good. That's why it is a good case study. It is all right to talk simplistic policy, but this is the first case study that we've managed to get our hands on, and I think it is an excellent one because it is teaching the American carriers something about the way the Europeans operate, as Walter has said.

For the first time they are understanding what whipsawing really means. It is not just referred to in an FCC policy document; this is a practical, real-life example. So, hopefully, they have learned something. I will wait to see.

MR. BOLTER: I think that Europe is sort of fortunate that they've had some of these smaller, less influential (in an economic sense) countries involved in that proposal. I think the rest of Europe is trying to reassess not only new opportunities for whipsawing, but also the chance to make international competition even more concentrated than it has been, what with AT&T now much freer to move into other markets. In addition, the English seem to be in an ideal position to do some whipsawing of their own. So I think there is an awful lot of shaking-out among the European countries that haven't been heard from, and among the market participants that have newfound freedom to gain advantage over their competitors, perhaps to the disadvantage of Ma Bell and our balance of payments.

*QUESTION: Did the FCC letters touch upon the theory or justification for any governmental interferece in support of a nonregulated or deregulated service? In other words, is in fact the FCC not regulating enhanced services? What business did it have, or what justification did it give, to tell the carriers providing a service not subject to regulation not to deal with the foreigners with respect to that service?*

MR. BOLTER: All I can say is, consistency has never been the hallmark of FCC or other governmental policies. I don't know that that's a reasonable basis on which to look at that situation.

*QUESTION: The French are proposing to have a regional satellite system called TELECOM. The British also are proposing a regional system called Unispace or UNISAT, I believe. Can either of these systems survive without international traffic over the Atlantic? Can the economies of either country, or the telecommunications of either country, really support a large satellite system?*

MR. BOLTER: I don't know. I'm not familiar enough with the numbers, but it's pretty clear that these systems are kind of analogous to Orion. In a sense, they can see the advantages of going around INTELSAT on the dense North Atlantic route.

Even if they were self-sufficient without that traffic, I don't know why they wouldn't want to entertain the possibilities of bypass.

MR. PEARCE: I agree. I'm not as familiar with the French proposal as I am with the British proposal, but British TELECOM is the single most powerful and relevant entity in Western Europe because of the ties between our two countries.

Again, I have not seen the figures but I am much more optimistic about any British proposal than I am about the French proposal in the North Atlantic simply because of our cultural ties. Certainly the British, as Walter said, will be routing traffic on their own satellite system. They will be rigging the system. It will be government supported, at least initially, as I understand it, because it is prestigious to have satellite communication systems and launch capacity. The United States has traditionally led in this field, and the Europeans don't want to do anything to perpetuate that leadership.

I agree with Walter. I think that the jury is out on both of these proposals, but, if I were to bet, I would bet for the British system simply because they are incredibly powerful in the North Atlantic basin.

MR. BOLTER: One could see the British as being as motivated as the United States to have the sense to break from the Europeans and start movement towards some competition—as per Heritage or Orion. I for one am suspicious; the U.K. is in the best position and further outside in Europe, and it is a natural hub for traffic. If you think about it, there are clearly economic advantages to being the first to break with the European cartel. So it may be philosophy, but I suspect it is economics that is motivating the British.

*QUESTION: If we send a Telex from here to West Germany, how does it go? Does it go through the U.K. or directly to West Germany?*

MR. PEARCE: The point I was making was that it is routine from West Europe to the United States. The difference does not exist going the other way as far as I understand it. The case before the European Community only talks about Telex traffic coming from Germany to the United States, and then from the Federal Republic via London to the United States.

*QUESTION: In view of the TAT-4 decision, what degree of success do you think carriers, other than AT&T, will have in obtaining operating agreements for switched voice service?*

MR. BOLTER: I don't know why the Commission's decision would have any effect on the incentives of the Europeans to give operating agreements.

Chapter Six

# The Free Flow of Information: Economic Necessity or Political Ideal?

# Joseph Rawley

*Joseph Rawley is Co-publisher,* High Point Enterprise *newspaper, High Point, North Carolina. Mr. Rawley received his B.S. and M.B.A. degrees from Wake Forest University and is presently working towards a Ph.D. in mass communication research at the University of North Carolina in Chapel Hill. He is a member of the U.S. National Commission for UNESCO, Chairman of the International Relations Subcommittee of the American Newspaper Publishers Association (ANPA), Telecommunications Committee, and a Vice Chairman of the International Press Telecommunications Council.*

These remarks will touch briefly on three areas: (1) the concept of a "free flow of information"; (2) UNESCO and international organizations; and (3) NTIA's report to the Congress.

## Free Flow

As a concept, the "free flow of information" has been labeled the "highest level of generality." The ambiguity of the idea has prompted one author to call the term "an inert principle" which is "too blunt to be an effective policy instrument." The recent NTIA report to the Congress on U.S. long-range international telecommunications and information goals concedes that "the phrase admits to a variety of interpretations."

I would like to talk about two popular uses of the term "free flow." Those interpretations are arbitrarily labeled: (1) the market view; and (2) the ideological view.

The market view concerns trade barriers. It advocates the international transfer of information without payment of an import tariff or tax on the real or imputed value of the information. It proposes the international exchange of information without a "customs house." The market view reflects the marketplace, where there is room for negotiation. According to the market view, data flow policies can be debated in such forums as the General Agreement on Tariffs and Trade (GATT).

Occasionally, compromise may be necessary.

On the other hand, the ideological view is concerned with the unfettered circulation of news, opinion, and ideas—the freedom of speech and of the press. The ideological view is held to be non-negotiable. Compromise is not acceptable. The ideological view has to do with fundamental human rights—the right to hold opinions, to express ideas, and to communicate.

"Free flow" has come to be regarded in international forums as an enigmatic Western "code word." Yet even in the West, the language is inexact. For example, those who write about transborder data flow and trade protectionism rarely use the expression "free flow" in the same sense that it is used in the Declaration of Talloires.

When we consider all of the information carried on international data networks, there is a subset of that information which we could call "news." General information can be viewed as a commodity which usually has value. News and opinion can be a commodity with value— but it is also a commodity whose availability has been associated with civil and political liberties. News is an ingredient of democracy.

This distinction has prompted various special treatments for news material in telecommunication networks—special treatment that appeared for the first time nearly a century ago for press telegraph services in Europe. Internationally, news and non-news data move through the same communication infrastructures. Electronically, they look alike. There has been a great deal of speculation lately in some press groups studying these issues about whether or not news mixed with other data in international networks can be singled out for special treatment. Theoretically it can. However, the regulation of data networks usually applies to infrastructures and services—not to content. Policies governing the use of a service generally apply to all users of the service. I would argue that in most cases where private leased lines are not involved, press users will be subject to the same regulation as other users.

We have a good example in the case of satellite-based point-to-multipoint international service for small- to medium-bandwidth (voice-grade circuit) users. INTELSAT has both the facilities and an applicable tariff for such multi-destinational service, but that service is not offered by national PTTs or by U.S. international record carriers (IRCs). Such a service is ideally suited to the structure of media organizations which gather news in one location and deliver it to a large number of other locations.

Where matters of international news and information flow are concerned, there seems to be a movement of important and substantive discussion away from the ideological forums, like UNESCO, to market forums such as the GATT, the Council of Europe, and the OECD.

You are familiar with press involvement in the ideological debate—in such organizations as UNESCO. Let me take a few minutes to tell you about press involvement with international market issues. In the committee structure of The American Newspaper Publishers Association (ANPA) there is a group which deals with international press telecommunications issues. Our last meeting was attended by representatives from seven news agencies, including Agence-France Presse, Canadian Press, and Reuters. The meeting agenda included such items as:

1. a report on Nippon Telegraph and Telephone activity in developing Integrated Services Digital Network (ISDN);
2. Canadian press use of satellite facilities for news distribution;
3. possible domestic press representation in the U.S. CCITT organization; and
4. shared use and resale of services on international leased lines.

The ANPA submitted comments to the Department of Commerce in response to the Notice of Inquiry associated with the NTIA report, and ANPA was not the only press organization to respond.

ANPA was a founding member of the International Press Telecommunication Council (IPTC), a London-based organization. ANPA members remain very active in that group. The Director of the IPTC chairs UNESCO's working group on international telecommunication tariffs. Several other members of the IPTC are working as UNESCO telecommunication consultants for various press projects. The IPTC is a paid and accredited organizational member of the CCITT and is particularly active in CCITT Study Group III (concerned with tariff policy).

In other words, the U.S. press community is not standing back from involvement in press telecommunication market issues. We are concerned about barriers to the international flow of news whether those barriers arise as a result of market or ideological pressures.

### UNESCO and the Marketplace

I have been asked to discuss "threats to the media and to press freedom from UNESCO." Please permit me to return to that subject in a moment, after some comments about the record of the marketplace.

Earlier this year, the Department of State made a report to the Congress, concerning UNESCO, as required by the Beard Amendment (Public Law 97-241). The report stated that, based on an evaluation of UNESCO activities over the past several years, the organization is not implementing any anti-free-press measures. That is, UNESCO is not implementing any policy, "the effect of which is to license journalists or their publications, to censor or otherwise restrict the free flow of information within or among countries, or to impose mandatory codes of journalistic practices or ethics."

It is interesting to compare those conclusions with market related data flow activities last year. To cite some recent developments:

1. An international record carrier (RCA) filed a request with the FCC to abolish several provisions of Press Bulletin Service. The filing seeks to eliminate subspeed leased services which are, in many cases, the only means for news exchange with lesser developed countries.

2. The Council of European PTTs (CEPT) told European press agencies they would not be allowed to lease transponder space or operate small receive-only earth stations in the 4-to-6 GHz bands.

3. The West German Bundespost proposed volume-based tariffs for leased lines that would raise Associated Press and Reuters costs by up to seven times present rates.

4. Terrestrial tariffs at the national level were recognized as the major obstacle in a UNESCO-INTELSAT global news exchange project.

The list could go on at length. It seems to indicate that market actions can have as much or more impact on the international distribution of news as actions taken in such ideological forums as UNESCO. Ironically, UNESCO's Director-General recently wrote to the communication administrations of member states urging lower telecommunication tariffs for the press.

Before leaving the subject of UNESCO, it would be inappropriate to brush aside problems that do exist in that forum. U.S. and Western free-press advocates will remain diligent because UNESCO continues to sponsor a seemingly endless series of conferences dealing with ideological stands that are at odds with democratic values. It is noteworthy that of the 42 alleged Soviet agents recently expelled from France by the Mitterrand government, three worked in the UNESCO Secretariat and nine were UNESCO national delegation members.

From that standpoint of press interests and UNESCO, there is one issue that has caused a great deal of concern. Recent UNESCO activities, particularly in the International Program for the Development of Communications (IPDC), are aimed at strengthening government media operations. At present, little attention is given to assisting non-government media development. Two major projects of the IPDC are directed toward establishing international government-controlled news agencies. That activity will be monitored closely in the West.

**NTIA Report**

In these remarks, I have tried to show that the U.S. press community is concerned about both market and ideological issues relating to the flow of news. That is why we are interested in such a major development as the NTIA report to the Congress. I will address my closing remarks to that report.

Although virtually every daily newspaper in this country publishes news about international events, only a handful of news agencies and larger newspapers regularly use international data networks. The telecommunications managers of those companies probably favor the creation of a "super-agency" that could deal comprehensively with international communication policy—a market approach. Journalists would not favor such an approach, and in these conclusions I want to reflect the views of journalists.

Concerning the future organizational structure for telecommunication affairs, the present multi-agency approach to policymaking has evolved over a long period and is able to consider and respond to diverse views. The FCC's Anthony Rutkowski has said that the present system "provides a delicate balance between the Legislative and Executive Branches, and between advocates of private sector and government interests." I believe that, in the face of all the facts, most members of the press community would favor a strengthening and restructuring of the existing interagency working group arrangement—or some similar but more streamlined approach.

Concerning long-range international telecommunications and information goals, the U.S. objective should be to regulate (or deregulate) international telecommunications considering the interest, convenience, and necessity of American users and without regard to considerations imposed by foreign telecommunications administrations. If the principles that now allow American users great freedom in the use of domestic facilities are valid, then they should also be valid for those same users in international applications. Donald Till, Director of Communication, *The Washington Post*, points out that "It is not likely that the U.S. can directly influence foreign administrations by negotiation. There is substantial evidence, however, that by its example, the U.S. can influence the thinking of foreign administrations . . . over time . . . such that both American and foreign telecommunications users benefit from unilateral U.S. actions which serve to promote the free flow of information."

Finally, returning to the point of departure, the free flow concept must be redefined in internationally understandable terms before it can be a useful instrument of policy. The NTIA report reduces the principles of U.S. policy to two, one of which is the free flow issue. The concept is vital to both press and industry, but in different senses. The title of this session, which was determined before I was asked to be on the program, is "The Free Flow of Information, a Business Necessity or a Political Ideal." I take issue with the notion that the two are mutually exclusive. They are simply two different issues which must be dealt with separately before sound policy can be formulated.

# Hugh Donaghue

*Hugh Donaghue is Vice President, Government Programs and International Trade Relations, Control Data Corporation. After graduating from Boston College, he was awarded a Government Fellowship at the University of Illinois where he received a Master's degree in Applied Mathematics. He serves as a member of the State Department's Advisory Committee on International Investment, Technology, and Development, and chairs its Subcommittee on Transborder Data Flows. He is also a member of the Committee on Transborder Data Flows for the U.S. Council for International Business, and is Vice Chairman of Policies of the International Chamber of Commerce.*

I am going to try to place my remarks in a little broader context than that contained in the NTIA report. I think that the report itself sets out a number of issues and expresses some perceptive viewpoints of the NTIA authors and others who contributed to it, and I think they did a fairly good job of that. But I look at the report as the first step in the establishment of a dialogue on a number of telecommunications policy issues that we are going to be discussing over the next decade.

I would like to frame my remarks in a slightly different perspective, and start with an observation concerning the change that is taking place around us as we enter this so-called "information age."

This change has social and political ramifications, and, certainly to many of us in business, a whole host of economic ramifications.

We are just beginning to see the effects upon our lives of the introduction of new computer and telecommunications concepts and applications. The privacy issue, both domestic and international, is just one outcome of this particular development. I'll get into that later when I address the privacy aspect of it. There are, however, a whole host of new developments that will affect our lives as we enter the information age.

In the geopolitical area, we live with instant worldwide information, so we know more about what's going on in all parts of the world than we ever did before, and in some instances probably more than we'd like to.

When you have a President shot here in Washington, D.C. and some of our domestic reporters finding out about it when they hear from their foreign news bureaus that it has occurred, it shows you how rapidly information is transmitted around our world.

And there is the question of the adequacy of today's legal systems to cope with many of these issues that we are going to be facing. On the economic side, we have the question of whether the information gap as perceived by many nations equates to an economic gap. We have seen in the United Nations that they consider the New World Information Order as part of the New World Economic Order.

In this country we are beginning to see changes in the workplace brought about by automation coinciding with the desire of many unions to move into the white collar area as a new source of manpower and revenues. They are calling for such new rules and regulations in the workplace as are dictated by the rapid development and increased use of video display terminals and by some of the perceived problems that have arisen as a result.

### Privacy

Now let's look at the privacy issue as described in the NTIA report and also as it has been developing in the other nations of the world. I remember back in the 1960s when the computer industry introduced magnetic discs, and for the first time it became apparent that here was a means of storing a great deal more information about individuals than had ever been stored before. At that time discussions were held between the Internal Revenue Service and the Justice Department to try to coordinate their record-keeping. Many of us in the profession objected very strenuously to that kind of development because we were concerned about the "big brother" syndrome, that is, the ability of the U.S. to gather, store, and use information against its citizens in ways never possible before. We are beginning to find that's the same concept that's affecting countries around the world. That's why you see countries adressing the privacy issue when it involves automated records and transmission rather than the written word and use of the mails. It's the concept of the "big brother" syndrome that's brought that on.

In turn, most legislation on transborder data flow dealing with the privacy issue has developed as countries instituted domestic privacy legislation. They came to realize that a great deal of personal information was not stored in their own country but was stored in the computers of the parent corporations, often outside their borders. Therefore, in their desire to maintain privacy protection for their citizens, they applied their laws extra-territorially by not allowing those data to be stored and processed abroad unless the companies that were doing so would accord the same rights as if those data were stored within the country itself.

The problem that we have in the U.S. business community has not been with privacy legislation itself. But we have had concerns about the administrative burdens it might pose because of the number of different national laws, and the difference in our legal systems.

All the European legislation to date has been omnibus in nature, following Napoleonic law, whereas the United States has developed legislation based on common law and, therefore, our laws, such as the Privacy Act of 1974, have been formulated to correct specific abuses of privacy practices. We have done an excellent job on that, though not to the satisfaction of the Europeans.

As a result of legislative initiatives going on in Europe, many of us in the private sector, working with our government, helped develop a set of privacy guidelines that were eventually adopted by the OECD in Europe. At the same time, the Council of Europe developed a treaty based upon a similar set of principles, and these are outlined in the NTIA report's discussion of transborder data flows.

Today we have the Council of Europe treaty which many of us expect to go into effect sometime this year [1983]. And we also have the OECD guidelines which are essentially the same as the treaty with regard to the principles involved, and these have been endorsed by at least 160 U.S. organizations to date.

The companies that I have talked to in the United States feel that the assurance to their employees, whether here or abroad, that we respect the privacy of individuals has been paramount; that is what led us to encourage the OECD guidelines.

As a result of the studies that preceded development of privacy legislation, many countries in Europe began to look at different kinds of data that were being transmitted and stored abroad. I won't recite numerous anecdotes about their findings, but just to cite one example, the French Government found that its annual budget was being processed in Cleveland, Ohio. That naturally raised some concern among a number of French bureaucrats as to whether it was really a rational thing to do. I can tell you it's not being done any longer. Some countries, as they started to look at the flows of data across their borders, began to question whether or not their sovereignty might even be at stake with certain kinds of information being transmitted outside of their countries.

These questions are still being debated and there are no good answers. The OECD has undertaken an economic study to try to determine the benefits of transborder data flow versus the risks, and that's an issue that will probably be debated for the next several years.

### Taxation of Information

There is another issue, however, that is closer at hand and that I suspect will be resolved by some countries in a few years, and this is the taxation of information. As the NTIA study points out, there are two basic kinds of data that are distributed. One is the sale of data products where somebody has either a computer database or has products generated by computers that are actually sold on the open marketplace with taxes paid on those sales.

The other is the intermediate kind of data, such as data flows from a subsidiary to a parent and back. There are many countries that would like to tap those flows as a new source of revenue. As we move into this information age, we are moving very rapidly towards a service economy. Therefore, when nations look for new sources of revenue, they look at services; and the underlying basic elements of services are data and information flows.

### Employment

In other areas, a different perception of transborder data flow has raised serious issues. Canada has looked at it as an employment issue. The concept there has been that the transmission and processing of data south of the border equals the export of jobs.

Bankers were able to demonstrate that if all banking transactions were processed in Canada rather than in the branches of Canadian banks in the United States, it would create a number of very prestigious white collar jobs in Canada. Therefore, we have the Canadian Banking Act legislation that essentially forces the processing of data in Canada.

### Foreign Parent/Subsidiary Relationship

Then we have the foreign parent/subsidiary relationship where many countries look at the development of this new technology as taking away the independence of the subsidiaries that they host in their countries. Their reasoning goes somthing like this: in the past when corporate communication was by mail or telex, the direction from corporate headquarters to a subsidiary was minimal. Therefore, management of that subsidiary took into account local social, political, and economic factors in the decisionmaking process about the operation of *that* subsidiary. Now, a subsidiary has become merely an input unit that feeds all the data back to some sterile corporate headquarters where decisions are made without consideration of local factors. As a result, some countries have instituted non-tariff barriers to these flows, and there will be legislation that will restrict certain kinds of flow.

### The U.S. and the New World Information Order

These developments raise questions in my mind as to future issues that I think we are going to need to address. Some of them actually are counter to the recommendations of the NTIA report, but I'm not saying that the NTIA report is wrong. I think it simply reflects a situation that has existed over the last few years, and so those recommendations stand at the moment.

The question is, will they stand the test of time as we move into this information age? There are a host of them, but I simply would like to put forth four for your consideration:

1. Is our present legal system adequate to handle the issues that we are facing? We have just found over the last couple of years that the Communications Act of 1934, which served us so well until recently, seems no longer totally valid in today's environment, and therefore many changes, including complete rewrites, have been debated.

2. What is wrong with a worldwide treaty on the privacy issue? We have taken the position that it would never be accepted in the United States, and the NTIA report reflects that. I suggest, however, that times and legal systems are changing. We can accept treaties in a number of other areas; privacy is going to be one of the more important issues of the information age, so we should address the issue of whether or not a treaty is in order.

3. Do corporations need all the data they are gathering in order to conduct their international business today? My boss constantly tells me she would like to see a lot of this data filtered out. Maybe we ought to start the filter at the subsidiary and leave the bulk of the information there, only transmitting to headquarters what is really necessary for corporate decisions.

4. Finally, are we ready to adapt to this new era or are we going to insist upon laws and regulations that were designed to lead us through the industrial age but not necessarily the informaton age?

# Chapter Six Discussion

*QUESTION: There has been a lot of talk about information leaving countries, but what about information coming into countries? Direct broadcast satellite private-station ownership is an example. Would someone talk about that a bit?*

MR. RAWLEY: International direct broadcast satellite exists in a sense today because of the many available entertainment services (e.g., HBO). I believe that all of our traditional theories and assumptions, both market and ideological, are going to be very much altered by technology. I think technology is really the driving force and the issue that you're talking about. I don't know the right or the wrong of it except to say that technology is certainly going to alter our traditional assumptions and theories.

*QUESTION: Hugh Donaghue, you mentioned treaties. Do you envision bilateral agreements with countries or broad multilateral treaties and, if so, what sorts of provisions would these agreements have?*

MR. DONAGHUE: I mentioned the OECD guidelines, and the Council of Europe Treaty which, as I said, will go into effect sometime this year. When it does, it is going to ease the burden of transmission of personal data across the borders of those countries which are signatories to the treaty. Even though the same set of principles has been endorsed and adopted by United States corporations under the OECD guidelines, we are still not signatories to the treaty.

In my discussion with both the data commissioners and others in Europe who are involved in this process, they have told me that those who are not signatories to that treaty will be somewhat like second-class citizens. In other words, we will have to abide by national legislation. So there is a burden upon us that would not exist if we were a signatory to the treaty. When they developed the treaty, they took an action that I don't recall being done before under the rules of the Council of Europe, and that was to allow endorsement of the treaty by parties who were not members of the Council of Europe.

I've been told by our government that there is no way that we would sign this treaty given our current attitude, as it is more regulation in a deregulatory environment. On the other hand, I have heard many instances here in the United States of companies and individuals who have been quite concerned about the lack of broader privacy protection for our own citizens, and indeed that's what brought about the Privacy Act of 1974.

In the last Administration several attempts were made to expand upon privacy laws outside the public sector where they now apply. So I raise the question, is it time to reexamine our values in this area? As we enter into the information age, it may be time to take a look at the entire privacy issue as information flows expand, and ask ourselves if we should throw away some of the old rules and be willing to consider new ones such as endorsing the Council of Europe Treaty.

Chapter Seven

# Can a Trade War Be Avoided?

# Richard Wiley

*Richard Wiley is a Partner, Wiley, Johnson, and Rein, Washington, D.C. Mr. Wiley graduated from Northwestern University and holds law degrees from Northwestern and Georgetown universities. Prior to joining Kirkland and Ellis, Mr. Wiley served as Chairman of the Federal Communications Commission (1974-1977). His tenure with the FCC began in 1970 as the Commission's General Counsel. In addition to his FCC service, Mr. Wiley also was appointed by both Presidents Ford and Nixon to the Council of the Administrative Conference of the United States.*

The last ten years have witnessed an explosive, even revolutionary, growth in the United States telecommunications industry, both in product offerings and in the provision of services. Much of this expansion can be traced to the creative confluence of communications and computer technologies and, concomitantly, to the advent of competition and progressive deregulation of many aspects of the industry.

A vibrant commercial environment can be expected to result from these developments. Indeed, anticipation runs so high that it has become commonplace to predict that "information" will be at once *the* basic and growth industry of the future, employing more people and generating more revenue than any other sector of the U.S. economy.

In the past, exports have not been essential to the economic health of telecommunications companies in this country. The tremendous domestic demand for goods and services has enabled U.S. suppliers to experience phenomenal expansion without the need to even look beyond their own national borders. However, the lucrative potential of our burgeoning telecommunications markets has not been lost on other industrialized countries. Many of these nations, due to their comparatively small domestic markets and import-dependent economies, have aggressively sought out opportunities for international trade. Indeed, they have been quite successful in recent years in increasing their share of the world and United States telecommunications markets. Growing foreign competition with U.S. telecommunication suppliers both at home and abroad, coupled with deregulation of our domestic market, has tended to underscore what many Americans perceive as a serious imbalance in trade opportunities. The assertion is that telecommunications and related fields in the U.S. are open to participation by foreign firms without extensive limitation while, in many other developed nations, the marketplace is essentially closed to our suppliers. Moreover, at the same time that the United States is expanding opportunities for wide-open competition, these nations are maintaining restrictive trade practices which are protectionist in effect, if not intent.

## Perspectives on Telecommunications Trade

Part of the problem underlying the telecommunications trade debate may be a basic difference in attitude. The United States traditionally has been a leading advocate of free trade and open access to markets, consistent with its free-enterprise philosophy. Many other nations, on the other hand, tend to view unrestricted trade in, for example, telecommunications goods and services, as representing an opportunity for foreign states—in particular, the U.S.—to trench on their national sovereignty and disrupt their cultural integrity. The fear of being overwhelmed by foreign influences that either reflect values incompatible with domestic mores or that might otherwise dilute a nation's self-identity underlies the desire of some states to maintain cultural independence.

Apart from political considerations, of course, these nations also seek to maintain and increase their indigenous employment levels and positive trade balances, and to retain a major share of expanding telecommunications markets for themselves and their industries. Whether erected for economic, political, or cultural reasons, however, barriers to international trade unavoidably translate into real and potential losses of competitive opportunities for U.S. firms. Unfortunately, too, protectionist policies adopted by one nation tend to engender similar policies in others. Moreover, the simple threat of such barriers can chill investment and thus have long-term adverse consequences for all.

## Barriers to Telecommunications Trade

Congressional hearings in the U.S. over the past four years have brought to light various practices by foreign governments which restrict international trade in telecommunications goods and services.

Among the most salient examples of actual and potential barriers to trade in both goods and services are the following:

1. legislation limiting the use of data processing facilities outside the host country;
2. private line surcharges and public network rates that favor domestic over international traffic;
3. unnecessarily strict technical standards for interconnection of terminal equipment;
4. "buy national" policies; and
5. "industry-targeting" practices aimed at promoting a country's domestic telecommunications industry (through subsidies, loans, tax breaks, and joint government-business ventures).

### Reciprocity and U.S. Congress

In the belief that many foreign markets are becoming increasingly restricted, a number of bills were introduced in both Houses of the 97th Congress that would have mandated "reciprocity" or "equitable market access" in telecommunications trade between the United States and its trading partners. While a variety of provisions were included in these bills, virtually all aimed to have the same result: to confer authority on the Federal Communications Commission to restrict the entry of foreign telecommunications carriers, facilities, services, or products into domestic telecommunications markets except upon terms and conditions which are "comparable" or "reasonably equivalent" to those applicable to U.S. entry into the foreign markets involved.

In general, the concept of reciprocity is fundamental to the rules of trade as established by the General Agreement on Tariffs and Trade (or GATT, as it is commonly known). In this context, reciprocity signifies the negotiated granting of a balanced set of mutual rights and concessions by the parties to an agreement. On Capitol Hill, however, the principle has been modified to a product-specific or sector-specific policy to be used as a defensive weapon to overcome perceived protectionist barriers to trade.

The gist of such "mirror image" reciprocity is deceptively simple— telecommunications markets in the United States would be closed to those nations which refuse to open theirs to American-based competition. The underlying intent, however, is to create a set of provisional restrictions that will increase U.S. leverage in future negotiations in order to remove trade barriers in other nations. The theory is that, in the absence of such a mechanism, little incentive would seem to exist on the part of our trading partners to offer concessions in return for access to a U.S. telecommunications market that is likely to be open in any event.

Legislation expanding the FCC's power over international telecommunications trade also has been introduced in the current Congress. However, it appears that a more moderate point of view concerning reciprocity has begun to prevail. Recently the Senate passed the International Trade and Investment Act, which strengthens the President's power to retaliate against unfair foreign trading practices and foreign investment policies abroad, but does not mandate trade sanctions. Similarly, the recently proposed international telecommunications act of 1983, or S. 999, deleted the provisions which were in last year's counterpart that had called for sectoral reciprocity.

### Arguments Pro and Con on Reciprocity

This emerging congressional approach to potential trade barriers reflects a substantially negative reaction among a wide range of government and industry representatives to the concept of mirror-image reciprocity. These objections recite the fact that sectoral reciprocity would be contrary to the traditional American commitment to free trade and liberalization of foreign markets through negotiated settlements, such as the GATT.

In particular, the United States has promised to treat any GATT signatory's commerce no worse than that of any other foreign nation. A policy of reciprocity obviously would result in treating the products of some GATT signatories less favorably than others, depending upon their own regulations.

Moreover, limiting reciprocity to a single economic sector, such as telecommunications, inevitably would create a number of problems. Most importantly, it would fragment the U.S. approach to trade negotiations. Nations obviously differ in terms of domestic resources and production capabilities and, as a result, their exports also differ. Thus, trade negotiations and practices which are restricted to one or two products cannot result in any kind of overall reciprocity or equity.

Furthermore, by creating a myriad set of rules monitoring all the anomalies of foreign law and practice which burden international telecommunications markets for U.S. suppliers, sectoral reciprocity legislation could encourage bilateral, as opposed to multilateral, resolution of telecommunications trade controversies. Such congressional action could be interpreted as indicating a U.S. intent to deal with telecommunications outside the GATT framework.

I should note that while no GATT rules, principles, or procedures currently are applicable to trade in services, the United States actively sought expansion of GATT coverage to this area, as well as to direct investments, at last fall's ministerial meeting of GATT in Geneva. Although the U.S. delegation was not successful in this regard, the GATT members did agree preliminarily to study the issue and to consider regulating services in two years.

Any move toward sectoral reciprocity by GATT's strongest ally, at a time when the issue of services is still under study, would signal an ambiguous commitment by the U.S. to the multilateral negotiation process.

Finally, a sectoral approach could result in different regulations—those of the FCC and other U.S. governmental entities—applying to a single foreign product, depending on the specific situation involved. Endorsement of mirror-image reciprocity also could give rise to the problem of inappropriate delegation of authority. Indeed, the vesting of substantial discretion in an independent regulatory agency like FCC might make it difficult to formulate and conduct a unified and coherent trade policy. Moreover, the FCC has neither the expertise nor the resources needed to assess the laws and practices operative in foreign markets, nor does it have, in my opinion, an awareness of broader considerations of trade and foreign policy which is necessary to make threshold judgments in the area.

In this regard, I have noted the recent flurry of proposals for consolidating governmental authority over international telecommunications. As you know, NTIA, in its recent and very comprehensive report, has advocated the establishment of a centralized policy authority with the power to mediate differences among the agencies and to represent our nation at all international conferences dealing with telecommunications and information issues. The proposal of S. 999 is that this authority should be placed within the White House itself. For the time being, the establishment of a centralized executive branch authority may well be a preferred alternative to creation of a new Cabinet-level department to deal exclusively with trade or some combination of commerce and trade, as other pending bills propose. If in the long-term, White House-level authority proves to be inadequate, then Cabinet restructuring should be considered. Incidentally, if a White House authority is established, I would not agree with NTIA that the new office should have the power to veto FCC decisions.

## Alternatives to Sectoral Reciprocity

Great difficulty seems to exist in finding a reciprocity law that achieves the desired objectives without causing other problems of equal significance. This problem has been compounded by the suggestion that traditional means of retaliation against foreign nations for trade discrimination under the Trade Act of 1974 are too limited to be of much use. For example, doubts have been raised over the ability of the President to take action in areas subject to the regulatory authority of an independent agency and against foreign suppliers of a service, rather than the service itself.

As noted earlier, legislation that would "clarify" the President's existing authority over trade matters has already passed the Senate. This bill, and others like it, would allow him to retaliate against restrictions on U.S. entry to foreign markets by taking action against any goods or sector, including *services*, on a nondiscriminatory basis, or solely against the foreign country involved, regardless of whether such goods or services were involved in the offending practice. This legislation is consistent with the Reagan Administration's policies and is supported by it. Prospects for passage are uncertain due to opposition by some members of key House committees.

Apart from such expansion of Presidential authority, the Administration generally believes that U.S. trade objectives should be secured through broader trade legislation and international agreements rather than by the passage of laws which target particular industries and lines of commerce. Specifically, U.S. Trade Representative Bill Brock has endorsed an approach that he calls "global reciprocity." This term apparently refers to the process of negotiating agreements on a multilateral basis, GATT-style, across several industries so that the aggregate of benefits derived by each party substantially equals concessions made by any other entity. The Administration favors this kind of "reciprocity" instead of the mirror-image or sector-specific approach.

Bilateral consultation with some of our major trading partners is another potentially fruitful avenue to be considered. Representatives of the Japanese Ministry of International Trade & Industry (MITI) and our government met several times last year to address issues such as the structure of and trends in the high-technology industries, cooperative research and development, industry targeting, trade distorting barriers, and access to capital markets. In February, the two governments adopted a "work plan" which affirmed the principle of free trade in high technology and called for the implementation of a number of concrete steps to alleviate specific trade problems in this area. Recently the two nations also have agreed to the formation of a joint Committee on

Industry-Related Policies and Their Effects on Trade.

The Committee's efforts will be devoted to providing policymakers with its assessment of potential trade- and investment-related effects of actions, such as "industry-targeting," that are designed to foster domestic industries.

Finally, the use of private initiatives by suppliers of telecommunications goods and services frequently has been suggested by industry spokesmen as offering better prospects for improved foreign market access than any kind of reciprocity legislation. The conclusion last year of operating agreements for the joint provision of data packet switching service between British Telecommunications International and two new U.S. carriers for international services may augur well for this kind of approach. Indeed, the Senate-passed trade bill would establish a procedure for the Administration to receive trade negotiating advice from private business.

In the final analysis, while widespread support exists for the principle of overall equality and quantity of trade opportunities between nations in telecommunications goods and services, I think that there is also general recognition that mirror-image reciprocity is not ultimately in our best interests. This is not to say that such an approach is without support in Congress or in the country at large. In fact, the impetus toward passage of a strong sectoral reciprocity law for telecommunications products could gain new force if Japan fails to honor its commitment to afford greater access to U.S. firms that seek to compete for NTT's high technology product requirements.

On the other hand, if a genuine willingness to discuss greater mutuality in market access begins to develop, either within the GATT context or otherwise, much of the pressure built up behind the plethora of reciprocity bills will likely dissipate of its own accord. Given the high stakes involved in international telecommunications, including continued global cooperation and harmony, I believe that such a movement could prove to be of great benefit not only to the U.S. but to the world at large.

# Phillip Grub

*Phillip Grub is Aryamehr Professor of Multinational Management, The George Washington University. Dr. Grub received his doctorate in business administration from The George Washington University and has been, since 1980, the Chairman of the Board of Governors of the African Institute for Economic Development. He is a management consultant to industry and government, domestic and foreign, on problems of international trade policy, export promotion, tourism, long-range planning, economic development, and multinational corporate policy.*

*Portions of this paper have been abstracted from "Transborder Data Flows: An Endangered Species," by the author and Suzanne R. Settle, published in* The Multinational Enterprise in Transition, *Darwin Press.*

The title of this session, "Can a Trade War Be Avoided?" is a moot question. The war has been going on for more than a decade; however, it has only been in the past few years that the United States has come to recognize its seriousness.

Once the undisputed leader in telecommunications, computing, electronics, and other high-technology industries, our position has gradually eroded to the point where the future of the United States' competition in these areas is being questioned. Aside from the pure open competition in the marketplace, American firms are finding increased difficulty due to local legislation that is, in effect, nothing more than a non-tariff barrier designed to protect domestic markets and often-inefficient industries. These actions have been masked in different guises ranging from the question of privacy to incompatibility of equipment and services.

Why has this become a problem? The answer is multifold. Reasons include the rising tide of nationalistic sentiment, increased competition from both developed and developing countries, direct and indirect subsidies by foreign governments to local industry, increased technology transfer from the United States abroad, "targeting" of selected industries (primarily by Japan) with concomitant support for their development, a lack of understanding on the part of the United States Congress of the competitive state of the world marketplace, and a failure of many American companies to exploit fully the present and potential foreign markets.

## The Data Protection Movement

The status of competition can well be noted in the case of transborder data flows, which in turn has its impact on the use and purchase of U.S. equipment and services as well as on the operating efficiency of American multinational corporations in their global pursuits.

A new challenge to the structure and operations of multinational corporations (MNCs) has been taking shape during the past decade in the critical area of international communications. Essentially a policy issue, this latest challenge goes by a variety of names: informatics, transborder data flows (TBDF), or international information flows. Whatever label is used, the issue revolves around the transfer of information across national boundaries using advanced computer and telecommunications technologies.

Among developed and developing countries alike, the protection of national sovereignty constitutes the highest priority on the national agenda. Global interdependence, and its primary agents, multinational enterprises, have served to heighten national sensitivities in this regard and to reinforce general goals of governmental autonomy.

In what has become known as the data protection movement, many countries have either enacted or are considering legislation to restrict flows of information across their borders in support of certain national interests. Due to the dominant role the United States has played in the use and supply of information resources, it is not surprising that American firms have become caught in the cross fire of this data protection movement.

Industry has responded, but many firms do not realize the impact that this legislation may have on their operations. It is not only the fact that vast quantities of data, the content of which may be highly sensitive, are regularly transmitted throughout the world in total disregard of national boundaries, but that the principal agents of data transmission are nonnational, usually American, entities. Although privacy issues appear to be the most compelling reasons for the imposition of controls on transborder data flows, there are a number of other, less visible, factors contributing to the regulatory trend.

The spectrum of purposes served by data protection legislation is broad and extends from the protection of privacy to protection of national sovereignty, balance of payments, employment, technology, social and cultural values, telecommunications policy, and national defense.

## Data Protection Regulations and MNCs

The immediate implications for multinational firms of the expanding TBDF regulatory framework are clear; those firms transmitting name-linked data, as opposed to anonymous data, are confronted and must comply with a variety of national data protection laws and standards. This patchwork of laws serves as a barrier to the free flow of information through multinational computer systems, which may increase the costs and decrease the efficiency of multinational operations.

Multinational computer/communications systems must often be redesigned or restructured in accordance with the new nationally imposed procedures for handling information. Requirements may include all or some combination of the following: (1) the registration of personal data files with a central regulatory authority; (2) limits on data collection to clearly defined purposes; (3) access to data files by subjects and/or governmental authorities for purposes of inspection; (4) sufficient security precautions to prevent unauthorized access to data bases; and (5) local purchase of equipment or services requirements.

Multinational firms generally accept the central objective of data privacy protection legislation, which many feel is simply an extension of existing corporate policy. Their major concern involves the effects of overlapping (often conflicting) national laws, as well as the wider impact the new regulations will have on corporate information flows. Because multinationals operate on a global basis, they are highly visible and, as a consequence, feel more vulnerable for the following reasons:

1. MNCs operating in *any* country with data protection laws may be obliged to extend compliance to *every* country where they have operations, resulting in communications with a much higher degree of transparency than would otherwise be normal or acceptable for the firm.
2. Licensing or registration requirements legitimize government supervision and scrutiny of corporate information systems. Further, registering the patterns and destinations of flows within their organizations to comply with privacy rules may expose much wider corporate policies and practices.
3. The right of access by data authorities to corporate data processing operations for security safeguards checks may lead to disclosure of nonpersonal data, since name-linked data may not be segregated from other types

of data; even the disclosure of personal information may involve a great deal of related collateral information of a proprietary nature.*

While some industries, such as banking and insurance, would appear to be more heavily impacted by laws regulating the flow of personal information by virtue of their organization, geographic dispersion, products and services offered, and the volume and types of data they process, the fact that TBDF can so easily be disrupted poses potential problems for the producers of data processing and telecommunications goods and services and manufacturing firms as well.

These problems can be magnified in the event that countries impose trade restrictions on the flow of information under the guise of, or in addition to, their data privacy laws. A number of the subordinate issues of TBDF are actually hidden trade issues which have little to do with the protection of privacy. Some examples include (1) requirements for local data processing; (2) local equipment specifications and interface standards; (3) increased tariffs on private leased lines and a denial of service of those lines in favor of PTT networks; (4) refusal to allow connection between internal (domestic) networks and international carriers; (5) denial of market access to foreign firms for reasons of inadequate security procedures; and (6) denial of access by foreign vendors to regional computer/communications networks (such as EURONET).

Discussions with a number of corporate executives indicate that such trade-related restrictions are indeed being imposed, with effects ranging from a loss of business at the extreme to higher costs in doing business at a minimum.

One U.S. information services firm indicated that Canadian banking laws were responsible for the loss of at least two clients, due to requirements for the local storage of data. Since the company maintains storage facilities in the U.S., its only option was to place equipment on the bank site, thus increasing up-front costs. The company has not yet decided whether data storage facilities will be placed in Canada. The same firm has been threatened with limits on ports of entry in Mexico and thus anticipates difficulty in expanding its market share.

A major American bank has encountered problems in Germany and Brazil. A new German law requiring that private international leased lines coming into the country terminate in a single computer system and that incoming data be processed locally prior to distribution

*See prepared statement by G. Russell Pipe, President of Transnational Data Reporting Service, in *International Data Flow*, Hearings before the Subcommittee on Government Information and Individual Rights, March 27, 1980, pp. 399-421.

within Germany literally forced the bank's subsidiary to switch from its private line to the local PTT network.

In Brazil, the American bank has had to "donate" American check processing equipment to its local branch; the government denied approval to purchase the equipment for balance of payments reasons. The result for the bank was a 31 percent increase in costs. In another instance, the bank was denied approval for the purchase of a U.S.-made computer which would have resulted in considerable savings. Instead, it was forced to purchase a Brazilian computer with capacity beyond the bank's needs, resulting in a reduction of expected savings by several hundred thousand dollars.

Two American computer companies, Control Data and Tymshare, have encountered regulatory difficulties in Japan. In both cases, restriction imposed by the Japanese international record carrier, KDD, on lines leased from KDD had the effect of delaying operations for five years and limiting the types of services each U.S. firm could offer to Japanese customers. Both companies have expressed concern that the new KDD usage-sensitive network, known as VENUS, will preclude the use of private fixed-cost leased lines. Tymshare expects the new service to cost ten times more than its existing network.

Eaton Corporation has voiced concern that the forced use of national PTT services may have the effect of limiting access by international firms to adequate information networks, thus giving local firms an unfair competitive advantage. Further, the costs of using PTT services are much higher than those for private lines. U.S. carriers charge approximately $4,100 per month for their portion of private lines between the U.S. and Europe while the Europeans charge nearly $5,800 and the Japanese charge approximately $11,000. A shift from flat-rate charges to usage-based charges would also escalate communications costs, as would the imposition of tariffs on data transmissions. Eaton has estimated that the company's communications costs in the United Kingdom will increase by 85 percent due to tariffs.

Those companies with decentralized international operations have had an easier time of complying with data privacy and local storage and processing requirements, but they are by no means immune to other TBDF-related problems. A major U.S. MNC, for example, has been required to purchase locally manufactured computers at two to three hundred percent higher cost.

Other areas of corporate concern revolve around the interoperability of equipment, security in the transmission of confidential data, the reliability of the public PTT services as opposed to private services, and the question of liability in the transmission of data via the PTT networks. This latter issue is particularly important for the banking industry. One banker made the point that if PTTs insist that U.S. firms use their facilities, they should be willing to assume more of the financial liability for transfer problems, such as delays or missed payments.

The interviews indicated that while some companies have begun to include data flow considerations in their marketing and strategic planning, the vast majority of multinationals have yet to do so. According to two executives, TBDF problems are poorly understood or, indeed, barely recognized because many firms have paid inadequate attention to their internal computer/telecommunications needs. A better understanding of the nature, frequency, and volume of information flows in support of business activity is a prerequisite to understanding the impact of TBDF restrictions on international operations.

Since all international operations are dependent on the timely and efficient transfer of information, it is imperative that business devote top-level management attention to the variety of foreign measures threatening the free flow of information. In addition to monitoring the specific actions of governments on a country-by-country basis, companies must assess their information requirements within the context of a changing, and more restrictive, global environment. Finally, companies must factor this assessment into their strategic planning to be better able to deal with future problems or prospects.

## The Future Challenge

If we are to deal effectively with the competitive situation confronting us today, reaction must come from three sources: government, industry, and labor.

First, *government* must recognize the competitive threat in the area of international telecommunications, information technology, and the high-tech industry in general. In so doing, it must:

1. Preserve our competitive strength in the fast-growing service sector.
2. Recognize the consequences of a "no action" policy, or the United States will fast become another Britain.
3. Realize that government must work more closely with industry to encourage greater research and development as well as innovation, and must encourage technology to be exploited at home rather than exported.
4. Face up to the realities of linkages between economic aid given by other countries, particularly to the LDCs, and the trade competitiveness of the aid-giving nations. Japanese aid to Burma is

probably the most concrete example of a trading nation capturing the market through aid assistance.

5. In trade negotiations, have a concrete policy concerning telecommunications, transborder data flows, and our information technology industry. Non-tariff barriers that currently exist are quite evident; however, research must be undertaken to provide valid data that can be supported in negotiations.

Secondly, *industry* must make renewed efforts to meet compeition head-on and become more dynamic in its sales and marketing efforts. Specifically, it must:

1. Enhance marketing efforts and not just concentrate on big sales. Much can be gained (and is being gained by Japan) through low-volume initial sales, particularly to LDCs, to obtain entry and then build upon that entry as local systems become more sophisticated.

2. Concentrate more effort on the future rather than on the short-term bottom-line results. Again, analysis indicates that Japanese corporate strength lies in emphasis on long-term growth strategies with heavy concentration upon greater productivity and optimizing technological breakthroughs.

3. Show a concerted willingness to take risks in new product development areas. For example, Japan would not have gotten the jump on robotics if American industry had taken the initiative in this arena. Now we are struggling to catch up.

4. Act more like industrial entrepreneurs than bureaucrats and, in so doing, be global- and future-oriented. In short, industry must face up to the realities of the challenge with which they are confronted with foresight rather than reactive measures.

Third, *labor* must recognize that survival of American industry, and not workers' short-term gains, is in their long-range interests.

1. Emphasis by the unions should be on greater productivity; future benefits and raises must be based upon a more realistic contribution to overall profitability.

2. Lessons need to be learned from competition, primarily Japan, that there is a need for supportive measures on the part of labor rather than destructive tactics in their negotiations with corporations.

3. Creative thinking is needed on the part of labor leaders to assist in keeping industry here at home rather than demanding a climate that forces companies to go abroad or otherwise lose their competitive position.

In summation, technology is indeed a precious asset that should be utilized to its utmost effectiveness. If utilized properly, American firms can more than offset much of the competition from abroad that is based merely upon low wages and tax holidays. While our high-technology industries, of which telecommunications is an integral part, cannot resolve our entire trade balance, unemployment, or trade competitiveness problems, the application and utilization of many of these technologies is a key means for a more productive and competitive U.S. economy, both now and in the future.

Chapter Eight

# The Government's Role
# in Research and Development

# Fred Weingarten

*Fred Weingarten is Program Manager, Communication
and Information Technology Program, Office of Technology Assessment (OTA), U.S. Congress. Dr. Weingarten
holds a Ph.D. in Mathematics from Oregon State University
and has written and spoken nationally and internationally
on issues of computer impacts and information policy. At
OTA he was the principal author of the report* Computer
Based National Information Systems *which projected for
Congress the general trends in information policy over the
next decade.*

The reason I was asked to comment on this subject is that right now
my program at the Office of Technology Assessment (OTA) is doing a
study of research and development in telecommunications in computers. We have been asked by the House Science and Technology
Committee and the House Commerce and Energy Committee—telecommunications is one of its various responsibilities—to take a look at
the implications of changing industrial structure and technology for
research and development and science policy within the U.S.

For those of you who may not know, OTA is one of a small number
of support agencies that work for the Congress—we are bipartisan, and
bicameral. We have a board of twelve members. Six of them are Senators, and six are Representatives—three of each from each party. So
they keep us on our toes and hopefully keep us in a rather neutral mode.

Our specific Communications and Information Technology program is responsible for all telecommunications and information policy
research at OTA. Our studies commonly take one to two years, and
involve the efforts of a number of staff and outside consultants and contracts. So we view these things as long-term concerns.

That leads me to my first comment on the NTIA report. I am very
sympathetic to what its staff faced. We ourselves are trying to do a
research and development study. We are looking at research and development, and telecommunications and computers, and we are several

months along on that study. I can say that spending a couple of months trying to put together a report that somehow analyzes all issues and recommends some options is an impossible job. I am sure NTIA wishes that it could have gone much more deeply into the issues.

The National Academy of Sciences, the National Science Board of NSF, and many professional societies have all made attempts to do R&D studies, and many of them have run up against the fact that it is a large fuzzy issue—a difficult field to approach. I will organize and put in my own language the issues as framed by NTIA (NTIA might not admit that this is the way they structured it, but this is what I see coming out of the report): (1) There are changes in the industry that are simply due to deregulation and certain kinds of technological developments. (2) There are changes in the technology itself. In fact, some of the pressures in deregulation in telecommunications arise out of that changing nature of telecommunications technology. (3) Finally, there is a change, or at least a perceived change, in the position of the U.S. and the international economy; and as Veronica Ahern mentioned [see Chapter One] this comes around to a set of ideas that we are calling "industrial policy"—whatever that might mean. High technology, in particular, as evidenced by communications and computers, is viewed as an inherent basis for our competitive posture in the future international economy.

Given all those changes, what are the implications for federal science policy, and federal R&D policy in general, including both overt programs of support such as those of the National Science Foundation and the indirect effects of tax policy, antitrust policy, and so forth, on the private sector and R&D?

Now, as I said, I see that as a very difficult problem to address: I am going to talk about three fundamental attributes of any study of this sort that one needs to pay attention to.

## Fundamental Distinctions

First is the need to make distinctions. I think a lot of writers on R&D and science policy fail to make fundamental distinctions that are very important to policy analysis. For instance, there is the distinction between science and technology. Because I have a background as a scientist and worked for the National Science Foundation, I am sensitive to this distinction.

I find that a lot of policy analysts, lawyers, and economists write about R&D and don't perceive the difference between basic research, applied research, and development. In fact, there are even finer subcategories in that spectrum. The fact that the categories overlap and we can't really draw a precise boundary doesn't mean they're not different.

Secondly, there are different fields of science, specifically different fields of science that support telecommunications and computers. I'm reminded of an exercise that I went through at the National Science Foundation in the early 1970s when "energy" suddenly became the key word. We all scurried around to find out how much basic research was conducted at the National Science Foundation that somehow underlay the energy problem.

We found out that 80 percent of the basic research at the National Science Foundation was, by some bureaucratic process, related to energy. We said we all wanted to be related to energy because that was where the bucks were. We even wanted to make some sort of logical connection between algebraic topology and energy supply. It took a few steps.

Nowadays when thinking about information technology R&D we need to include hardware technology, software technology, basic solid-state physics, computational mathematics, computer architecture, and so on. These are all different fields that have different characteristics. And the U.S. is in a different position with respect to the rest of the world in each of these areas.

These distinctions really do matter because each field represents different types of research done by different types of people and organizations; and if one wants to measure the health of U.S. science, one has to make those distinctions.

An example: There is a comment in the NTIA report about making the U.S. national labs more closely connected to industrial needs. Well, there are national labs like Kitt Peak, the Fermi Lab, and SLAC whose fundamental goal is basic research—I don't really know how one would make Kitt Peak Astronomical Observatory more appropriate to industrial concerns.

Moreover, there are other labs like Los Alamos and Livermore which, although they do some other kinds of research, have a fundamental national defense mission. One certainly isn't going to reorient Livermore away from weapons and into industrial research without some basic reorientation of federal policy and, probably, without a major fight with the Departments of Energy and Defense.

That leads us to another type of distinction—there are different federal agencies involved, depending on whether you are talking about science or technology, basic or applied research, and defense or civilian work. The National Science Foundation and the Defense Department both fund research in computers. Although there is a great deal of overlap, NSF's basic role in the American society is quite different from that of Defense. So there are differences in their motivations for supporting research, the way they support it, and the kind of encouragements or discouragements they provide.

### A Sense of History

The second aspect that I think needs to underlie any study is a sense of history. The super-computer debate, I guess, is my favorite current example.

My original technical background was in computer architecture. I've been around the field off an on for almost 25 years, and I have never known a year in which there was not a super-computer or a super-computer industry. There have always been super-computers around. They have always been few in number. There have never been large numbers of manufacturers because there's no market. If you look at how many super-computers there are around, you'll find a few dozen.

In the early days, there were a few, period. I remember year after year in the early 1970s, Watson, the chief executive officer of IBM would go to stockholder meetings and get upbraided because IBM didn't make super-computers. Somebody says it is not profitable. Somebody else says it is prestigious; IBM is the biggest company, so IBM ought to make them anyway.

So there has always been a long debate. That doesn't mean that there is not a legitimate policy debate right now about whether we need additional federal efforts to develop the next computer generation. On the other hand, the federal government has always played a major role in the development of this technology.

The 64K bit chip is another example. I don't think we really know whether Japanese success with the 64K chip was a result of any lead in that particular technology. Might it have been the result of marketing success, or production investment strategies, or general industrial policy? I have articles on my desk right now arguing all sides of that case.

### Assumptions Open to Analysis

Finally, I think we make a lot of connections and a lot of assumptions about R&D that are open to analysis. I believe many of them, but they should still be open to question as we try to develop major policy options. An example is the connection between R&D and the development of industrial products, or the "commercialization" of R&D.

We know that somehow knowledge is a raw material, just as iron ore is the raw material for the steel industry. But we also know that increasing the quantity of iron ore in the U.S. is probably not the key to revitalizing the U.S. steel industry. Yet the connection between raw material and production is a lot closer than the connection between R&D and entrepreneurial activity on the part of U.S. industry in general.

I believe that basic and applied research are, in fact, fundamental drivers of industrial innovation, but many economists disagree. If you don't understand what and where the links between research and product innovation are, it is hard to promote federal policy. You can stimulate all the science you wish, but industry may still be moving along slowly and not commercializing the results. In fact, the French, the Japanese, and the Candians may be doing a better job in commercializing U.S. technology and science.

We also don't know the connection between patents and innovation. The report talks a bit about patents, but we really don't know that patents, particularly in the area of software and computers, are either major barriers to or incentives for commercialization of technology. There may be very superficial links in some cases to entrepreneurial activity, at least in this country.

We don't understand the fact that measures of patent activity can be accurate measures of industrial R&D, or the status of parties in different countries, or different habits and traditions in industry, or simply different attitudes toward this indication of property.

We don't understand manpower needs. We talk about the shortage of engineers and shortage of scientists but we don't define it well. A lot of statistics suggest that there is *not* an enormous shortage. How much manpower do we need? It depends on what kind of research we want to do, and in what areas. If we wanted to put $50 million into super-computer research next year, as people have suggested, who would do the work? I can count the top-level computer architects right now on two hands. So I don't know where that $50 million is going to go unless we expect that the purpose of it is to develop, within the next five or ten years, a new generation of experts in this field.

In fact, some people have suggested that that is the real motivation of the Japanese "Fifth Generation" project—not to build the super-computers of the next decade but to build a generation of super-computer architects that will continue on for several decades. But quantity isn't everything. For example, in the area of super-computers, the U.S. has a major resource, Seymore Cray. For the last 20 years Cray has been a key leader of U.S. research in this field, and we have led the world. So it doesn't necessarily take quantity—if one has the quality.

We also don't understand the relationship of size—the critical mass. A lot of talk has appeared in the press about Bell Labs. Bell Labs *is* a major producer of basic research; and undoubtedly Bell does very good work. But also underlying some of those debates is the assumption that a laboratory, in order to produce useful work, has to be larger than some minimal critical mass. I don't think we really understand the nature of science or research well enough to make that immediate leap of faith.

\* \* \*

My objective today was to raise some analytical questions. I understand the magnitude of the effort that NTIA has undertaken. So the comments are certainly not meant to be overly critical about the report. I think it is an important first step that NTIA has made in bringing some of these R&D issues to the forefront, particularly within an industrial policy perspective.

# Elliot Maxwell

*Elliot Maxwell is a telecommunications consultant, Washington, D.C. Mr. Maxwell received his B.A. from Brown University and a J.D. from Yale Law School. He served as Deputy Chief, Office of Science and Technology at the Federal Communications Commission and was a Special Assistant to the Chairman of the FCC, 1978-1980. Prior to that he was Senior Counsel, Select Committee on Intelligence Activities for the U.S. Senate, and Counsel, Select Committee to Study Governmental Operations with Respect to Intelligence Activities, U.S. Senate.*

One thing about this session is that it is a low-technology presentation on the subject of high technology. In theory, everyone should be able to stay at home and receive this session via satellite teleconferencing, respond to it via electronic mail encrypted by the data encryption standard, or listen to it over NASA's mobile radio satellite or a spread spectrum radio developed by the Department of Defense. Unfortunately, you have people talking at you without even a microphone.

What I will try to do is endorse the purposes of this section of the report, make some general comments about it and several of the options presented, and point to further work that needs to be done.

## Foreign Competition in High Technology

It is very clear that the authors know that high technology in telecommunications is going to be enormously important for Americans in the future. It is important for increases in productivity, the spurring of exports, and the creation of jobs.

The report also points out that there are very strong competitors in this area doing everything they possibly can to improve their positions. I've just finished doing a report on U.S.-Asia trade in telecommunications and went through an exercise identifying some of the techniques that our rivals have used to bolster their trade in telecommunications.

The list is very long. Rather than citing particular examples, I will just run through the types of things that have been done and give some of the difficulties that may be encountered.

In the area of finance and fiscal support: grants; manipulation of credit; direct funding for research and development; salary assistance for scientists and technical personnel; funds for feasibility studies to move new products into production; aid for development and distribution; government assurances on production or government funding of losses in production; and tax forgiveness on export profits.

There are requirements for licensing and delays in customs or equipment approvals. There are often elaborate requirements dealing with market penetration by foreign entities in some of the foreign markets that are of greatest importance to us. These include questions of technology transfer, limits on foreign ownership, and domestic sales restrictions. There are guidelines as to the employment of nationals, import ceilings for products and components, local content rules, export minimums, and controls on use of particular product distribution channels.

In some countries there are restrictions on foreign participation in research and development joint ventures between the government and private sector. Foreign firms are also discriminated against by not having equal access to bidding information and by an inability to participate in government-controlled market segmentation. Use of technical standards and standards for safety and human factors are also barriers to foreign entry.

There are restrictions on telecommunications services that can be offered. There are, for example, restrictions on the use of particular equipment on particular lines and other questions of interconnection. And the report doesn't deal with restrictions on information transfer that have not been the subject of transborder data flow questions, such as services that are more "content" oriented rather than managerial-information oriented. We have focused on the passage of data that are useful for management; we have spent less time trying to develop an analytic framework for trade in video and audio services, movies, and other services that in the United States are protected by the First Amendment.

The list is very long. But I believe the report does not detail what the United States has done—or can do.

## U.S. Involvement in High Technology

The United States has in its own arsenal a very substantial list of tools which can be used in the trade arena. But the report only implies—

it doesn't state it as explicitly as I might have—that these tools, these weapons for trade, the positive instruments for encouraging U.S. high-technology industries, have not been used consistently or coherently. They have not been applied in a rigorous way. And we have not scrutinized them to see how better to use them to develop our high-tech areas.

It may be instructive to see what one former head of the Department of Commerce did in applying some of those tools. He established a bureau which advised private sector firms in obtaining foreign loans and investments. He set up an office that analyzed foreign markets and an office for searching for foreign or raw materials. He created a worldwide intelligence network on the action of the U.S. foreign competitors. That Secretary of Commerce was Herbert Hoover. And if he could use government in these ways, we can. The history of U.S. use of these tools is quite long, as is the list of the tools themselves. They include tax policies—for example, trying to increase tax credits for industry—and patent law policies. There are policies governing regulation and deregulation as well as antitrust policies. While we have protested Japanese telephone procurement policies overseas, our Post Office's decision to "buy American" with respect to optical character readers and the Defense Department's interest in a U.S. supplier of fiber optic cable does not look very different in Japanese eyes.

There are also quotas, voluntary markets agreements, and subsidies, but if there has been a difference it is that (unlike certain foreign governments) we haven't used them in a concerted way to move toward higher value production.

The scale of this government action is enormous. In 1977, the government bought 56 percent of radio and communications equipment produced in the United States. It bought 12 percent of the engineering and scientific instruments produced in the United States.

In 1980, government procurement of electrical equipment and systems was one-half of the total value sold. This provides the government with a great deal of power in that marketplace.

Another part of governmental activity normally goes underreported. In 1950, the cost of special tax credits and tax depreciation was $8 billion or about one percent of the gross national product. By 1980 it was $62 billion or 3 percent of the gross national product. In 1950, subsidized loans and loan guarantees cost about $3 million. By 1980, it had grown to $3.6 billion. Government subsidies and tax expenditures to promote certain industries went from approximately $77 billion in 1980, or from about 9 percent of the gross national product, to close to 14 percent of the gross national product in 1982. But there does not appear to have been a focus on moving to higher value production or on improving our competitiveness in international trade.

I would like to give you two figures that illustrate this. According to one source, the U.S. timber industry receives $455 million in tax breaks. The U.S. timber industry has been an important source of trade, but it can hardly be called a high-tech industry. In contrast there are relatively few tax breaks for the semiconductor industry. There is five times as much government spending on R&D for commercial fisheries as there is for the U.S. steel industry.

Given these numbers, it might be useful to look at the role of the U.S. Department of Defense with respect to industrial policy. Since 1979, DOD has instituted a $300 million program in very large scale integration (VLSI). The Air Force has a "factory of the future" program with a funding of roughly $75 million. DOD has a $40 million budget per year for optical fiber research.

One should not minimize the very positive things resulting from DOD research. In digital telecommunications, very fast integrated circuits, and high performance materials, we have a bountiful legacy from DOD research. Yet DOD's rationale and the concerns of Japan's Ministry of International Trade & Industry (MITI) have been quite different.

While MITI is engaged in research on international trade it has also encouraged strong competition domestically. DOD, by and large, with some small exceptions such as the Sperry-Burroughs computer bake-off, is not as interested in domestic competition as it is in the existence of high quality and stable defense contractors. This is reflected in the very high percentage of contracts at DOD which certainly help maintain stability.

MITI has also supported the diffusion of technology into commercial production. This has not been a prime concern for DOD. In fact, given attempts to control exports, DOD has restricted the commercial application of technology. In certain instances, such as with the recent agreement to allow the manufacture of F-15 fighter aircraft in Japan, the Defense Department encouraged the export of materials technology for policy reasons. But that export may have substantial detrimental effects on the U.S. aircraft industry in the future. One wonders how much discussion focused on that issue.

Unlike commercial technology, in DOD research there may well be classification problems. In addition, a vast number of scientific personnel are drawn away from other areas that might have more powerful positive effects on international trade.

### Recommendations For the Future

I would like to touch upon some of the recommendations that were made in the NTIA report to try to highlight our country's unfinished agenda. Most of the recommendations seem quite defensible, although the scale of the recommendations doesn't match the apocalyptic visions suggested by the report.

Clearly R&D must be strengthened. Government-supported R&D has barely stayed ahead of inflation since 1969. It suffers enormously from stop-and-start policies such as we are now seeing in the energy area. It is, unfortunately, a politically sensitive part of the budgetary process, to our detriment. If the Japanese suddenly proclaimed a ten-year program on antigravity devices, then there would be a rush to introduce bills in Congress for appropriations for antigravity devices—while our lead in other areas was nibbled away. We seem unable to plan and to hold to the plan without fits and starts. To the extent that we lose a sense of continuity, we suffer. To the extent that we start and stop this support, we suffer.

Secondly, I believe the report is dead right on encouraging a rethinking about antitrust policy. Some steps have been taken, for example, to encourage limited partnerships in R&D. But as Bobby Inman, head of Microelectronics and Computer Technology Corporation (MCC), told a group of Congressmen, "The Antitrust Division has given us a yellow light."

If one wishes to encourage entrepreneurial spirit, a yellow light is not, perhaps, the color of choice. We have clearly not changed our antitrust policy dramatically. We must reflect on how one encourages entrepreneurial spirit while protecting legitimate goals of antitrust, particularly with respect to ventures more directly oriented to competing in international markets.

There are two other recommendations that I want to stress. One is the need to have better information gathering. At this point, there is really no place in the government that one looks to for gathering information about what foreign competitors are doing. There is no one place analyzing public and private sector activities in the United States. As the National Research Council suggests, we must study not only basic research but ways to improve our productivity all along the production line, from research to development to marketing to distribution. As the Council points out, our capacity to innovate is tied to developments across that range of activities rather than restricted to basic research. To the extent that our competitors are funding development, production, and marketing, they may overcome a substantial edge that we have in basic research.

Information gathering and analysis are clearly roles for the government to play. Yet recent developments have not provided us with much encouragement about the amount of government funding that will go into information gathering.

Government also has a role to play in the area of "human capital." The report recommends encouraging the training of teachers and encouraging better science and math education. The facts on science and math education are very, very grim. Sixty-five percent of the physics teachers left the classroom in the period from 1971 to 1981 and roughly 50 percent of the math teachers followed during that same period. Whether or not we have enough engineers, we are certainly facing a shortage of qualified engineering and computer science teachers.

Although the President endorsed recent calls for improvements in education, the programmatic recommendations are downplayed when compared with proposals for tuition vouchers and the introduction of school prayer. We face enormous challenges and prayer may not be the solution.

We face today not a missile gap but a technical literacy gap that will affect not only our high school or college graduates but our industrial managers as well.

As a lawyer I hate to be critical of lawyers, but lawyers now play a disproportionate role in the management of industrial enterprise. In the German manufacturing sector roughly 44 percent of the managers have engineering backgrounds. This is far different in the United States. One finds greater numbers of lawyers and fewer people familiar with the needs of production. In the long run it will not be the government that plays the most significant role in technical developments; it will be the individual firm. And the individual firm will have to rely on the individual managers who must be technically literate and must be able to identify, with the aid of others, appropriate frontier technologies. We are going to have to do a fairly substantial job in education that goes far beyond the report's recommendations.

There is another part of training that the report doesn't talk about at all. That is the work force within the government. I wonder how many of the people who worked on the NTIA report are still working in this area. I am concerned about turnover that might well affect the ability of the government to gather information, develop expertise, and implement more effective policies.

The Japanese Ministry of Posts and Telecommunications has just sent a manager for its satellite program to the United States for six months. He will spend several months with the FCC and three months traveling around the United States to various satellite-related companies. He will return to Japan with a great deal of knowledge about U.S. satellite policy and U.S. satellite development.

As an alumnus of the U.S. government I shudder to think of the reactions at a budgetary hearing if it were proposed that several branch managers should be sent to Japan for six months. We will continue to have a less effective government role in this area until we pay attention to the development of the government work force.

The report omits other things the government can be doing. If one looks at the development of cellular radio one finds a 1960s technology finally emerging commercially in the 1980s. This was due, in part, to lag time due to faulty regulation. That lag time provides market opportunities for foreign competitors. We have to think about how the regulatory process affects innovation and our capacity to compete internationally. At the same time, the regulatory agencies must be charged with considering the effects of their actions on international trade.

There is nothing in the FCC charter that suggests international competition should play any role whatsoever in its deliberations. It would seem to be easy to remedy that. It would seem simple to have one part of the Commerce Department, i.e., the International Trade Administration, talking more to NTIA about these issues.

# Chapter Eight Discussion

*QUESTION: I assume that you have talked to some federal government people recently. Do you have any indications that this Administration is at all interested in the kind of industrial policy role—strong industrial policy role—that you described?*

MR. MAXWELL: One of the difficulties is that industrial policy is like pornography. It is in the mind of the beholder. What is "industrial policy"? Would a substantial increase in the emphasis on science education have industrial policy implications? The answer is yes. Does industrial policy mean that the government would identify a particular segment and say, for example, that we are going to go all out for fiber optics tomorrow? Not necessarily. We have an industrial policy by default now. Even gathering information for NTIA's high-tech report is part of it. At the very least I would like to think carefully about better ways to use mechanisms that already exist.

*QUESTION: You made a remark about the lack of technical management in a lot of industries. Is that because the industries don't perceive that as a high goal, or are they really driven to that situation by a lot of other things going on in this society?*

MR. MAXWELL: The latter. Industry is not driven so much by the nature of the production process or the nature of the product developed. Companies increasingly have had to think more about legal implications and financial implications as opposed to quality control or increasing productivity.

# Chapter Nine

# National Security: Hostage to Telecommunications Deregulation?

# Vice Admiral Jon Boyes

*Vice Admiral Jon Boyes (U.S.N., Ret.) is President, Armed Forces Communications and Electronics Association (AFCEA). Admiral Boyes graduated from the U.S. Naval Academy and had a distinguished naval career which included being Commander of the Navy's first all-nuclear submarine division and various top-level commands in military communications. Admiral Boyes received a Ph.D. in International Affairs from the University of Maryland.*

Each one of these speakers has been asked to hold himself to about ten minutes and give his main points. That will give the audience an opportunity to bring up some questons.

We see two major considerations resulting from the recent telecommunications decisions on the AT&T divestiture and telephone deregulation. We lump them under economic concerns or national defense. We are not going to deal here with the economic situation.

We all know about the uncertainties of deregulation. Certainly we have seen some bad examples of past deregulatory actions, and we have seen some good ones. The primary measurement of the impact of the recent telephone deregulation on national defense is going to be the quality and reliability of service that will be available to the President and to the military services. The question we will attempt to address is: will this quality and reliability be better or worse than before deregulation?

Now, that question brings into focus the responsibilities of many enterprises that are coming into being in the telecommunications world. We have to ask ourselves, based on the historical precedents, what the oil, forest, mineral, and transportation entrepreneurs did to our society. Now, what will the telecommunications entrepreneurial people do, and will they be responsible? It is particularly important that we consider that aspect because of the possible drastic impacts on national defense.

We move from there, then, to the role of the Federal Communications Commission. What role are they going to play in this whole deregulation process—essentially being regulators—and more important to us from a national defense standpoint, what will the FCC's relationship to national defense be? Will the FCC be more active and positive than it has been in the past? True, we now have a Commissioner who is a little bit more active;* but does that mean that she is going to be positive? Is she really going to be concerned about the national defense?

Then, of course, we turn to Congress, and we look at them very carefully. We wonder about the proposed Senate Report 9882 of March 11, 1983. We look at the proposed Senate Bill 999 and House Resolution 2527. There is an awareness in these Houses, but not much really is said about national defense.

We have carefully picked these speakers because while on some points they agree, some of their views will contradict each other. We hope thereby to get some questions from the floor.

---

*Mimi Weyforth Dawson has been named Defense Commissioner, to act as liaison with defense community concerns.

# Richard Foster

*Richard Foster is Senior Director, Strategic Studies Center, Research and Analysis Division, SRI International. Mr. Foster, a graduate of the University of California (Berkeley), is the Founder and Director of the Strategic Studies Center for interdisciplinary research at SRI and is Editor-in-Chief of* Comparative Strategy. *Prior to joining SRI, he was associated with Marquardt Aircraft and was a partner and management consultant in the firm Foster and Derian.*

As a word of background, SRI has been engaged in analyses of the role of the common carrier national telecommunications system in support of our national security objectives for over 25 years. The scope of the studies included all aspects of national security and emergency preparedness (NS/EP) needs, including national security policy and defense doctrine.

One of the more important factors that entered into these series of studies for the government, for industry, and for the military was the need to focus on the changing national security and emergency preparedness doctrines and supporting communication needs, and those needs have changed radically. The most radical change in the last two decades was the introduction of small, efficient nuclear weapons accompanied by a dramatic increase in ICBM accuracy and number of warheads per ICBM in the 1970s. These improvements nullified a lot of the past efforts to support continuity of government (COG) and continuity of command ($C^3$). Known, fixed points, no matter how hard, can now be destroyed along with the communications that support these fixed command structures. This has led to a stress on mobility, concealment, and other means of protecting COG and $C^3$ centers, with new requirements for ubiquitous communications support over the entire U.S.

Common carrier communications support for government communications, such as COG and C$^3$, has historically depended on a single manager, essentially the AT&T organization, vertically and horizontally integrated, which was set up early in this century as a public service monopoly. AT&T planned, designed, manufactured, operated, and managed most of the nation's voice telecommunications and many of the overseas tie-ins. But divestiture of the 22 Bell Operating Companies (BOCs) has changed the relationship between government users and the common carriers.

### Deregulation and National Security

In the future, how will these now-fractionated national telecommunications networks relate to national security requirements? In the past there existed a single national system capable of universal connectivity, with standards established for every system element. This total system was planned for the future, designed, manufactured, installed, operated, maintained, and modernized on a continuous basis. Thus, the common carrier system could be gradually yet continuously adapted to the changing needs of national security. Arrangements were made by AT&T with the Department of Defense, the military departments, and other government agencies to provide end-to-end services. The FCC cooperated through general tariff support for many of the actions necessary to enable the building of a basic core system for the national security needs.

This dependence on the common carrier system has not been too well understood although over 90 percent of all government communications are common carrier dependent. Without common carrier support it would be very difficult indeed to manage and direct military forces and provide for COG in the continental U.S. However, the concept of a single manager of a regulated public service monopoly is now being modified by a combination of government actions.

The FCC has shifted its emphasis from regulation to deregulation (I must confess I am a bit confused about the idea of "regulated competition"). But be that as it may, the *Carterphone* decision and FCC decisions made in the 1970s, including the FCC Computer Inquiry II (CI 2) in the late 1970s, followed by the 1982 AT&T/Department of Justice divestiture agreement, broke up the regulated monopoly into a complex of separate local telephone companies and competitive "long lines" companies. The result has been that we are going to be left with nobody planning and managing the system as a whole.

Nor has government yet filled the role of becoming, if you like, the national common carrier planning manager to meet NS/EP needs. The government itself over the last few years has fundamentally changed the entire doctrine and operation of how to fight a nuclear war should we be attacked. Our new concept of deterrence is based on the objective of forcing the Soviets to believe that they would have to fight a prolonged nuclear war, and the temptation of a short war "instant victory" by a pre emptive strike (which in part would be targeted to decapitate the government high command) would be radically lessened. This is a bipartisan doctrine; the changes were initiated under President Carter in 1979 with publication of Presidential Directive 53 on national security telecommunications policy. A series of other Presidential directives followed in 1980 on targeting, on continuity of government, on mobilization, and on civil defense, all of which have been endorsed and reissued by the Reagan Administration. All of these new doctrines require enduring communication systems in the common carrier networks as called for in PD 53.

During this same time frame, we have eliminated the single manager for our national telecommunications system, and the government policy apparatus has been quite fractionated. There is now no single government focal point for telecommunications policy as a whole. Many are in the act—the FCC, Congress, the Department of Justice, Judge Greene from the Federal Courts, the Office of Science and Technology Policy (OSTP), the Federal Emergency Management Agency (FEMA), the National Communications System (NCS), the Defense Communications Agency (DCA), the military services, the Departments of State and Commerce, the NTIA, the CIA, and fifty state governments and PUCs.

Thus, we have changed from a single-manager concept which stressed public-service accountability, to a series of competitive networks and subsystems, with government-sponsored committees attempting to coordinate government interests and government requirements with private interests and capabilities. This committee arrangement cannot replace the need for a strong single manager who can address the multiple, end-to-end communications needs of the government and the nation as a whole. Since military requirements, to a large extent, are by necessity emerging and changing, there is going to have to be very close cooperation between common carriers, government, and military users. This must be a continuous process or there will be a fundamental separation between the common carrier system and the military and other government users.

## National Security and Technology

And there is another problem to be faced. For many years the U.S. has held the technological lead in telecommunications. To a large extent, this was due to the regulated monopoly environment and Bell Laboratories. However, an earlier antitrust settlement caused the government to order the Bell Labs to make available its patents to other firms. One phenomenon resulting from this sharing of patents has been that in the last 20 years foreign companies and countries have made use of these patents and have put them to active use in competition with the U.S. firms in the U.S. Recently, fiber optics communications was a case in point and raised a question regarding the degree to which we have sustained our "industrial mobilization base."

SRI made a study recently for DOD of the U.S. mobilization base for fiber optics and other such systems. We found that to a large extent competitive, including foreign, firms are now increasingly important suppliers of technology to the U.S. market. In the event of mobilization where we would want to rapidly increase our fiber optics capacity, we might find ourselves in a difficult situation if our national systems depended on foreign support. It is never good policy to depend on foreign suppliers for critical material in the event of national mobilization.

## National Security and Industrial Incentive

Finally, there is the question of incentives for the private sector to support NS/EP needs. If the only incentive is financial, then the "public service" factor will gradually disappear. In fact, we as a nation are now converting a very large public service institution—AT&T—into just one more competitor in the marketplace. In the marketplace we eventually get down to maximizing profits, not services.

I think we will find fewer and fewer firms—and people—motivated by a public service ethic, one that drives them to do whatever is necessary to design their common carrier communications system to fit the future needs of the government and the military. Instead the marketing ethic will become dominant, and sales to the government will become the goal. How that will work in terms of a national system, and whether it will result in a coherent national system compatible with NS/EP needs in the future is open to question.

It is rather interesting to note that by 1984 the U.S. will be the only developed country without a national telecommunications system under a single manager. The others, of course, are primarily state owned and controlled, in both capitalist and socialist countries.

We also can't neglect the fact that the Communications Act of 1934 is still the law of the land. Set forth in Title I are the purposes of the Act in creating the Federal Communications Commission: *to regulate* interstate (and foreign) communications for the purposes of promoting commerce and the safety of life and property, and *for the purpose of national defense.* The objective of the FCC and Title I was not to deregulate and enhance competition, but to regulate to enhance these broad public purposes. It would appear to me that we have reached a point where some of the provisions of the Communications Act of 1934 have become moot. What takes place in the Federal Courts, in the Department of Justice, in the various government committees, and in competitive marketing efforts will have more effect on NS/EP needs than the FCC under the Communications Act. The situation is increasingly irreversible and chaotic and has now reached a point where a new and radical review of the Communications Act in the Congress is necessary. Today, we are trying to plan and manage our national telecommunications system upon which our NS/EP operations depend through "government by committee," even to the point where we are trying to replace a single national manager with a series of government and industrial committees. How well these committees will work in managing anything, I will leave to your judgment.

# Brigadier General Robert Petty

*Brigadier General Robert Petty is Director, Defense Communications System Organization, Defense Communications Agency, Washington, D.C. General Petty earned a B.S. degree from Texas Agricultural and Mechanical College and an M.S. from The George Washington University. Among his many assignments, he commanded the 2176th Communications Squadron at Prestwick Airfield, Scotland; was Chief of Operations of DCA, Washington; Commander of the 2130th Communications Group at Royal Air Force Station, Croughton, England; Vice Commander, European Communications Area, Kapaun Air Station, Germany; and Commander, Air Force Communications Command's Continental Communications Division, Griffiss Air Force Base, New York.*

My purpose is to discuss the communications needs or requirements of the Department of Defense (DOD) and then to talk briefly about the possible impacts of deregulation and divestiture on our ability to acquire, maintain, operate, restore, and reconstitute communications for national security emergency preparedness needs.

Let me begin by stating what is probably obvious, and that is that deregulation and divestiture are introducing many new variables into the command, control, communications business. This afternoon I would like to tell you about the federal government's national security and emergency preparedness communications needs and how the effects of deregulation and divestiture may impact our ability to successfully satisfy these needs.

## The Importance of Telecommunications for National Security

It has been the policy of the United States Government to rely on the private sector to provide all telecommunications services whenever and wherever possible. Accordingly, as the federal government's telecommunications needs in the United States have evolved, it has depended primarily upon the commercial carriers to satisfy those requirements. For example, in planning, engineering, operating, and managing the long-haul, point-to-point domestic telecommunications requirements of the National Command Authorities, including the President, the DOD leases more than 95 percent of its domestic defense communications systems from commercial carriers. Indeed, through the Defense Communications Agency the DOD leases long-haul domestic communications at an annual cost of more than $750 million.

More important than this obvious DOD financial stake in the telecommunications industry is the fact that the entire federal government is heavily dependent upon rapid, efficient commercial communications in performing its national defense and security and emergency preparedness missions. Existing federal emergency systems designed to provide critical communications depend primarily upon facilities or services provided by the commercial telecommunications industry. For example, Defense Communications System (DCS) components such as AUTOVON, its voice network, AUTODIN, its data network, and JCSAN, its JCS network, are all totally dependent upon commercial carriers.

Furthermore, the President and the major command and control missions in the United States such as the Strategic Air Command and the North American Air Defense Command rely heavily upon commercial carriers for communications. In fact, Strategic Air Command's Primary Alerting System, which is employed to communicate with and among SAC's worldwide bomber and missile forces, relies totally upon commercial telecommunications resources.

These factors demonstrate that the federal government must engage in extensive dealings with, and is significantly affected by the structure of, the private sector in performing the missions of insuring that we have adequate telecommunications capability to protect our nation during peacetime, to defend and reconstitute the nation if we are attacked, and to maintain preparedness to both deal with natural disasters and deter enemy attack. Furthermore, while the government shares all telecommunications users' desire for a variety of low-cost, innovative telecommunications services, it has broader needs to which the commercial telecommunications industry must respond.

A recognition of these broader needs resulted in a Presidential determination that this nation must have a commercial telecommunications industry that can provide connectivity between the National Command Authority and our military forces before, during, and after nuclear attack to provide flexibility of response.

We must also be able to support mobilization of strategic forces in all circumstances; to effect operational control of strategic forces during any nuclear conflict; to support the conduct of worldwide intelligence collection and diplomatic affairs; to support continuity of government during and after nuclear war or natural disaster; to reconstitute any part or all of the nation during and after nuclear war and natural or man-made disaster; and to protect at all times the sensitive information transmitted over the telecommunications system.

With an understanding of the federal government's national security and emergency preparedness communications needs, and an awareness of its reliance upon the commercial telecommunications industry to meet those needs, it becomes clear why the effects of deregulation and divestiture are important to national defense and security and emergency preparedness.

From our perspective, the most critical factor determining whether the expanding telecommunications industry can provide national security and emergency communications will be the ability of all industry entities to engage in prior joint planning and preparation to subsequently respond in a prompt, coordinated manner on an industry-wide basis.

In our view, to obtain effective emergency communications it is absolutely essential that extensive preplanning and pre-emergency arrangements be accomplished by all carriers; that a robust and survivable nationwide telecommunications network be provided; that the capability to manage and control the network so as to reroute, restore, or rapidly initiate new service be continued and markedly improved to meet the changing threat; and that technical standards continually be developed and established so that all portions of the nation's telecommunications resources are capable of interoperation and universal connectivity. These are critical factors in the ability of the telecommunications industry to provide national security and emergency communications.

### Before Deregulation & Divestiture

Since the Disaster Relief Act of 1974 was passed there has been an annual average of 32 Presidentially declared disasters and 12 declared emergencies. In that past, to obtain responsive telecommunications in Presidentially declared emergencies such as earthquakes, floods, and Mount St. Helens; and man-made crises such as assassination attempts and the Cuban and Vietnamese refugee relocations, we turned to a telephone industry dominated by a single entity—the nationwide Bell system—which possessed a central management organization able to draw manpower and equipment from anywhere in the U.S.

Standardized equipment, training, and installation methods and maintenance practices existed, which insured the expedited utilization of available resources, thereby permitting rapid restoration or initiation of service in any location. Moreover, expensive and detailed network planning, from customer premises to customer premises, was performed by the Bell system, with the participation and cooperation of the Independent Telephone Companies.

The ability of the telecommunications industry to react quickly and effectively to meet our needs in times of crisis or emergency was thus directly dependent upon and related to the extent of advance planning by the telecommunications carriers involved. Workable intercompany operating procedures, pre-positioned equipment, and standardized personnel training had been accomplished in advance so that the industry could get the people and equipment to where they were needed and in a hurry.

Detailed plans for network restoration, to include the rerouting of voice and data circuits on different paths all the way to the end instrument, had been developed and were ready for instantaneous implementation. Mechanisms to assure that the paperwork eventually caught up with the orders placed and that the necessary funding was provided were also pre-established.

### Effects of Deregulation & Divestiture

With these views in mind concerning telecommunications services as they have existed in the past, let's turn now to the elements of that service which are important to DOD and examine the known or probable effects of deregulation and divestiture. There are four elements of service that we are concerned about.

The first is customer-premise equipment, which in its simplest terms, is all terminal equipment located on a customer's premises. This ranges from a telephone to a Number One Electronic Switch. The second element is inside wiring service, or the on-premise connection between the customer's equipment and the transmission systems. The third element is intra-exchange or local service—the exchange system through which the customer completes local calls and accesses the fourth element, which is interexchange or long distance service.

The FCC's Computer Inquiry II decision and Judge Greene's approval and entry of the Modified Final Judgment affect these four elements. Computer II restricts how we can obtain end-to-end service from AT&T and the Bell Operating Companies. One result of this restriction is that obtaining service is more difficult and time-consuming. Similarly, restoration of disrupted services during peacetime, natural disasters, or national emergencies may take longer because increased coordination with more than one commercial company will be necessary.

Moreover, an extensive survey indicates that more frequent outages occur on circuits provided by multiple carriers as opposed to one carrier providing end-to-end service. Time required to restore service is also extended considerably. During one five-month period, 8.3 percent of high-priority government circuits within the continental United States which were provided by a single carrier sustained outages, while 31 percent of the same priority circuits provided by a combination of carriers experienced outages. Further, the single-carrier circuits were in service 97 percent of the five-month period, while multiple-carrier circuits had a circuit availability of only 88 percent.

The second area of operational concern in the Computer II decision is the future status of customer-premise equipment and inside wiring. Many telephone companies may no longer provide these services. This may require the government to stockpile customer-premise equipment and obtain private contracts for the purpose of wiring and rewiring government facilities. Further, similar arrangements may be needed for the maintenance of customer-premise equipment and inside wiring.

The third area of concern is cost, which although not quantified is surely evident. We expect increased installation and maintenance charges, increased management staff to coordinate these new activities, and the cost of buying and storing customer-premise equipment. All these are problems of a yet undetermined magnitude. DOD and the Federal Aviation Administration (FAA) are already experiencing cost increases of 10 to 12 percent.

Other impacts of the Modified Final Judgment are also far-reaching. These include the potential inability of any Bell system entity to own all elements of an end-to-end service, the loss of central network and contingency planning capability, and the inability to devise technical standards to insure that the nationwide telecommunications facilities will interoperate as a system.

Finally, we see a vastly increased government role being required in the coordination of new service; routing of day-to-day services; and directing the initiation, restoration, or rerouting of emergency services. We also see the need to establish a national coordinating mechanism to develop industry-wide responses to national security and emergency preparedness requirements.

In summary, deregulation and divestiture have introduced many new variables and uncertainties in the command, control, communications business. The effects are significant but not unsolvable. We in DOD are working hard to maintain a national telecommunications system responsive to our national defense and security and emergency preparedness missions and will continue to rely on the private sector to provide these critical telecommunications services whenever and wherever possible.

So far, I have outlined requirements and potential or actual problems resulting from deregulation and divestiture. Mr. MacPherson, the DCA regulatory counsel, will now turn to legal and policy ramifications and what we are doing to try to solve those problems.

# J. Randolph MacPherson

*J. Randolph MacPherson is Regulatory Counsel, Defense Communications Agency, Washington, D.C. Mr. MacPherson earned a B.S. and a law degree from the University of Santa Clara, and a Master of Laws from The George Washington University. He was a captain in the U.S. Army Judge Advocate General (JAG) Corps. Before assuming his present position, he was a trial attorney and then chief trial attorney for the Defense Communications Agency.*

Let me tell you the perspective I bring to this. As a lawyer and policy advisor to Lieutenant General William J. Hilsman, who is Director of the Defense Communications Agency, and also a lawyer who works for the General Counsel of the Defense Department, it is my job to represent the military departments and agencies before Congress, in the courts, and in the regulatory proceedings to see that the problems Richard Foster raised are solved, and also to see that the operational needs of General Petty and his counterparts and the other military departments and agencies are met. In order to do that, the first thing one has to do is simplify the problem as much as possible.

## Defense Department Concerns

The problem is that the Defense Department has historically relied upon end-to-end service. Whatever that may be, whether from San Francisco to Los Angeles, from Washington, D.C., to someplace in Europe, or just local service to meet a local disaster, the Defense Department has gotten its service from either one company or from one central entity responding to those needs. This applies to emergency requirements and to day-to-day operational requirements in military posts, camps, and stations.

Understanding that, you go down one more level: What kinds of end-to-end service do the Defense Department and other government agencies get? They really have gotten three. The first is where a single entity "provides" end-to-end service. What I mean by that is a single entity owns, operates, and maintains all of those four elements of service that General Petty mentioned.

The second kind of end-to-end service we have gotten is the category I call "be responsible for." A single system manager doesn't own all the elements of service but puts them all together and is the single point of contact who is responsible to the user.

The third category is "coordinate." It is like the contractor who comes in to direct remodeling on your home. He will call a plumber and an electrician and get them there on the same day, but he is not actually going to do what the electrician does or what the plumber does. He facilitates everybody's response.

The vast majority of the Defense Department's requirements are in the second category—"be responsible for." Even in the day of the Bell system monopoly, many critical Defense Department needs, such as the Strategic Air Command (SAC) Primary Alert System, had many independent telephone companies integrated into that system. Those companies also owned portions of the system. The Bell system was acting as the system manager.

Having figured out what the problem is and what kinds of end-to-end service we get, we have to look at deregulation and the divestiture and find out what that may do to us. The first thing one has to do is contrast the domestic environment with the international environment.

Internationally, we have been in a fragmented world for many years. There are multiple U.S. carriers. There are multiple foreign entities. To get our end-to-end service, we have had to develop arrangements whereby a single entity—in this case, a U.S. carrier—could give us end-to-end technically sufficient service. We have been able to do that.

Now, can we do that domestically? In the domestic environment we grew up with the Bell system. We always turned to it. It has provided 85 to 90 percent of the service in this country. But my answer is: Yes, we can do that. Why? Well, when the divestiture was announced in 1982, we could have continued to resist as the Defense Department had historically done. At first we did object to the lawsuit. We tried to stop it. I was called into court to testify to reports we wrote which were designed to kill the lawsuit. But then we decided that it was better to stop complaining about the trends and start trying to do something about making sure we could meet our needs within a clearly changing environment.

**Defense Department Solutions**

We have been working in the last year and a half in five major areas. I would like to quickly run through those, because in my view they will solve our problems.

First of all, following the settlement we put together a Defense Department task force. We brought in operational representatives of all the military departments and agencies. That included agencies such as the National Security Agency and the White House Communications Agency, which provides all the communications for the President when he travels. It also included an entity called the National Communication System which is a coordinating role that the DOD plays on behalf of eleven federal agencies, including FEMA (Federal Emergency Management Agency), NASA, and GSA.

Through that task force, we worked very hard to influence what Judge Greene was doing in his court. Judge Greene agreed that we had substantial concerns and gave us the authority to deal with AT&T and Justice and come back to him if necessary to assure our concerns were met in the reorganization plan. We have had substantial input into the reorganization plan that calls for the divested Bell Operating Companies (BOCs) to provide a single point of contact to do many things for us. We have also asked for changes in the reorganization plan to insure that the single point of contact has the directional authority over the BOCs in emergency circumstances and to meet critical national security needs. Six of the seven changes we asked for, including all the important ones, were made. The end result is that because of our efforts, we will have a single point of contact with the divested Bell companies. In my view, it can do things for us in the post-divestiture environment that a single point of contact could not really have done in the predivestiture environment.

I think a major effort was made; and I think at least insofar as the Bell Operating Companies are concerned, we may eventually be better-off after divestiture than we were before. Of course, the Bell Operating Companies are only going to provide local service and CPE if they choose, and probably inside wiring. That doesn't take care of all our problems.

So we have been working on legislation: Senate Bill 898, House Bill 5158, and Senate Bill 2469. We have been up on the Hill on all of these. Extensive defense-related legislation was included in each one. But there is almost no defense legislation in the latest bill, Senate Bill 999. That was really deliberate by the Senate, which is not unsympathetic to our needs. But in the past, there has never been a unified FCC–executive branch duo before the Congress. If we could agree with Justice or

Commerce, the FCC opposes. If we get an agreement with the FCC, Justice or Commerce opposes.

What the Senate and the House want us to do is get together on a unified view. We are extremely close to that. In the last week, I spent most of my time negotiating with the FCC; and as of last night, Commissioner Dawson and the Chief of the Common Carrier Bureau have agreed to legislative provisions that will serve our needs. As of today, the Commerce Department has agreed. I expect the Justice Department to do so shortly.

When we testify next week on S. 999, I fully expect the Commission and ourselves jointly to say that we have a unified view on the kind of legislation necessary to insure that national security and emergency preparedness communications needs are met in the post-divestiture, deregulated or less regulated environment.*

A third area in which we have been working was alluded to before— the President's National Security Telecommunications Advisory Committee (NSTAC). We have been fighting for legislation for years so one can't presume that the mere fact that we have a chance now means it's going to occur. More importantly, while legislation clearly was not going to make it last year, there were problems without it; so we could not sit idly by. My job was to find out how we could jointly plan with less regulated multiple carriers in this new environment if we did not have legislation. The one avenue available to us was an advisory committee. So through establishment of the NSTAC we now have a legal framework for joint planning that is moving very quickly in two major areas. It is focusing on a national coordinating mechanism to bring together all carriers in a post-divestiture environment into a national coordinating center—roughly termed an "operations-type" center—to coordinate an industry-wide response to national security and emergency preparedness telecommunications needs.

Industry, through the chief executive officers of all the key corporations, such as AT&T, MCI, Southern Pacific, GTE, IBM, and Control Data (the firms which will be in the enhanced service market), has made substantial commitments to the NSTAC at no expense to the government.

These CEOs have developed an extensive report, down to detailed cost estimates of typewriters and desks, for a national coordinating mechanism. The Presidential Advisory Committee will receive that report in July, and we fully expect them to make recommendations to

_____

*As the speaker had hoped, a unified policy position was presented. See U.S. Senate, Committee on Commerce, Science, and Transportation; Subcommittee on Communications. *The International Telecommunications Act of 1983: Hearings on S. 999.* (May 10 and 11, 1983). 98th Congress, 1st Session.

the President to establish such a center and mechanism which will bring together all these less regulated carriers into an industrywide mechanism to meet our needs.

We are also working with the FCC—working with a great deal more success in recent years than we had in prior years. We just got a waiver from the Computer II requirements to continue to get end-to-end critical national security and emergency preparedness service. For the first time, the FCC Defense Commissioner, the Chief of the Common Carrier Bureau, and we worked constructively to solve NSEP problems. Why for the first time? I think because for one of the few times in the history of the Defense Department we thoroughly got our act together before we went to the Commission for help. Instead of screaming "NSEP is collapsing!" we took a comprehensive, coordinated look at our problem.

We came to the Commission after having worked with the Justice Department and AT&T to reach an agreement on how best to meet our needs; and the Commission, in less than 120 days, turned around and gave us precisely what we asked for. This is the dawn of a new era in my view, one that I think will last for some time.

We are also involved in proceedings regarding embedded CPE and inside wiring; and the Defense Commissioner is representing our concerns in the debates within the Commission. We have also filed in the Bell Operating Companies separate subsidiary proceedings, again, stating our operational need for end-to-end service and the entities that can provide that.

The Justice Department has filed in the divestiture proceeding saying precisely the opposite of our view. We said no separate subsidiaries; they said yes; but they have come to us this time saying, "We are willing to sit down and talk to try to shape a resolution whereby we get what we want"—the separate subsidiary—"but that can still meet your end-to-end operational needs." This is also a change.

Finally, we are working in the contractual area. Recognizing that this world is going to change and there are going to be other carriers out there, we are also seeking to save a lot of money, as General Petty alluded to. We can save money if we work hard in the contractual area.

We have gone to the telecommunications industry and said we have hundreds of routine low-dollar requirements every month. We need people who are interested in providing those on an end-to-end basis. Eighteen entities in the industry responded and we think eleven of them are capable of doing it.

This week we have gone out again with another solicitation to the industry that says that we need people who can provide end-to-end emergency service on short or no notice. Who is interested in doing that? I expect to get the same kind of response there—multiple companies who are interested in doing it.

The GTE Service Corporation, the Continental Service Corporation—these are companies who are going to be interested in doing that. So I believe by the end of this year we will have contractual arrangements in place for both routine requirements and emergency requirements that will allow the Defense Department to get its end-to-end requirements, as well as other agencies' end-to-end requirements, in a post-divestiture, post-deregulated environment.

# Chapter Nine Discussion

ADMIRAL BOYES: Well, hopefully, we have done two things. We have answered the questions that I have posed in the beginning, and we have also given you a little bit of ammunition to fire back at us.

QUESTION: *Why is Mr. MacPherson optimistic while the other two gentlemen are not?*

GENERAL PETTY: Well, I guess I should say that I was not attempting to express optimism or pessimism. I was really trying to state more what historically has been the case and then to weave into that the requirements that we continue to have; and then, of course, we orchestrated this so that Mr. MacPherson could tell you what we see as the answer to those problems. So I was only trying to outline that situation. I share his views, obviously.

QUESTION: *I wish you would sound happier.*

ADMIRAL BOYES: Well, most military guys are pessimistic.

MR. MACPHERSON: You have to keep in mind that military men are not inherently trusting of lawyers. They see lawyers as having created this problem and then they have to rely on lawyers to solve the problem. So the natural reaction is to be little bit hesitant to say, "I think he has got it all under control."

ADMIRAL BOYES: I always argue that it's the best of all professions. They design the law; they implement the law; they operate the law; they pass on the law without much responsibility for the law; and then they make all the money.

MR. FOSTER: The real problem is that this is a very difficult and complex system to comprehend, to design, and to manage; to think that we can do it quickly is almost subversive.

The first thing is defining when an emergency exists. An emergency exists every time the President moves. That is an emergency.

The second thing is that having done what we have done, we are going to pay a price for it. If competition is supposed to increase the quality of service while decreasing cost, that may be some time in the future.

So the question is, what really is the intent of the break-up of the system? What *was* the intent? Was it to increase service? Was it to decrease cost? Just what was it? In any case, I think the impact will come out gradually as service is provided and paid for in the future.

My guess, generally, is that we have just seen the beginning of the added costs of support for continuity of government and military with this whole new telecommunications world we are living in now, where the continental United States could become the battlefield, insuring the Soviets that they can win the war with one blow. This is a most dangerous situation to be in, one which could decapitate the government— where the Soviets could snatch the communications and isolate the command structure, whatever it was, with a few weapons. Unfortunately, that was our situation just recently.

We have begun to repair that; and this is such an enormously difficult problem that to add the problem of trying to figure out how to find a new manager for the system is going to be very difficult, and, frankly, dangerous. It is something we didn't have to do to ourselves in our defense posture. This is already costing a lot of money.

*QUESTION: What role does research and development play in addressing this problem or non-problem? What specifically should be done in terms of the national security aspect? Where should we be going that we are not going?*

GENERAL PETTY: Well, I think that the only serviceable kinds of communication systems are those that are proliferated very, very widely. I don't really believe there is any research and development ever conceived that would produce a communication system that's not vulnerable. So my view would be that we should continue to strive for a very widely proliferated, distributed communication system rather than trying to concentrate a lot of resources.

MR. FOSTER: I should add that from our perspective, coming from circumstances where we had a monolithic, monopolistic carrier, a new multiplicity of carriers to be coordinated and connected presents a big problem.

*QUESTION: Sort of a follow-up to that with regard to adding multidimensionals, particularly with regard to command carriers. Do you actually feel that there was some degree of cross-subsystem from the entire Bell system? Do you feel a multiplicity of carriers will be able to provide service without any subsystem, or will there be a need for the government to go in and pay more in order to provide information?*

MR. MACPHERSON: The answer is yes. The government will have to pay more. We have an initiative under way right now designed to deal with those kinds of problems, and I think it is entirely proper for the government to pay for such special requirements.

MR. FOSTER: Well, one of the problems, I think, is that a series of disconnected subsystem networks do not a national system make, and you can't invent interoperability after you have been hit.

Yet I know there are many expensive studies addressed to solve that problem. I have been looking at how it might be solved, but to maintain a national system and integrate all of the subsystems prepared for continuity of government is not going to be an easy task and certainly is going to take a lot more funding, if you like, from the government than in the previous system.

That new concept requires exactly the system characteristics noted by General Petty. I don't know where the bottom will lie, where the President might be, where the command structure might land. So one has to be able to have interactivity wherever one is.

*QUESTION: I have a political question to ask. The antitrust suits brought by Justice against AT&T—there was a series of them. In the last one, why didn't the alliance form that time?*

MR. MACPHERSON: I would have to start by saying that Judge Greene will disagree with you that the alliance hasn't been formed. I would say he felt the same alliance had been formed. The political difference might have been that because AT&T took our report and used it as an exhibit in the case, this judge grabbed ahold of it and dug into the situation and prevented the formation of any kind of alliance in the way you put it; but I think also the Defense Department recognized that the world was going to change with or without us. Technology was changing and the Department had no control over that. So these kinds of things were going to occur with or without us.

MR. FOSTER: There were not only Department of Justice suits but also suits by other companies claiming damages, and there was a rather remarkable suit that led to about $1.8 billion awarded to MCI. That was a very salutary effect on management.

The circumstance is that the government put AT&T in business. In effect, that so-called "monopolistic" position was a decision made by the government. So over a long period of time, what the government agreed to put into being, it took to rend asunder.

Part Two

# Long-Range Goals in International Telecommunications and Information: An Outline for United States Policy

# Long-Range Goals

in

# INTERNATIONAL TELECOMMUNICATIONS

# AND

# INFORMATION

## An Outline for United States Policy

PRINTED AT THE DIRECTION OF

HON. BOB PACKWOOD, *Chairman*

FOR THE USE OF THE

# COMMITTEE ON COMMERCE, SCIENCE, AND TRANSPORTATION

## UNITED STATES SENATE

MARCH 11, 1983

Printed for the use of the
Committee on Commerce, Science, and Transportation

U.S. GOVERNMENT PRINTING OFFICE
WASHINGTON: 1983

17-333 0

COMMITTEE ON COMMERCE, SCIENCE, AND TRANSPORTATION

BOB PACKWOOD, Oregon, *Chairman*

BARRY GOLDWATER, Arizona
JOHN C. DANFORTH, Missouri
NANCY LANDON KASSEBAUM, Kansas
LARRY PRESSLER, South Dakota
SLADE GORTON, Washington
TED STEVENS, Alaska
BOB KASTEN, Wisconsin
PAUL S. TRIBLE, Jr., Virginia

ERNEST F. HOLLINGS, South Carolina
RUSSELL B. LONG, Louisiana
DANIEL K. INOUYE, Hawaii
WENDELL H. FORD, Kentucky
DONALD W. RIEGEL, Jr., Michigan
J. JAMES EXON, Nebraska
HOWELL HEFLIN, Alabama
FRANK R. LAUTENBERG, New Jersey

WILLIAM M. DIEFENDERFER, *Chief Counsel*
RALPH B. EVERETT, *Minority Chief Counsel*

(II)

190

# LETTER OF TRANSMITTAL

U.S. SENATE,
COMMITTEE ON COMMERCE, SCIENCE,
AND TRANSPORTATION,
*Washington, D.C., March 11, 1983.*

DEAR COLLEAGUE: I am submitting herewith the report of the National Telecommunications and Information Administration (NTIA) on U.S. long-range international telecommunications and information goals.

NTIA submitted the report in accordance with section 202 of the Communications Amendments Act of 1982 (Public Law 97–259). This document is a reflection of the importance Congress places on U.S. ascertainment of the goals and objectives of its international telecommunications and information policies. Congress believes that the U.S. Government should be organized in such a way so as to maximize the ability of the United States to realize its goals in international telecommunications.

The United States faces a rising challenge to its technological telecommunications leadership from foreign firms, many of them directly or indirectly supported by their governments. In the area of information services, there has been an increase in barriers to U.S. service offerings, limits on transmission facilities, problems of entry into foreign markets and restrictions on the flow of information across national boundaries.

It is in this context that world expenditures in telecommunications are expected to exceed $78 billion. The U.S. Government must establish a long-range strategy that will promote and protect U.S. long-range economic interests. The stakes are too high to do otherwise.

This report should serve as a basis for action by Congress and the executive branch.

Cordially,

BOB PACKWOOD, *Chairman.*

# LETTER OF SUBMITTAL

U.S. DEPARTMENT OF COMMERCE,
ASSISTANT SECRETARY FOR
COMMUNICATIONS AND INFORMATION,
*Washington, D.C., February 25, 1983.*

Hon. ROBERT W. PACKWOOD,
*Chairman, Committee on Commerce, Science, and Transportation,*
*U.S. Senate, Washington, D.C.*

DEAR MR. CHAIRMAN: In accordance with section 202 of the Communications Amendments Act of 1982 (Public Law 97–259), I respectfully submit the following report on U.S. long-range international telecommunications and information goals.

This extensive report is in three parts. The first part sets forth information concerning the challenges and opportunities we now confront in this key high-technology field. Second, some of the difficulties that have arisen in conjunction with past U.S. policies and approaches are discussed. Particular emphasis is accorded the problems that we have faced in seeking to work affirmatively within the increasingly politicized International Telecommunication Union. The direct and opportunity costs attributable to the present dispersion of Government policy authority in this sector are also assessed, and means by which improvements could be achieved are analyzed.

The third part of the report consists of a number of specific issue papers. They deal with important issues currently of interest in the United States and on other nations. I trust that these papers, together with the other parts of the report, will prove of value to the Committee as it studies U.S. policies and developments in the international telecommunications and information field.

Sincerely,

BERNARD J. WUNDER, Jr.

(V)

## NTIA SPECIAL STUDY STAFF

Kenneth W. Leeson, *Director*
Robert F. Aldrich
Melvin Barmat
Bohdan Bulwaka
Jack E. Cole
Richard J. Feldman
Richard M. Firestone
Richard J. O'Rourke, Jr.
Richard D. Parlow

Kenneth G. Robinson
Roger K. Salaman
Suzanne R. Settle
Helen A. Shaw
Richard H. Shay
Francis S. Urbany
William F. Utlaut
Charles K. Wilk
Marilyn I. Wilson

## CONSULTANT STAFF

Paul L. Laskin

Harrison H. Schmitt

## SUPPORT STAFF

Lois H. Adams
Denise F. Becker
Phyllis M. Littleford

Lorraine A. McAllan
Steven W. Pomerantz

(VI)

194

# CONTENTS

(VII)

Prologue

DISTURBING TRENDS, U.S. INTERESTS, AND THE NEED FOR ACTION

United States economic, defense, and political interests in international telecommunications and information services have become increasingly vulnerable to adverse foreign actions as a consequence of events over the past decade. Steps have been taken by both developed and developing nations to restrict the free flow of information across their borders. Japan, France, West Germany, Canada and other countries today are successfully targeting specific sectors of our telecommunications and information industries, generating intense subsidized competition here while imposing protectionist restrictions against American producers. The economic strengths conferred by sheltered foreign markets are in fact being used to deny American firms a full and fair chance to compete effectively both at home and abroad. Decisionmaking within the International Telecommunication Union (ITU) and other specialized UN agencies has also begun to be needlessly politicized due to block voting by lesser developed countries. The one-nation, one-vote premise upon which these multilateral international bodies ostensibly function admits to further politicization contrary to the interests of developed nations, especially the United States.

These specific national and international developments are more than isolated instances posing resolvable short-run problems for the United States. Collectively, they reflect the emergence of restrictive trends in the international telecommunications and information environment. Projected into the future, a gradual erosion of the United States position in the telecommunications, information flow, and associated high-technology markets may result, absent prompt remedial action.

The dispersal of responsibility and the lack of policy authority at the highest levels of our Government have prevented the United States from responding effectively and quickly to this escalating challenge to its defense, economic, and political interests. It has also adversely affected the ability of U.S. firms to

XII

function effectively abroad by signalling to foreign administrations that these key "sunrise, high-tech" industries are not valued sufficiently by the Nation's political leadership to warrant full collateral support of industry's efforts. It is important that remedial measures be initiated now. If we wait another ten years before we counter these adverse trends — after seven more critical international conferences and many more attacks on the free trade of goods, services, and ideas — it will be too late. The likely impact on U.S. defense capabilities, on employment and economic growth, and on freedom itself will be catastrophic.

The list of specific adverse events that buttresses these harsh conclusions is long. However, it is critical that policymakers in the Executive, as well as in Congress, become familiar with those of greatest significance. These events are set forth below in chronological order.

o    1970:   Technology Targeting   —   Japan includes "knowledge intensive industries" in its national economic policy and planning, thus recognizing the importance of information products in shaping future Japanese economic development.

o    1972:   Information Control   --   Brazil establishes a Coordinating Commission on Data Processing Activities (CAPRE) to promote development of its indigenous telecommunications and information infrastructures and to control the flow of information in its economy. The resulting policies severely limit access to the Brazilian market and serve as models for other developing countries in promoting their own telecommunications and information sectors.

o    1973:   Information Control   —   European countries commence enacting data protection laws designed to control international flows of personal data ostensibly to safeguard personal privacy. Some laws affect non-personal corporate data as well, however, thus potentially handicapping U.S.-based multinationals.

o    1973:   ITU Politicization   --   The politicization of the ITU, a process that began in 1965, continues with the strengthening of developing country voting blocs and the expulsion of Portugal and South Africa from the Torremolinos Plenipotentiary Conference. One-fourth of the Conference is consumed by heated debates over membership and other political topics, not radio frequency management issues.

XIII

o    1976:    Trade Restriction  —  At its Sixth Plenary Session, the International Telegraph and Telephone Consultative Committee (CCITT) of the ITU adopts recommendations prohibiting resale and shared use of private lines.

o    1976:    Trade Restriction  —  Canada denies tax deductions to Canadian businesses for advertisements aimed at Canadian viewers, but broadcast on foreign stations.  A significant reduction in the revenues of U.S. border broadcast stations results.

o    1976:    Information Control  --  A variety of measures surface in UNESCO supposedly to reverse perceived North-South inequalities in the telecommunications and information fields.    Included are proposals for a New World Information and Communication Order and a code of ethics and, indeed, the licensing of journalists.

o    1978:    Trade Restriction  —  Japan unilaterally imposes restrictive conditions on leased channel service sought by Tymshare, Inc., and Control Data Corporation.  Each leased circuit must terminate at a single facility in the United States, thereby preventing these U.S. data processing companies from offering a full line of services in the Japanese market.

o    1978:    Technology Targeting  —  The Nora-Minc Report to the President of France expresses the need for a national strategy to control the impact of "telematics" on society, develop indigenous computer and telecommunications capabilities, and respond to the "renewal of the IBM challenge."

o    1979:    Information Control  --  A Canadian government study, the Clyne Report, recommends that "the government should act immediately to regulate transborder data flows to ensure that we do not lose control of information vital to the maintenance of national sovereignty."

o    1979:    Technology Targeting  —  The Japanese Ministry of International Trade and Industry (MITI) issues "MITI Vision for the 1980s."  This policy report recommends targeting the computer and data processing industries as crucial to Japan's long-term economic progress.

o    1979:    ITU Politicization  —  The World Administrative Radio Conference fails to resolve national differences regarding the use of the geostationary satellite orbit.  Passed is a resolution sponsored by a block of lesser developed countries to convene a conference to "guarantee in practice for all countries equitable access to the

XIV

geostationary satellite orbit and the frequency bands allocated to the space services."

o   1979:   Trade Restriction  — The European Commission (EC) issues a report recommending a community-wide strategy to develop telecommunications and information markets, to improve European capabilities in information services, and harmonize standards. EURONET, a community-wide data communications network, reflects the goal of providing purely European services in the EC market.

o   1979:   Trade Restriction  -- European countries refuse to include the Post, Telegraph, and Telephone (PTT) administrations as "government agencies," thus subject to the GATT goverment procurement code.

o   1980:   Trade Restriction  — The Canadian Banking Act is enacted and prevents transactions being processed outside Canada unless processing is done domestically as well. Prior approval before financial data can be sent out of the country is also required.

o   1980:   Information Control  -- The MacBride Commission Report on international communications is transmitted to the UNESCO Director General. Its findings stridently support Third World demands for "more justice, more equity, more reciprocity in information exchange, less dependence in communication flows, less downwards diffusion of message, more self-reliance and cultural identity, more benefits for all mankind," but suggest severe restraints on Western news media.

o   1980:   Information Control  — The Council of Europe adopts a treaty concerning protection of individual privacy to be legally binding when ratified by five member nations. Once ratified, this treaty could seriously restrict flows of personal data to non-member countries.

o   1980:   Trade Restriction  -- A French report by Alain Madec asserts transborder data flows reinforce the economic strength of multinational companies and "even more than trade in products, mean the decay of the state." The report presents a scheme for analyzing information as a commodity, which may serve as the basis for imposing customs duties and value-added taxes on transborder data flows.

o   1981:   Technology Targeting  — MITI sponsors the Fifth Generation Computer Conference and outlines a ten-year

XV

government-industry R&D program by which the Japanese hope to leapfrog the U.S. computer industry.

o       1981:   Trade Restriction   —   The United States Trade Representative compiles an inventory of over 100 non-tariff trade barriers posing current and potential problems for the telecommunications, data processing, and information services areas.

o       1982:   ITU Politicization   --   Amendments to the ITU Convention at the Nairobi Plenipotentiary Conference expand the purposes of the ITU to include provision of technical assistance to developing countries. Also changed are certain election procedures for directors of the International Consultative Committees who will no longer be elected by their technical peers in plenary sessions, but by all participants in plenipotentiary conferences.

o       1982:   Trade Restriction   —   West German Bundespost regulations go into effect which condition private leased line access to international lines on the local processing of data before international transmission. These regulations serve the dual purpose of protecting the domestic data processing industry and increasing PTT revenues from new volume sensitive services.

This list is not only a litany of concerted actions taken by other nations. It is also an indictment of the lack of U.S. policy coordination in the face of ever-increasing economic and political challenges. The report that follow sets out in detail how we reached the adverse situation in which we find ourselves, what our policy and organizational options are, and which of these options offer the best chance of enhancing U.S. and free world interests.

There is great international strength in U.S. ideas, technology, and free enterprise. There is great weakness and danger in complacency and indecision.

Introduction

## OBJECTIVES AND ORGANIZATION OF
## THE REPORT

The primary objective of this report is to provide a comprehensive delineation of the goals, policies, strategies, and principal issues in the international telecommunications and information field in order to improve the formulation and execution of Government policy. While this report constitutes an important step, the only effective way to ensure consistent and effective policy is for private enterprise, Congress, and the Executive branch to assert a level of commitment to the field commensurate with its significance for U.S. interests and to see that a proper organizational scheme is established with clear responsibility for maintaining high performance in policy formulation and implementation on an ongoing basis.

### ORGANIZATION

This report contains three major parts. The introductory section explains the background of the study, why it was undertaken, and the procedures followed in its preparation.

Part I, International Trends and Long-Range Goals, contains a discussion of some of events and trends highlighted in the Prologue and a general discussion of goals, policy, and strategy.

Part II describes the international process through which the United States seeks, through collaboration and compromise with other countries, to advance its interests. It discusses the International Telecommunication Union and the challenges that have to be met in this key organization in the coming decade. This part also analyzes the problems of Government structure and organization that must be promptly addressed and soundly resolved to ensure comprehensive, consistent, and effectively executed policy.

(1)

2

Part III contains detailed discussions of important issues on which specific policies and strategies must be developed. These issues include:

1.  international telecommunications facilities and networks, their structure, technological characteristics, and the international institutions and organizations that affect their development;

2.  international telecommunications services;

3.  trade issues in telecommunications and information equipment and services; market access, non-tariff barriers, foreign investment, and U.S. trade disincentives;

4.  information issues, including mass media topics, that affect the international flow of information, such as privacy protection and intellectual property rights;

5.  research and development in telecommunications and information, and technology transfer; and,

6.  national security, defense, and emergency preparedness.

BACKGROUND

Title II of the Communications Amendments Act of 1982 directs the National Telecommunications and Information Administration (NTIA) to:

> conduct a comprehensive study of the long-range international telecommunications and information goals of the United States, the specific international telecommunications and information policies necessary to promote those goals and the strategies that will ensure that the United States achieve them.[1]

The Act further states that NTIA shall

> conduct a review of the structures, procedures, and mechanisms which are used by the United States to develop international telecommunications and information policy.[2]

In response to this directive, the Assistant Secretary of Commerce for Communications and Information established a "Special Project on Long-Range Goals" to plan and execute the comprehensive study. This Special Project has drawn on the technical, economic, and legal expertise of NTIA's Offices of International Policy, Domestic Policy, Spectrum Management, and the Chief Counsel, as well as NTIA's Institute for Telecommunication Sciences.

3

NTIA sought additional contributions to the study by soliciting comments from outside the agency. There were two efforts in this regard: one directed toward other agencies of Government and one directed toward the general public.

## Request of Assistance from Government Agencies

At a meeting of the Senior Interagency Group on International Communications and Information Policy on November 16, 1982, Assistant Secretary Wunder reported on NTIA's efforts to conduct the comprehensive study of long-range telecommunications and information goals.[3] A study outline was distributed and other agencies asked to assist in completing the report. Informal consultations were subsequently held with some of the agencies; others contributed written comments.

## Notice of Inquiry

To obtain additional information and comments from the general public, NTIA published a Notice of Inquiry in the Federal Register on November 2, 1982.[4] The Notice contained a list of the subjects to be covered in the study, as well as several specific questions on matters involved in international telecommunications and information.[5]

Forty-four submissions were made in response to the Notice of Inquiry.[6] They ranged in content from broad expressions of the significance of the topic addressed and offers to provide assistance at some future time, to detailed responses on each of the subjects raised and questions posed.

## Underlying Themes in the Responses

The responses reflect a diversity of opinion on the relative significance of particular issues, on goals and strategies, and on Government organization. This diversity reflects the wide variety of activity and interests implicit in a competitive, free-enterprise system. Some underlying themes, however, commanded general support, including:

o     International telecommunications and information policy has critical implications for U.S. political, social, and economic interests.

o     The Government is not functioning effectively in response to increasing international challenges.

4

o       Domestic U.S. policy to foster free enterprise and competition serves
        as an appropriate model for international goals; while many major
        nations are embracing these policies, gaining complete acceptance on
        an international scale will be a gradual process and require persuasion
        by example and patient negotiation.

o       Active and effective U.S. participation in bilateral consultations and
        multilateral organizations is necessary to advance our interests;
        better preparation for such deliberations, however, is clearly
        required.

o       The fundamental principle of free flow of information remains an
        essential element of U.S. international telecommunications and
        information policy. Viewing information as a "commodity" as well as
        a means of conveying free thought and expression, however, presents
        new issues yet to be fully explored or evaluated.

o       It is in the long-range political, social, and economic interests of the
        United States to help developing countries provide the
        telecommunications and information services their people seek and
        need.

Specific contributions obtained from responses to the Notice of Inquiry are
incorporated wherever relevant in the remainder of the report.


NOTES TO THE INTRODUCTION

[1]U.S., Communications Amendments Act of 1982, Public Law 97-259, Title II,
September 13, 1982, page 1099.

[2]Id. at p. 1100.

[3]The meeting was chaired by the Under Secretary of State for Security Assistance,
Science and Technology. Among the agencies represented were the Departments
of State, Commerce, Defense, and Justice, the Federal Communications
Commission, Office of Management and Budget, National Security Council, Central
Intelligence Agency, Office of Science and Technology Policy, National
Aeronautics and Space Administration, Agency for International Development, and
the United States Information Agency.

[4]Federal Register, 2 November 1982, Volume 47, Number 212, pp. 49,694-49,696.

[5]The Notice is reproduced in its entirety in an appendix to this report. It noted
that consideration would be given in the study to issues such as the appropriate role
of Government, the public interest, economic interests of the United States,
interests of users of telecommunications and information goods and services,
orderly mechanisms for establishing international agreements on technical
standards, procedures for effective preparation of U.S. delegations to
international meetings, and social and political concerns raised by developments in
international telecommunications and information, especially with regard to the
problems and needs of developing countries.

[6]A list of the respondents is contained in an appendix to this report.

Chapter One

## INTERNATIONAL TRENDS IN
## TELECOMMUNICATIONS AND INFORMATION

A number of international telecommunications and information developments have serious implications for U.S. interests. These sectors are crucial for the United States and a strong presence in international telecommunications and information markets is essential to our economic vitality. The long-held leadership position of the United States has been challenged by other countries, however, which also consider these sectors of vital national importance.

This section highlights the significance of these high-technology, "sunrise" sectors for the U.S. economy and the growing foreign competition we confront. It discusses the twin underlying trends which pose major problems for U.S. policy:

(1)   the growing prevalence of trade barriers and other protectionist policies once reserved for traditional labor-intensive, "smokestack" industries; and,

(2)   the increased politicization of the issues in international forums.

Meeting these challenges calls for concerted Government action; instead, basic deficiencies in the coordination of U.S. policy and the level of attention it receives have been exposed.

### Significance for U.S. Interests

Relative to other parts of our economy, the telecommunications and information sectors have experienced rapid, indeed, exponential growth in the past two decades and become driving forces of change in contemporary society. Technological advances, for example, have triggered the shift from an industrial to a service-oriented economy. Services-related industries are information intensive and thus depend heavily on advanced communications and computer systems to provide necessary access to and transfer of information. The strong link between the information and telecommunications sectors extends beyond the domestic sphere, however, to international markets as well.

(5)

# 6

As world leaders in information and telecommunications technologies, U.S. firms have employed their technological talents to serve foreign markets and consumers. Exports of information and telecommunications goods and services have made vital contributions to the U.S. balance of trade. International telecommunications and information flows are also crucial to the efficient operation of U.S.-based multinational firms. Virtually all firms with overseas operations rely heavily on international information flows to conduct business. Reliable and cost-effective access to the telecommunication facilities and services in the countries where subsidiaries are located is thus necessary. Net earnings from such U.S. overseas holdings amounted to $24.1 billion in 1981. These firms also accounted for a significant proportion of U.S. revenues from services exports.

The information and telecommunications sectors are not only important as growth sectors themselves. They also function as supporting factors in the growth of other industries -- and constitute major contributors to restoring the strength and productivity of the U.S. economy. Until the 1970s, U.S. firms dominated international markets in high technology goods and services. Since then, however, foreign firms have made inroads in several key areas, including semiconductors, robotics, microcomputers, lasers, and satellite communications. Japan's early market lead in 64K random access memory (RAM) chips is just one example of such increasing foreign competition.

## Protectionism and Other Anticompetitive Practices

An increasing number of countries have targeted the information and telecommunications sectors for special government support and protection against foreign competition, in recognition of their critical role in future development. As a result, a variety of anticompetitive measures are currently in place including:

o    denying or restricting access by U.S. firms to foreign telecommunications and information equipment and services markets;

o    devising technical interface and equipment standards which needlessly preclude or hamper use of foreign-owned equipment in connection with domestic public telecommunications networks;

o    extending concessionary export financing for domestic firms;

7

o        imposing local equipment purchase requirements or local content requirements;

o        providing extraordinary tax incentives, direct subsidies, or low cost loans for research and development to local firms;

o        restrictive government procurement; and,

o        imposing higher rates for private–line services for the purpose of excluding U.S. competition.

The current global recession, with its attendant pressures on national economic policies, has only aggravated the tendency to erect protectionist barriers in the telecommunications and information sectors.   In addition to outright protectionism, the United States faces anticompetitive policies growing out of the regulatory traditions of telecommunications markets.   In most other countries, telecommunications facilities are owned and services are controlled by the government, and the interests of some government-owned post, telegraph, and telephone (PTT) entities have hindered the development of open markets.  Some nations, including Britain, Australia, and Japan, have voiced an intention to move rapidly toward more freely competitive conditions.  Other PTTs, however, seem intent on maintaining their traditional monopolies. While U.S. experience suggests competition can expand overall demand for telecommunications services, some abroad are concerned lest their present revenues be eroded as a result of foreign competition.

Finally, many countries have become more concerned about maintaining sovereignty over the transmission of information across their borders, ostensibly for national security and socio–cultural reasons.  U.S. firms operating overseas, for example, are concerned about the possible adverse impact of recent European data protection laws.  Designed in theory to protect individual privacy in the face of sophisticated data processing techniques, these laws either expressly prohibit or authorize restrictions on the export of personal data.  A potential consequence of these broadly phrased data protection laws, however, might be needless interruptions or restrictions on international transfers of non–personal data.

The serious danger exists that the cumulative effect of these protectionist and other barriers to U.S. competition will be to curtail trade and direct investment in telecommunications and information equipment and services, reduce the flexibility with which users apply telecommunications and information

8

technologies, and lead to further restrictions on the free flow of information. An immediate problem is the disincentives to foreign investment created by uncertainty about future trade barriers.

### Politicization of International Forums

As the international institution directly responsible for managing the technical aspects of international telecommunications, the International Telecommunication Union (ITU) has become a focus for Third World efforts not only to gain needed assistance in the telecommunications field, but also to further other, often unrelated, political ends. What was once chiefly a forum for the quiet exchange of engineering views and judgments has become embroiled in many of the same controversies affecting other international forums. The attempted expulsion of Israel at the 1982 Plenipotentiary Conference in Nairobi is the most recent example. At Nairobi, there was also a concerted, and successful, effort by Third World countries to expand the role of the ITU to include the provision of technical assistance to developing countries.

Other international organizations have placed international information and telecommunications issues at the forefront of their agendas. These include the Organization for Economic Cooperation and Development (OECD), the Council of Europe, the United Nations Educational, Scientific, and Cultural Organization (UNESCO), the United Nations Center on Transnational Corporations (UNCTC), and the Intergovernmental Bureau for Informatics (IBI). (Profiles of these and other organizations are set forth in an Appendix to this report.)

The importance accorded the telecommunications and information sectors, and the diversity of national interests and levels of development reflected in these international organizations, have elevated international discussion to a highly sensitive, political level of attention.

Activities in the special agencies of the U.N. clearly reflect Third World interests. Among developing countries, there is widespread sentiment that the existing international framework does not serve to lessen global inequalities in telecommunications and information resources and capabilities. A majority of Third World governments have focused their efforts on redressing the North-South imbalance in these critical sectors by collective actions.

9

The call for a New World Information Order through UNESCO is just one example of such collective action. Agenda-setting in the IBI and the UNCTC is another; both institutions are concerned primarily with the problems of developing countries.

In 1980, the OECD adopted a set of voluntary guidelines for corporations and governments to follow with regard to the protection of individual privacy. In contrast to these voluntary guidelines is a proposed treaty, covering the same subject, for the member countries of the Council of Europe. Pending ratification, this treaty could seriously restrict flows of personal data to non-member countries.

The increasing politicization of the international forums in which telecommunications and information issues are debated poses problems for the orderly management, by consensus, of those issues for the benefit of all nations. Most international organizations operate on the one-nation, one-vote principle. It is thus likely the United States will continue to experience difficulties in respect of decisions and actions taken at the international level. The growing number of international organizations involved with telecommunications and information issues also increases the likelihood any international "rules of the road" developed governing the activities of nations and private entities will impinge upon U.S. interests.

### U.S. Government Response

As indicated elsewhere in this report, the U.S. Government has undertaken false starts in seeking to prepare itself to respond to these situations. Policy has evolved in piecemeal fashion. Problems have been aggravated by inadequate high level attention and insufficient coordination among the diverse departments and agencies involved. The net result too often has been confusion, needless jurisdictional disputes, and consequent lack of adequate preparation -- all of which place the United States at a serious disadvantage. Reexamination of our strategy and Government organization for pursuing U.S. telecommunications and information goals is required. The interests at stake demand high level attention and serious political commitment to ensure that, U.S. interests are not compromised by default.

Chapter Two

## GOALS, POLICIES, AND STRATEGIES

Our basic long-range telecommunications and information policy goals are those which, if achieved, will provide a stable national and international environment commensurate with our basic principles of national existence. These policy goals are defined both directly by Constitutional, Legislative, and Executive parameters and indirectly by obvious national interest considerations. Our principal policy goals include assuring:

o      the free flow of information worldwide, subject only to the most compelling national security and personal privacy limitations.

o      the necessary growth of the national security, public service, and commercial interests of the United States occurs in a manner commensurate with our leadership role in the world.

o      that information flow to developing nations contributes fully to the elimination of hunger, poverty, disease, and ignorance and facilitates their sound economic development.

o      there is a free and competitive marketplace for telecommunications and information services equipment and facilities.

o      there are efficient non-political international organizations for the development, management, expansion, and non-discriminatory access to international telecommunications facilities and networks.

o      that human well-being and understanding grow as rapidly as possible through international telecommunications services.

These goals are fundamentally compatible and can be pursued individually or together. The national interest may require, however, that some goals be accorded priority over others; and these priorities may also shift from time to time. Hence, there will always be a need to balance these various goals in formulating and implementing international telecommunications and information policy.

(11)

# 12

## TWO PRINCIPLES FOR POLICY

In working to attain the goals enumerated above, U.S. telecommunications and information policy has been moving with reasonable consistency and to a greater degree than any other nation toward reliance on two broad principles: free flow of information and free competitive market enterprise. Thus, in general, individual policy decisions formulated to achieve long-range goals in international telecommunications and information reflect efforts to:

o    enhance the free (without restriction or control) flow of information across national borders, with limited exceptions condoned only for the most compelling reasons; and

o    promote an international environment for the provision of telecommunications and information facilities, services, and equipment — and for the production and dissemination of information itself — in which maximum reliance is placed on free enterprise, open and competitive markets, and free trade and investment with minimum direct government involvement or regulation.

These principles currently guide U.S. policy in many parts of the international telecommunications and information sector. With respect to international facilities and services, our basic policy was succinctly stated in a recent report by the Senate Committee on Commerce, Science, and Transportation:

The policy of the United States is to rely wherever and whenever possible on marketplace competition and the private sector to provide international telecommunications services, and to reduce or eliminate unnecessary regulation. This is based upon the Committee's belief that competition enhances technological innovation, efficiency, and provision of services to the public at reasonable rates. When it is necessary to regulate international telecommunications services, it must be the absolute minimum necessary to achieve the purposes of the act.[1]

Despite a tradition of heavy Government regulation of the international telecommunications industry, a policy of fostering maximum feasible competition has been adopted and implemented by the Federal Communications Commission (FCC) as the basis for regulation of international facilities and services.[2]

13

U.S. policy emphasizes fundamental marketplace principles in other areas as well. With respect to international trade in equipment and services, the United States is the foremost advocate of liberalizing and reducing barriers among the countries of the world. Similarly, U.S. policy for research and development in this sector relies heavily on technological innovation achieved primarily through private initiatives.

Finally, with respect to mass media and other issues of information policy, the United States persistently has called for worldwide recognition of the principle of free flow of information with minimum government interference. In addition to its economic benefits, free flow of information in the "marketplace of ideas" serves to promote cultural development and to strengthen political liberty and effective self-government.

Reliance on the marketplace and free flows of information establishes basic guidance for formulating policy. In some cases, however, achieving U.S. goals requires limited Government intervention. Where market structure necessitates, some Government oversight (e.g., natural monopoly), where close cooperation between the United States and other sovereign nations is vital (e.g., for the allocation of radio spectrum), or where the unfettered marketplace will not necessarily achieve important ends (e.g., in matters of national security or foreign policy), governments must intervene in telecommunications and information activities. Nevertheless, there is consensus within the United States that reliance on market principles is generally consistent with our international telecommunications and information objectives, and that, when government intervention is required, it should be structured to minimize interference with economic efficiency, competition, and the free flow of information.

## PROBLEMS IN APPLYING THE PRINCIPLES

Two significant problems are encountered when policy is based on market principles and free flow of information. First, there is not yet a consensus among other countries that these principles should apply to telecommunications and

14

information services, and second, the concept of free flow of information admits to a number of interpretations. Each of these points merits elaboration.

### Foreign Resistance to Market Principles and Free Flow

Throughout the international telecommunications and information arena, the United States has encountered resistance by other countries to the application of marketplace and free flow principles. In the International Telecommunication Union (ITU) and other forums where countries collaborate on the planning of facilities and services, it has been difficult to obtain agreement on competitive, efficiency-enhancing policies. Most countries continue to follow a monopolistic approach to telecommunications service. Some major countries commendably have begun to move toward reduced government control. The majority, however, remain unconvinced of the benefits of competition. As a result, the foreign telecommunications administrations (PTTs) have refused to conclude operating agreements with new U.S. entrants in the international services market, or have subjected them to severe regulation. There is also some danger that some PTTs will seek to use their monopoly power unfairly to exploit the increasingly competitive environment of the United States.

Second, in the area of radio spectrum and satellite orbit management, the developing countries have increasingly opposed the allocation of frequencies and orbital positions on the basis of economic efficiency. This opposition reflects the growing politicization of the ITU and a commensurate reduction of its effectiveness in solving technical problems.

Third, international trade in equipment and services is increasingly disrupted by industry-targeting policies of other governments, including the use of subsidized export financing and the erection of protectionist non-tariff trade barriers. There is significant concern in this country that, without a reduction in such practices, our continued adherence to a policy of open markets and minimal government intervention will ultimately harm U.S. interests.

Finally, in the area of mass media and information policy, UN organizations have drafted proposed "codes of conduct" in support of restrictive policies. We

15

believe these codes fail to strike a reasonable balance between legitimate concerns over sovereignty and the fundamental doctrine of free flow of information advocated by the United States. In addition, there is a trend toward greater government control of "transborder data flows" of both commercial and personal information circulating among computers located in different countries.

Despite the disparity in acceptance of marketplace and free flow principles between the United States and other countries, NTIA believes that we should continue to adhere to these principles as guideposts for U.S. telecommunications and information policy in coming years. The principles themselves should not be abandoned, although the strategy for their implementation requires improvement.

### Free Flow of Information

A basic difficulty with grounding U.S. policy on the concept of free flow of information is the variety of interpretations of this phrase. This variety can be attributed, in part, to the peculiar characteristics of information. Under certain conditions, information assumes the attributes of an intangible "commodity," with market-determined value — a product that commands a price from its consumers. Under other circumstances, it constitutes an "intermediate resource" applied at various stages in the process of producing other goods and services. Under still other conditions, it conveys fundamental beliefs or rudimentary ideas to which economic value cannot be objectively assigned and for which regulations to achieve economic goals may clash with basic rights of free thought and expression.

Among the meanings that might be attributed to "free flow" are:

o   An extension of the First Amendment prohibition against laws "abridging the freedom of speech, or of the press," and in the sense expressed by Article 19 of the Universal Declaration of Human Rights;

o   The absence of impediments imposed inadvertently as a consequence of regulations not directed at information flows per se;

o   The absence of laws or regulations that intentionally impose restrictive conditions on the location of data-processing facilities, or on the transmission beyond borders of certain kinds of information

16

(the motivations may be purely economic and not political, and content may be of no particular concern to the regulators);

o    The absence of governmental attempts to require disclosure—for economic, social or political reasons -- of the content of information being processed or transmitted;

o    The availability of information without direct cost to the recipient.

United States policy in international telecommunications and information should continue to be grounded on the basic principle of free flow of information. Clarification of how this principle applies in various circumstances, however, can be made.

o    Free flow of information means unrestricted flow of information. It does not refer to matters concerning the allocation among recipients of the costs of production and distribution.

o    With regard to freedom of speech and press, and international flows of information via the print and broadcast media, policy will continue to provide unequivocal support for free flows.

o    With regard to information as an economic commodity, policymakers should recognize that it is rarely necessary to regulate information itself in order to achieve legitimate economic objectives. Ordinarily, the costs of such regulation outweigh any economic or social benefits.

The U. S. position on this last matter, consistent with the long-range goals of promoting telecommunications and information technology as a contributor to efficient resource utilization, would be to oppose strongly any actions interfering with the ability of producers and users to make optimum use of information as a productive resource. This will lead to a more efficient utilization of resources. It will also lead to greater revenues for both private entities and, ultimately, for taxing authorities.

Adopting free flow of information as a basic principle of policy has not meant, nor will it in the future mean, that the United States does not concede the need for exceptions for certain reasons. The requirements of maintaining national security is one example. Here, too, however, any impediments should be held to an absolute minimum and imposed only when doing so will clearly and efficiently achieve the desired objective.

17

In summary, although the "free flow of information" principle is subject to several possible interpretations, it stands essentially for the least possible control of information by governments for any reason. How this general position will apply in individual circumstances -- and the many "new" circumstances created by advancing technology — is a matter for on-going consideration.

## POLICY IN SPECIFIC AREAS

The report covers six major areas relevant to international telecommunications and information. These are: (1) research and development, (2) facilities and networks, (3) international telecommunications services, (4) trade in merchandise and services, (5) information, and (6) national security. Each of these areas are discussed in separate portions of this report. These are the principal findings and recommendations:

### Research and Development

An important objective of U.S. research and development policy is maintaining scientific and technological leadership in the telecommunications and information industries. Traditionally, the United States has relied heavily on private initiative to assure adequate innovation. In the future, private initiative must remain the primary source of technological development. There are two factors, however, that create a need for Government attention to reinforce and complement the activities industry has undertaken: (1) the high cost, high risk nature of R&D in telecommunications and computers, and (2) the "targeting" policies of other governments that have accelerated the rate of technological advance of competitors. In recognition of these factors, the following general policies are appropriate for supporting the overall goals listed earlier:

o      Heighten Federal support for R&D through

           - increased direct Federal funding of basic research
           - improved tax credits
           - liberalized patent rights for corporations;

18

o     Establish a mechanism to obtain outside advice for Federal R&D activities;

o     Continue aggressive support for joint research activities among government, universities, and business;

o     Permit greater cooperation among U.S. business through joint R&D ventures;

o     Provide Federal assistance in support of R&D activities in small innovative firms;

o     Improve data gathering on the position of the U.S. relative to other countries in technological standing.

Many of these points are endorsements of Federal actions already underway. This Administration's basic economic policies, however, have also had an affirmative impact. By sharply reducing inflation and restoring needed stability and predictability to Government decisionmaking generally, the Reagan Administration has gone far toward providing a commercial environment conducive to long-term product development and basic research rather than short-term profit seeking as engendered by previous eclectic economic policies.

Facilities and Networks

With respect to facilities and networks, five issues are discussed: (1) allocation of spectrum resources; (2) allocation of satellite orbital resources; (3) facilities planning and authorization; (4) Comsat and Intelsat issues; and (5) integrated services digital networks (ISDN).

Policy in the provision of international facilities and networks in general should track closely fundamental principles favoring market competition. Emphasis should be placed on the efficient use of scarce resources, flexible planning responsive to technological changes, alleviation of bottlenecks in facilities, and dissolution of unnecessary or unfair monopoly advantages. Future facilities, particularly ISDN, should be carefully designed to accommodate the needs of users and to maximize the likelihood of competition which will benefit those users. Specifically, in:

19

o      Allocation of Spectrum and Geostationary Orbit Position

         –     We should adhere to current policies that favor allocation on the basis of efficiency and established need, while assuring that the needs of future users will be effectively met.

o      Facilities Planning

         –     We should seek new ways to facilitate consultation with other administrations while reducing or eliminating unnecessary regulatory delays.

o      Comsat/Intelsat

         –     The United States should continue support for the Intelsat system.

         –     We should promote unrestricted ownership of earth stations in the United States.

o      Integrated Services Digital Network

         –     The Government in close cooperation with private sector users and service providers should develop a more formal policy regarding the evolution of ISDN to assure greater U.S. influence in the international process of developing network configuration and standards.

International Telecommunications Services

It is the policy of the United States to place maximum reliance on marketplace competition wherever possible in the provision of international telecommunications services and to reduce or eliminate unnecessary regulation. The United States, however, must retain sufficient Government oversight authority to assure the success of its competitive policies and to safeguard vital U.S. interests in national security, foreign policy, trade, and technological leadership. With respect to international services, the United States should:

o      assure that private line service remains a network option for international telecommunications and that ISDN provides comparable or superior choices;

o      support the efforts of new U.S. service providers to obtain international operating agreements and prevent any carrier from entering exclusive contracts with foreign administrations;

20

o      continue a uniform accounting and settlement policy for switched services;

o      retain sufficient oversight and take appropriate steps to protect U.S. carriers and service providers from unfair competition by foreign government-affiliated entities;

o      ensure nondiscriminatory interconnection and fair competition in international voice service; and,

o      maintain a strong U.S. role in the CCITT.

## Trade in Equipment and Services

The telecommunications and information industries require greater attention in overall U.S. trade policy. Telecommunications and information equipment and services in the past decade have assumed much greater importance both in the U.S. economy as a whole and in the U.S. balance of trade. Although U.S. trade policy in this sector (as in others) adheres firmly to the principles of free trade and open competition, our ability to continue making trade policy on this basis is being tested by the proliferation of trade barriers throughout the world.

In the telecommunications sector, barriers to trade and investment in equipment and to the international supply and use of services have long existed. They pose especially pressing problems today, as the U.S. industry is deregulated and focuses increasingly on serving both domestic and foreign customers. In the information sector — computers and data processing — U.S. industry's leading position is being challenged by the development of hardware manufacturing and data processing capabilities in other countries, often aided by concerted industry-targeting policies.

These problems have grown in importance at the same time the overall world economic picture has darkened. Protectionist sentiments are increasingly prevalent. It is thus crucial that the telecommunications and information industries be given greater attention on the U.S. trade policy agenda. In particular, the United States should:

o      place a high priority on the reduction of non-tariff trade barriers affecting the telecommunications and information industries through

21

vigorous multilateral and bilateral negotiations in the GATT and elsewhere, but without insisting on rigid sectoral reciprocity;

o    take appropriate actions — including, if necessary, the amendment of U.S. trade laws — to protect U.S. telecommunications and information industries from unfair industry-targeting practices and other anticompetitive policies of other countries;

o    augment the U.S. export promotion effort in the telecommunications and information sectors by identifying and reducing or eliminating U.S. barriers to exports; and

o    assure the integration of telecommunications and information services into the overall U.S. trade effort, by identifying the barriers encountered by U. S. suppliers and users of such services abroad and vigorously seeking their reduction.

Information

The basic recommendations regarding information have already been presented above in the chapter on "Free Flow of Information." On the specific subjects discussed, the following recommendations apply:

o    Press Freedom. U.S. policy will continue uncompromised support for a free press and free international flows of information.

o    Communications and Development. Private initiative is providing the expertise and guidance needed to develop the telecommunications and information sectors of developing countries. Greater efforts by the private sector will be mutually beneficial. In addition, Government agencies responsible for foreign aid should review the priority accorded assistance for communications development.

o    Direct Broadcast by Satellite (DBS). U.S. preparations for the 1983 Region 2 Regional Administrative Radio Conference on DBS planning are well underway, but the recent UN vote on DBS should encourage increased concentration on the political aspects of our groundwork. Several U.S. Government agencies involved in international broadcasting have been investigating the potential of DBS. This activity should continue with appropriate safeguards and notification bounds of existing arrangements to protect the interests of U.S. businesses in this area.

o    Privacy Protection. U.S. policy should continue to recognize the need for personal privacy protection, and support efforts of individual countries to implement safeguards according to their own legal traditions.

22

o    Valuation and Taxation of Information. Consistent with the objective
of promoting the role of telecommunications and information
technology, the United States strongly opposes any actions that would
interfere with the ability of producers and users to make optimum
use of information as a productive resource.

o    Encryption. Efforts should be undertaken to formulate a clear U.S.
policy on encryption that will accommodate both the legitimate
concerns raised by national security and the needs of users of
international facilities and networks.

o    Intellectual Property Rights. The United States should maintain
close contact and cooperation with other countries to ensure the
development of mutually acceptable forms of protection for property
rights for new forms of intellectual property and continue within the
bounds of existing arrangements to protect the interests of U.S.
businesses in this area. In this regard, the Government should ratify
promptly the Brussels Convention concerning unauthorized
commercial reception and use of copyrighted material transmitted by
satellite.

## National Security

National security concerns bear on each of the areas discussed in this
report. Ensuring national security is a fundamental goal, and telecommunications
and information are crucial factors in achieving that goal. Included within the
scope of national security are not only national defense and related military
concerns, but also the conduct of foreign policy, the economic strength of the
nation, and emergency preparedness.

As telecommunications and information technology evolves and the field
becomes more competitive, steps will have to be taken to assure the specific needs
of the national security community are satisfied. These include ensuring the
availability of reliable and economical telecommunications networks, the security
of messages transmitted, and adequate procedures for restoring networks in case of
national or international emergency. In addition, a more effective means of
including the defense community in the process of formulating and executing
international telecommunications and information policy is vital.

## 23

### STRATEGY

The issues covered thus far — long-range goals, guiding principles for policy formulation and general statements of policy in key areas affecting international telecommunications and information — constitute the substance of policy. The remaining issue, strategy, pertains largely to the execution of policy. What plans and actions will be necessary to work effectively toward the long-range goals and objectives?

#### Government Role

Successful implementation of policy requires an effective Government role -- a commitment to provide proper leadership. An effective role need not imply an expanded role. Leadership can be improved without retreating from the policy of minimum Government intervention. By elevating the level of attention devoted to international telecommunications, clarifying responsibilities and authority, and establishing an effective, well-coordinated organizational structure, many of the problems now characterizing Government activities in this area can be reduced or eliminated.

The Government's role in international telecommunications and information should be to provide what private efforts cannot. In particular, Government should establish overall policy in the national interest and, through consultation and negotiation with other governments, ensure the development of an open international setting conducive to competitive private enterprise and initiative.

It is essential to establish in Government an organizational structure that will provide effective, on-going policy formulation and implementation. This must be done, first, because the Government is an important factor in the field. It uses some 40 percent of the radio spectrum and annually purchases nearly half the output of the electronics industry. It is also the largest single user of international telecommunications services. See 1983 U.S. Industrial Outlook at pp. 29-1, 46-1. Not only is the Government thus a major player and likely to remain so, how effectively the United States organizes its telecommunications policy structure

24

also bears directly on the ability of U.S. firms to compete effectively abroad. It signals the importance that the U.S. Government attaches to these issues. And, implicitly, it is one measure of the willingness and ability of the Government to afford American enterprise any necessary collateral support. Taking these factors into consideration therefore, the optimal Government structure should be characterized by:

o    high-level attention and responsibility;

o    a central locus of coordination and decisionmaking with the necessary authority for implementing policy;

o    provision for an adequate degree of continuity of expert and technical staff over time;

o    a well-trained staff of negotiators versed in the broad range of international telecommunications and information issues;

o    a means of reaching decisions promptly in response to a broad range of relevant factors, including  domestic policy, general foreign policy, trade, national security, labor and employment, international finance;

o    mechanisms to enable specific problems of private entities to be addressed expeditiously and effectively;

o    efficient means of gathering and using data and information.

Consultation and Negotiation

The United States cannot unilaterally mandate competition in international telecommunications services. Attempts to do so will meet with frustration and may invite responses in this and other fields inimical to U.S. interests. Thus, advancing U.S. interests internationally and seeking adoption by other governments of policies advocated by the United States should be accomplished through example and through consultation and negotiation with other nations.

Beyond Technical Issues

In view of the many issues involved in international telecommunications and information, policy can no longer be based solely on technical considerations, if indeed that was ever the case. The attention accorded sectoral issues in this report reflects the dimensions of the problem. It must be recognized instead as an area in which developments affect a broad range of U.S. interests, including foreign policy, trade and economic relationships, and defense and national security concerns.

### Need for Positive Action.

U.S. strategy can no longer be limited to ad hoc "damage control" -- mere attempts to shore up a gradually deteriorating situation. Given the importance of this sector to the U.S. economy, it is necessary instead actively to promote our policies and objectives through positive, preemptive actions.

### Private-Sector Input

As a source of expertise, advice, and information, the private sector must play a more prominent role in policy development than in the past. As the direct beneficiaries or victims of many policy decisions, private firms have a critical stake in the nature and effectiveness of Government decisionmaking and are thus in a position to give sound advice born of experience.

### International Organizations

Although the United States increasingly finds itself defending a minority view in international organizations, it cannot simply walk away from these forums. Rather, it must assess the nature and extent of U.S. participation and concentrate on those organizations and issues where the most beneficial results can be achieved. An across-the-board reconsideration of the extent and nature of participation in the pertinent international organizations is thus needed to determine the settings in which U.S. goals in international telecommunications and information can most effectively be pursued.

## International Rules

Progress in this area obviously will not come easily. Foreign resistance to marketplace principles is often solidly entrenched and international support for free flows of information is by no means on the rise. In this climate, an impatient push for comprehensive agreements might well produce the opposite of the desired results. It could produce restrictive "rules of the road" that codify anticompetitive practices, inhibit free flow of information, restrict free expression, and stifle the development of new technologies. With the exception of trade negotiations in the proven forum of the GATT, the United States should thus seek to avoid the development of any omnibus, all-encompassing treaties or manifestos that would impose a rigid structure on an area in which problems and opportunities cannot be effectively anticipated given the rapid pace of technological and commercial change. Instead, strategy should support the attainment of broad objectives on an issue-by-issue basis, through consistent, coordinated preparation and positive action. Such a strategy will promote the gradual, natural evolution of an open competitive, international regime in telecommunications and information, one that will accommodate technological change and respond well to the needs of users.

The achievement of basic long-range telecommunications and information policy goals for the United States also requires an adequate foundation of national science and technology. The construction and support of this foundation requires the implementation of the following basic goals:

o   ensuring tax, regulatory, patent, and antitrust legal environments which encourage near-term private sector investment in marketable technologies;

o   providing Federal sponsorship and funding for necessary "centers of excellence" where government, industry, and academia can work cooperatively to advance the technological state of the art;

o   securing Federal Government funding of broadbase high-risk, basic research in academia and in Federal laboratories which can produce the defense and market technologies of the future;

o   encouraging private sector financing of the modernization of academic research plant and equipment; and o    facilitating Federal and private sector cooperative funding of **grants,** loans, and supplemental salaries for students, researchers, and faculty.

GENERAL CONSIDERATIONS
ON STRATEGY

Two broad issues require attention in devising effective strategies for attaining the long-range goals: Government structure and international diplomacy and negotiation. The first, taken up in detail elsewhere in this report, pertains to the way the Federal Government formulates policy and devises plans for discharging its responsibilities on an on-going basis. The second pertains to the way in which the United States advances its policies through bilateral and multilateral contact with other governments. A case in point is United States involvement in the ITU.

Those responsible to devise the plans by which the United States will achieve its international telecommunications goals must weigh several factors.

Three Policy Arenas  —  Domestic, International, Foreign

First, they must recognize that there are three jurisdictions in which international policy in telecommunications and information is made:

(1)    the domestic setting, where the U.S. Government enjoys complete sovereignty in establishing and implementing policy;

(2)    the international or intergovernmental setting, where the U.S. Government must seek, in cooperation with other sovereign nations, to establish and implement mutually acceptable policies; and,

(3)    the foreign setting, namely, domestic settings of other countries where the U.S. Government has no formal or direct control and where the indigenous government has sovereignty.

Decisions made in all three of these jurisdictions have a direct and significant effect on U.S. interests in telecommunications and information.

28

Establishing international telecommunications and information services constitutes a cooperative venture among the United States and other sovereign nations. Unfortunately, not all countries currently share U.S. views regarding the most efficient and effective means to provide and regulate of such services.

In most countries, telecommunications equipment, services offerings, and rates are controlled by a single government-owned monopoly. There are a growing number of countries, including Great Britain, Ireland, Japan, and Australia where there have been positive and commendable moves to reduce direct government control and allow greater competition in telecommunications. Many postal, telegraph, and telephone authorities (PTTs), however, remain unconvinced of the benefits of competition and deregulation, the basis of much of U.S. policy in recent years. As the bulk of international telecommunications and information arrangements are made in the international and foreign jurisdictions, unilateral extension of U.S. policies to the international setting is obviously impractical.

Strategies appropriate for pursuing our international goals favoring competition and diversity of service thus must include:

(1) Demonstrating the benefits of U.S. policy, including greater efficiency, ensuring variety of service to users, stimulating aggregate demand for services, fostering rapid deployment of new technologies --in short, promoting an efficient, innovative telecommunications and information sector;

(2) Undertaking patient, persistent and affirmative negotiations and consultation with foreign administrations that function as our partners in establishing international links;

(3) Strongly opposing any attempts by foreign administrations to exert their own monopoly power in the U.S. competitive setting; and,

(4) Ensuring effective U.S. participation in international standards setting organizations to ensure continuing compatibility of networks and services and to ensure standards conducive to maximum possible competition are adopted.

### Developing International Rules

Here, two basic choices are presented. The first is to undertake global negotiations among all countries, specify the general terms and conditions applicable to international telecommunications and information, to codify them, and then have individual countries and private entities adjust their behavior accordingly. The second choice is to follow an "atomistic approach," where the regime is left to develop gradually, with decisions and agreements reached, bilaterally and in appropriate international forums, on individual topics, according to the particular circumstances?

An impatient push for comprehensive agreements might well produce the opposite of the desired results. Such an agreement could produce restrictive "rules of the road" that institutionalize anticompetitive practices, inhibit free flow of information, restrict free expression, or stifle the development of new technologies. Thus, in determining issues suitable for negotiation and formal agreement, careful consideration should be given to the trade-off between (a) positive effects (e.g., reducing uncertainty and risk, improving the business climate), and (b) negative effects (e.g., imposing too rigid a structure on a technologically dynamic area, stifling innovation, and reducing entrepreneurial opportunities). Too many do not fully understand the forces involved in international telecommunications and information. It will be important, therefore, to proceed to any discussions and negotiations with an adequate appreciation of the changes due to technological advances. Developing such an understanding should be a primary factor for international discussions.

It is especially important for the United States to avoid the development of omnibus, all encompassing treaties or manifestos that would impose a rigid structure on a technologically dynamic area.

### Negotiating Posture

Is preemptive negotiation preferable to reactive negotiation? Should discussion and agreement be undertaken in anticipation of problems, even on individual issues, or would this prove too stultifying and costly and the identification of potential problems too difficult? Would it be more effective to await tangible problems and then engage in discussions or negotiations with the countries and entities involved? Are there characteristics peculiar to certain

30

issues that render them compatible with one or the other postures -- preemptive or reactive — and should they be so divided?

U.S. activities in international telecommunications and information have tended to be reactive, and there is some advantage to such an approach. When dealing from a position of technological or economic advantage, it is wise to approach the question of negotiation with caution. If, relative to the other parties to the negotiation, a country has most to give, and already has most of what it is liable to get, striking a satisfactory bargain may require a good deal of careful forethought. In fact, the safest option may be to abstain from negotiations altogether. Increasingly, however, this situation of advantage does not characterize the United States for aspects of international telecommunications and information. Thus, in general, U.S. strategy no longer should be limited to "damage control" — attempts to shore-up a gradually deteriorating situation. Given the strategic importance of this sector to the United States, the time has come to more actively promote our policies and objectives through positive, preemptive actions.

Assuming a more active posture in international deliberations will require attention be given to the following questions, on a case-by-case basis. First, should delegations go to international meetings prepared with initiatives, suggestions, and proposals, or would low visibility and less initiative be preferable? Second, what tactical advantages are inherent in being the proposer of an idea, rather than having to react to or argue against the proposals of others? Third, should greater effort be made to participate actively in studies, commissions, and international deliberations to channel their course more effectively, or should participation be avoided because the results may ultimately have to be disavowed.

### Institutional Separations

Is it desirable, or possible, to maintain the current institutional separations among major blocks of the international telecommunications and information field — telecommunications, trade, mass media, computers and transborder data flow — and to act on them separately? Or, are these separations becoming obsolete and meaningless, even misleading?

31

A major theme of this report is that progress in working toward long-range goals in international telecommunications and information will be enhanced by viewing the wide range of issues as part of the same general phenomenon. While each requires separate attention and under certain circumstances may be the primary responsibility of one Government agency, it is vital to coordinate efforts in the various areas to assure consistency in policies adopted.

Another facet of this issue of traditional separations of activity in the field pertains to industrial structure and existing institutions. A strategy that bases international agreements and practices regarding international telecommunications and information on existing institutional arrangements may tend artificially to perpetuate industrial structures technological advances would otherwise change. This problem arises domestically as well. In the past, regulatory schemes based on conventional technologies and traditional notions of which commercial activities are the "proper" domain of particular industries, have inhibited the natural evolution of new industrial structure. The traditional lines that divide financial services, mass media or common carrier communications services, and data processing, for example, today are maintained more by regulatory fiat than by technological or economic necessity. As in the case of establishing technical standards, there are trade-offs. Agreeing on the ground rules and boundaries for industries establishes predictable procedures and thus reduces uncertaintly. But it also inhibits the natural development of innovative institutional arrangements that would otherwise emerge due to technological change. Basing U. S. policy on the related principles of free market competition and the unfettered free flow of information is far more likely to accommodate the natural evolution of international commercial institutions and activities.

### Bilateral or Multilateral Efforts

To what extent would interests be better served by pursuing bilateral discussions and negotiations rather than working through multilateral organizations? For which issues is the one approach to be preferred over the other?

32

For some purposes, particularly in setting international technical standards, working through multilateral organizations is essential. In solving particular problems, however, direct bilateral discussions are generally preferable. These can be conducted away from the large, visible arenas of multilateral organizations where political posturing is on the rise and where powerful and sometimes hostile blocs and coalitions abound. A more definite strategy on this question ought to be developed.

## Selecting the Appropriate Forums

Which international organizations should serve as appropriate vehicles for advancing U.S. interests in international telecommunications and information? This is a question that requires careful consideration in the effort to devise effective strategy. A review of U.S. participation in the ITU is provided. This is one of the most important international standards-setting organizations and one that may pose difficulties for the United States in coming years.

In addition to the ITU, we have identified over a dozen international organizations that have some involvement in international telecommunications and information. Profiles of each of these are given in an appendix to this report. We recommend that to improve strategy, U.S. participation in each be reviewed, to determine where U.S. interests in international telecommunications and information can be advanced most effectively .

## Technology as Arbiter

It has been argued that technology will foil attempts by governments to exert effective control over international flows of information. To begin with, there are many communications channels (cable, microwave, and satellite circuits) reaching into each country and tying it to the rest of the world. Digital transmission methods will homogenize all messages (voice, record, data, video), producing an undifferentiable stream of binary signals transmitted through packet-switched networks that send bits and pieces of each message over different routes for reassembly at the destination. Cryptographic techniques will be improved. The miniaturization of components, such a silicon chips, will make it possible to store large amounts of information on minute media for convenient transport. Because of these developments, as the argument goes, it will be infeasible for governments

33

to enforce laws that may tend to restrict, intentionally or unintentionally, communications of any kind among countries. Moreover, increasing personal interchanges among nations will expand awareness of the new goods and services competitive, high-technology markets can provide. Governments may thus prove unable to deny their nationals access to the benefits afforded them abroad. There may be something to this argument.

There are good reasons for not relying solely on technology to be the final arbiter of international relations, however. Using technology to circumvent the laws of a country may merely encourage the development of technologies of surveillance. These, though costly and disruptive, may go far toward closing technological loopholes. Second, enforcement of laws may be accomplished through unannounced audits, where violations of laws may be uncovered irrespective of the technologies used in everyday operations. Third, for corporations with foreign-based subsidiaries, complying with the laws of a host country is simply a necessary matter of good business practice. If violations of laws on communications are discovered, the penalties could jeopardize the overall standing of the corporation, in the country of violation and elsewhere.

## Strategic Concerns

Finally, U.S. strategists have been forced to recognize that in an area such as telecommunications and information processing, in which a "national capacity" is widely viewed as being of strategic importance to a country's economic well-being and security, attempts to dissuade governments from taking restrictive measures based on arguments of "optimization" of global resources may not be adequate. Arguments in support of an open international system on the grounds that all will benefit by exploiting comparative advantages, specialization, and an international division of labor will, by themselves, not always prove persuasive.

### NOTES FOR CHAPTER TWO

[1] Senate Committee on Commerce, Science, and Transportation, International Telecommunications Act of 1982, S. Rept. No. 669, 97th Cong., 2d Sess., p. 9 (1981).

[2] See, e.g., the Record Carrier Competition Act of 1981, 47 U.S.C. §222(b)(1); Authorized User, 90 FCC 2d 1394 (1982); Overseas Communications Services, ___ FCC 2d ___ (1983).

Chapter Three

U.S. PARTICIPATION IN THE INTERNATIONAL TELECOMMUNICATION UNION (ITU)
AND PREPARATION FOR INTERNATIONAL RADIO CONFERENCES

BACKGROUND

Statement of Issues

To support its study of Long-Range International Telecommunications and Information Goals of the United States, NTIA requested public comments on the following questions:

o    Should we consider the feasibility and desirability of alternatives to the ITU, and if so, what alternatives are reasonably available?

o    What are the deficiencies in U.S. preparations for international conferences, and what measures should  be taken to improve such preparations?

A  review  of  the  public  comments  indicates  that  many  respondents considered the two questions to be closely related.  Those that addressed the matter endorsed continued participation in the ITU, but with a concerted effort by the United States to improve  its preparations and thus increase its effectiveness in ITU proceedings.  Additionally, several respondents acknowledged the need to examine  alternatives,    although  only  one  advanced  specific  proposals  for consideration.   On the question of improved preparations, however, specific recommendations were made by all respondents who addressed the matter.

Several issues recur  throughout  the  replies  to  the  questions concerning participation in the ITU and preparation for international radio conferences.  The issues are:

(1)    Alternatives to the ITU;

(2)    Effectiveness  of  U.S.  participation  in  ITU  and  in  international conferences;

(3)    Need  for  a  central  Government  authority  and  structure  for coordinating  and  formulating  international  telecommunications policy;

(35)

36

(4)     Need for greater private sector and industry involvement in the ITU and international conferences;

(5)     Need for bilateral and multilateral dialogues in international telecommunications with other countries; and,

(6)     Need for the Government to signal other administrations abroad that it accords great importance to telecommunications and has organized its resources accordingly.

These issues, as well as others that were identified, will be addressed in this section.

Basis for Concern

A specialized agency of the United Nations, the ITU is the international institution chartered to foster cooperation and coordination in the field of telecommunications, which includes administration of treaties concerning the allocation of the radio frequency spectrum. As described in greater detail in Attachment 1, the ITU contains a number of permanent organs and is in charge of organizing various international conferences. The latter include the Plenipotentiary Conference, annual Administrative Council meetings, and Administrative Radio Conferences of a regional or worldwide character. The permanent organs are the General Secretariat, the International Frequency Registration Board, and the International Consultative Committees (CCIs) for Radio (CCIR) and Telegraph and Telephone (CCITT).

Although political issues have previously surfaced in the conference work of the ITU (see Attachment 1), the extraordinary degree of politicization characterizing the 1982 Nairobi Plenipotentiary Conference has raised anew U.S. concerns about continued participation in the ITU and has provoked an examination of alternatives. The problems of Nairobi are discussed in greater detail in the next section.

With regard to effectiveness of U.S. preparations for international radio conferences, a number of questions were raised following the 1979 World Administrative Radio Conference (WARC 1979), and during the Senate ratification

37

hearings on the resulting Radio Regulations (Geneva, 1979). These concerns were stated in a study for Congress by the Office of Technology Assessment (OTA). See "Radiofrequency Use and Management: Impacts from the World Administrative Radio Conference of 1979," U.S. Office of Technology Assessment, Washington, D.C. OTA covered a wide range of issues while focusing on two major areas:

(1)     A perceived absence of high-level Government oversight and accountability for effective policy development and coordination on a consistent and continuing basis; and

(2)     A perceived lack of an on-going conference preparatory structure focusing on high-level responsibility and accountability.

The issue of U.S. preparations for international radio, telegraph, and telephone conferences is important and relevant given the very heavy updated schedule for such conferences established by the 1982 Plenipotentiary. Comprehensive preparatory efforts will be necessary since the U.S. will participate in most of the conferences. Many of them are of a controversial "planning nature" for important radio services determined to be necessary by the WARC 1979. In addition, important meetings concerning public voice and data communications via switched telephone and telegraph networks are forthcoming, which will have important consequences, both domestically and internationally, for the United States.

Radio conferences deal with major topics in radio spectrum and geostationary satellite orbit positions and other radio communication principles. Telegraph and telephone conferences deal with equally important matters concerning tariff principles, and operational questions relating to switched systems and protocols for voice, data, and video services using wire, cable, and fiber optic networks. At present, telegraph and telephone conferences are held less frequently than radio conferences, and major effort is concentrated in the CCITT where recommendations, regulations, and standards pertaining to end-to-end performance of communication systems, interconnection of systems, and maintenance of the world network for telephone, telegraph, and data communications are made.

38

The technical standards and recommendations made by the CCITT are very important to the U.S. in at least two major ways. First, they affect international telecommunications equipment trade. Because the CCITT standards are recommendations extensively used on a worldwide basis, countries and particularly developing countries use them as a basis for telecommunication equipment procurement. Second, and although in the strictest sense CCITT recommendations pertain only to the international interworking of networks, the complexities and interrelation in present day networks are such that international regulations have major impact on national networks.

Until recently the major participation by the United States in CCITT has been through representatives of AT&T, with minimal State Department oversight. With increased competition among telecommunications services and equipment providers, however, companies have urged Government to take a more active role in U.S. CCITT preparation for international meetings, to serve as a neutral mediator between sometimes conflicting industry viewpoints and thus to develop more effective national policy decisions.

While Government involvement in the CCITT has increased, mainly on the part of NTIA and the FCC, it remains limited. To achieve national planning for CCITT, however, it is important to obtain broad input from telecommunication equipment and services providers and Government to ensure an adequate share of the world's $60 billion equipment market for the U.S., and the development of new networks and services along lines consistent with U.S. interests. Fast evolving integrated services digital networks (ISDN) are an example of a significant new development which will provide voice, data, and video services via a unified digital network consisting of radio, electronic, and optical line networks. Services provided will range from basic telephone to advanced packet switching, and eventually will penetrate most households and businesses in the developed, and increasingly the developing, world. Issues concerning ISDN are discussed elsewhere in this report.

## The Plenipotentiary Conference in Nairobi

In 1982, the ITU Plenipotentiary Conference met for six-weeks in Nairobi, Kenya, ostensibly to consider revising the ITU Convention, a treaty governing the ITU's functions. Several modifications to the Convention based on initiatives taken by developing countries have resulted in an increased politicization of the ITU, however, and a continued drift from its traditional role of dealing with technical aspects of international telecommunications.

The issue of Israel's participation was a major problem. A proposal to expel Israel from ITU conferences and meetings consumed an inordinate amount of time (almost half of the time allocated for the entire conference). This proposal was defeated by a narrow margin of only four votes despite the fact that expulsion is contrary to the Convention, contrary to the principle of universality of membership, and not within the legal scope of the Plenipotentiary Conference.

Block voting was apparent during consideration of the expulsion proposal. The measure was defeated only through major political and diplomatic efforts on the part of Western European and other governments, a maximum effort by the U.S. Delegation in Nairobi, a worldwide diplomatic effort by the U.S. State Department, and the public pronouncement by the U.S. Secretary of State that if Israel were expelled from the ITU, the United States would leave the Plenipotentiary Conference, withhold further financial payments, and reassess its participation in the ITU. The tensions caused during this debate spilled over and had ramifications in the substantive part of the Conference.

Several modifications were made to the Convention which were contrary to U.S. proposals. They reflect the differing concerns and priorities of developing countries. These changes included:

(1) Expansion of the membership of the Administrative Council;

(2) Expansion of the general budget to accommodate increased technical assistance and cooperation activities, as promoted by developing countries;

(3) Revision of the election procedures for the directors of the International Consultative Committees, subjecting them to elections in the political atmosphere of a Plenipotentiary Conference rather than by plenary sessions of their technical peers; and

40

(4)     New language "taking into account the special needs of developing countries and the geographical situation of particular countries with respect to the geostationary satellite orbit."

Previously, the ITU's role had not been to offer direct technical assistance from its ordinary budget except for limited activities, but to foster provision of such assistance from appropriate United Nations programs and resources. The purpose of the ITU was formally modified, however, with the addition to Article 4 of the statement "as well as to promote and to offer technical assistance to developing countries in the field of telecommunications." Greater emphasis on technical assistance, perhaps to the detriment of its traditional role, is an example of the changing role of the ITU.

Dissatisfied with decisions taken at the Plenipotentiary Conference, the United States stated the following reservation to the Convention:

The United States of America, deeply troubled by developments at the 1982 ITU Plenipotentiary Conference, reserves the right to make appropriate specific reservations and statements prior to ratification of the ITU Convention. The general concern of the United States of America is based on the Union's regrettable and pervasive lack of realistic fiscal planning, the politicization of the Union, and a requirement that the Union provide technical cooperation and assistance which should be appropriately provided through the United Nations Development Programme and the private sector. This reservation is necessarily general in nature due to the Conference's inability to complete its substantive work by the time required for submission of reservations.

At the Nairobi Plenipotentiary Conference, the United States came very close to withdrawing from the Conference and reassessing its continued participation in the ITU. A similar possibility of withdrawal cannot be discounted with respect to several of the forthcoming ITU Administrative "planning" Conferences, where telecommunications issues vital to U.S. interests are at stake. WARC '79 was not competent to deal with detailed planning issues; it therefore referred several controversial items, such as planning   of the shortwave broadcasting bands and planning of the geostationary orbit for broadcast and fixed satellite services, to specialized conferences. Given the recent experience in

41

Nairobi, the demonstrated tendency of developing countries to favor rigid "a priori" planning, and the numerical majority of developing countries in a one-nation, one-vote conference forum, the distinct possibility exists that decisions could be taken in the ITU which are not in the interests of the United States and other countries with similar goals. It is, therefore, imperative for the United States to anticipate contingencies, examine alternatives, and be prepared, in case the cooperative approach for the benefit of all members breaks down.

A frank and open dialogue at the highest levels of the U.S. Government will send a clear message to the ITU that the United States is very concerned over the changing role of the organization. As this issue is openly discussed in the United States, perhaps moderating influences in the ITU will recognize the interdependence of interests and become more active in achieving a cooperative approach.

### Discussion of Continued Participation in ITU

Although several comments addressed the issue of increased politicization of certain organs of the ITU, all of the respondents unanimously urged continued participation by the United States in the activities of the ITU, citing the numerous telecommunications goals that have been achieved, and the considerable influence that the U.S. still has in the decisions of the organization. Representative comments included:

"Current ITU mechanisms function well."

"the United States should concentrate on maximizing its effectiveness in what still appears to be a workable and extremely important forum."

"The ITU should continue to serve as a planning vehicle. . . "

"its coordination functions are extremely important and need to be continued with strong U.S. support."

While indicating support for continued ITU participation, the need seriously to examine alternatives was recognized in the comments of the National

42

Association of Broadcasters, Southern Pacific Communications, Comsat, and American Telephone and Telegraph. Comsat presented three broad alternatives:

(1)  Work more effectively within the present ITU structure;

(2)  Seek to change the ITU structure;

(3)  Withdraw from the ITU either unilaterally or in conjunction with others, and use new arrangements to fulfill the needed functions.

Most of the respondents cautioned any alternative to the ITU should be given careful thought and attention and it should have the broad support of developed countries.

NTIA also proposed alternatives which are discussed in Attachment 3. The first two alternatives explore the advantages, disadvantages, and related aspects of U.S. withdrawal from the ITU either alone or with one or more other major telecommunication administrations. The third alternative examines the possibility of remaining in the ITU, but endorsing conference decisions on a selective basis, only when they are in the national interest.

At some point, continued U.S. membership in the ITU may become untenable. NTIA is of the view that the only prudent approach is to maintain a parallel effort. On the one hand, we should seek improvements within the ITU; at the same time, however, we should explore and develop contingency approaches to serve our national interests in the event the ITU continues its drift to greater politicization. Prior to any final decision made on U.S. withdrawal, the advantages and disadvantages would require in-depth study utilizing the widest range of consideration by all interested Government and private sector parties.

Proposals for Increasing U.S. Effectiveness in the ITU

Rather than alternatives to the ITU, most respondents called for increasing U.S. effectiveness and influence in the organization and trying to "make the ITU work." Most parties argued that increased effectiveness would result from an improved and comprehensive preparatory effort for all ITU activities (i.e.,

43

conferences and meetings of the permanent organs). The comments indicate that the issues of greatest concern to the private sector when dealing with improved preparatory efforts are:

(1)     To establish a central point for all international telecommunications policy activities;

(2)     To achieve greater private sector and industry involvement in all phases; and

(3)     To attain more dialogue with other countries.

Many of the other suggestions for increasing effectiveness through improved preparations were oriented specifically to radio conference preparations. These will be treated and discussed in the another section of this report.

NTIA also believes that U.S. effectiveness in the ITU could be increased, and suggests the following initiatives.

Through redoubled efforts in the ITU Administrative Council, the United States and other major contributors sharing the same goals have an opportunity to influence the organization's future direction. Many decisions of the Council are crucial to the activities of other organs of the ITU, as evidenced by the Nairobi Plenipotentiary Conference, which tasked the Administrative Council to consider and act on a wide range of important issues.

The Council has a current membership of 41 countries. To influence its decisions, NTIA believes the United States must provide leadership and achieve better coordination between Council members. This could serve as a counterpoint to the narrow and politically motivated interests that are being more frequently expressed.    Better coordination among Western European and other government (WEOG) members, for example, would enable representatives to meet before each Administrative Council meeting and establish common positions on agenda matters, coordinate strategy, and exchange views. Although control of the Council may not be possible nor even desirable, a coordinated effort by major contributors may prove more effective.

44

Retaining an American presence in the top elected offices of the ITU is another condition necessary to maintain U.S. influence. After the change of the method for electing Directors of the CCIs at the Nairobi Plenipotentiary Conference, it is incumbent upon the United States to attract qualified candidates and to promote their candidacy sufficiently in advance to develop widespread recognition and support.

ITU preparatory activities must be part of an ongoing Government international telecommunications policy coordination structure. Such a structure would put radio conference preparation in the context of other interrelated telecommunications preparatory activities (such as UNESCO, COPUOS, OECD, CEPT, and others) and undertake regular, systematic development and coordination of policy objectives, strategies, and resources in the international area. This structure could be a centralized authority with supporting secretariat that has accountability for international conference preparations in telecommunications matters. Such a proposal is presented in this report in the section on Government Organization.

To make the preparatory process more accessible and the dialogue all-encompassing, regular briefings on ITU activities should be given key Congressional staff. Additionally, regular briefings, workshops, or exchange programs for the private sector could be given by the Government to assure that goals and policy are based on a continuing input from all interested parties. Perhaps the most important prerequisite for increasing U.S. effectiveness in the ITU, however, is the realization of the critical importance of international telecommunications by the top levels of Government and industry, and their subsequent commitment of priority and resources.

Discussion of U.S. Preparations for Radio Conferences

As previously noted, many respondents considered the questions of U.S. participation in the ITU and preparation for radio conferences to be closely related. Most felt that effective participation could be increased by improved preparation for both.

45

The current U.S. procedure for preparing for ITU Radio Conferences is described in Attachment 4. In response to one of the principal findings of the OTA study — the perceived absence of high level government attention to policy development and coordination — several changes were made to the preparatory process. The State Department, in cooperation with other Government agencies, formalized and established two policy groups: (1) the Senior Level Interagency Committee (responsible for broad policy direction of all U.S. activities relating to international telecommunications); and (2) the Coordinating Committee for Future Radio Conferences (responsible for day-to-day management of radio conference preparatory activities). These groups are not staffed, however, and a more permanent structure may be a better alternative. Furthermore, because the United States will be participating in a large number of radio conferences in the future (see Attachment 2), it is necessary to identify and remedy any other deficiencies that may exist in the preparatory process.

The public comments for improving U.S. preparations for international radio conferences reiterated some of the previous OTA findings. Eight general issues were identified as requiring consideration:

(1)  The level of preparatory effort should be maintained or expanded. (National Association of Broadcasters, Satellite Business Systems, Southern Pacific Communications, Xerox, Computer and Business Equipment Manufacturing Association, and RCA);

(2)  There should be adequate timing and schedule for early development of conference goals and positions (RCA Globcom, Satellite Business Systems, American Library Association, and Southern Pacific Communications);

(3)  There should be adequate input and consultation with private sector and industry during all phases of the preparatory effort (National Academy of Sciences, RCA Globcom, University of Colorado, American Telephone and Telegraph Company, Southern Pacific Communications, CBS, Comsat, and RCA);

(4)  There should be a permanent staff devoted to conference preparation (American Telephone and Telegraph Company, and RCA);

(5)  An entity with central responsibility for preparatory effort should be established (American Library Association, Computer and Business Equipment Manufacturers Association, TRT Telecommunications, IBM, and RCA);

46

(6)     There should be early appointments of chairmen and delegations **and** greater use of individuals from the private sector (Arinc, University of Colorado, Comsat, Michael R. Gardner, Esq. (Chairman of the U.S. Nairobi Plenipotentiary Delegation), and American Library Association);

(7)     There should be extensive bilateral and multilateral contacts with other countries before the actual conferences (Satellite Business Systems, Computer and Business Equipment Manufacturers Association, Comsat, and Southern Pacific Communications);

(8)     The United States should capture the initiative and shed its defensive posture (Comsat).

The options identified by NTIA in the next section are based on a careful review of the OTA study, public comments in this proceeding, extensive participation in past ITU conferences and preparations, and staff analysis of the matter.

### THE UNITED STATES AND THE ITU IN 1990
### LONG RANGE GOALS

The next seven years will be a critical and pivotal period for the United States in the field of international telecommunications. By the end of the decade, a number of decisions and actions will have been taken in the ITU with far reaching consequences for our national interests. Planning decisions of the World Administrative Radio Conference for the HF Broadcasting Service, for example, will have a direct bearing on the ability of the U.S. Government effectively to pursue and achieve its public diplomacy and foreign policy objectives through the use of shortwave broadcasting. Likewise, ITU planning conferences dealing with the Broadcasting Satellite and Fixed Satellite Services, and decisions regarding the use of the geostationary orbit, could have an enormous impact on the ability and opportunity of the U.S. telecommunications industry to serve domestic and international markets with U.S.-developed technology and new services. These important conferences, together with decisions by the 1989 Plenipotentiary Conference, will determine whether the organization will serve the needs of all its members or whether it will be significantly dominated by administrations whose highly political objectives conflict with those of the developed world.

47

At several recent ITU conferences, developing countries with increasing success have pursued concepts, such as expanded technical assistance, special consideration, and long-term "a priori" reservation of spectrum resources. These concepts are at variance with previously established ITU principles which advocate the most efficient use of spectrum resources according to actual need. Absent changes in current trends, by 1990, the developing countries could be in a position to block U.S. objectives significantly. It is of the highest priority, therefore, for the United States to establish a set of long range goals for the ITU.

NTIA believes that there are two long range goals. First, by 1990 the politicization trend must be reversed and the United States and other like-minded major donors must reestablish influence over the direction of the ITU as an international organization that serves the needs of all its members, including both developing and developed countries. Second, as a parallel effort in the event unacceptable politicization continues, the United States must have available a fully developed and workable alternative to the ITU.

To achieve the first goal, the United States must take several actions to improve its effectiveness in the ITU. These actions include: greater coordination by major contributors prior to meetings of the ITU's Administrative Council; more effective advocacy within developing countries of U.S. positions for radio conferences and greater priority for bilateral contacts; greater focusing of CCI participation to support U.S. positions for specific conferences; and, significant attention to preparation for the 1989 Plenipotentiary Conference. At that Plenipotentiary Conference, issues of major importance to the United States will include:

(1)    The principles that will guide the ITU in the 1990s;

(2)    Maintenance of fiscal austerity and budgetary restraint;

(3)    Continued U.S. presence in the Administrative Council;

(4)    Continued U.S. presence in the top elected offices of the ITU; and

(5)    The role of technical assistance and cooperation.

48

The United States came very close to withdrawing from the 1982 Plenipotentiary Conference in Nairobi and reassessing its future participation in the ITU because of the Israeli expulsion attempt. Had the withdrawal occurred, it would have been without prior preparation of alternatives. In order to be fully prepared for any similar eventuality, as its second long range goal the United States must have alternatives to the ITU available in case they are needed.

If by 1990 the first long range goal is achieved, with the support of like-minded administrations, the United States will have successfully passed through a critical and pivotal period in international telecommunications, and it will be in a strong and collaborative position of leadership in the ITU for the 1990s. If the ITU becomes more politicized, however, the United States will be in a position to implement alternatives that will be compatible with national interests.

Proposals for Improving U.S. Preparations for Radio Conferences

Several specific actions or changes to the existing preparatory structure should be accomplished in order to improve preparatory efforts for international radio conferences.

The Senior Level Interagency Committee (see Attachment 4) constitutes an initial step toward focusing high level Government attention on international telecommunications policy development and coordination. To eliminate other concerns — including continuing attention to preparations and adequate access by interested parties to policy formulation during all phases — we should broaden the conference preparatory structure to coordinate all interrelated telecommunications issues on an ongoing basis .

A Government structure with centralized authority to coordinate telecommunications policy was mentioned previously in the discussion on increasing U.S. effectiveness in the ITU. Besides strengthening radio conference preparations through a sharing of information on tactics, strategy, potential supporters or adversaries, and experience gained in applicable negotiations in other forums (such as UNESCO, COPUOS, OECD, CEPT, and others), the centralized structure would also satisfy the private sector's need for access to a central preparatory authority

49

during all phases of radio conference preparations. It would also signal internationally both the importance we accord these issues and our ability to act effectively and promptly to safeguard U.S. interests.

An experienced and balanced U.S. Delegation and its chairman should be organized and nominated in a timely fashion -- at least one year in advance -- to eliminate the transition effects in preparation, and to allow ample time for Delegation members to become familiar with all issues and aspects likely to arise at the conference, as well as to contribute to specific U.S. proposals. Composition of the Delegation obviously should take into account the nature of the particular conference and be balanced among qualified Government and private sector representatives representing a broad, multidisciplinary range of backgrounds.

Influential developed and developing countries would be identified for ongoing bilateral contacts of both a technical and political nature. Extensive contacts with countries having different or similar points-of-view would: (a) acquaint the United States with those attitudes and positions most likely to occur at a conference; (b) provide an opportunity for a meaningful exchange of views on national needs and positions outside of conference pressures; (c) provide an opportunity to build a reservoir of trust and familiarity among participants; and (d) enable us to enlist like-minded countries with similar goals to multiply the effects of bilateral contacts in regions or areas of special influence. The private sector's international contacts and resources could be utilized to a greater extent in conference preparations, and pre-conference bilateral negotiations and discussions, as well as during the actual conferences.

The early definition and dissemination of broad U.S. goals and objectives would prove beneficial as it would focus the work of the CCIR and CCITT and thus secure greater support of U.S. positions at future conferences. Greater attention to the coordination of CCI and conference preparatory activities would assure that the efforts are mutually supportive and not at cross purposes. Furthermore, a better and wider dissemination of documentation in the private sector is necessary especially in the activities of the CCIs.

50

Conclusions and Recommendations

Based on all of the material considered in this Study of Long-Range International Telecommunications and Information Goals of the United States, NTIA concludes that:

(1)     At present, the United States should remain in the ITU but promptly initiate several specific actions to increase its effectiveness;

(2)     Because politicization of the ITU is at cross purposes with U.S. national interests, alternatives require further study to develop feasible courses of action which could be implemented quickly;

(3)     U.S. effectiveness in the ITU can be increased through improved preparation and participation in all activities and would aid the private sector;

(4)     The greatest private sector concerns are access to all phases of the preparatory effort and greater participation given the major implications for their interests;

(5)     A number of reasonable actions can be taken within the current organizational structure of the Government to increase U.S. effectiveness in the ITU and improve preparations for radio and other conferences;

(6)     A new organizational structure is necessary, however, to centralize effectively U.S. telecommunications policy.

To increase and broaden U.S. effectiveness in the ITU, as well as in other international forums where telecommunications matters are considered, it is proposed that:

(1)     Congress take appropriate action to establish, within the Federal Government, an international telecommunications policy structure (as described in greater detail in this report in the section on organization and structure of the U.S. Government), which would have centralized accountability and which would on a regular and systematic basis coordinate U.S. policy objectives, positions, and strategies on all international telecommunications matters while taking into account the views of the private sector and the Legislative branch. NTIA's further study of alternatives to the ITU would be one of the first items for coordination;

51

(2)    An action plan and strategy should be developed to enhance U.S. leadership in the Administrative Council of the ITU;

(3)    As a matter of priority, a strategy should be developed to assure U.S. presence in the senior elected offices of the ITU;

To improve U.S. preparations for ITU radio conferences, it is proposed that action be taken to:

(4)    Assure that Delegations are formed in an expeditious manner — at least one year in advance -- and a policy is established that would be adhered to for all future radio conferences;

(5)    Establish a program and schedule for expanded bilateral and multilateral discussions with both developed and developing countries in support of future conferences;

(6)    Develop a program for utilizing private sector participation to a greater extent;

(7)    Provide guidance to and review of United States and CCIR and CCITT considerations for international meetings in order to focus their input effectively in meeting U.S. policy and technical objectives in ITU matters;

(8)    Identify and document each of the activities and functions of the ITU that are necessary and beneficial to U.S. telecommunication operations and development;

(9)    Determine which activities and functions carried out within the ITU could be conducted outside the ITU either in other international or regional organizations or through bilateral or multilateral agreements with other countries;

(10)    Determine the feasibility of establishing particular alternative mechanisms to the ITU; the likelihood that other countries would cooperate with the United States outside the ITU; and which countries, in addition to the United States, would consider withdrawing from the ITU. Also determine the U.S. costs and effectiveness of conducting these activities outside the ITU and compare this with the costs and effectiveness of participating in the ITU;

(11)    Examine ways for the United States to work within the ITU structure and improve its influence and effectiveness using the information, suggestions, and comments developed in this report to Congress;

52

(12)     Examine ways for the United States to change the ITU structure to one more amiable to U.S. interests and seek to improve U.S. influence and effectiveness under the modified structure; and,

(13)     Establish a U.S. policy framework providing incentives for the private sector — including the telecommunication service and equipment industry, together with the financial community — to package U.S. technology and know-how and engage Third World countries in mutually profitable joint ventures to improve their telecommunication services. Not only would this enhance the competitiveness of the U.S. industry in world markets and improve U.S. balance of trade, but it would also favor U.S. objectives within the ITU. By addressing the Third World problems at their source — improved telecommunication infrastructures -- the current North/South debate over the role of the ITU and differences in objectives to be achieved might be alleviated. In other words, treat the source of the problems outside the ITU. If successful, the current focus of debate within ITU will be altered and U.S. influence increased.

## APPENDIXES

(1)     The International Telecommunication Union (ITU)

A specialized agency of the United Nations, the ITU was created in 1932 by the merger of two existing organizations, the International Telegraph Union (founded in 1865) and the signatories of the International Radiotelegraph Convention. It was created for the purpose of achieving agreement and cooperation among nations on the use of telecommunications. The fundamental governing principles and purposes are contained in the ITU Convention, and prior to the 1982 Plenipotentiary Conference, they were:

1.     to maintain and extend international cooperation for the improvement and rational use of telecommunications of all kinds;

2.     to promote the development of technical facilities and their most efficient operation with a view to improving the efficiency of telecommunications services, increasing their usefulness and making them, so far as possible, generally available to the public; and

3.     to harmonize the actions of nations in the attainment of those ends.

53

The ITU Convention specifies that to achieve its purposes the following actions are necessary: allocation, registration, and coordinated utilization of the radio frequency spectrum; planned development of telecommunications facilities, particularly those using space techniques; collaboration in setting telecommunications rates; and conducting studies, collecting and publishing public information, adopting resolutions, and formulating regulations.

The structure of the ITU consists of a combination of conferences and permanent organs. The plenipotentiary conference is the supreme body of the ITU. It convenes every five to nine years to consider the Convention, formulate general policies, establish guidelines, elect members and senior officials and conclude agreements with other organizations. In the intervals between plenipotentiary conferences, the Administrative Council yearly acts on behalf of the entire membership in formulating policy and overseeing the work. Administrative conferences, of a regional or worldwide character, are convened as the need arises to consider specific telecommunications matters. Deliberations in all conference activities are based on a one-nation, one-vote procedure. The final acts of plenipotentiary or administrative conferences become treaties following ratification by the membership. Treaties are binding on member nations only with their stated and formal agreement. In the United States, for example, treaties become binding only after the advice and consent of a two-thirds majority of the Senate and final ratification by the President.

The permanent organs of the ITU are: the General Secretariat, the International Frequency Registration Board, and the International Consultative Committees (CCIs) for Radio (CCIR) and Telephone and Telegraph (CCITT). The work of the CCIs is conducted by technical experts in each of the specialized areas of interest and their outputs form the basis for standards and specifications that are generally accepted by all members. Within the CCIs, deliberations are usually conducted on a consensus basis.

The history of the ITU can be categorized into three major periods. Prior to World War II, a group of Western-oriented nations, including the United States, had preeminent influence in ITU affairs. A majority of members were in agreement on

54

telecommunication matters and it was rarely necessary to bring issues to a vote. Between World War II and 1960, with the demise of colonialism, many nations with differing political values joined the ITU. Although this period witnessed the introduction of politics into the work of the ITU, the Western-oriented coalition, led often by the United States which fundamentally based its proposals on technical rather than political principles, was usually able to prevail. The period between 1960 and the present is characterized by a very marked increase in the membership of the ITU (from 78 members in 1947 to 125 members in 1965, 146 members in 1973, and 157 in 1982). Many newly-independent nations (developing countries) were former colonies with limited telecommunications infrastructures, trained personnel or established institutions. Thus, the newest ITU members have brought with them different national concerns and priorities in telecommunications matters. With their significant majority in a one-nation, one-vote forum, the developing countries are now in a position to exert greater control over the direction and purpose of the ITU.

Although the United States has protected and advanced its interests in the ITU, the effort is becoming increasingly difficult. It has required the commitment and expenditure of substantial resources by Government and industry, while future success and benefits are uncertain. The United States position has always been that the ITU is a forum of international cooperation for the benefit of all members. The work of the International Consultative Committees has most consistently reflected this cooperative spirit. Politically motivated actions in certain organs of the ITU, however, are increasingly challenging the United States' position.

At the 1973 Plenipotentiary Conference, a voting bloc of 77 non-aligned and developing countries was formed. This bloc frequently used its voting power to achieve political ends such as the expulsion of South Africa and Portugal in contravention to the ITU Convention, cancellation of the membership of trust territories, and consideration of other political items. The pattern continued at the 1974 Maritime Radio Conference where a voting bloc of 45 developing countries was formed. Their actions were such that the United States and seven

55

other countries with major maritime interests were forced to take a reservation on a major operational telecommunications issue that had been decided on political rather than technical grounds.

Block voting did not play a major role at the 1979 World Administrative Radio Conference. For the most part decisions were made on a consensus basis and the United States achieved in whole or in a large part all of its specific objectives. Nevertheless, it was necessary to take several substantive reservations to the Final Acts of the Conference and several of the most controversial issues were deferred for consideration by previously scheduled "planning" conferences.

56

(2)    Schedule of Future ITU Conferences

1983

1.    World Administrative Radio Conference for Mobile Services (Geneva, 28 February-18 March 1983).

This conference will consider and revise the existing Radio Regulations dealing with distress and safety communications in the maritime mobile and aeronautical mobile services. A prominent issue will be to facilitate an improved, maritime distress, communication system. The U.S. Coast Guard is the party most affected by this conference.

2.    Regional Administrative Radio Conference for the Planning of the Broadcasting-Satellite Service in Region 2 (Geneva, 13 June - 15 July 1983).

For the purposes of ITU radiocommunications, the world is divided into three regions: Region 1 (Europe, Africa, and the entire territory of the U.S.S.R.); Region 2 (the Americas); and Region 3 (Asia and Australia). This conference will consider the stated frequency (12.2-12.7 and 17.3-17.8 GHz bands) and geostationary orbit requirements of North and South American countries and plan the use of the broadcast-satellite service for Region 2. A key issue for the U.S. will be to maintain flexibility in any plan so as not to preclude the introduction of new technology. Those segments of the U.S. telecommunications industry intending to serve the direct broadcast satellite (DBS) television market are the parties most affected by this conference.

1984

3.    First Session of the World Administrative Radio Conference for the Planning of HF Bands allocated to the Broadcasting Service (January 1984, for five weeks).

For the bands allocated to high frequency (HF) broadcasting, this conference will establish technical parameters and select a planning method which will process requirements at the second session. Critical issues for the U.S. include: the deleterious effects of jamming, the restrictive attributes of a long-term, "a priori" plan, and the ability of the U.S. Government to conduct its public diplomacy through shortwave broadcasting. Private and Government (Voice of America, Board for International Broadcasting) shortwave broadcasters are the parties most affected by this conference.

57

4.  Second Session of the Regional Administrative Conference for FM Sound Broadcasting in the VHF Band (Region 1 and certain countries concerned in Region 3) (end of October 1984 for six weeks).

    This is a regional conference not involving U.S. participation.

1985

5.  First Session of the World Administrative Radio Conference on Use of the Geostationary Satellite Orbit and the Planning of the Space Services Utilizing It (end of June to mid-August 1985, for six weeks).

    This conference will consider which space services and frequency bands should be planned and it will establish principles, technical parameters and criteria for planning. Presently, the greatest interest appears to be focused on planning of the fixed-satellites service in 4/6 GHz. The restrictive attributes of "a priori" planning will also be an important issue and probably be considered by this conference. This is one of the most important ITU conferences from the standpoint of the U.S. and a wide range of U.S. private sector and Government interests will be directly affected.

1986

6.  First Session of the Regional Administrative Planning Conference for the Broadcasting Service in the Band 1605 - 1705 kHz in Region 2 (first half of 1986, for three weeks).

    This conference is scheduled to plan, for North and South America, the spectrum reallocated by WARC 1979 to the broadcast service for AM radiobroadcast use. U.S. broadcasters desiring to provide new service in the band 1605-1705 kHz will be directly affected by this planning conference.

7.  Second Session of the World Administrative Radio Conference for the Planning of HF Bands allocated to the Broadcasting Service (October-November 1986, for seven weeks).

    This will be the second session of the planning conference for HF broadcasting and it is scheduled to accomplish and implement planning based on the decisions of the first session.

58

8. First Session of the Regional Administrative Conference to review and revise the Provisions of the Final Acts of the African VHF/UHF Broadcasting Conference (Geneva, 1983) (first half of 1987, for three weeks).

   This is a regional conference not involving U.S. participation.

9. World Administrative Radio Conference for the Mobile Services (mid-August to end of September 1987, for six weeks).

   This conference is scheduled to consider a broad range of issues affecting land, aeronautical, and maritime mobile services. Depending upon the issues considered, a variety of U.S. interests may be affected.

10. Regional Administrative Conference to establish Criteria for the Shared Use of the VHF and UHF Bands allocated to Fixed, Broadcasting and Mobile Services in Region 3 (end of November 1987, for four weeks).

    This is a regional conference not involving U.S. participation.

1988

11. Second Session of the World Administrative Radio Conference on the Use of the Geostationary Satellite Orbit and on the Planning of Space Services Utilizing It (end of June - beginning of August 1988, for six weeks).

    This will be the second session of the planning conference for space services and it is scheduled to accomplish and implement planning based on the decisions of the first session. Depending on the space services considered and planning method adopted, this conference will have a significant impact on a wide range of private sector and U.S. Government interests.

12 Second Session of the Regional Administrative Planning Conference for the Broadcasting Service in the Band 1605 - 1705 kHz in Region 2 (third quarter of 1988, for four weeks).

   This will be the second session of the planning conference for AM broadcasting (North and South America only). U.S. broadcasters intending to provide AM radio service in the band 1605-1705 kHz will be directly affected by the outcome of this conference.

59

13.  World Administrative Telegraph and Telephone Conference (beginning of December 1988, for two weeks.

This conference is scheduled to consider proposals for a regulatory framework for new telecommunications services which have resulted from technological advances in the fields of telegraph and telephone. U.S. international message carriers will be directly affected by this conference/

1989

14.  Plenipotentiary Conference (beginning of 1989, for six weeks).

This conference will consider and revise the Convention which is the basic charter of the ITU. Actions and decisions of the Plenipotentiary Conference will determine the future course of the ITU and its relevance for the U.S. issues of major importance will include: maintenance of fiscal austerity and budgetary restraint; continued U.S. presence in the Administrative Council and top elected offices of the ITU; the role of technical assistance and cooperation. Most segments of the U.S. telecommunications industry and the Government will be affected by this conference.

15.  Second Session of the Regional Administrative Conference to review and revise the Provisions of the Final Acts of the African VHF/UHF Broadcasting Conference (Geneva, 1973) (September 1989, for four weeks).

This is a regional conference not involving U.S. participation.

60

## Potential Alternatives to the ITU

**Alternative 1.** The United States unilaterally withdraws from ITU membership and no other administrations follow.

The fundamental issue is whether the U.S. in fact could successfully meet its international telecommunications needs if it were unilaterally to cease ITU membership. If this is feasible, the option of withdrawing would provide maximum negotiating leverage in conducting hard bargaining to shape ITU decisions acceptable to the U.S. Before any final decision is made on U.S. withdrawal from the ITU, the following list of advantages and disadvantages would require in-depth study utilizing the widest range of inputs from all interested Government and private sector parties.

### Advantages

1. United States possesses the financial and technological base to meet national operational requirements.

2. There would be no serious, adverse near-term (36 years) impact on U.S. system operations. As specific problems are identified in "going-it-alone," United States could adopt responses and initiatives appropriate to the situation. Real problems would be identified and solved directly and not masked by "conventional wisdom" that remaining in the ITU is the only way to go.

3. Financial and other resources expended in support of ITU activities by the U.S. Government and private sector could instead be applied to meeting specific operational needs such as negotiating bilateral and multilateral arrangements for terrestrial and space systems.

4. The United States would be seen by the world as an industrial power with resources and resolve sufficiently to define and satisfy its own sovereign needs.

5. The United States would continue to participate in commercial operating consortia where the decisionmaking process is based on weighted voting commensurate with participation, e.g., Intelsat, Inmarsat. As new needs arise, new organizations could be created, e.g., Aerosat or new services could be supplied by existing organizations. These organizations would

continue to require that system equipment be procured competitively, thus preserving opportunities for U.S. equipment suppliers.

6.   U.S. technological leadership would continue and trickle down to the world community as other countries, to satisfy their own needs economically, would follow the U.S. lead.

7.   Given U.S. prominence as an economic trading power, foreign nations wishing to interconnect with U.S. systems would find it necessary to agree on mutually acceptable terms.

8.   The United States would continue to work through other existing international organizations, e.g., IMO/ICAO which are mission-oriented and where technical and economic considerations influence communications systems decisions and commercial elements are well represented.

9.   To influence ITU decisions, the U.S. could advance its views through friendly ITU members and through regional organizations such as CITEL and CEPT. Although this would present some difficulties, preferences on technical criteria and operating standards could be submitted to the International Consultative Committees through OECD, URSI, ICAO, IMO, etc.

10.  To minimize coordination and interference problems, the U.S. could generally adhere to the ITU Radio Regulations but selectively depart when necessary.

11.  Foreign administrations once confronted with the workability of the above process may moderate their views and accept renewed participation by the United States in the ITU on terms more compatible to our interests.

### Disadvantages

1.   Unilateral withdrawal by the United States could destabilize the ITU as an effective regulatory regime and produce a chaotic situation that would ultimately work to our disadvantage.

2.   The United States would be viewed as supernationalistic and insensitive to the legitimate concerns and interests of other nations and the principle of international cooperation.

3.   Such a move could expand the number of bilateral and multilateral arrangements required to accommodate U.S. operational requirements with possible increase in overall administrative costs as compared with continued ITU participation.

62

4. It may also adversely affect the ability of U.S. equipment manufacturers to supply foreign markets and undermine the ability of U.S. industry to capitalize on its technological leadership.

5. The United States would lose its ability directly to influence ITU decisions relating to spectrum/orbit usage, technical and operating standards in the CCIs, etc.

6. U.S. private sector system operators would be denied the international recognition and protection for their systems now accorded by the ITU radio regulations; thus they may be reluctant to commit system investments, particularly with respect to space communications, without assurance of Government indemnification in event of interference or other impairment of their operations.

7. Over the long-term, going-it-alone may prove unworkable with the possibility that U.S. would be compelled to seek readmission to the ITU perhaps on less favorable terms with lessened credibility and influence as a world telecommunications leader.

Alternative 2.   The United States withdraws from ITU and one or more major telecommunications administrations follow.

The advantages and disadvantages of going-it-alone identified in Alternative 1 would be generally applicable under Alternative 2. However, on balance, the likelihood of successfully operating outside of the ITU would be increased. The United States and other participating administrations would have the means collectively to ensure that the enterprise would not fail.

Of course, if Alternative 1 were not practical then critical to the success of Alternative 2 would be the task of convincing other administrations to withdraw from ITU membership. The likelihood of achieving this could only be determined on the basis of actual, high-level initiatives and consultations with other administrations. At this time, the possiblity of withdrawal from the ITU is being discussed within at least one European administration.

Were the United States to be joined by even a few other major telecommunication administrations, the likelihood of the ITU continuing as an effective international regulatory body would be greatly diminished. This suggests that at some point, an acceptable reapproachment could be reached with the ITU

63

and our membership in the Union renewed but on more compatible terms. Hence, any scenario which envisions several major members leaving the Union could be viewed as an interim or short-term arrangement, for possibly three-six years.

The essential functions to be carried out under interim arrangements would be limited to international radio frequency coordination and recording among participating members. There would be no CCI-type activity on a continuing basis. Instead, issues of technical or operating standards could be dealt with on an as-needed basis.

An organization to support the interim arrangement would need the following features:

- Have a foundation charter or working agreement.

- Be capable of being activated quickly.

- Be a model of simplicity free of extensive administrative overhead and procedural detail.

- Provide for the coordination and recording of frequency/orbit usage by its members.

- Provide a means of reflecting arrangements entered into by members with non-members.

- Distribute for the short-term various essential functions among participating members, the cost of which to be borne directly by the administration responsible for carrying out the function.

- A centralizing coordination office, probably located in Europe, to oversee general operations and to facilitate dialogue/coordination with the ITU as necessary.

In the event it proved necessary to remain outside the ITU for an extended period of time, more permanent financing arrangements would be required. In the short-term administrations could reasonably be expected to absorb the costs of carrying out the various distributed functions within their existing frequency management structures.

64

Alternative 3. The United States remains in the ITU but endorses decisions on a more selective basis.

A third alternative is for the United States to remain in the ITU, but be much more selective than in the past in endorsing and adhering to conference decisions. The essential advantage of this approach would be the continuing presence of the United States to work directly within the ITU to influence outcomes in the decision-making process. The United States wields considerable influence now and can be expected to do so in the future, especially in the CCI technical areas.

With respect to decisions taken at administrative conferences, the United States would not necessarily follow majority decisions. We could be more selective in observing and endorsing only those decisions found to be acceptable. For example, should the 1983 BSS RARC adopt a plan unacceptable to the United States, we could simply reserve our right to satisfy our needs as we see fit by not signing the final acts and thereby not being bound by any moral or treaty obligation to observe the conference results.

In some respects selective adoption of ITU decisions would not be dissimilar from the Alternative 1 approach of going-it alone. Within the context of ITU membership, the United States would simply do what is necessary to protect our vital national interests.

By remaining in the ITU, however, there would be more pressure to "conform" to ITU decisions. This might result in somewhat different approaches as to how we might otherwise meet our national needs if freed from the necessity of accommodating ITU processes.

If the United States were to leave the ITU, there would be greater incentive, even the necessity, of finding different or new ways of transacting business such as establishing more focused areas of common-user undertakings.

A list of advantages and disadvantages associated with the Alternative 3 approach is set forth below.

65

## Advantages

1. Ability to directly influence results has been generally successful in the past, and it is reasonable to expect we will continue to exert leadership, especially in the CCI's.

2. Can selectively accept/reject WARC/RARC Final Acts or provisions thereof.

3. Have freedom to do what is necessary to satisfy our national interests.

4. Taking long-view, interests of all members can be accommodated; vital U.S. interests have not been compromised to date.

5. Remaining in allows time to develop support for alternative structures.

6. Costs of continuing participation are acceptable.

## Disadvantages

1. Developing countries continue to nibble away at our interests while enhancing theirs.

2. Only a dramatic break with ITU (even if only for a limited interval) will demonstrate seriousness with which we regard present trends; best hope of achieving acceptable accommodation as developing countries do not regard United States as serious about leaving the Union.

3. United States pays more-and-more for results that are less-and-less satisfactory.

4. Lose incentive to finding new approaches to best satisfy U.S. needs and interests.

5. Lose opportunity to build a new organization responsive to U.S. needs and interests.

### Current U.S. Radio Conference Preparatory Procedures

In its preparatory efforts for international radio conferences, one of the first concerted actions by the United States is to secure adoption, by the ITU's Administrative Council, of a conference agenda which will service U.S. goals and interests. Domestically, preparatory actions to define government and nongovernment needs are undertaken by NTIA and the FCC respectively. NTIA

66

utilizes the advice of the Interdepartment Radio Advisory Committee (IRAC) to define spectrum allocation or radio service planning needs which are necessary to support the mandated missions of the Government. The FCC utilizes its Notices of Inquiry and Rulemaking procedures to ascertain the needs of the private sector which includes equipment manufacturers, carriers and users. Continuous coordination is maintained between both efforts to assure that preparations are in the national interest. Individual proposals, which are usually similar as a result of the resolution of any conflicts in the coordination process, are submitted by NTIA and the FCC to the Department of State. The State Department is responsible for submitting the U.S. proposal to the ITU and for nominating a United States Delegation and recommending its chairman. Delegation responsibilities include drafting of position papers, conducting bilateral and multilateral meetings, and participating in the conference.

To prepare technical bases for the conferences, the United States participates extensively in meetings of the CCIR, IFRB seminars, and Panels of Experts. Additionally, to coordinate regional positions or consider specialized issues of a particular radio conference, the United States participates in meetings of the following international organizations: IMO, ICAO, CITEL, CEPT, and NATO/ARFA.

With a view towards improving and strengthening U.S. preparations and taking note of the concerns raised previously, the State Department, in cooperation with other Government agencies, formalized and established two policy committees. The Senior Level Interagency Committee, chaired by the Under Secretary of State for Security Assistance, Science and Technology, is responsible for broad policy direction, review of major options and alternatives, and final decisions as to U.S. proposals for all activities relating to international communications and information matters. Day-to-day management of radio conferences preparatory activities is provided by the Coordinating Committee for Future Radio Conferences which consists of senior level staff of State, NTIA, and FCC.

Chapter Four

## ORGANIZATION AND STRUCTURE OF THE U.S. GOVERNMENT

### BACKGROUND

The ability of the U.S. Government as currently organized and structured to establish and achieve long-term international telecommunications and information policy goals and objectives is being severely questioned today. Spokespersons from private industry, members of Congress, Executive branch policymakers, even representatives of foreign governments, are highly critical of U.S. performance to date. They are especially concerned about Government capability to protect vital national interests in future negotiations, conferences, regulatory proceedings, and legislative initiatives.

More than two dozen departments and agencies of the Federal Government are involved in the development, implementation, and operation of U.S. international telecommunications and information policy.[1]  For some it is a primary mission; for others an occasional sidelight.  But each has different expertise, tools, and available forums with which to seek its goals, and each brings a different perspective, if not constituency, to an issue.  While the argument is made that diversity and cross-fertilization yield strength, a review of international telecommunications policymaking in the U.S. suggests that they also breed confusion, conflicts, jurisdictional disputes, lack of coordination, and lack of adequate preparation. These concerns are not new.

During its 1946 investigation of international communications problems, the Senate Committee on Interstate Commerce sought "to obtain a well-rounded and over-all viewpoint from the Government agencies. . . ."[2]  The Committee's Interim Report noted, however, that:

> During the course of the hearings it became obvious that the affected Government departments were not of one mind with respect to the policy that should be laid down by this Government to govern American international communications . . . . The Executive had

68

constituted an interdepartmental committee to study the problem and make recommendations . . . (but) this interdepartmental committee had failed to reach complete agreement.[3]

The Interim Report continued:

The committee regards with favorable anticipation the recent creation of another interdepartmental committee and trusts that this agency will be able to shortly recommend to the President a unified departmental view.[4]

In 1951 President Truman's Communications Policy Board considered, among other questions, how the U.S. Government could "strengthen its organization to cope" with the major domestic and international telecommunications issues facing the Nation.[5] In what sounds like contemporary criticism, the Board reported that:

In our efforts to discover the current state of Government telecommunications policy as preliminary to recommending needed steps toward a total national communications policy, we once more encountered dispersion, confusion, gaps, and deficiencies in the product and performance of those agencies charged with telecommunications policy responsibilities.[6]

In anticipation of developing national policy for dealing with other nations in seeking international telecommunications agreements, the Board found that:

Just as the United States has no clear policy for apportioning its own share of spectrum space, so it has lacked satisfactory means of determining policy as a basis for negotiations with other nations.[7]

As for maintaining a sound private telecommunications industry, the Board found "there has been no long-range study of the question, no long-range planning. No agency of Government is in a position to take a comprehensive view of this problem."[8] Similarly, a 1968 Presidential Task Force on Communications Policy reported:

Traditionally, government has viewed telecommunications primarily as a mission-support function, rather than a focus for public policy. The result has been that policy has evolved as a patchwork of limited, largely ad hoc responses to specific issues, rather than a cohesive framework for planning. Government organization for the formulation and implementation of communications policies reflects this evolution. . . . The patchwork nature of the present structure is not conducive to optimum performance of the telecommunications activities and requirements of the Federal Government.

From these hearings, reports, and studies of the Forties, Fifties, and Sixties, to the 1982 report of the Senate Commerce Committee on S. 2469 ("The International Telecommunications Act of 1982"), the 1980 report of the House Government Operations Committee (International Information Flow: Forging a New Framework), and the Office of Technology Assessment study (Radio Frequency Use and Management, Impacts from the World Administrative Radio Conference of 1979), the persistent lack of an effective Government organization to develop, adopt, and implement U.S. international telecommunications policy has been widely discussed.

To recognize that these organizational problems are long–standing and difficult to resolve, however, does not diminish the necessity for prompt attention and comprehensive efforts to establish a more effective government structure to deal with them. Telecommunications and information have become increasingly vital components of our national security, international trade and economic well-being, and critical to our relations with allies and other countries alike. At one time, the United States might have been able to afford the direct and opportunity costs implicit in the present disordered and dispersed telecommunications policymaking structure. American industry, too, may not have required in its dealings with other nations the collateral support which the fact or perception of organized high-level Government can provide. Whatever else may be true, however, we have today reached a point where the persistent inability of Government to get its own telecommunications policy "house" in order threatens severely to affect the future efficient development of key high-tech, "sunrise" industries upon whose effectiveness so much of our economy, security, and national life stands to depend.

72

Department of State

The Secretary of State serves as principal foreign policy adviser to the President, and is responsible for the overall direction, coordination, and supervision of U.S. foreign relations. The conduct of international telecommunications and information policy has been treated as a minor subset of that function. Executive Order 12046 in 1978 appeared to reaffirm this view, in its direct grants of telecommunications authority to the Secretary of State:

> With respect to telecommunications, the Secretary of State shall exercise primary authority for the conduct of foreign policy, including the determination of United States positions and the conduct of United States participation in negotiations with foreign governments and international bodies. In exercising this responsibility the Secretary of State shall coordinate with other agencies as appropriate, and in particular, shall give full consideration to the Federal Communications Commission's regulatory and policy responsibility in this area.
>
> . . .
>
> (The Secretary of State shall) [e]xercise the supervision provided for in Section 201(a)(4) of the Communications Satellite Act of 1962, as amended (47 U.S.C. 721(a)(4)); be responsible, although the Secretary of Commerce is the chief point of liaison, for instructing the Communications Satellite Corporation in its role as the designated United States representative to the International Telecommunications Satellite Organization; and direct the foreign relations of the United States with respect to actions under the Communications Satellite Act of 1962, as amended. [Emphasis added.][16]

Executive Order 12046 reaffirmed this view by its mandate to the Secretary of Commerce as well:

> The Secretary (of Commerce) shall provide advice and assistance to the Secretary of State on international telecommunications policies to strengthen the position and serve the best interests of the United States, in support of the Secretary of State's responsibility for the conduct of foreign affairs.[17]

The Department of State heads or names the head of U.S. delegations to international telecommunications conferences and negotiations; delegation members are selected by the State Department after consultation with involved Federal agencies and consideration of the input of the private sector. At times other agencies have been designated by the State Department to represent the United States at specific meetings or for special purposes.

In light of growing criticism of the international telecommunications policymaking performance of the Executive Branch, an Interagency Group on International Communications and Information Policy, chaired by the Under Secretary of State for Security Assistance, Science, and Technology, was created. It was designed as "a senior-level group which ensures coordinated development of policy by the interested departments and agencies of the Executive Branch which includes participation of the Federal Communications Commission."[18] Those who attend its irregularly scheduled meetings include representatives of the Departments of State, Commerce, and Defense, USTR, OMB, OSTP, NSC, NASA, the Board for International Broadcasting, USIA, AID, CIA, and the FCC.

## Federal Communications Commission

The FCC was created by the Communications Act of 1934[19] as an independent regulatory agency responsible directly to the Congress. Although its seven (soon to be five)[20] Commissioners are appointed by the President, once confirmed by the Senate for seven-year terms, they do not serve at the pleasure of the President. The FCC thus is not a part of the Executive branch, nor is it necessarily bound to Administration policies. The FCC was created:

> For the purpose of regulating interstate and foreign commerce in communication by wire and radio so as to make available, so far as possible, to all the people of the United States a rapid, efficient, nation-wide, and world-wide wire and radio communication service with adequate facilities at reasonable charges, for the purpose of the National defense, for the purpose of promoting safety of life and property through the use of wire and radio communication, and for the purpose of securing a more effective execution of this policy by centralizing authority heretofore granted by law to several agencies and by granting additional authority with respect to interstate and foreign commerce in wire and radio communication.[21]

74

The FCC carries out these responsibilities for international telecommunications by approving the construction and operation of communications facilities, the offering of services, and the tariffs, or rates, charged therefore, by allocating and assigning radio frequencies to non-Federal Government users,[22] and by participating in international negotiations and conferences. The FCC also establishes rules and regulations for international telecommunications, has attempted to engage in facilities planning and coordination, and significantly influences U.S. policy and the reactions of foreign entities by virtue of the speeches and statements of the Chairman and Commissioners. The Communications Satellite Act of 1962[23] gives the FCC regulatory responsibilities over the common carrier activities of Comsat as well.[24]

The Commission's international functions have been divided among eight bureaus and offices: the Common Carrier Bureau, Office of Science and Technology, and the Mass Media Bureau, which perform the bulk of the international activities, and the Office of Plans and Policy, Office of General Counsel, Private Radio Bureau, Field Operations Bureau and Office of the Managing Director which are also involved. In 1981 an Assistant to the Chairman for International Affairs was appointed to coordinate FCC planning and activities, as well as to advise the Commissioners in international communications policy. An internal International Telecommunications Coordinating Committee also was created within the FCC "to assist in focusing the varying international functions of the involved Commission elements."[25]

## United States Trade Representative

The United States Trade Representative is a Cabinet-level official with the rank of Ambassador who has responsibility for setting and administering overall international trade policy. The agency he heads (USTR) was first established in 1963 as the Office of the Special Representative for Trade Negotiations, and functions now as part of the Executive Office of the President.

Presidential Reorganization Plan No. 3 of 1979 (implemented by Executive Order 12188) has given USTR primary responsibility "for developing, and for coordinating the implementation of, United States international trade policy," saying that he shall serve "as the principal advisor to the President on international trade policy and shall advise the President on the impact of other policies of the United States Government on international trade," as well as having "lead responsibility for the conduct of international trade negotiations."[26] Whether the policy, advice, or negotiations are on trade in telecommunications equipment, telecommunications and information services, or any of the multitude of industries increasingly dependent on international telecommunications, the USTR is in the midst of international telecommunications policymaking.

While the Presidential Reorganization Plan establishing the Office of the United States Trade Representative uses terms such as "primary responsibility," "principal advisor," and "lead responsibility," it nonetheless assigns trade functions to the Secretary of Commerce, and states specifically as to the Secretary of State:

> Nothing in this reorganization plan is intended to derogate from the responsibility of the Secretary of State for advising the President on foreign policy matters, including the foreign policy aspects of international trade and trade-related matters.[27]

Elegant distinctions on occasion are drawn among the trade "facilitation," "promotion," and "negotiation" responsibilities of these players. Again, however, the question of overlapping responsibilities for international telecommunications policymaking is aggravated rather than resolved by this reorganization document. Nor has any serious attempt been made to reconcile the delegations of authority here with the potentially conflicting grants of authority found in other reorganization plans and Executive Orders, such as Executive Order 12046 discussed earlier.

## Cabinet Council on Commerce and Trade

The Cabinet Council on Commerce and Trade is one of five Cabinet Councils formed by President Reagan in 1981. The purpose underlying the creation of the Cabinet Councils was to establish an orderly process for reviewing issues requiring a decision by the President, who acts as the Chairman of each Council.

76

The Cabinet Councils were designed to operate as subgroups of the full Cabinet. The creation of the five Cabinet Councils has resulted in a rerouting of certain issues within the Federal bureaucracy. Issues formerly decided in OMB now receive consideration on a substantially higher political level with more White House control.

The Secretary of Commerce serves as the Chairman pro tempore of the Cabinet Council on Commerce and Trade. The other members include the Secretary of State, the Secretary of the Treasury, the Attorney General, the Secretaries of Agriculture, Labor, and Transportation, the U.S. Trade Representative, and the Chairman of the Council of Economic Advisers. The Vice President, the Counsellor to the President, and the Chief of Staff are ex officio members of the Council.

Although the Cabinet Council on Commerce and Trade was active the first six or eight months of its existence, with no definite schedule of meetings, it has been relatively inactive subsequently. The largest percentage of issues discussed in the Cabinet Council on Commerce and Trade concern trade; however, the focus has been on "smokestack" industries such as steel and automobiles rather than communications. The AT&T litigation and proposed domestic telecommunications legislation (S. 898 and H.R. 5158, 97th Congress) were issues discussed in the Cabinet Council on Commerce and Trade, along with the role of the Postal Service in electronic mail, and proposals on home recording and cable copyright.

Also addressed but not resolved was the organization of the Executive Branch to deal with international telecommunications policy and the ambiguity of Executive Order 12046. This problem was passed to a working group of staff members to resolve, and no recommendation has been resubmitted to the Cabinet Council.

PROBLEMS

Executive Branch Policymaking

The traditional organization of policy development in the Federal Government encourages the labelling of issues as foreign policy, trade,

77

telecommunications, spectrum, information, national security, etc. For example, foreign policy issues are handled by the Department of State; trade issues by the U.S. Trade Representative and by the International Trade Administration within the Department of Commerce; telecommunications by the FCC and NTIA; and so on.

International telecommunications issues, however, are typically complex and rarely so easily categorized. The Computer and Business Equipment Manufacturers Association (CBEMA) recognized this in its comments submitted in response to NTIA's November 2, 1982 Notice of Inquiry:

> The Executive Branch of the U.S. Government, as currently structured, is designed to deal with well bounded problems and policies in domestic communications, international trade in traditional raw materials and manufactured goods, and the legitimate "informational interests" of citizens and enterprises. However, it is ill-equipped to deal with problems and policies which cut across the boundaries of those areas or the agencies chartered to deal with them. The existing executive agencies lack the charter or experiential background necessary to deal with issues of the contemporary technology involving international channels for information, the information that flows in those channels, and the processes which might occur during transit.[28]

Choosing a label for an issue may well determine not only where in the Executive branch policy will be developed, but also what expertise and point of view will be applied in the process.

Former Under Secretary of State for Security Assistance, Science and Technology, Matthew Nimetz, summarized the difficulties inherent in the Executive Order 12046 when he, in 1980, explained to the Subcommittee on Government Information and Individual Rights of the House Government Operations Committee the division of Executive Branch authority. After reviewing the overlapping delegations of authority in the Executive Order, Nimetz testified:

> So, I see two focuses. One is that we have primary responsibility for foreign affairs, and in negotiations. The Secretary of Commerce — under whose authority NTIA falls -- is the primary policymaker in the communications area. And we certainly defer to their authority and expertise. It is not the simplest area to describe. You have to go through the Executive Order rather carefully to parcel it out.[29]

78

The House Committee was less than satisfied. It responded in its Report:

> While State and Commerce are carefully parceling out their responsibilities, the private sector is understandably confused about where to go to ensure effective contributions to policy development and to get help for particular problems.[30]

Indeed the Subcommittee had received highly critical private industry testimony. For example, the Association of Data Processing Service Organizations (ADAPSO) wrote:

> The United States enters discussions, debates and participates in other fora involving international computer services with no real coordinated national policy and with many disjointed representations. As a result, independent American firms do not have the support of a unified national policy when they negotiate with foreign governments or PTTS. . . .[31]

Tymshare Incorporated told the Subcommittee of its lengthy difficulties dealing with the Japanese Government and the Japanese international telephone agency (the KDD) when trying to establish a computer services venture in Japan. They then described having "worked extensively with the numerous U.S. Government agencies apparently involved in the area of international information flow, in an attempt to get some useful assistance."[32] Their experience and resultant attitude is significant:

> Unfortunately, our disappointment and frustration due to the apparent lack of interest, assistance, and results from any U.S. Government agency was in some ways more frustrating than the agonies in dealing with the Japanese. We really had hoped and expected some form of support and assistance from our U.S. Government agencies. We were thoroughly disappointed by their reluctance to be involved and to take action but were most frustrated by the refusal of each agency to acknowledge that they had any responsibility or authority to provide such assistance.[33]

The fact that the forty-eight Federal Government delegates to WARC-79 were drawn from nine different agencies (FCC, NTIA and other parts of the Commerce Department, Defense, State, NASA, ICA, Transportation, the National Science Foundation and the White House Office of Science and Technology Policy) further illustrates the broad range of concerns involved and the need for coordinating mechanisms in the U.S. Government to deal with international telecommunications issues. The Interagency Group on International Communications and Information Policy, described earlier, was created to try and deal with the lack of effective Executive branch coordination. Yet as the Report on S. 2469 by the Senate Committee on Commerce, Science, and Transportation recently noted, "there is no statutory or administrative basis for the interdepartmental group."[34] Its activities are not necessarily treated as priority matters by the participating agencies, nor given adequate high-level attention. Despite the international ferment in telecommunications issues in recent months, the Group has met only sporadically.

While issues before the Interagency Group may not receive enough high-level attention, the only other established mechanism for coordinating international policy development efforts, the Cabinet Council on Commerce and Trade, suffers from the opposite problem. Only the rare issue will warrant the study and attention of a multitude of Cabinet-level officers, and none will be able to have continuous monitoring, feedback, industry input, etc. over extended periods of time.

At the State Department, the former Under Secretary for Security Assistance, Science and Technology told a House hearing that he had "responsibility for ensuring a comprehensive U.S. international communications policy and ensuring close collaboration with other interested agencies."[35] At the same time, however, he announced a transfer of principal responsibility for transborder data flow problems affecting the interests of U.S. firms to the Bureau of Economic and Business Affairs, which is responsible to the Under Secretary for Economic Affairs. He also noted that "Other Bureaus will, of course, retain their lead roles in such matters as advanced technology, legal matters, and management of U.S. participation in international organizations."[36]

The House Committee on Government Operations responded that these Bureaus are scattered throughout the State Department, report to different authorities, and represent the U.S. in various forums. The attached organization chart of offices within the State Department concerned with international communications policy gives a picture of the complexity, overlapping responsibilities and diffused authority within that Department alone.

80

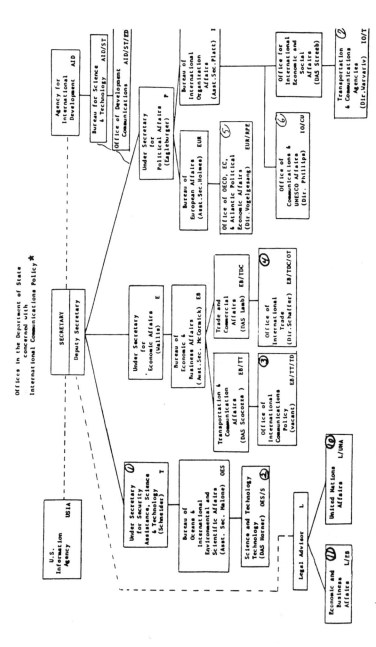

Offices in the Department of State concerned with International Communications Policy *

* Senate Comm. on Commerce, Science, and Transportation, International Telecommunications Act of 1982, S. Rep. No. 97-669, 97th Cong., 2d Sess. 18 (1982).

81

One of the areas where the lack of effective Executive Branch policymaking is raising the greatest concern is in preparation for international conferences and negotiations. Vital U.S. interests are at stake in meetings of organizations such as the ITU, UNESCO, and the OECD. Yet as another section of this report details, the U.S. Government seems ill-prepared to meet the challenges presented.

In view of the international telecommunications policymaking structure of the Executive Branch, both between and within agencies, it is not surprising that private industry is often confused. Spokespersons from the private sector cite the fragmented, ambiguous grants of authority, and consequent problems of lack of coordination, myopia, and lack of accountability. They call for an ultimate arbiter of U.S. policy, with sufficient resources of both expertise and power, who can then serve as a focal point for private sector input and for foreign negotiations. In recognition of their vital importance to the nation, international telecommunications policy decisions require high level attention in the Executive branch.

## The Executive Branch and the Independent FCC

Structural deficiencies within the Executive branch have long been discussed, and many remedies have been proposed to improve the development and implementation of U.S. international telecommunications policy. Another structural "flaw," with us since the Communications Act of 1934, however, has only recently become significant, or at least been recognized as such. Irrespective of any policy developed within the Executive Branch, the FCC, independent of direct Presidential control, may effectively establish international policy on its own, and may advance or thwart Administration policies. The FCC was established by the Communications Act of 1934, in part, ". . . for the purpose of securing a more effective execution of this policy by centralizing authority heretofore granted by law to several agencies. . . ."[37]

But while the need for centralized authority was recognized even then, the Congress, nonetheless, carefully divided responsibility for allocating the radio frequency spectrum between the FCC for non-Federal Government users and the

82

President (since delegated to NTIA) for Federal Government users. See 47 U.S.C. Sec. 305.

As a practical matter, responsibility for international telecommunications policymaking also has been divided between the FCC and the Executive branch, although with no clear dividing lines such as those which exist for frequency allocation authority. The FCC has increasingly taken an affirmative policymaking role, not one limited to its regulatory or adjudicatory model, in part because of the failure of the Executive branch itself to develop and implement policy in a coherent manner. Control Data Corporation, for example, has written in terms of the FCC acting "to fill the vacuum" left by the failure of other Government entities, even though some such actions "are generally considered to be outside the statutory scheme set forth by the Communications Act of 1934, and cannot lead to the resolution of existing problems in the international telecommunications and information flow area."[38]

As international telecommunications has grown dramatically, so too has the significance of FCC policy decisions, not merely for telecommunications, but also in their impact on national security, trade, and foreign policy. Therefore, as the General Accounting Office reported in its recent analysis of the FCC's international telecommunications activities:

> Under its normal process for authorizing communications facilities, FCC considers factors such as technological development and consumer economies that can result from these developments. However, in several proceedings over the last few years, FCC has had to go beyond its traditional areas of expertise to consider foreign affairs, national security, and U.S. trade policy.[39]

The GAO cited as just one example the facilities authorization proceeding in which the FCC reviewed AT&T's proposed award of a contract for fiber optic cable to Western Electric instead of to a lower-bidding Japanese firm. The Departments of Defense, State, and Commerce, and the USTR, among others, discussed the national security, foreign policy, and international trade issues at stake, but it was the FCC which had final authority to decide the matter.

83

In carrying out his foreign policy functions with respect to telecommunications, the Secretary of State is required by Executive Order 12046 to "coordinate with other agencies as appropriate," and in particular to "give full consideration to the Federal Communications Commission's regulatory and policy responsibility in this area."[40] No similar statutory or other requirement mandates that the FCC must take foreign policy, trade, and national security concerns into account, nor even that it must seek or consider the views of the Executive Branch agencies whose primary functions these are. Concerns such as national security, of course, are generally considered important components of the broad "public interest" mandate under which the FCC operates. The statute gives the FCC little clear guidance, however, concerning the decisional weight it should accord such concerns. Rather, the FCC is obliged on an ad hoc basis to endeavor to balance Executive branch needs (as to which it lacks full knowledge) with a diversity of other matters, a process often as frustrating to the FCC as to the pertinent Executive agency.[41]

OPTIONS

Maintain the Status Quo

Despite the preceding review of some of the problems and criticisms of the organization of the U.S. Government to deal with international telecommunications policymaking, one obvious option which must be considered by Congress and the President is maintaining the present structure.

Telecommunications policymaking responsibilities are fractionalized, with consequent problems of insufficient planning, coordination, and final decision-making authority. The present system is clearly inadequate to meet current needs. However, given the diversity of institutions and Congressional committees involved, not to mention private sector constituencies, the transaction costs of major changes obviously could prove substantial.

84

### Executive Branch Policymaking

Increased Coordination. The focus of the analysis thus far has been on the structure of the Government, looking at the multiple and overlapping grants of authority both to various Government agencies and within those agencies. Many have expressed concern not only with the number and diversity of agencies interested in international telecommunications and information issues, however, but rather with the general lack of adequate coordination, communication, and cooperation among those agencies. The formal mandates of the Secretaries of Commerce and State and of the USTR, among others, all require coordination of efforts, but without setting forth specific mechanisms by which this is to occur.[42] As a practical matter, all too often coordination falls victim to questions of jurisdictional disputes between departments and agencies, lack of adequate high-level attention, varying agency priorities, time pressures, and lack of resources.

Expressing what has become a commonly-held point-of-view, the Computer and Business Equipment Manufacturers Association told NTIA:

> CBEMA believes that until such time as there is a central authority in the United States vested with the responsibility of coordinating and articulating overall international communications and information policy, negotiating international rules with our trading partners, and participating in the development of appropriate means by which those rules will be enforced, the U.S. will continue to be of a disadvantage.[43]

Alternative proposals which could be considered to overcome the lack of Executive Branch coordination and cooperation include:

(1) Formalizing the present Interagency Group on International Communications and Information Policy and strengthening its mandate.

(2) Setting up another interagency council, task force, or body headed by either the Secretary of State, the Secretary of Commerce, or the USTR, or their senior level designee.

(3) Charging the President's National Security Adviser, OMB, or another Executive Office entity with coordinating interagency efforts.

(4) Designating a Special Assistant to the President for International Communications Policy with a small professional staff.

85

(5)    Giving all responsibility for international communications policy to either the Department of State or Department of Commerce.

(6)    Creation of a Department of Communications.

Each alternative is designed to establish the specific process and to hold a specific individual responsible for the coordination which broad agency mandates have not accomplished. Each would provide a focus for private sector input. Yet each seeks consensus, which may translate to the lowest common denominator and produce inherently weak policies, or fails to address what occurs in the absence of consensus. Will the agencies continue to speak with more than one voice, so that the Congress, the FCC, U.S. industry, and foreign entities are unsure what Executive Branch policy is? There must be established within the Federal government by whatever mechanism or structure a focal point for the handling of international communication matters. At the current time, the private sector, foreign governments, and even the U.S. government itself are not altogether clear as to which part of the Federal government deals with these matters and has the authority to express the views of the United States.

Consolidation of Authority. In reviewing the record to date, one could argue that efforts merely to improve coordination and communication among the many diverse Government entities with a hand in international telecommunications policymaking are superficial and doomed to failure because they fail to deal with the underlying cause of the problem. What is missing is not coordination, but coordinated decisionmaking, the development of a single Executive Branch position on an issue which is then accepted and followed throughout the Administration. This requires not only a person charged with obtaining various agency views and drawing on agency expertise, but also with the specific authority to arbitrate differences and finally determine the Administration's policy, a policy which individual agencies are not free to contradict, ignore, or undermine.

The guiding principles in establishing such authority are:

(1)    the authority must be centralized in a single place;

(2)    the coordinating entity, agency or person must have a clear and strong grant of authority and responsibility for coordinating international telecommunications and information policy;

86

(3)    the entity, agency or person must have the power to mediate differences among agencies and make final decisions;

(4)    the entity should establish a formalized interagency policy advisory body, supported by a secretariat, and which meets regularly to assist in the formulation and implementation of policy.

(5)    there should be a clear and regular structure for industry input.

In addition, the coordinating entity should be responsible for representing the U. S. at all international conferences dealing with telecommunications and information issues, and the head of the entity should be clearly identified as the President's principal adviser on international telecommunications and information issues.

Private sector input is also a critical element in the development of effective and responsive policy. In the view of Michael R. Gardner, Chairman U.S. Delegation, Nairobi Plenipotentiary Conference:

> A Council on International Telecommunication should be established by the White House consisting of ten to twelve leaders from diverse segments of the telecommunication industry. This Council should have as its primary goal the task of forging a new and much needed alliance between the U.S. telecommunication industry and segments of the federal government appropriately involved in international telecommunication. By forging a more open and meaningful partnership between industry and government, a new form of entrepreneurial diplomacy should guide the joint activities of government and industry in the international policy fora and the worldwide marketplace for telecommunication.

While many agree with the need to consolidate final decisionmaking authority, there is no consensus as to where in the Executive branch that authority should be vested. Within existing institutional structures, potential designees include the Secretary of State, the Secretary of Commerce, the President's National Security Adviser, and the U. S. Trade Representative. Consideration can also be given to establishing a new Special Assistant or Adviser to the President, or a new Board or Office within the Executive Office of the President, or even a Department of Communications. Each would bring a different expertise and perspective to the issues.

87

Recognizing the previously discussed problems of labeling issues as merely foreign policy or trade or national security or telecommunications, however, the question must be raised as to whether even the granting of final decisionmaking authority is sufficient. Will the designated official have sufficient access to the diverse expertise housed in other agencies in order to exercise that decisionmaking responsibility wisely? Or must adequate staff expertise on the array of interrelated issues be consolidated along with the final authority?

Having been granted responsibility of preparing for and representing the United States at international negotiations, this centralized authority will require the additional staff to meet the crowded international conference agenda which has already been set. A strong case has been made for the establishment in Government of a permanent conference preparation staff, whether consolidated at one agency or drawn on a continuing basis from existing entities. The skills, knowledge of the issues and players, and the continuity of representation, all under the control of a high level political appointee, would greatly strengthen U.S. capability to achieve the goals set for international negotiations.[44]

A possible way to implement the approach described above is indicated in the following diagram. By clearly designating central accountability and by coordinating interrelated policy objectives, strategies, and resources on a systematic and regular basis, U.S. actions internationally will be mutually supportive and better achieve U.S. goals.

The senior level policy authority would be supported by a policy advisory body comprised of concerned and affected Government agencies, thus providing a full opportunity for policy input from all interested agencies.

From the senior level policy authority, the advisory body would receive broad policy guidance on the Administration's goals and objectives for international telecommunications. The policy authority might also task the advisory body, where policy voids exist, to make appropriate policy recommendations. In this way, the advisory body would be responsive in a timely manner to any changes in the Administration's positions and such information would be disseminated quickly and comprehensively to the appropriate activities. The advisory body, in turn, would

88

**EXAMPLE**

**EXECUTIVE BRANCH STRUCTURE
COORDINATED DECISIONMAKING**

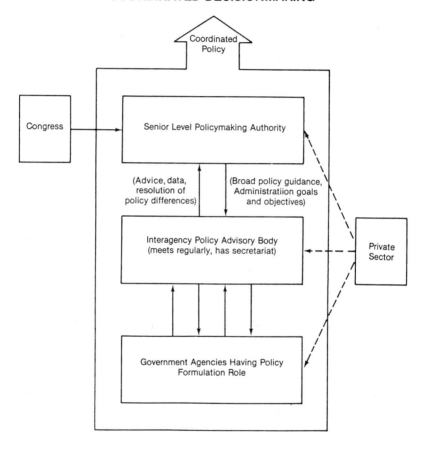

refer for resolution and guidance to the senior level authority those policy issues which appear to elicit differing or conflicting positions on the part of advisory body members.

The advisory body would meet on a regular basis, possibly twice a month. It would have a small professional staff to oversee policy development activities and a secretariat to support its distribution of papers and agenda items among the membership. The Secretariat would also keep consolidated and centralized records of advisory body actions and policy statements. Its terms of reference should be broad, to encompass at a minimum, all of the major interrelated telecommunications issues identified by NTIA in its Notice of Inquiry.

Some channel would also be established to take note of the views of the Legislative branch and private sector and facilitate meaningful interaction in the policy formulation process. The private sector could have access in a number of ways. The senior level policy authority might establish an advisory group or the private sector could organize itself into a telecommunications council and make its views known on issues of importance or concern. Contact with the Legislative branch could be in the form of periodic briefings and discussions.

### The Executive Branch and the Independent FCC

The options discussed above may solve or alleviate structural deficiencies within the Executive branch. If they yield an Executive branch speaking with one voice, they will also have solved a major problem for the FCC, which is often confronted with competing, if not conflicting, views of individual federal agencies. Today the FCC, without the mandate or expertise to do so, must balance concerns of national security versus trade policy, or foreign relations versus balance of payments effects. Instead, the FCC should be presented with a single Administration position which already represents the trade-offs and cost/benefit analyses which are the Executive's function to make.

Given a single, clear representation of the Administration's views on the foreign policy, security, trade, or other implications of contemplated action, however, the FCC is still under no legal mandate to consider the Administration's position, let alone defer to it. Nor is the FCC specifically required to consider the foreign policy or trade implications of its decisions. Legislation is possible to require the FCC specifically to weigh these factors in its deliberations and to require consideration of the views of the Executive branch agencies. It would be very difficult, of course, to measure the impact of such requirements on the outcome of future FCC deliberations. To provide greater assurance of Executive branch influence or control might require the establishment of a Presidential veto power over FCC international telecommunications actions.

The first question in exploring a grant of authority to the President to override FCC decisions is what are the appropriate reasons for the exercise of the veto. Possible grounds for intervention include national security, foreign policy, international trade, economic well-being, or any combination thereof. Second, within what time limits must the President act? Clearly the President cannot be expected to review each proceeding nor would the marketplace be able to function if every FCC order were left as only tentative. Setting an automatic effective date of 15 or 30 days after the FCC issues an order -- unless the President takes affirmative action -- would provide sufficient certainty. Finally, a decision must be made on the extent to which the power to exercise the veto may be delegated. Delegation could again spark battles over "turf" and control in the Executive branch, and if multiple grounds for intervention are provided, the risk would exist of having many Executive agencies all looking over the FCC's shoulder. It is also important to note that a veto power can only void an FCC decision. It cannot modify the decision nor deal with a failure to act.[45] To do so would require affirmative policymaking authority in the Executive branch.

Another option, therefore, is to transfer the bulk of the FCC's international telecommunications policymaking responsibility into the Executive branch. The execution of that policy, such as the issuance of licenses or the approval of facilities within guidelines set by the Administration, could remain at the FCC. The underlying policy formulation, and the consideration of issues such as national security, foreign policy, trade, and economics, however, would be within the control of the President. Without a controlling Executive branch statement of policy, the FCC would be powerless to act. New policy initiatives thus could not be undertaken by an independent agency which was not subject to direct Presidential oversight. Many of the traditional regulatory criteria applied by the FCC have now been dwarfed in significance in the international area by concerns

91

such as security and trade. Therefore, the traditional public utility regulatory model may no longer be the appropriate one for international telecommunications policymaking, and the FCC may no longer be the proper situs for that responsibility.

The various organizational and operational options discussed in this chapter are graphically represented in the following charts.

# THE EXECUTIVE BRANCH AND THE INDEPENDENT FCC STATUS QUO

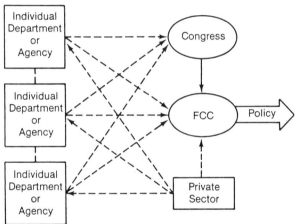

# COORDINATED EXECUTIVE BRANCH DECISIONMAKING

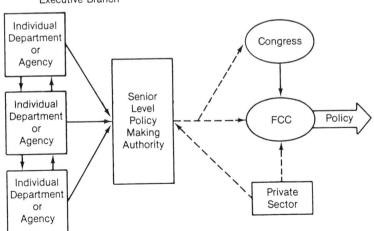

92

## PRESIDENTIAL VETO

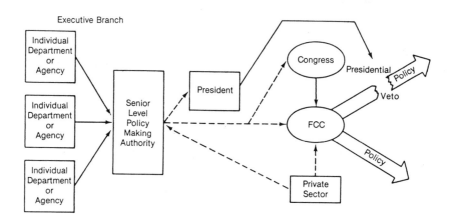

## EXECUTIVE BRANCH POLICYMAKING, FCC IMPLEMENTATION

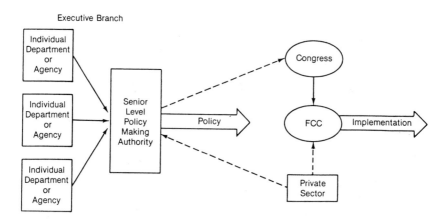

93

## NOTES TO CHAPTER FOUR

[1] A nonexhaustive list includes: Department of Commerce, Department of State, United States Trade Representative, Federal Communications Commission, Department of Defense, National Security Council, Office of Science and Technology Policy, Office of Management and Budget, Department of Justice, United States Information Agency, Board for International Broadcasting, National Aeronautics and Space Administration, Department of Transportation, Department of the Treasury, Department of Energy, United States Postal Service, Postal Rate Commission, Federal Reserve System, National Science Foundation, General Services Administration, Small Business Administration, Office of Technology Assessment, General Accounting Office, International Trade Commission, International Development Cooperation Agency.

[2] Senate Comm. on Interstate Commerce, Investigation of International Communications by Wire and Radio, Interim Report, S. Rep. No. 1907, 79th Cong., 2d Sess. 3 (1946).

[3] Id.

[4] Id. at 4.

[5] President's Communications Policy Board, Telecommunications, A Program for Progress, at 9 (1951).

[6] Id. at 184.

[7] Id. at 10.

[8] Id. at 11.

[9] President's Task Force on Communications Policy, Final Report, ch. 9, at 2,10 (1968).

[10] Allocation and assignment of spectrum space to all non-Federal entities is the responsibility of the FCC.

[11] See Executive Order 12046, 3 CFR 158 (1978 comp.).

[12] 47 U.S.C. § 721(a).

[13] 3 CFR 197 (1977 comp.).

[14] 3 CFR 158 (1978 comp.).

94

[15]See discussion infra.

[16]Executive Order 12046, §§ 5-201, 5-202, 3 CFR 158, 164 (1978 comp.).

[17]Id. § 2-404 at 161.

[18]1 Foreign Affairs Manual 145 (h)(3) (Dec. 29, 1981).

[19]47 U.S.C. §151 et seq.

[20]See Omnibus Budget Reconciliation Act of 1982, Pub. L. No. 97-253, § 501 (1982).

[21]47 U.S.C. § 151.

[22]The allocation and assignment of spectrum space to Federal government entities is performed by NTIA under a delegation of Presidential authority.

[23]47 U.S.C. §701 et seq.

[24]See discussion infra.

[25]General Accounting Office, The Federal Communications Commission's International Telecommunications Activities, Report to the Chairman, House Subcomm. on Government Information and Individual Rights at 6 (April 19, 1982).

[26]3 CFR 513 (1979 comp.).

[27]Id. at 516.

[28]Computer and Business Equipment Manufacturers Association, Comments in Response to National Telecommunications and Information Administration's Notice of Inquiry of Nov. 2, 1982, at 4 (Dec. 3, 1982).

[29]House Comm. on Government Operations, International Information Flow: Forging a New Framework, H.R. Rep. No. 96-1535, 96th Cong., 2d Sess. 43 (1980).

[30]Id. at 44.

[31]Letter from Jerome L. Dreyer, Executive Vice President, ADAPSO, to Hon. Richardson Preyer, Chairman, House Subcomm. on Government Information and Individual Rights, May 30, 1980, in International Data Flow, Hearings before the House Subcomm. on Government Information and Individual Rights, 96th Cong., 2d Sess. at 703 (1980).

[32]Statement of Warren E. Burton, Vice President, Tymshare, Inc. before the House Subcomm. on Government Information and Individual Rights, March 10, 1980, in International Data Flow, Hearings before the House Subcomm. on Government Information and Individual Rights, 96th Cong., 2d Sess. at 75 (1980).

[33] Id.

[34] Senate Comm. on Commerce, Science, and Transportation, International Telecommunications Act of 1982, S. Rep. No. 97-669, 97th Cong., 2d Sess. 17 (1982).

[35] Testimony of Matthew Nimetz, Under Secretary of State for Security Assistance, Science and Technology before the House Subcomm. on Government Information and Individual Rights, March 27, 1980, at 13.

[36] Id.

[37] 47 U.S.C. § 151.

[38] Statement of Philip C. Onstad, Control Data Corporation, before the House Subcomm. on Government Information and Individual Rights, March 10, 1980, in International Data Flow, Hearings before the House Subcomm. on Government Information and Individual Rights, 96th Cong., 2d Sess. at 53 (1980).

[39] General Accounting Office, The Federal Communications Commission's International Telecommunications Activities, Report to the Chairman, House Subcomm. on Government Information and Individual Rights at 3 (April 19, 1982).

[40] Executive Order 12046, § 5-201, 3 CFR 158, 164 (1978 comp.).

[41] As the State Department told the Congress in this regard:

As an independent regulatory agency, the FCC is not in a position to determine the foreign policy and national security implications of plans for international facilities and services.[47]

Letter from J. Brian Atwood, Assistant Secretary of State, to Hon. Richardson Preyer, Chairman, House Subcomm. on Government Information and Individual Rights, August 21, 1980, in International Data Flow, Hearings before the House Subcomm. on Government Information and Individual Rights, 96th Cong., 2d Sess. at app. 4 (1980).

[42] See, e.g., Sections 2-404, 2-405 and 5-201 of E. O. 12046 and Sections 1(b)(1) and 1(b)(3) of Reorganization Plan No. 3 of 1979.

[43] Computer and Business Equipment Manufacturers Association, Comments in Response to National Telecommunications and Information Administration's Notice of Inquiry of Nov. 2, 1982, at 5 (Dec. 3, 1982).

[44] See the chapter on U.S. Participation in the ITU and preparation for radio conferences, infra.

[45] For a detailed discussion of the use of a Presidential veto in the facilities planning context, see the chapter on Facilities and Networks, infra.

Chapter Five

FACILITIES AND NETWORKS

International telecommunications facilities -- chiefly undersea cables and geostationary satellites — link the United States with overseas networks and are owned jointly by United States carriers and foreign telecommunications administrations. Each generally owns half of each link extending to the imaginary midpoint for undersea cables and from earth station to spacecraft in the case of satellite circuits. Establishing international telecommunications facilities is thus a cooperative undertaking involving entities of two or more nations -- private, regulated firms in the case of the United States, and the government or government-designated monopolies in other countries.

Satellite planning for most international communications (capacity, cost, quantity, etc.) is undertaken through the International Telecommunications Satellite Organization (Intelsat), which is jointly owned and administered by operating entities of 108 nations. Undersea cable systems for use by the United States are planned for by the American Telephone and Telegraph Company in consultation with United States international record carriers (e.g., Western Union International, RCA Global Communications, Inc., ITT World Communications, Inc., TRT Telecommunications, Inc., FTC Communications, Inc.) and the relevant foreign telecommunications authorities.

This chapter reviews the major issues involved in the establishment of international facilities and networks by focusing on:

o      Allocation of spectrum resources;

o      Allocation of satellite orbital resources;

o      Facilities planning and authorization;

o      Comsat and Intelsat issues; and

o      Integrated Services Digital Networks (ISDN).

(97)

98

## BACKGROUND

The last two decades have witnessed rapid development of telecommunications and information technology. Increases in capacities and lowered unit costs are the most obvious results of these technological advances.

The first modern transoceanic submarine cable capable of providing voice services was placed in operation across the North Atlantic in 1956 (TAT-1). It was capable of providing only 36 basic 4 kHz two-way voice circuits. The latest North Atlantic submarine cable, now under construction, is TAT-7 with a capacity of over 4,000 voice circuits. It is expected that the next generation of submarine cables, using fiber optic and digital technology, will be available for transoceanic use in the late 1980s. This digital cable should be capable of providing (in a basic configuration) over 12,000 voice grade circuits, or a mixture of voice and television transmission. Conversation "throughput" is expected to be increased several-fold through the use of more efficient speech encoding and interpolation techniques.[1]

The technology of international satellites has also developed rapidly. The first commercial international communications satellite, known as Early Bird, was launched by NASA for Intelsat in 1965 and had a total capacity of 240 voice grade circuits or one TV channel. Each of the current, or fifth generation Intelsat satellites can be configured to provide more than 12,000 voice grade circuits plus two TV channels. The capacity and flexibility of these satellites will be enhanced by advanced earth segment technology such as time division multiple access (TDMA), compandors, and speech interpolation systems.[2]

Flexible regulation of the radio frequency spectrum and of the geosynchronous orbit (GSO) is necessary on an international scale to ensure the viability of both domestic and international satellite systems. The growth in technology has fostered continuing increases in efficiency, both in the use of the spectrum and the GSO. It is vital to U.S. national interests to assure international regulatory features are adopted that support efficient use of the GSO, guarantee equitable access, and ensure the orderly introduction of new technologies to the benefit of all users.

99

A recurring problem is the obsolescence of existing U.S. legislation in light of (1) the increasing importance of international telecommunications and information to the nation's economic well-being and national interest, and (2) the changes that permit transformation from regulated monopoly conditions to full and fair competition in a deregulated environment.

MAJOR ISSUES IN THE ESTABLISHMENT OF
INTERNATIONAL FACILITIES AND NETWORKS

Allocation of Spectrum Resources

Allocation of the electromagnetic spectrum for specific radio services is accomplished at periodic World Administrative Radio Conferences (WARC) and Regional Administrative Radio Conferences (RARC) of the International Telecommunication Union (ITU). The ITU allocation table divides the world into three regions and makes a basic distribution of the frequency spectrum up to 275 GHz.[3] This spectrum is divided into 544 separate frequency band allocations. These allocations are made to 37 different radio services on either an exclusive or shared basis.

The basic allocation table was reviewed in 1959 and again during the 1979 WARC. The ITU allocation table may be changed in limited ways as a result of specialized conferences held more frequently, when the terms of reference permit such action. Most specialized conferences, however, are devoted to development of specific details for frequency use by a specific radio service and work within the framework of the overall allocation table.

The U.S. National Table of Frequency Allocations is a separate allocation table for use in the United States. This document follows the general framework of the ITU Allocation Table to the extent unique U.S. operations permit. In those instances where the U.S. allocation table differs from the international table, operations must be on a non-interference basis relative to other administrations operating in accordance with the ITU allocation table or in accordance with bi- or multilateral operating agreements. As a matter of practice, the United States deviates from the ITU allocation table only where operations are unlikely to cause interference outside of U.S. borders.

<u>Economic  Significance  of  Spectrum  Allocation  Tables.</u>  The telecommunications  equipment  manufacturing  industry  obviously  has  a  vital interest in the allocation of radio spectrum on a national and international basis as it determines both potential demand for products and the cost of the equipment involved.  When new radio equipment approaches the developmental stage, the new system  must  be  designed  to  operate  in  a  frequency  band  allocated  to  that particular radio service.  If the system is to be marketed worldwide, it must be designed to operate in internationally allocated frequency bands.  This presents major economic considerations because the wider the area of the world where a new product can be used, the greater the potential market, the larger the production quantities, and, in many cases, the lower the cost of each unit produced. This prospect of lower costs influences buyers and sellers and produces an incentive to strive for spectrum allocations which are consistent worldwide.  Due to these factors many ITU disputes over spectrum allocation issues relate to how much spectrum in what frequency range a particular radio service will be allocated, as well as uniform applicability to all regions.

<u>Political Aspects of Spectrum Allocation Tables.</u>  Different nations clearly have different internal and international telecommunications needs; they tend to be guided by their internal needs when negotiating for spectrum allocations at international  conferences.    Additional  problems  arise  when  the  spectrum requirements  for  national  security  operations  are  the  basis  for  a  particular allocation.[4]

Currently, the use of spectrum on an international basis is accomplished through specific coordination and notification procedures.  Frequencies are registered to whomever first coordinates the use with other countries for a particular frequency at a designated location and subsequently notifies the International Frequency Registration Board (IFRB). This process has satisfied the

101

needs of most administrations, although questions have arisen concerning the complexity of the process by those with limited spectrum management resources. Questions have also been raised by some lesser developed countries concerning the ability of the present process to accommodate their future needs which, in turn, has stimulated interest on their part in long-term "a priori planning" for the spectrum and GSO.

Current Policy on Allocation of Spectrum Resources. U.S. policy for international spectrum management takes into account a large number of specific policy objectives. These objectives fall into several categories.

(1) The first category of objectives involves obtaining international recognition and protection of new and existing radio systems, as for example, the new U.S.-developed Global Positionary System (GPS), which has the potential of replacing a number of existing radio navigational aids.

(2) The second category involves the adoption of frequency allocations that realistically advance our economic and national security goals.

(3) The third category involves the introduction of spectrum conservation measures to permit more efficient use of the radio spectrum, as for example, the introduction of single side band modulation in the aeronautical and maritime services.

(4) A fourth category of U.S. policy objectives concerns the conduct of future spectrum planning conferences, which will further refine how some radio services will be operated in the future.

The last category has received significant attention on the part of Congress and the public given that a number of developing countries are now seeking detailed frequency planning which would reserve spectrum assets for their future use. This approach is wasteful of spectrum assets and would inhibit technological progress.

U.S. preparation for international conferences — the process of developing concrete U.S. spectrum allocation proposals -- involves developing comprehensive information on the current use, needs, and rate of development of radio services, assessing the state of the art, and reviewing the operational practices used by these services. The ability of radio services to share allocations must be under constant evaluation if the most efficient applications are to be fostered. When U.S. requirements for international telecommunications systems or allocations are presented, coordinating these proposals with other nations materially enhances the likelihood of their acceptance.

Since the International Spectrum Allocation Table is reviewed in its entirety only about every two decades, the task of forecasting detailed spectrum requirements is a substantial undertaking. As the rate of change in the state of the art continues, this challenge becomes more acute. The consequences of faulty projections can have a serious impact on the future of many different radio services.

Recommendations on Allocation of Spectrum Resources. U.S. policy seeks to ensure timely application of the latest technology to minimize transmission bottlenecks and spectrum scarcity. The policy of allocating the spectrum in response to demonstrated economic, national security, and foreign policy needs and future requirements is most effective and should be maintained. Management of these allocations should be grounded on sound procedures that afford users flexibility, equitable access to meet operational needs, and facilitate the systematic introduction of new technologies beneficial to all.

The overall importance of planning for future radio spectrum requirements, both nationally and internationally, cannot be overstated. Service allocations and management procedures are the keystone to the entire spectrum management structure. The United States thus must continue to improve its overall ability adequately to prepare sound international proposals and to obtain international support. In few other areas of spectrum management is it more difficult to correct mistakes. A full discussion of methods to improve U.S. performance in attaining its goals at future scheduled radio and other ITU conferences (such as DBS-RARC-83, Mobile WARC-83, HF Broadcasting WARC-84, Space-WARC 85/88) is presented elsewhere in this report.

Allocation of Geostationary Orbit Resources

During the last five years there has been much discussion concerning "equitable access" to the geostationary orbit (GSO). The twentieth anniversary of the orbiting of the first successful geostationary satellite, NASA's Syncom II, will be marked in 1983. In these two decades there has been and continues to be a remarkable growth in the number and diversity of types of satellites which have been placed in orbit.

Most satellites relaying communications are located in the geostationary orbit. These satellites have created an institutional and structural revolution in the field of telecommunications and information, both domestically and internationally. The global connectivity made possible by satellites has had a fundamental impact on the practical delivery of communications.

Although many space services utilize the geostationary orbit, the Fixed Satellite Service (FSS)[5] is the largest in terms of total satellites. Dramatic growth in GSO use has occurred over the past 15 years, particularly in telephone, data transmission, and video distribution. This growth has occurred largely in developed countries, although developing countries have shared in this growth through their participation in Intelsat, through special leasing arrangements, or through construction of their own satellites. In 1981, Intelsat served 160 countries, territories, or possessions either directly or indirectly. Several developing countries (e.g., Mexico, Brazil, Indonesia, India, and China) are already operating or have firmly planned domestic satellite systems. Regional satellite systems, such as Arabsat, have planned launch dates, and interest in an African regional satellite system has been expressed. In addition, Intelsat is considering plans to offer nonpreemptable domestic leased satellite services. This activity exemplifies the extensive interest and growing demand for use of the GSO by developing countries.

The current method of orbital assignment in the ITU for both geostationary and non-geostationary satellites is similar to but more flexible than procedures used for international notification of radio stations on earth. These procedures are used to obtain international interference protection of the satellite, to avoid interference to other satellite networks, and to inform administrations of others' plans. The procedures are technical in nature and involve parameters including satellite location, transmitter power, operating frequencies, antenna coverage, and receiver sensitivity.

The satellite notification process involves three phases — advance publication, coordination, and notification. In the first phase, the ITU's IFRB circulates to all administrations the information submitted by a country on its planned satellite network. After a six month comment period, the proposing administration coordinates with others to resolve any potential interference problems. After an additional six months and the resolution of all potential interference problems, the proposing administration submits notification of the satellite operation to the IFRB. This notification is an administration's "license" or "assignment" to use the orbit (and frequencies), and forms a basis for commenting on potential interference by the planned networks of other administrations.

A first step in considering potential orbit allocation scenarios involves an assessment of available GSO capacity. In order to provide a common baseline and because analog TV and telephony are the two most common uses of the FSS, system capacity is most commonly measured in equivalent 40 MHz transponders, which relate to one TV or 1000 equivalent voice grade channels. This measure of orbital capacity represents substantial simplification. It provides a reasonable means of estimating the potential for orbital crowding, however, since it understates actual achievable capacity for modern systems.

In analyzing the subject of the total capacity of the geostationary orbit, it is instructive to estimate current in-orbit capacity along with an estimate of its present usage. As a means of providing some insight into this information, two elements or blocks of orbit capacity now being used are:

(a)     the Intelsat system, and

(b)     the systems for the Western hemispheric arc to provide fixed domestic satellite service to the U.S., Canada, and Latin America, which have been, or are in the planning process.

Japan, Intelsat, the United States, and the Soviet Union have undertaken analyses of the capacity of the GSO. The results of some of these analyses show:

o        Achievable capacity is very great, something in the order of 5 to 20 x $10^6$ telephone channels, and this could be increased if standards were adopted which maximize satellite orbit capacity in relation to service area.

o        The U.S.S.R. study estimates the maximum theoretical capacity in television channels to be in the order of 400 to 1,176 per degree of orbit.

These estimates have all been based on certain technical assumptions, all of which are practical and many of which are in operating systems. The analyses mentioned above have indicated that there are certain directions in which satellite system design and operation should evolve if further orbit capacity is to be achieved. These include the following:

o        The use of cross polarization to achieve frequency re-use;

o        Increasing the number of areas served from a given orbit location;

o        Increasing use of limited coverage beams;

o        Better control of satellite and earth station antenna side-lobes;

o        Further improvement in satellite station keeping; and

o        Increase in intersystem noise allowance.

Current Situation concerning GSO Allocation. There have been comments and observations regarding possible "crowding" of the GSO. These comments have fueled fears, particularly among developing countries, that no orbital slot will be available at such time as they may launch their own satellites. At the 1979 WARC, the LDCs proposed and obtained concurrence on a resolution to convene a conference to "guarantee in practice for all countries equitable access to the geostationary satellite orbit and the frequency bands allocated to the space services."[6] The 1982 ITU Plenipotentiary scheduled sessions for 1985 and 1988 on this topic. Many technologists and policymakers in the developed nations believe:

o    There are a number of techniques and improvements which can be
     implemented over time to increase availability of capacity
     dramatically.

o    No satellite system in the relevant frequency bands has yet been
     denied access to the GSO.

o    The United States, in its domestic regulatory procedures, is breaking
     ground in forcing the implementation of improved orbit utilization
     technology techniques.

o    The actual number of satellites which may be accommodated in the
     GSO in any particular frequency band is very large and is being
     increased constantly through the use of improved technology.

o    Effective management procedures that have the flexibility to take
     into account changing requirements, technology, and operational
     arrangements offer the best means of ensuring both efficient use of
     and equitable access to the GSO.

The fact that several countries located on the equator have claimed
sovereignty over the GSO has further complicated the situation.    The United
States and most of the world have opposed the notion of sovereignty.  The issue
was addressed at the UNISPACE '82 Conference and its report stated: "Clearly,
such a planning method should take into account the specific needs of the
developing countries, as well as the special geographical situation of particular
countries."[7] These ideas were subsequently adopted by the ITU Plenipotentiary in
Nairobi although they were consistently opposed by the United States, other
Western, and, indeed, Eastern Bloc countries.

Finally, and importantly, the LDC's have been and will continue to be the
direct beneficiaries of hundreds of millions of dollars of R&D funds spent on
satellite system design, which will lead to reduced costs for the systems they
select to implement.  Many of these funds are directed toward those technologies
which lead to enhanced capacity.  This capacity, however, cannot be enhanced if
restrictive orbit planning methods are adopted.

107

Recommendations on Allocation of Geostationary Orbit Resources. The current regulatory scheme for obtaining access to the GSO is contained in the ITU Radio Regulations as revised at the 1979 WARC. It is based on accommodating orbit access on the basis of defined needs. Because of concerns of the developing countries that all available orbit locations may be used by the developed countries, however, there is growing concern in the United States that many LDCs will use the 1985/8 ITU Space WARC to establish a plan in which orbit and spectrum are pre-assigned rather than employed on the basis of need. It is the U.S. view that such an approach would be detrimental to space communications development and to the interest of all users.

The United States has supported and continues to support the concept of equitable access to the GSO. The United States, in preparing for the 1985/8 Space WARC[8] must develop proposals that promote flexibility and use of the orbit on an "as needed" basis. Most importantly, the United States must develop technical information and rationales that will assure the LDCs these procedures will provide "equitable access" to the orbit better than a pre-planned, long-term assignment approach.

### Facilities Planning and Authorization

International satellite systems are planned within Intelsat, while cable systems landing in and used by the United States are planned jointly by U.S. carriers and their foreign correspondents. The Federal Communications Commission (FCC) has exclusive authority to permit U.S. carriers' construction of new or additional domestic or international facilities. It also authorizes U.S. entities to provide basic services[9] over existing or new domestic and international facilities. The FCC, however, has no jurisdiction over the non-U.S. activities of foreign telecommunications entities. Nor, of course, can the FCC authorize U.S. carrier entry into, or provision of service in, foreign markets.

The planning and construction of new international facilities as well as the provision of international services requires a joint effort between U.S. carriers and their foreign correspondents, or between Comsat and the other members of Intelsat and Inmarsat. The FCC is placed "in the middle" of these joint activities. Moreover, the primary statutes[10] which authorize Commission action provide little guidance regarding the manner and extent to which national interest, foreign policy, national security, and international comity concerns must be balanced by the FCC in conjunction with its international facility and service authorization activities. While each of these concerns constitutes one component of the broad "public interest" standard under which the FCC operates, there are instances where it requested and followed Executive Branch advice on these subjects and other instances where such views were neither sought nor, when offered, accorded proper weight.

The ownership and management of satellites and cable facilities pose major differences in terms of  their operations and capabilities, their economic characteristics, and planning. Submarine cables landing in the United States are owned and operated by the U.S. service carriers and their foreign correspondents, generally on a 50-50 basis. They provide point-to-point communications between two countries or continents, and are traditionally planned for and operated primarily under the control of those entities, in conjunction with any other administrations which purchase transmission capacity for extension to their domestic communications networks.[11] The total cost of a submarine cable system, with a typical design life of about 24 years, is established by including manufacturing and laying costs, operating and management costs, research and development, repairs, and other directly associated expenses. The costs of cable circuits have thus been relatively simple to determine.

International communications satellites are primarily planned, owned, and operated by the international organization Intelsat. Ownership of Intelsat is vested, according to use, in the various Signatories to the Intelsat Operating Agreement. Comsat, the U.S. Signatory, owns the largest share of the Organization. A single modern satellite can simultaneously accommodate many point-to-point or point-to-multipoint communications paths, thus providing great operational flexibility. Since earth stations accessing the Intelsat system are not owned by Intelsat, however, but by the individual administrations, significant international technical cooperation is necessary and has become routine. Furthermore, the cost of an Intelsat circuit is not as simply determined, since a major objective is the establishment of universal and flexible access to its global communications network. Earth station costs of each nation also are different. Finally, Intelsat prices reflect a significant amount of averaging among satellites and ocean regions, so that efficient high volume routes provide some subsidy to low volume routes. Economic and operational comparisons between satellites and cables thus have been, and are likely to remain, complex and controversial.

Current Policy Concerning Facilities Planning and Authorization. U.S. regulation of international communications is now accomplished by the FCC as required by the Communications Act of 1934 (as amended), the Communications Satellite Act of 1962, and the International Maritime Satellite Act of 1978.[12] With the exception of the amended Section 222[13], the regulatory scheme imposed by the 1934 Act does not distinguish between domestic and international common carrier facilities and services. Hence, the same broad "public interest" standard contained in the 1934 Act applies to all facilities and services, and there is no explicit legislative requirement for the FCC to take into account considerations such as the U.S. national interest or foreign correspondent requirements.[14] The Comsat Act also does not address the legal obligations imposed by the Intelsat Agreements, which were created after the Act was passed; neither the Interim nor Permanent Agreements were ratified by the Senate.

The FCC's public interest analysis regarding the licensing of international facilities and services has a major impact upon the plans, investments, and revenues of many foreign telecommunication entities. The FCC participates in the development of U.S. guidance to Comsat regarding Intelsat facilities and services. The FCC has also actively participated in the North Atlantic Consultative Process for the planning of both satellite and cable facilities although it lacks jurisdiction, obviously, over the activities of foreign telecommunication entities in these joint enterprises. It is difficult for the FCC to engage in meaningful unilateral review of international satellite facilities for which Comsat seeks authorization, when

110

Intelsat has already approved the long-range planning for such facilities. This has led to greater FCC focus upon submarine cable facility applications, although, similarly, it also has proved difficult not to authorize cable facilities which are deemed necessary by U.S. service carriers and their foreign correspondents.

Because of the continuing problems with the FCC's application of outdated legislation, an alternative approach to the planning and authorization of international facilities was sought by a group of European Administrations. Starting with a 1974 meeting with U.S. Government representatives (including the FCC, the Office of Telecommunications Policy, NTIA's predecessor, and the Department of State), they sought to devise a procedure wherein cable and satellite planning for the North Atlantic region could include consultations with both U.S. carriers and Government representatives at an early stage. This procedure has evolved into a formal arrangement[15] now called the North Atlantic Consultative Process.[16]

By the late 1970s, the FCC processes for approval of international telecommunications facilities in general, and for Intelsat V and TAT-7 in particular, were the subject of much controversy in the United States as well as in Europe. Pursuant to a Congressional request, the General Accounting Office reviewed the overall situation and issued a final report in March, 1978.[17] The report made several cogent observations and recommendations, some of which have affected continued FCC activities and have been incorporated in proposed legislation.

There has been some attempt to extend the Consultative Process to the Pacific Ocean Basin and elsewhere. To date, the other nations of these areas have not indicated a high receptivity to the concept. The FCC has instituted a proceeding,[18] however, that attempts to involve joint cable/satellite planning for the Pacific Basin by U.S. carriers only. Whether such one-sided planning can be useful in the long term is unclear.

There are serious drawbacks in the current process which necessitate an improved long-term resolution of the international facilities and services planning and authorization process. These drawbacks include:

111

o      Excessive economic control by the FCC over the international
       communications marketplace, evidenced by extensive allocation of
       cable and satellite market shares and detailed country-by-country
       approval of carrier plans;

o      Undue FCC focus on engineering and economic factors, and too little
       consideration of national interest, foreign policy, and national
       security concerns; and

o      The difficulties of addressing the facility and access needs of new
       and potential service providers when the cooperation of foreign
       correspondents is required, and when such new entrants seek to
       compete with those U. S. carriers owning existing facilities.

In summary, there is excessive economic regulation and it inhibits attainable
market competition, diversity, and innovation. As a result, the existing process is
inadequate to promote U.S. national interests.

Options concerning Facilities Planning and Organization. Resolving the
problems in the planning and authorization of international facilities and services
hinges on two questions. First, how can the advantages of full and fair competition
and attendant deregulation be achieved, when there is one legislated monopolist,
and one de facto monopolist, among U.S. carriers, and when the overseas
correspondents of U.S. carriers are also monopolists? Second, in either the current
U.S. regulatory regime or in a future, more competitive, deregulatory environment,
how can the national interest, foreign policy, public interest, and national security
be protected and promoted?

As these two questions have come to be understood and appreciated,
alternatives to the current statutory process for international facility approval
have been advanced. Before describing specific options to resolve the problems
with the process as it is currently implemented, however, the detailed goals the
U. S. should attempt to achieve in the planning, construction, and use of
international facilities should be considered. These goals are:

o      Access for U.S. telecommunications users to international facilities
       in sufficient diversity, quantity, and quality to ensure the low-cost,
       reliable choice of desired services.

112

o    Minimal governmental regulation or oversight over U. S. carriers
     cooperating with foreign entities in the  planning, construction, and
     operation of facilities.

o    Encouragement of intermodal (cable vs. satellite) and inter-company
     competition.

o    Statutory recognition of the growing importance of international
     facilities to U. S. national interests, foreign policy, and national
     security.

o    Prohibition of the construction of inefficient or unnecessary facilities
     and other improper activities by "bottleneck" carriers in order to
     protect U.S. telecommunications users.

o    Government recognition and amelioration of the  disadvantages of
     competitive U. S. carriers attempting to negotiate with monopoly
     foreign correspondents while still accommodating the needs of
     international comity.

Some of the alternatives to the current statutory process for international
facility approval, which have already been proposed as options by others include:

o    Maintain the status quo; permit the Commission to continue the
     consultative process, and take other ad hoc actions as  necessary.

o    Make sections 214, 309, and 319 of the 1934 Act inapplicable to
     international facilities and services, thereby allowing facility choice
     to be determined by the carriers in response to marketplace forces
     and foreign regulatory actions.

o    Create a Government/industry task force for the planning of
     international facilities.

o    Require the FCC, or a joint U. S. Government group (e.g., FCC,
     State, Commerce/NTIA), to develop detailed guidelines, including
     cost comparison methodology for international underseas cable and
     satellite systems, and specific operational criteria, which would form
     the basis of Commission decisions on facility construction and
     operations.

o    Retain section 214 substantially as is, but add an "alternative"
     international facility construction and authorization process
     permitting carriers to invest in and construct facilities without prior
     FCC approval, and with post-construction regulatory review.
     Carriers would then be free to select either avenue, weighing the
     benefits and risks of each.

113

Recommendation for Facilities Planning and Organization. None of the alternative approaches is perfect, nor will any single one solve all extant and foreseeable problems. Maintaining the status quo would be particularly troubling. The FCC has neither the legislative mandate nor the expertise to negotiate effectively with foreign governments. Furthermore, pending litigation could well require the FCC to discontinue the consultative process.[19] Existing legislation requires lengthy regulatory proceedings entailing costly uncertainties about projects involving hundreds of millions of dollars. Finally, the existing legislation permits the FCC to act without adequate consideration of the national interest or foreign policy of the United States at a time when these concerns are of increasing importance in international telecommunications.

## COMSAT/INTELSAT

### Historical Background

The Communications Satellite Act of 1962 was enacted after intense Congressional debate, at a time when the Soviet Union was considered to be leading the "space race" by being the first to place both an artificial satellite and a man into earth orbit. The 1962 Act was intended to lead to a demonstration of United States supremacy in the practical uses of space technology. Other factors influencing the legislation included the imminent 1963 World Administrative Radio Conference for space applications, the desire to show the advantages of private over governmental ownership, and a U.S. commitment to help developing countries. The 1962 Act provides for the

> establishment, ownership and regulation of a private corporation which would be the United States participant in a commercial satellite system. This system is to be established in cooperation and conjunction with other countries and is to be a part of an improved global communications network. It would be responsive to public needs and national objectives serving the communications needs of the United States and other countries and contribute to world peace and understanding.[20]

114

The corporation conceived in the 1962 Act is the Communications Satellite Corporation (Comsat). The ownership and operation of the global satellite system has devolved to the International Telecommunication Satellite Organization (Intelsat), which, in turn, is owned by 108 national Signatories, including Comsat.

The ownership of the U.S. corporation was the major subject of controversy surrounding the legislation. Indeed, an unsuccessful filibuster was carried out by a group of Senators who believed that the Government-financed research and development leading to the operational system should not be given to a private corporation, particularly the existing international common carriers, but instead to a Government owned, TVA-type entity. A compromise was reached, whereby half of the initial Comsat stock was offered for sale to the public, and the other half to telecommunications carriers "authorized" by the FCC. The board of directors was to consist of six members elected by public shareholders, six selected by carrier owners and three appointed by the President.

The 1962 Act also assigns to the FCC regulation of the corporation and the satellite system [21], while national interest, foreign policy, and national security oversight responsibilities are assigned to the President. NASA is directed to provide assistance to the corporation.

Growth of Intelsat—the Global System. The global communications satellite system envisioned by the 1962 Act has become an unqualified, outstanding success on institutional, financial, and operational grounds, and must be considered a triumph of U.S. foreign policy.

The initial institutional concept — to base the system on a series of bilateral arrangements -- was rejected by major foreign communications correspondents at the outset, and a joint ownership/consortium arrangement was instituted in its place. A multilateral, interim agreement took effect in August, 1964, and was called the International Telecommunications Satellite Consortium (Intelsat).[22] Nineteen entities, including Comsat, participated in the interim arrangements. This agreement made Comsat the majority owner and manager of the system, with ownership based upon usage of the system. The interim arrangements also included a time schedule for arriving at Definitive Agreements.

115

As a result of three international conferences, agreements for Intelsat's permanent arrangements were finalized in August 1971.[23] The agreements:

> preserv[e] the commercial nature and viability of the system, would give participants a greater measure of responsibility in determining policy, would provide for the establishment of an integrated management body responsible only to the Organization and independent of any signatory, and would afford fair opportunities in the supply of equipment for the system. The final texts . . . provide for a four-tier structure comprising:

> (a) an Assembly of Parties composed of representatives of Governments to consider general policy and scheduled to meet every two years;

> (b) an annual Meeting of Signatories of the Operating Agreement (the telecommunications entities);

> (c) a Board of Governors (about 25) which will meet several times a year and have responsibility for the design, development, construction, establishment, operation and maintenance of the system;

> (d) an executive organ. During a transitional period of 6 years the United States Communications Satellite Corporation (Comsat) will perform technical and operational management functions under contract, its performance being monitored by a Secretary General who, in addition, will be responsible for the other management functions. After the transitional period, a Director General will assume responsibility for all management functions, acting in accordance with the policies and directives of the Board of Governors.

> In the Assembly of Parties and in the Meeting of Signatories each Party or Signatory, as the case may be, will have one vote. Decisions on matters of substance will be taken by a two-thirds majority. In the Board of Governors, voting will be related to investment which, in turn, will be related to use of the system.[24]

As of January, 1983, membership in Intelsat included 108 nations. On the operational side, Intelsat has been successful. The initial "Early Bird" Satellite, which was something of a technical gamble, was launched into equatorial geosynchronous orbit in 1965. It had a capacity of 240 voice circuits or one television channel. The first of the Intelsat V series was launched in December 1980 and has a potential capacity of 12,000 circuits and two television channels. Intelsat now carries the major portion of the world's intercontinental communications traffic on almost 30,000 circuits. There are more than 1,000 satellite paths connecting over 220 antennas in 136 countries using Intelsat satellites. Circuit use has been growing at approximately 25 percent per year, although economic conditions have lowered this rate to about 20 percent. In addition, more than 20 nations now use spare Intelsat space segment facilities for their domestic services.

Corresponding to this substantial traffic growth in operations is the financial growth of the organization. Its current capitalization is over $1.1 billion, and the worldwide investment of its users in earth stations is probably double this amount. Ongoing programs have required raising the capital ceiling to $2.3 billion. Finally, there has been a continuing reduction in charges for satellite users. The annual price of a 1965 Early Bird channel was $32,000, while the 1982/3 price for an equivalent but technically superior channel is $4,680.

The 1978 International Maritime Satellite (Inmarsat) Act. In 1970-71, the Radio Subcommittee of the Intergovernmental Maritime Consultative Organization commenced a long process, significantly stimulated by the success of MARISAT,[25] that culminated in a convention and operating agreement establishing the International Maritime Satellite Organization (Inmarsat). The organization came into being on July 16, 1979.

Following the 1976 international conference, where agreement on the convention had been reached, domestic debate began on designation of the U.S. representative. Those supporting Comsat believed that a single voice, speaking with the experience of MARISAT and Intelsat behind it, would best represent the United States. Others, concerned about potential conflicts of interest if this role were added to the many already assumed by Comsat, and desiring to bring the experience and financial strength of all the U.S. international and maritime carriers to the enterprise, supported a consortium approach for U.S.

117

representation. After considerable debate, Congress designated Comsat as the U.S. representative to Inmarsat.

    Current and Future Issues. It is more than two decades — and five generations of satellites -- since the United States formulated its original satellite policy, based on a chosen U.S. entity and a single global system. Both the U.S. company, Comsat, and the global system, Intelsat, have prospered.

    At the same time, the satellite communications environment has evolved in unforeseen ways. As satellite technology has developed, opportunities for competition in the provision of services have increased. Today, competition is a reality in the U.S. domestic, if not the international, satellite market.

    The remainder of this chapter reviews a number of current issues in international satellite communications. These issues would not have arisen absent fundamental changes in U.S. regulatory philosophy regarding competition in the telecommunications field. They also resulted from a number of historical trends that reflect the growing sophistication of all participants in the Intelsat system.

    First, Comsat began to explore new fields of activity in addition to its statutory mandate. In the late 1960s, Comsat put forth the idea of a pilot program for the U.S. domestic satellite market. In 1973, the corporation obtained approval to launch a maritime communications satellite, MARISAT. More recently, Comsat's business activities have continued to diversify.

    Second, users became increasingly impatient with various "middlemen" in the international satellite market. On the one hand, large customers such as the U.S. Department of Defense sought to buy satellite service directly from Comsat as "authorized users," rather than indirectly through the carriers designated by the FCC. On the other hand, the carriers themselves have begun looking for ways to circumvent Comsat and secure direct access to the Intelsat system.

    Finally, countries other than the United States began to launch satellites in partial competition with those of the Intelsat system. Increasingly, U.S. carriers became interested in such regional satellite systems and called for changes in the U.S. policy vis-a-vis such non-Intelsat systems.

118

Unlike other aspects of international telecommunications, the United States can be effective in trying to create a competitive domestic environment in international satellite communications. The provisions of the Intelsat Agreements permit the U.S. and other nations to decide for themselves, as sovereigns:

o    Which entity or entities will be the ultimate source of capital investment[26] for national Intelsat space segment allotments.

o    Who shall own and operate national earth stations in the Intelsat system.

o    How many national earth stations will operate in the Intelsat system.

o    The composition of national delegations to various Intelsat meetings.

The major conditions that must be satisfied by the Agreements in this regard are that all earth stations operate within Intelsat standards, that a single entity serve as Signatory for each nation, and that the Signatory or Party assume responsibility for all national allotments.[27] In structuring and demonstrating the advantages of a competitive environment, the United States can provide significant advancement to the goal of competition in telecommunications on a broad international front. The major issues currently being debated include:

o    Regional satellite systems;

o    Provision by Intelsat of services other than "fixed satellite";

o    The "Authorized User" question; and

o    Ownership of earth segment by Comsat, carriers, and/or users.

Each of these issues is briefly discussed below.

Regional Satellite Systems

During the negotiations leading to Intelsat's permanent arrangements, the United States sought to make a single global system a mandatory element of the Agreements.[28] This issue was among the most contentious of the negotiations. A compromise was struck concerning the Preamble's stated desire to achieve "a

119

single global" system, and language permitting thorough, although non-binding consultations regarding international use of non-Intelsat space segment are incorporated into Article XIV(d) of the Intergovernmental Agreement.

Article XIV(d) requires that non-Intelsat satellite systems used by members for international public telecommunications services be technically compatible with the Intelsat system. It also describes a process whereby organs of Intelsat can express "findings" and "recommendations" regarding the potential for "significant economic harm" to Intelsat by the use of such non-Intelsat space segment, as well as whether the establishment of Intelsat links is prejudiced by such use. There is no specific prohibition or penalty based upon negative findings. Intelsat members may thus legally use non-Intelsat space segment for international services regardless of the finding of economic harm, as long as they adhere to the Article XIV(d) process.

Beginning in 1979, several groups of nations (Arabs for Arabsat, Southeast Asians for Palapa, Algeria for Intersputnik and Europeans for ECS/Eutelsat) completed the Article XIV(d) process. More than two years later, after pressure from U.S. applicants and other government agencies, the Department of State set forth a policy modification regarding the use of non-Intelsat space segment for international telecommunications. In a July, 1981, letter to the FCC Chairman, the Under Secretary of State acknowledged that:

> members may decide to rely on space segment facilities separate from the Intelsat global system to meet their international public telecommunications service requirements.

and that:

> Certain exceptional circumstances may exist where it would be in the interest of the United States to use domestic satellites for public international telecommunications with nearby countries. [emphasis added] [29]

The policy described in the letter quoted above affirms this country's strong support for Intelsat, but recognizes that under certain exceptional circumstances, it would be in the interest of the United States and other countries to authorize the

120

use of domestic satellites for international communications. Many of the respondents to NTIA's Notice of Inquiry agreed that the United States should continue to support Intelsat, but suggested that U.S. carriers should be able to use competitive, non-Intelsat space segment for regional communications.

Provision of New International Satellite Services

Intelsat was organized primarily to provide international fixed public message satellite services. On a preemptible basis it has been using its spare space segment capacity to provide domestic services to many nations. In addition, however, Intelsat has shown an interest in entering the field of international mobile satellite service, which is permitted by the definitive agreements.

Two issues concerning the provision of mobile satellite services that are of particular interest to the United States:

o   Second Generation Space Segment for Inmarsat; and

o   Aeronautical Satellite Services.

The first generation Inmarsat space segment is composed of the residual capacity of three Marisat spacecraft, a European built and launched MARECS, and several maritime subsystems on Intelsat V spacecraft. Inmarsat is now engaged in advanced planning for its second generation space segment. One of the issues in the Inmarsat Council is whether again to consider Intelsat as a potential supplier.

The use of satellites for communications between commercial aircraft and the ground has been considered for at least fifteen years. At this time, the Inmarsat Director General is holding exploratory talks with the staff of the International Civil Aviation Organization (ICAO) concerning a future joint aeronautical/maritime satellite system. Intelsat's staff is also holding discussions with ICAO. Inmarsat's discussions with ICAO were directed by Recommendation 4, which was sponsored by the United States in the Inmarsat Convention.

In addition to mobile satellite services, Intelsat is in the midst of planning and designing a new fixed service. Traditional Intelsat service is characterized by one or a few very large antennae serving as a gateway for traffic to each country

121

in the system. In the U.S. domestic arena, advances in technology, innovative spectrum engineering, and the spur of competition have led to "customer premises" services. Similar service is expected to be provided on a regional basis in Europe by the Eutelsat organization. The primary advantage of customer-premises service is the elimination of costly and technically degrading terrestrial end links, which are particularly troublesome for wide bandwidth and high speed data transmission services. Intelsat is now considering alternative design changes to Intelsat VA and VI spacecraft that would allow the organization to offer this type of service at or near customer premises on an international/intercontinental basis for several geographical areas.

Comsat by statute is the chosen instrument of U.S. participation in the Intelsat system. Comsat's role in these activities is currently subject to oversight and instruction by the U.S. Government. This mechanism should be continued.

The Authorized User Question

In Section 305(a) of the 1962 Act, the Congress authorized Comsat to:

(1)  plan, initiate, construct, own, manage, and operate itself or in conjunction with foreign governments or business entities a commercial communications satellite system;

(2)  furnish, for hire, channels of communication to United States communications common carriers and to other authorized entities, foreign and domestic; and

(3)  own and operate satellite terminal stations when licensed by the Commission . . . .

Exactly who would be Comsat's customers was the subject of much controversy following the passage of the Act. In 1967, the FCC decided that the Act gave it the authority to designate such entities. The FCC determined that Comsat, for the time being, should only serve other carriers, except under unique or unusual circumstances. The FCC promised to revisit this determination, however, "in light of experience gained."

122

By 1979, use of satellite communications had grown substantially, and many users believed they would save money by eliminating the "middleman." In December 1979, the Department of Defense petitioned the FCC for a declaratory ruling designating the Federal Government an authorized user of Comsat's services and facilities.[30] In October 1979, Aeronautical Radio, Inc. (Arinc) had also petitioned to become an authorized user. In May 1980, the FCC released a Notice of Proposed Rulemaking on this subject. The FCC proposed that following a corporate restructuring, a Comsat unit would be allowed to offer space segment and earth station facilities and services directly to "large users." The FCC also proposed concurrent elimination of FCC-prescribed satellite fill factors and mandatory composite rate formulation.

In August 1982, the FCC issued its Authorized User Report and Order.[31] It directed Comsat to remove user-type restrictions in its tariff for services terminating at earth stations. It required, however, that only a separated Comsat subsidiary could offer "end-to-end" service. Prescribed fill factors and mandatory composite rates were eliminated. The provision of services by Comsat directly to individual non-carrier users was authorized.

Earth Station Ownership

The 1962 Act limits earth station ownership to Comsat and carriers. Paragraph 201(c) of the Act gave the FCC authority to determine whether Comsat or the terrestrial carriers or both would own the U.S. earth stations associated with the global system.

Under an "interim" earth station ownership policy[32] established in 1966, Comsat operated the stations and owned 50 percent of each. With minor exceptions, the remaining 50 percent was owned by the terrestrial carriers connecting with the space segment service. This arrangement led to the establishment of an Earth Station Ownership Committee (ESOC), that has made major decisions concerning U. S. earth stations in the Intelsat system.

This ownership policy was adopted because existing technology required expensive stations (about $10 million each), and because multiple access to a single satellite caused significant loss in capacity. Technology, however, has changed. Earth stations costing $1.5 million or less today have routine access to the Intelsat space segment, and techniques have been developed to minimize the deleterious effect of multiple access. Furthermore, the "new" business service being planned by Intelsat will employ even less expensive earth stations located at or near customer premises.

In August, 1982, as part of the Comsat structure and authorized user decisions, the FCC instituted a Notice of Inquiry on earth station ownership.[33]

## INTEGRATED SERVICES DIGITAL NETWORK

National and international work toward an Integrated Services Digital Network (ISDN) is being carried out in various forums and countries around the world. Yet, ISDN is still only a concept. Many technical and standardization problems exist. Likewise, many domestic and international policy decisions must be made before ISDN comes into reality. As the network of the future, ISDN is a vital consideration in a study of long-range goals.

### The ISDN Concept

The core concept of ISDN is a network that will be based on and evolve from the telephony integrated digital network (IDN) by progressively incorporating additional functions and network features, including those of any other dedicated networks, so as to provide for existing and new services (CCITT Recommendation G705). Telephone networks around the world have evolved through two distinct stages, and are embarking on the third. The first stage was completely analog, both transmission and switching, and was designed for voice transmission. The second stage began evolving with the introduction of digital transmission and switching. It is identified as IDN and, in addition to voice, carries services such as data and facsimile. The third stage will encompass end-to-end digital connectivity and provide the backbone of ISDN.

124

There are three factors motivating ISDN. They are: (1) new or expanded services which can be offered, (2) the economy or lower cost of offering the services because of digital network characteristics, and (3) new technology which can permit the new services to be offered at reasonable cost. Combining these factors results in economic benefits through services integration.

Since the present telephone networks already carry various services, there currently exists a form of integrated services network. And, thus, it is not the evolution and digitization of the network in itself that has made ISDN a major subject of national and international importance and a subject of debate. Rather it is the philosophy in the planning and design of the future network and of subscriber access to that network, including the interconnection of constituent (telephone and non-telephone) networks as well as peripheral networks (e.g., private networks).

Although all ISDN services have not yet been defined, or perhaps even envisaged, these services are expected to fall into the following categories:

o     Digitized voice, with voice encryption a future possibility.

o     Facsimile and graphics.

o     Video. Whether digital TV will be provided is uncertain because of the large bandwidth required. Other video services are planned, however.

o     Other services, including telemetry, videotex, software transfer, electronic mail, data base access, computers, and other terminals.

Because the ISDN concept is now only defined in very general terms, it is open to different opinions and interpretations. One reason for this is that some countries are better able to implement a total digital approach than others, because they do not have a large plant investment in the latest analog switch technology. Other reasons arise in the differences between countries in the degree of governmental control of telecommunication resources and their political and economic philosophy. The differences in interpretation of the ISDN concept are indicative of the nature of issues and standardization which will have to be addressed. Some examples of the conflicting views about the scope and impact of ISDN are:

125

o    There will be a single, worldwide ISDN.

o    Each country will have an ISDN with a (high) degree of international connectability.

o    Several ISDN's may exist within a single country with varying degrees of connectability.

o    The ISDN will operate in parallel with dedicated public networks and private networks and compete with them for customers.

o    All services will be provided by the ISDN with little room left for other telecommunication service providers and networks.

## Foreign ISDN Influence

The drive toward establishing an ISDN has varying strength in different parts of the world.   In the United States, the common carriers are adding interfaces to end-office analog switches to permit digital operation, while some countries, such as France, have essentially planned to leapfrog a technical generation by establishing a new digital telephone network.   Many European countries and Japan have done major planning for ISDN and in some cases have or are establishing pilot and experimental networks which include not only metallic but also optical fiber and satellite transmission.   A number of European countries seem serious about setting standards for ISDN soon.   The United States should continue to participate strongly in the activities of international standard-setting bodies, so that the interests of our domestic manufacturers, service providers, and network operators are recognized, and so that U.S. procompetitive policies will be taken into account.

## Domestic ISDN

In the United States, the emerging ISDN will evolve from the current and developing technology which includes digital switching, digital subscriber loops, digital transmission via lightwaves, satellites, digital data services and signalling systems.

126

The U.S. communications environment is characterized by a number of factors which do not, or only to a much lesser degree, exist in other countries. Some of the major factors that may effect ISDN are:

o    Distinction between basic and enhanced services.

o    Multiplicity of domestic common carriers and, hence, public networks.

o    Multiplicity of private networks that need to be connected to the public network(s).

o    Development of alternative local distribution schemes.

o    Multiplicity of international carriers.

These factors raise critical policy and standardization questions. Standards in an analog environment are more forgiving than is true in an all-digital communications world. Ensuring full and fair access to technical, interface, and other standards as well as operating protocols is critical to ensure competition.

The distinction between basic and enhanced services will, from the U.S. perspective, have to be considered by the CCITT on the subjects of services to be provided by ISDN and on service classification.

U.S. Domestic Issues

There are numerous issues relating to domestic ISDN implementation. Three major issues which appear to subsume a number of others are described in this section.

Impact on Procompetitive Policy. The evolution of the ISDN raises serious questions as to some of the assumptions underlying the U.S. procompetitive policy to date. One viewpoint has been expressed as follows:

> It will be increasingly difficult to ground service distinctions in regulating network facilities. The multi-service and multi-facility (integrated packet and circuit switching) environment increasingly relying on or utilizing new network storage and processing (not necessarily "computing") resources will frustrate attempts to regulate the "basic-enhanced" service dichotomy and related segregated facility provisions.[34]

127

General Competitive Access in the United States. There are two types of access of concern with regard to ISDN: (1) access by service providers, and (2) access by equipment providers. In the case of multiple service providers, to what extent will the U.S. requirements of full interconnection be reflected in the U.S. ISDN thereby providing maximum competitive access? In addition, will the same level of interconnection apply to private networks, by-pass carriers, broadcasters, and information service providers?

Opportunities for suppliers of customer premises equipment (CPE) could be limited not only by normal interconnect-type barriers, but also by the unique complexity of ISDN. An example of this concern has been described as follows:

> The ISDN also greatly complicates the segregation of service markets from CPE markets when standards, functional allocations and performance parameters of the ISDN significantly affect a CPE required. The concern is that the network service provided could configure network equipment so as to favor his own CPE, or (by placing most of the "intelligence" in network equipment) to reduce the role of the CPE and thus the size of the CPE market.[35]

Multiple ISDNs. The two major concerns relating to the existence of multiple U.S. domestic ISDNs are: (1) will they be interoperable, particularly in a deregulated market, and (2) how will the interoperability or lack thereof affect national security requirements?

### International and Global Considerations

In addition to the domestic issues, there are a number of more fundamental questions which arise in the international and global sphere:

> Underlying these policy issues are basic ideological and even philosophical questions. Will ISDNs be configured to allow major roles for competing private enterprises, or will the public service monopoly principle prevail? How are the inevitably divergent policies in different nations to be accommodated at the international level? Can countries favoring a dominant PTT role be expected (or entreated or pressured) to open their equipment and service markets to "free trade"? Will advocacy of a public sector monopoly approach justify technical standards-setting behavior which pro-competitive governments may regard as "protectionist"?

128

Viewing the longer-term and the broader world beyond the major industrial countries, even larger issues may loom. Should ISDNs be configured to serve developing countries as efficiently and powerfully as developed countries (even if the economics are less favorable?) Could affordable access to ISDNs (and its productivity-enhancing services) significantly improve the position of some developing countries in the world "economic order"? Might unfavorable terms of developing country access exacerbate north/south differences over the future shape of the world "information order"?[36]

Recommended Actions. The effort to establish basic parameters for the ISDN, and access thereto, is seen by many administrations around the world as an urgent matter. That is because it is viewed as essential that standards be agreed upon before national implementations have reached a point where compromise will be too difficult to achieve.

Progress in developing ISDN standards is underway within the CCITT. U.S. Government and industry participants have devoted considerable effort and have contributed significantly in this undertaking. However, because of the far-reaching impact of ISDN on competition, equipment and service trade, and U.S. technological leadership, it is important that the U.S. Government provide a reasonably specific policy framework on which future U.S. efforts to develop ISDN standards could be based. Toward this end the FCC, which is presently considering a Notice of Inquiry on ISDN development, should initiate it without delay.

NOTES TO CHAPTER FIVE

[1] These microchip-based techniques are both alternative and complementary methods of increasing the efficiency of the basic transmission medium to transmit voice type information.

[2] Ibid.

[3] A GHz = gigahertz = 1,000,000,000 cycles per second.

[4] The ITU Allocation Table does not specifically refer to military applications although these are generally recognized.

[5] The ITU definition for Fixed-Satellite Service: A radiocommunication service between earth stations at specified fixed points when one or more satellites are used; the fixed-satellite service may also include feeder links for other space radiocommunication services.

[6] 1979 WARC, Resolution 3.

[7] UNISPACE '82 Report.

129

[8]See discussion of ITU and Radio Conferences, infra.

[9]The FCC recently ruled that it would not regulate either domestic or international "enhanced" service providers as common carriers. See the following chapter for a full discussion of this ruling.

[10]Communications Act of 1934, 47 U.S.C § 151 et seq.; Communications Satellite Act of 1962, 47 U.S.C. § 701-744.

[11]In modern, high-capacity cables the ownership tends to become very diversified (e.g., TAT-7 has 18 European owners) and the destinations become more widespread (e.g., trans-Atlantic cables serve as transit facilities to Africa and Asia).

[12]A new Section 222 was inserted into the 1934 Act by the Record Carrier Competition Act of 1981.

[13]By contrast, Section 201(a)4 of the 1962 Act and Section 504(b) of the 1978 Act direct the President to ensure that the actions of Comsat are "consistent with the national interest and foreign policy of the United States." However, the President does not have a statutory role in oversight of FCC decisions regarding Comsat or any other carrier, except in a wartime emergency. The President delegated his responsibilities under the 1962 Act to the Departments of State and Commerce. No delegation of Presidential responsibilities under the 1978 Act has been made.

[14]47 U.S.C. §751 et seq.

[15]See, e.g., Overseas Communications, 71 FCC 2d 71.

[16]Certain aspects of this process were challenged in ITT World Communications, Inc. v. FCC, No. 80-0428 (D.D.C. Oct. 17, 1980).

[17]Report of the Controller General, "Greater Coordination and a More Effective Policy Needed for International Telecommunications Facilities," CED 78-87, March 31, 1978.

[18]CC Docket 81-343.

[19]ITT v. FCC, D.D.C. Oct 17, 1980.

[20]Senate Committee on Commerce, Report on Communications Satellite Act of 1962, S.Rep.No. 1584, 87th Cong., 2d Sess. 1 (1962).

[21]Because the ownership of the satellite system was expected to be based upon a series of bilateral arrangements similar to undersea cable agreements, some of the provisions of the Act cite the system and the corporation interchangeably.

[22]Agreement Establishing Interim Arrangements, August 20, 1964, 15 UST 1705, TIAS No. 5646.

[23]Definitive Agreements for the International Telecommunications Satellite Organization, entered into force 12 February 1973, 23 UST 3813, TIAS No. 7532.

[24]"Satellite Communications," October 1971, U.K. Stationery Office, Cmnd. 4799.

[25]MARISAT, Inmarsat's predecessor, was a satellite project launched by Comsat for use by the U.S. Navy as well as commercial maritime interests.

[26]In at least one, and perhaps several instances, the capital investment for Intelsat space segment allotments and earth stations, as well as their operation, are not provided by the Signatory of the nation wherein the services are delivered.

[27]The Intelsat Agreements state:

o    "Each State Party . . . shall designate a telecommunications entity . . . to sign the Operating Agreement. (Article IIb)

o    "Relations between . . . . the Signatory and the Party . . . shall be governed by applicable domestic law. (Article IIb)

o    "Each Signatory . . . to which an allotment [of space segment] has been made . . . shall be responsible for compliance with all the terms and conditions . . . unless . . . its designating party assumes such responsibility for allotments made with respect to all or some of the earth stations not owned or operated by such Signatory." (Article 15c)

[28]Whereas the 1962 Act describes and sets forth the structure of a single global satellite system, a clause added to Section 102(d) during final passage of the legislation at the behest of Senator Church suggests that additional systems could be desirable if the initial system were a failure or it were otherwise in the national interest.

[29]U.S. Department of State, Correspondence from the Under Secretary of State to the Chairman of the FCC, July 23, 1981.

[30]The U.S. Government is specifically noted as an authorized user in Section 305(b)(4) of the 1962 Act. On one previous occasion, the FCC had waived its restrictive policy. In 1978 (70 FCC 2d 2127), at the request of the Spanish International Network, the FCC authorized Comsat to provide Intelsat facilities at their earth stations directly to users of international television services. Several of the carriers appealed this decision in the courts.

[31]90 FCC 2d 1394 (1982).

[32]5 FCC2d 812 (1966).

[33]CC Docket 82-540.

[34]Martech Strategies, Inc., "ISDN — Integrated Services Digital Networks: Impacts and Industry Strategy," page 8-6, June 1982.

[35]Id. p. 8-6.

[36]Id. pg. 8-5.

Chapter Six

INTERNATIONAL TELECOMMUNICATIONS SERVICES

The provision of international telecommunications services is vital to the national interest of the United States, and the significance of these services in our economy is growing daily.    This section summarizes current U.S. policy on competition in international telecommunications services, and analyzes resulting issues and their future consequences for U.S. interests.

BACKGROUND

Since the late 1960s, there has been a fundamental shift in the philosophy underlying U.S. telecommunications policy from pervasive economic regulation toward reliance on unregulated marketplace competition.    This change has been soundly based on the premise that the benefits normally considered in the public interest -- a strong U.S. telecommunications industry with competitive and efficient rates, high quality of service, wide choice of services, and innovative technology -- can best be achieved through maximum possible reliance on competitive marketplace forces rather than through the regulatory processes of the Federal Communications Commission (FCC).

The FCC commenced the expansion of international telecommunications competition in December 1979.[1]    Since then the FCC has taken a number of actions to increase competition in both the international voice and record markets. The international record carriers have been granted additional domestic and international authority.    New firms have been authorized to provide international service and Western Union Telegraph was authorized to reenter the international market in accordance with the Record Carrier Competition Act of 1981.    In December 1982, AT&T was permitted to enter the international record market and the record carriers to enter the voice market.    The FCC has also undertaken a number of initiatives to restructure U.S. access to the Intelsat system.    In August

(131)

132

1982, it completely removed all restrictions on noncarrier access to Comsat. Comsat was also permitted to enter the end-to-end service market with certain structural safeguards.

The relationship between regulation and competition is an integral part of all of the issues discussed in this section. A central question that must be addressed is what minimal amount of regulation or residual Government oversight is needed to achieve the goal of promoting the maximum possible amount of competition.

Before discussing specific issues associated with international telecommunications services, it would be helpful to clarify a few basic considerations, namely: (1) the institutional differences between domestic and international telecommunications; (2) trends regarding monopoly and competition in foreign countries; and (3) different levels of competition in the international environment.

## Institutional Differences Between Domestic and International Telecommunications

Although international telecommunications service is a cooperative venture of the United States and other sovereign nations, not all the market opportunities existing in domestic telecommunications can be automatically achieved in the international arena. In a cooperative international venture, the United States cannot unilaterally mandate policies, structures, or market opportunities. While reliance on competitive market forces serves as the basis of communications policy in the United States, this is not generally the case overseas. In addition, safeguards intended to encourage fair competition, such as antitrust legislation, rate-of-return regulation of underlying facilities, and requirements for nondiscriminatory interconnection between carriers, are only applicable generally in the United States.

In most countries, telecommunications equipment, service offerings, rates, and conditions are controlled by a government-owned monopoly whose motivation and objectives are different from those of private firms in the United States. For example, in many countries, international telecommunications is run by the

133

government as a profit-maximizing business, and international revenues are used to subsidize postal and other domestic services, including domestic telecommunications services. This is not the case in the United States, and the differences must be addressed in policymaking, or they will obstruct the implementation of U.S. international telecommunications objectives.

International carriers in the United States have not only operated under different economic conditions and motivations, but have also been subject to a unique regulatory scheme. In the past, the foreign administrations have adjusted to U.S. conditions because of the very large American traffic streams and the need for access to U.S. technology. In part because of the changes in U.S. regulatory policy, however, this stance is being reviewed.

U.S. efforts to apply a deregulated competitive approach in the international arena are a matter of some concern to several foreign telecommunication administrations. They have reacted in various ways. For example, some have declined to interconnect promptly with new U.S. carriers; and some have tried to exploit the new U.S. environment by having U.S. service providers bid against each other for the exclusive right to carry data services.

## Monopoly and Competition in Foreign Countries

In July 1982, NTIA commissioned a study of 17 countries to determine the extent to which each was moving toward competition in the provision of telecommunications and information products and services.[2] Preliminary findings indicate that Japan has been considering a liberalization of its telecommunications marketplace and, indeed, plans to restructure Nippon Telephone and Telegraph Company, the domestic monopoly, into regional and long-distance enterprises (similar to the court-approved restructuring of AT&T) are now underway. Australia is also studying the possibility of adopting a more procompetitive policy, primarily in the domestic market. The Davidson Committee there, for example, recently proposed deregulation of customer premises terminal equipment and liberal entry criteria for private networks.

134

Canada and the United Kingdom have already begun moving toward certain limited forms of service competition. In the case of the United Kingdom, for example, British Telecom has been restructured (with the creation of a separate international subsidiary), a private specialized carrier, Mercury, has been authorized and, indeed, has recently been permitted direct access to Intelsat under liberal conditions. While British Telecom is likely to control a significant share of British telecommunications services for the foreseeable future, "privatising" the organization and fostering competition are major goals of the Thatcher government.

Most of the remaining countries in the study appear to favor the status quo. Some countries apparently wish to increase the role of the government monopoly. In those cases where there does exist some movement toward selective competition, the focus appears to be exclusively on the domestic market. Monopoly control of international service would be maintained. There is affirmative movement toward fostering a competitive environment in telecommunication services in some countries. Telecommunications deregulation has thus become in some senses a major American export especially given the positive experiences of the United States. In summary, however, the global environment is likely at best to be characterized by "selective competitive entry" (limited to certain service categories) and "administered competition," managed through government licensing and standards-approval authority for yet some time.

### Levels of Competition

Within the United States, competition in telecommunications service generally involves intensifying commercial rivalry among U.S. carriers. This level of competition, however, cannot be automatically projected to the international arena, where two additional levels of competition must be considered.

In the international market, U.S. carriers and service providers must also deal with foreign telecommunications administrations (usually government-owned monopolies). The issues at stake in this international tug-of-war include the division of revenues between U.S. carriers and foreign administrations, the types of

135

services authorized, the terms of interconnection, the technical characteristics of transmission facilities, and their place of manufacture.

The third level of competition occurs among the nations themselves -- the United States and foreign countries. The subjects of this level of competition include national security, employment, technological leadership, balance of trade, and influence in the determination of global telecommunications standards.

ISSUES

From the preceding background it should be apparent that some conflict exists between the desires of the United States to create a competitive market for international telecommunications services, and the perceived intention of some foreign administrations to maintain a monopoly market structure. How long this conflict will persist is unclear. The same technological forces chiefly responsible for competition in the United States are increasingly being felt abroad. If the implications of foreign monopoly power in telecommunications services are not fully recognized and adequately addressed, however, the United States may not be fully effective in its efforts to promote competition in these areas.

The issues discussed in this section include:

o    The Resale and Computer II Decisions;

o    International private leased service;

o    International operating agreements;

o    Financial arrangements for international switched services;

o    Foreign entry into U.S. international telecommunications service markets;

o    Competition in voice services; and

o    U.S. participation in CCI Standards Activity in a Deregulated Environment.

136

### The Resale and Computer II Decisions

As mentioned earlier, the FCC started taking steps towards improving international telecommunications competition beginning in December 1979. The actions that have generated the most debate are: (1) the FCC's Notice of Proposed Rulemaking for International Resale and Shared Use of Services and Facilities, and (2) the FCC's Second Computer Inquiry (Computer II), which commenced in 1976. Because they relate to subsequent issues, these two actions are discussed more fully.

Resale is the subscription to communications services and facilities by one entity and the reoffering of services and facilities to the public (with or without adding value) for profit. Sharing is a nonprofit arrangement in which several customers collectively use communications services and facilities provided by a carrier, with each user paying the communications related costs according to its pro rata usage. In 1976 the FCC required carriers to remove from their interstate tariffs restrictions prohibiting the resale and shared use of private lines. In that decision the FCC concluded that resale and shared use of private line services would yield a number of public benefits, including:

o   the curtailment of unwarranted price discrimination (i.e., charging different customers different prices for essentially the same service) and possibly provision of communications services at rates more closely aligned to actual costs;

o   better management of communications networks, and facilitating the availability of noncarrier management expertise by intermediaries to users;

o   the avoidance of waste of communications capacity; and

o   the creation of additional incentives for research and development of ancillary devices to be used with transmission lines.

In 1980 the FCC came to a similar decision regarding resale of domestic MTS and WATS service.[3]

The question of international resale and shared use was addressed as part of the 1976 decision but the issue was deferred in a 1977 reconsideration.[4] Among the

137

factors contributing to the FCC deferral was the international debate then underway. Resale and shared use had been subject to considerable debate in the International Telephone and Telegraph Consultative Committee (CCITT). In addition, many foreign administrations had expressed opposition to the initial FCC decision. The CCITT at its Sixth Plenary session in 1976 adopted its D.1 Recommendation prohibiting resale and shared use of international private lines and the United States concurred in this Recommendation. Because the issue was pending at the FCC, however, the United States added a footnote to the D.1 Recommendation, stating: "There is in the USA, a continuing discussion of issues related to the dedicated use of customer private leased circuits, and the U.S. delegation is pleased that this will be the subject of further study in Study Group III during this study period."[5] The footnote was intended to notify other CCITT members that the issue was under review in the United States and that we expected the Recommendation to be reviewed by the CCITT in its next plenary period (1977-1980).

In April 1980, the FCC again raised the subject of international resale, adopting a Notice of Proposed Rulemaking "to consider whether or to what extent common carriers subject to our jurisdiction which provide international communications services should be allowed to continue to restrict the resale and shared use of the services and facilities they offer under tariffs filed with the Commission."[6] The responses from U.S. parties divided along predictable lines. The established international record carriers, who benefit from the present resale restrictions, opposed the change. AT&T took the position that benefits could result from resale and sharing if the policy is carried out under competitive conditions. A large number of users also filed in the proceeding. In general, users supported the concept, although many recognized it was a controversial international issue and the larger users, especially, feared retaliation.

The benefits that would flow from resale and shared use include opening the possibility for a wider variety of services, promoting more efficient use of network facilities, and reducing the costs and potentially the prices charged users. Under the current CCITT restrictions, only large users can obtain the cost saving benefits of flat rate private lines. While the costs savings of resale and shared use could stimulate demand, foreign administrations also see it diverting traffic from the higher priced switched services. The additional revenues flowing from increased demand could offset any revenue losses associated with traffic diverted from switched to private line service. Some foreign administrations nevertheless fear that, on balance, they would lose.

The CCITT D.1 Recommendation was one agreed upon mechanism for preventing this diversion. Naturally, foreign administrations are concerned that, if the United States were to permit unlimited international resale and shared use, it would be difficult for them to prevent such activities, although they control one end of the facility. As a further measure, some administrations have threatened to retaliate by imposing volume-sensitive pricing for private lines or eliminating them altogether. Either action could greatly increase the annual cost for large users of international telecommunications such as DOD and U.S. companies that use leased channels throughout the world for their internal communications. It could also have a major effect on U.S. data processing firms providing services that compete with foreign companies, and in some cases with foreign administrations as well. In addition, possible small users' gains from resale services might be reduced or eliminated if volume-sensitive pricing were initiated.

The FCC's Computer II Rulemaking. Both the First Computer Inquiry (Computer I) and the Second Computer Inquiry (Computer II) represent efforts by the FCC to redefine and limit the scope of traditional common carrier regulation, taking into account the convergence of computer and telecommunications technology.

In Computer I, the FCC drew a distinction between communications services and data processing services, and concluded that the latter were not subject to common carrier regulation under Title II of the Communications Act. This determination applied to all domestic and international services provided over common carrier facilities. As the technology advanced, however, the criteria adopted in Computer I for distinguishing between "communications" and "data processing" services became increasingly obsolete. Accordingly, the FCC adopted new criteria for determining the scope of its Title II jurisdiction, based on a distinction between "basic" and "enhanced" services. Under Computer II, providers of basic services are regulated as communications common carriers, but enhanced services fall outside the scope of the FCC's Title II jurisdiction. The FCC defined the dichotomy as follows:

> We find that basic service is limited to the common carrier offering of transmission capacity for the movement of information, whereas enhanced service combines basic service with computer processing applications that act on the format, content, code, protocol or similar aspects of the subscriber's transmitted information, or provide the subscriber additional, different, or restructured information, or involves subscriber interaction with stored information.[7]

In Computer I the FCC decided not to regulate data processing services; in Computer II, it concluded that enhanced services (which encompass both data processing and some transmission component) should not be regulated. The FCC's action in Computer II has thus served to reduce further the scope of common carrier regulation in an increasingly competitive environment. In its reconsideration of the final Computer II order, the FCC indicated that the basic/enhanced dichotomy applies to international services as well as to domestic services.[8]

While a broad variety of new services would be deregulated, Computer II does not deregulate basic transmission service nor in any major way alter the FCC's Title II jurisdiction over the common carrier transmission facilities used to provide international services. The FCC structured Computer II so that carriers authorized to own international transmission facilities must provide basic services under traditional common carrier regulation. An international carrier must therefore separate or unbundle its enhanced services from its basic services so that other enhanced service vendors can use the basic transmission facilities in a manner consistent with the carrier's tariffs governing use of the facilities.

The Commission adopted its Computer II decision in April 1980. Parties have subsequently challenged a Commission determination that the

140

basic/enhanced dichotomy applies to international services. As recently as August 1982, the FCC affirmed that Computer II applies to international services.[9] Petitions were filed seeking reconsideration of the FCC's August 1982 Order.[10] Some petitioners contend the FCC has taken precipitous action without adequately considering the international ramifications. They argue, for example, that the FCC has, in effect, already ordered international resale and thereby prejudiced the outcome of its International Resale proceeding. If this were true, there would be cause for concern over possible foreign reactions.

Insofar as resale is concerned, the FCC has made clear that Computer II in no way alters existing prohibitions against international resale. When confronted with this issue, the FCC in its August 1982 Order stated that Computer II does not "prejudge issues pending before the Commission in International Resale." Order at para. 22. This is supported by the fact that the FCC has not required carriers to alter any tariff provisions restricting third party use that were in effect prior to Computer II. In addition, Chairman Fowler in a response dated October 20, 1982, to correspondence from Mr. Burtz, Director of the CCITT, stated that "[a] ny interpretation of Computer II to the effect that the Commission has established a new policy with respect to international resale or otherwise prejudiced the outcome of the International Resale Proceeding is simply incorrect."

It appears that some misunderstanding may exist among some foreign administrations as to the effect of the FCC's Computer II decision. The cause for this uncertainty is unclear. It is apparent, however, that some of the misunderstanding can be attributed to actions taken by certain U.S. carriers. Western Union International (WUI), for example, has appended to its Petition for Reconsideration of the FCC August 1982 Order correspondence from various foreign administrations expressing concern over the Computer II decision.[11] An examination of WUI's outgoing correspondence to these foreign administrations reveals, however, that concern on their part may be premised on misunderstandings as to what the FCC did in Computer II. Statements are made in WUI's correspondence that "the FCC has held that 'enhanced services' (i.e.,

141

value added services) may be shared and resold without limitation." WUI goes on to state it concerns that "this trend might broaden the boundaries of enhanced services to include basic services such as telex, message telephone, and leased channels . . . ."

These statements appear inconsistent with past statements of the FCC and inconsistent with the underlying theory of Computer II -- that basic services would continue to be regulated as common carrier services. In addition, the Commission has stated that "application of the basic/enhanced dichotomy to the international arena will not alter existing operational relationships between enhanced service providers and their foreign correspondents. Enhanced service providers will have to adhere to established practices with respect to offering international services." (August 1982 Order at n.7.) It appears, therefore, that some misunderstanding currently exists among foreign administrations as to the scope of FCC's Computer II decision. Any misunderstanding should be clarified so that it does not needlessly precipitate actions by foreign administrations that are adverse to U.S. interests.

Issues of major concern to the U.S. are (1) the continued availability of flat rate leased circuits, (2) the possibility some foreign monopoly administrations may exploit financial arrangements to the disadvantage of U.S. industry, and (3) the potential for unfair competition resulting from unregulated foreign-owned U.S. service providers acting in concert with their overseas affiliate. While these issues will be discussed in the following sections, certain observations are warranted here. First, application of the Computer II basic/enhanced dichotomy to international services is sound public policy. There is no need to subject enhanced services provided over common carrier facilities to a common carrier scheme of regulation. Experience gained over the last decade as a result of Computer I demonstrates this. Second, even though individual enhanced services are not subject to traditional common carrier regulation, regulatory action may be required to prevent foreign entities from utilizing U.S. transmission facilities to the competitive disadvantage of U.S. service vendors.

142

Whether the FCC can provide effective regulatory safeguards sufficient to protect U.S. interests in an unregulated environment remains to be seen. Under Computer II the FCC retains a full panopoly of regulatory authorities to license common carrier facilities and regulate their use. The court of appeals has affirmed the FCC's ancillary authority with respect to enhanced services where necessary to effectuate the FCC statutory mandate. AT&T v. FCC, 572 F.2d 17 (2d Cir. 1978). How the FCC will exercise its jurisdiction to safeguard U.S. international communications interests is unclear. The FCC appears to be proceeding on the assumption that so long as it retains jurisdiction to regulate the common carrier transmission facilities, over which enhanced services are provided, it will be able adequately to meet its responsibilities in accord with its statutory mandate.

Current Policy. Restrictions on third party use are currently contained in the tariffs of various international carriers. These restrictions serve to prohibit resale of private line services. The FCC is currently examining whether these resale restrictions should be removed.

The FCC has deregulated various services provided internationally. Computer II removes the provision of international enhanced services from the scope of common carrier regulation under Title II of the Communications Act. While the FCC has removed regulatory barriers to entry, an enhanced service may be offered internationally only if it is provided consistent with tariff provisions governing the use of common carrier transmission facilities and meets the approval of foreign administrations.

### International Private Leased Service

Private leased service[12] is one of three basic network options — public switched, packet switched, and private leased networks. Large users, both U.S. and foreign, make extensive use of all three options in order to satisfy different technical needs. Private leased service is especially important to maintain highly-sophisticated business networks, because of the following unique advantages:

143

(1)     Private lines permit the user to attach customer premises equipment of the latest technology, thereby maximizing circuit utilization. Private lines thus encourage innovative technology.

(2)     Private line circuits offer more efficient and technically superior services, including quicker response time and a broader range of applications.

(3)     Private lease offers substantial cost savings for a user with sufficient traffic to cover the relatively high fixed costs involved.

The continuation of international private leased service is a seldom-recognized but important U.S. concern. In part because of the controversy over application of the FCC's Computer II and international resale actions, some overseas administrations may review their policies concerning private leased service. Should this happen, the U.S. business community and the Department of Defense would face major cost increases for international telecommunications, estimated in DOD's case to be as high as 300-700 percent.

Private leased service is technically feasible even in an Integrated Services Digital Network (ISDN). Not all foreign administrations that favor ISDN are opposed to private leased service. In fact, there are distinct economic, technical, and political advantages to retention of private leased service by other countries. In order to retain this type of service within an ISDN environment, however, the U.S. Government must promote it vigorously, while encouraging broader participation in the ISDN development process.

## International Operating Agreements

One impediment to increased entry of  U.S. service providers  into international telecommunications markets has been the reluctance of foreign administrations to sign operating agreements with additional U.S. carriers. In most cases, an operating agreement must be negotiated by a U.S. carrier and foreign administration prior to the initiation of direct telecommunications service between countries.  The operating agreement usually sets all relevant financial and operating arrangements.

144

Most foreign administrations appear reluctant to operate with a large number of carriers, because there are added administrative and operating costs associated with each new carrier. Although not all European markets may be large enough to support an unlimited number of U.S. carriers, recent actions by some European administrations have nonetheless caused concern in the United States. The Nordic and Benelux countries recently indicated interest in possibly limiting the number of U.S. carriers for public data communications service between those countries and the United States, on the basis of competitive bids.

Even prior to deregulation, U.S. policy favored multiple suppliers in the record communications marketplace. The Nordic-Benelux proposals were originally perceived as a step backwards from the status quo, because they implied an interest in reducing the number of carriers of a particular service to only one -- creating single carrier exclusivity.

The positions of the Nordic and Benelux administrations were clarified after they became aware of several U.S. concerns. Informal discussions between representatives of the U.S. Government and the Nordic and Benelux administrations were held in Paris during January 1983. These discussions have led the U.S. to interpret each inquiry in the following manner:

> — The inquiry should not be understood as a formal request for competitive bids, but as a commercial inquiry seeking information about new services previously unavailable;
>
> — It is, similarly, not intended to lead to renegotiation of existing arrangements, but is a preliminary inquiry about interconnection with U.S. carriers for the new services;
>
> — Interconnection with multiple (four, five or more) U.S. carriers for new services is envisaged;
>
> — There is no intention to alter current arrangements in respect to accounting rates and their division.[13]

Current U.S. policy is to encourage an environment in which users are free to choose among competing suppliers on the basis of price and service quality. To this end, the United States favors an international market in which new carriers are free to enter, and long-term exclusive arrangements between foreign administrations and U.S. firms are not permitted.

## Financial Arrangements for International Switched Services

The mechanism used to divide the revenues earned by jointly-provided international telecommunications switched services between U.S. carriers and foreign administrations is known as the accounting and settlement process.[14] Unfortunately, without U.S. Government oversight, this process could be used by foreign administrations to "whipsaw" one U.S. carrier against another. The current policy of the FCC is intended to help prevent such exploitation.

U.S. carriers generally share revenues from the switched services with their foreign correspondents, based on a negotiated "accounting rate." This rate is distinguished from the "collection rate" (the rate the customer pays) at either terminal. During a given month, if the number of paid minutes from calls billed in both countries is equal, the U.S. carrier and its foreign correspondent would be entitled to the same amount of accounting rate revenues, and no transfer of funds would be required. If, however, the number of paid minutes is greater in one direction than the other, the carrier with the higher outbound paid minutes must make a payment to its correspondent.[15]

In 1980, for example, there were more inbound minutes (to the United States) of both telex and packet switched services than outbound, and more outbound (from the United States) telephone minutes and telegraph words than inbound. Therefore, the U.S. carrier industry as a whole was in a receivable or creditor position with respect to telex and packet switched services, and was in a payable or debtor position with respect to message telephone and telegraph services.

The term "whipsaw" has been defined by the FCC as "the ability of the foreign correspondent to utilize its monopoly power to play one carrier against others to gain concessions and benefits from the U.S. international carriers."[16] In the past, only international record carriers (IRCs) have been deemed vulnerable to "whipsawing"; switched international voice services were supplied by just one carrier, AT&T, in the continental United States. The FCC authorized the IRCs to provide voice services in its decision of December, 1982. Carriers such as Comsat, MCI, and others may also provide voice services if they can obtain the necessary operating agreements with foreign administrations.

In the past, the foreign administrations have had the potential power to "whipsaw" the IRCs for two reasons: (1) the foreign administrations are typically monopolists, with the power to choose which U.S. carriers they will have an operating agreement with; and (2) these administrations generally control the distribution of return traffic to the United States among those carriers with whom they have signed operating agreements.

As an example of "whipsawing," a foreign administration might insist that a new telex carrier agree to a telex accounting rate lower than the prevailing rate in order to be allowed to interconnect with that country. Alternatively, an established carrier might be threatened with a reduction in its share of return traffic if it did not agree to a lower telex accounting rate. Once the accounting rate for one carrier is lowered, other U.S. carriers would have to agree to reduced accounting rates, to avoid a loss of inbound telex traffic.

The process can then be repeated by the foreign administration, starting with a different carrier. In this fashion, one carrier can be played off against the others, with the foreign administration constantly gaining a larger share of total revenues. "Whipsawing" thus diverts revenues from the U.S. industry to the foreign administrations, and reduces the potential for any significant reduction in U.S. users' rates.

"Whipsawing" could actually result in increased rates for U.S. users. On one hand, the U.S. carriers may simply "swallow" their loss, with no resultant compensatory rise in the U.S. collection rate. On the other hand, the carriers may have to compensate for the revenue loss by raising the U.S. collection rate. In either event, however, the U.S. balance of payments is adversely affected.

The marketplace cannot adequately protect the U.S. industry from the monopolistic tactics of foreign administrations in the accounting and settlement process. Once it became evident that "whipsawing" could occur, some U.S.

147

Government intervention was necessary to protect the U.S. industry. The Government agency most deeply involved in the process has been the Federal Communications Commission (FCC).

To prevent "whipsawing," the FCC in 1980 reaffirmed a long-standing policy requiring uniform settlement rate agreements on parallel international routes.[17] This means that all carriers must abide by the same accounting and settlement arrangements for the same destination. However, the policy as reaffirmed by the Commission allows some departures from uniformity. The Commission has stated:

> We will consider, on a case-by-case basis, waivers of the policy of uniformity. Our consideration of a waiver request will be in accordance with the public interest standard and will include examination of the potential effects of a grant on the ratepayer, the carrier, and the industry.[18]

This uniform settlement policy prevents "whipsawing" by foreign administrations, while allowing for waivers if such action is demonstrably in the public interest. Such a policy strengthens the industry, promotes lower consumer rates, and contributes to a favorable U.S. balance of payments in telecommunication services. Under Computer II as presently interpreted, however, the uniform accounting and settlement policy would not apply to enhanced services.

## Foreign Entry into U.S. International Telecommunications Service Markets

In recent years, as U.S. deregulation has continued, the U.S. telecommunications service markets have become increasingly attractive to foreign entities. A number of U.S. carriers and Government agencies, as well as Congress, have expressed concern about the openness of U.S. service markets in contrast to the continuing lack of such openness abroad. In this situation, with the lack of truly reciprocal overseas markets, there may be a need to determine to what extent foreign entry into U.S. international telecommunication markets could result in unfair competition with U.S.-owned firms. This is an issue Congress, in any event, is likely to address.

148

In general, the United States has sought mutually open international markets in services as well as equipment, as a matter of sound trade policy. Open world markets offer the consumer lower prices, better quality, and greater diversity; new technologies may be more rapidly exploited; exports are stimulated; and worldwide employment opportunities are expanded. In such a mutually open environment, foreign entry into U.S. domestic and international telecommunications service markets would be highly beneficial. In services as in product markets, however, it is important to assure that competition is fair both in U.S. and foreign markets.

In the product area, if a foreign company engages in "dumping" — flooding the U.S. market with large amounts of an item at an unjustifiably low price —U.S. companies can take legal action. Equivalent legal protections do not exist for services. While consumers may benefit in the short run from "dumped" services, the practice could have serious long term effects if it weakens U.S. industry and endangers the success of procompetitive policies. The United States should therefore be prepared to act against unfair competition in U.S. markets by foreign-owned telecommunications service providers.

There is always some potential for anticompetitive conduct implicit in a market in which numerous firms are competing vigorously. When a telecommunications firm operating in the United States is owned by a foreign government,[19] additional competitive issues arise:

(1)     The foreign-owned firm may be able to benefit from discriminatory access to markets in the foreign country, through the parent foreign administration's monopoly control of the foreign half of international transmission facilities and networks.

(2)     Foreign-owned U.S. firms may be able to benefit from more favorable financial arrangements with the parent country than are afforded U.S. firms.

(3)     The foreign country may be willing to provide the foreign-owned firm with service between the United States and third countries at a lower cost than is offered to U.S.-owned firms (for example, service from the U.S. to Singapore, via Hong Kong).

(4)     The foreign-owned firm may be able to benefit from a disproportionate share of return traffic from the parent country or countries.

149

Some of the practices described above could have some distortional effects and might be difficult to detect. Unfair competition by foreign-owned firms could be detrimental to the interests of the United States, and could have adverse effects on trade and national security.

The FCC has deregulated domestic resale carriers. There are statutory restrictions on foreign ownership of firms holding radio frequency licenses (47 U.S.C. Sec 310(b)). Foreign entities, however, can obtain transmission capacity from common carriers to provide basic or enhanced services. The Commission's recent Authorized User decision allows noncarriers to obtain transmission capacity from Comsat. Since the Commission did not restrict the types of entities that could obtain satellite circuits directly from Comsat, foreign entities can obtain, on an end-to-end basis, an international satellite circuit for private or commercial use. A foreign firm could operate in conjunction with a foreign administration in a discriminatory manner to the detriment of U.S. service vendors.

Anticompetitive activities by a domestic firm that have an impact on U.S. commerce are subject to the antitrust laws, whether the firm is U.S. or foreign owned. The fact of non-U.S. ownership confers no immunity from possibly severe antitrust sanctions. At present antidumping laws do not apply to the telecommunications services market. There are no explicit statutory requirements governing disclosure of financing, ownership, and other relevant information that are unique to foreign-owned firms. Authority to investigate anticompetitive activity by foreign-owned or other providers of enhanced services would reside in the Commission's ancillary jurisdiction respecting competition in commerce (e.g., 47 U.S.C. Sec. 313, 314). The stated policy of the U.S. Government has been to sanction foreign investment in this country and participation in our economy by foreign firms. The United States thus does not oppose the involvement of foreign-owned entities in our competitive telecommunications marketplace. At the same time, the potential competitive issues posed by such involvement that may be unique to telecommunications should be recognized.

150

### Competition for Voice Services

During 1981, international record services in the U.S. accounted for only 19 percent of total international telecommunications revenues, whereas international voice service revenues were responsible for 81 percent[20] of the total. Congress and the FCC in recent years, however, have concentrated on increasing record service competition, and have paid comparatively little attention to competitive conditions in the voice market.

The Record Carrier Competition Act (RCCA) of 1981 amended Section 222 of the Communications Act of 1934, in order to improve domestic and international telecommunications competition in record service.[21] The new Act allows the Western Union Telegraph Company to compete in the international arena, and the IRCs to offer domestic telecommunications, without prior FCC authorization. It also requires nondiscriminatory interconnection among all record carriers. Recently, interpreting the general requirements of the RCCA, the FCC (a) required record carriers to unbundle their overseas transmission charges into separate domestic and international components, (b) established provisions to determine the charges for domestic handling of international traffic, and (c) established a formula to negate any advantage an IRC may derive from an operating agreement with a country that refuses to grant one to another U.S. carrier. The FCC has also released a Report and Order which eliminated the voice/record dichotomy in the provision of international service.[22]

Interconnection of voice services may be addressed by the FCC in the future. To ensure fair competition in the voice market, the FCC should, at a minimum, take steps similar to those adopted in the record communications business concerning interconnection. Unbundling of overseas transmission charges for voice services into separate domestic and international components as presently required for record services may be also necessary. These and other approaches to foster competition need to be evaluated.

### U.S. Participation in CCI Standards Activities in a Deregulated Environment

International consensus on technical and operating standards and tariff principles is reached in the International Telecommunication Union (ITU). The

151

results are incorporated in ITU regulations and in the recommendations of the International Radio Consultative Committee (CCIR) and the International Telephone and Telegraph Consultative Committee (CCITT).

United States participation in ITU activities is ultimately the responsibility of the Department of State. U.S. working groups of the CCIR and CCITT include representatives from industry, users, and various agencies of the Federal Government. The delegations are always headed by a U.S. Government representative.

In U.S. CCITT working groups, where preparations are made for international meetings, the Federal Government must act as organizer, mediator, and catalyst in arriving at consensus views among industry representatives. In U.S. CCIR preparatory groups, by contrast, industry plays a different role because the Federal Government has a direct responsibility for most matters covered in the CCIR. Although members of U.S. industry submit company papers and make presentations at international meetings, particularly CCITT meetings, only Federal officials can state the U.S. position. (There have recently been proposals to modify this restriction.)

The recommendations of these international committees are legally voluntary but are generally accepted throughout the world. Those in which the United States has concurred are the functional equivalent of international agreements. The U.S. Government ensures compliance with these international recommendations within the United States, principally by means of the authority granted the FCC under the Communications Act of 1934. The FCC powers consist primarily of tariff and certificate authority governing new carrier facilities and services (Title II) and radio licensing authority (Title III). In addition, radio frequencies for U.S. Government use are controlled and assigned by NTIA pursuant to section 305 of the 1934 Act and under authority granted it by Executive Order 12046. NTIA's responsibilities in this regard are carried out in accordance with ITU rules and recommendations.

152

## Recommendations

Some Government involvement in the international telecommunications arena is required to protect vital U.S. interests. Full and fair competition cannot be ensured without Government oversight, as long as foreign administrations resist movement toward a truly competitive international marketplace.

At present, the United States is promoting a competitive marketplace while much of the world still lags behind. Other governments have taken commendable initiatives to foster competition, although more needs to be done.

The United States should continue aggressively to seek a more competitive international communications marketplace. We must make clearer to other nations that competition does not constitute a threat to their sovereignty and that the benefits of competition are substantial. We should also indicate that the same technological forces driving competition in the United States are having similar effects abroad. A possible approach would be for the United States to have more high level discussions with those segments of foreign governments concerned with foreign policy and economic matters. These policymakers would have less of a vested interest in the existing telecommunications arrangements of their countries and could see the broader benefits of competition to users, consumers, and equipment suppliers.

153

NOTES TO CHAPTER SIX

[1]On December 12, 1979, the Commission took action in the following cases related to competition in international services:

 (1) International Audit and Study, 75 FCC 2d 726 (1980);

 (2) International Gateways, 76 FCC 2d 115 (1980);

 (3) International DATAPHONE, 75 FCC 2d 682 (1980);

 (4) Alternate Voice/Data Service and Interconnection with Domestic Network, 76 FCC 2d 166 (1980);

 (5) Interface of International and Domestic Telex and TWX Services, 76 FCC 2d 61 (1980);

 (6) New Telex Service Arrangement via Mexico and Canada, 75 FCC 2d 461 (1980);

 (7) Consortium Communications International, Inc., 76 FCC 2d 15 (1980); and

 (8) Regulation of Domestic Public Message Service, 75 FCC 2d 345 (1980)

[2]The NTIA study focused on Australia, Austria, Belgium, Brazil, Canada, France, West Germany, Hong Kong, Italy, Japan, Mexico, Philippines, Singapore, Sweden, Switzerland, the United Kingdom, and Venezuela.

[3]Resale and Shared Use of Common Carrier Services and Facilities, 60 FCC 2d 261 (1976); MTS/WATS Resale & Sharing, 80 F.C.C. 2d 54 (1980).

[4]Resale and Shared Use of Common Carrier Services and Facilities, 62 FCC 2d 588, 593 (1977) (reconsideration).

[5]CCITT Orange Book, Vol. II.1, "General Tariff Principles, Lease of Circuits for Private Services," p. 83 (VIth Plenary Assembly, Geneva 1977).

[6]International Resale, 77 FCC 2d 840 (1980) (notice).

[7]Amendment of Section 64.702 of the Commission's Rules and Regulations (Final Decision), 77 FCC 2d 384, (1980).

[8]Amendment of Section 64.702 of the Commission's Rules and Regulations (Reconsideration), 84 FCC 2d 50, 53 fn 4 (1980).

154

[9]FCC Memorandum Opinion and Order, "GTE Telenet Communications Corporation and Tymnet, Inc." Authority to extend Packet-Switched Services to Western Europe, released August 25, 1982.

[10]Petitions for reconsideration of the FCC Memorandum Opinion and Order of August 25, 1982, were filed by WUI, RCA Global Communications Inc., Association of Data Processing Organizations, Inc., and International Communications Association. These petitions were supported by Control Data Corporation and GTE Corporation. Aeronautical Radio, Inc., and IBM supported having Computer II apply to the international arena.

[11]Western Union International, Inc., Petition for Reconsideration in the matter of GTE Telenet Communications Corporation and in the matter of Tymnet, Inc., Appendix A, September 24, 1982.

[12]Private leased line service in this chapter refers to the use of voice grade circuit bandwidths and greater.

[13]Letters from Matthew V. Scocozza, Deputy Assistant Secretary for Transportation and Telecommunications, Department of State, to Nordic and Benelux Administrations, January 28, 1983.

[14]Leased channel services do not entail such a process. Each administration charges a monthly rate for its half-circuit (from the country to the theoretical midpoint of the path.)

[15]The description of the process has been simplified somewhat for purposes of explanation.

[16]Uniform Settlement Rates on Parallel International Communications Routes, 84 FCC 2d 121, 122 n. 3 (1980).

[17]Uniform Settlement Rates, 66 FCC 2d 359 (1977) (notice); 84 FCC 2d 121 (1980) (order).

[18]84 FCC 2d at 128.

[19]For example, Pacnet Communications Corporation (PACNET), a resale common carrier, is a wholly-owned subsidiary of Cable and Wireless PLC, of which the British government owns 49 percent. Cable and Wireless and its affiliates serve as the Recognized Private Operating Agency (RPOA) for a large number of countries around the world.

[20]Includes AT&T and four other voice carriers. See Federal Communications Commission, Statistics of Communications Common Carriers, Tables 14 and 25 (1981).

[21]Pub. L. No. 97-130 (Dec. 29, 1981); 47 U.S.C. § 222.

[22]FCC Report and Order, Overseas Communications Services, CC Docket No. 80-632, released December 22, 1982.

Chapter Seven

TRADE IN EQUIPMENT AND SERVICES

U.S. policies concerning trade in telecommunications and information equipment and services are developed under a separate rubric from other international telecommunications policies -- the rubric of international trade as a whole. Because of the distance between trade and telecommunications institutions -- between the USTR and the FCC, or between the GATT and the ITU -- there is some danger of a lack of coherence or consistency within the policymaking apparatus. Nonetheless, the importance of the telecommunications and information industries is increasingly recognized in trade circles.

The major part of this chapter is devoted to a discussion of trade in telecommunications and information equipment. At the end of the chapter, however, an effort is made to explain the special problems posed by service-related barriers to trade and investment.

## The U.S. Equipment Trade Position

The term "telecommunications and information equipment" could be interpreted to cover an almost unlimited variety of products that play a role in the transmission or processing of information.[1] In order to provide a manageable discussion, this chapter concentrates on three major equipment categories: (1) telecommunications equipment (SIC 3661 and 3662); (2) computing equipment (SIC 3573); and (3) electronic components (SIC 367).[2]

Each of these industries constitutes a large and rapidly growing sector of the U.S. economy. In 1982, product shipments amounted to $26 billion for telecommunications equipment, $33 billion for computing equipment, and $28 billion for electronic components. In the last decade, all three industries have grown much more rapidly than U.S. manufacturing as a whole. The telecommunications and electronics components sectors have experienced real annual growth of 8 percent and 10 percent respectively, while the computer industry has grown at an 18 percent annual rate. By contrast, the overall U.S. output of electrical and electronic machinery has averaged only 4.3 percent real growth, and U.S. manufacturing as a whole has inched along at 1.2 percent per year.[3] Estimates for the telecommunications equipment market in 1987 indicate a U.S. market of about $34 billion and a world market of just under $60 billion.

In the material that follows, a rough "trade picture" is drawn for each of the three industries, discussing (1) the trend of U.S. exports and imports over the last decade; (2) the importance of exports and imports relative to overall U.S. production and consumption in that industry; and (3) the U.S. share of world export markets. It will also be helpful to compare the trade status of these industries with that of U.S. manufacturers as a whole. Our manufacturers have become significantly more export-oriented, with manufacturing exports increasing from 6.6 percent of total shipments in 1973 to 10 percent in 1980.[4] Imports as a percentage of domestic consumption have increased in a similar fashion. However, the United States still has a long way to go before these percentages match those of most other industrialized countries.

Telecommunications Equipment. The Commerce Department classifies telecommunications equipment in two main categories, SIC 3661 and 3662, making an overall evaluation difficult. The first category, SIC 3661 ("telephone and telegraph equipment"), contains the type of equipment and facilities traditionally used for point-to-point communications, but it does not include a variety of advanced products such as fiber-optic cables, microwave systems, mobile radios, facsimile machines, and satellite facilities. These are included in SIC 3662 ("radio and television communicating equipment"), along with broadcasting and a wide variety of specialized equipment. This category has been modified for our purposes.[5]

In SIC 3661, U.S. exports have increased substantially since 1972, from about 2 percent of U.S. production to about 5.5 percent. Imports have increased mainly in the last five years, from less than 2 percent in 1977 to almost 5 percent of U.S. consumption in 1982. Both sets of figures, however, are substantially below those for U.S. exports and imports as a whole.

157

The relatively backward U.S. export position in this type of equipment can be attributed to a number of factors. First, the U.S. industry, while technologically formidable, has been severely handicapped by the voluntary, decades-long exile from the world market of the industry giant, Western Electric. Second, in most of the developed world, telecommunications continues to be a heavily regulated, highly concentrated industry, in which a single buyer (usually a "PTT" or government administrative agency) purchases most telecommunications equipment from a handful of favored suppliers, usually domestic. Thus, telecommunications equipment imports by developed countries have always been substar.tially smaller than in technologically similar industries.

In the modified SIC 3662 category, on the other hand, the export figures are more substantial: approximately 13 percent of 1982 production was exported. In the subclassification "broadcasting equipment" (including cable and closed circuit television systems), exports accounted for over 20 percent of U.S. production. In the subclassification "communications systems and equipment (except broadcast)," which includes fiber-optics, microwave, and satellite systems, as well as mobile radio and facsimile equipment, close to 15 percent of U.S. production was exported. If the SIC 3661 and modified 3662 categories are combined, it can be inferred that exports accounted for about 9 percent of 1982 industry shipments.

By contrast, as early as 1975, the other six major equipment exporting countries all exported over 10 percent of production, and the percentages have probably increased since then. In the SIC 3661 category, the U.S. share of 1981 telecommunications exports came to 13 percent -- smaller than those of Japan, West Germany, and Sweden. The same data indicate that, in the last five years, the U.S. share of telecommunications exports is growing faster than that of any other major exporting country except Canada and Japan. However, imports to the United States are growing even faster. As a result, the U.S. trade surplus in SIC 3661 telecommunications equipment is growing much slower than that of other leading countries, with the exception of Britain and Italy.

Computing Equipment. This sector includes all varieties of computing equipment, from desktop "personal" computers to large-scale supercomputers. It

158

also includes equipment such as disk drives and printers, which can be used for either computers or other office machinery such as word processors. Since 1977, computer exports have leveled off at 25-30 percent of total U. S. production, while imports have suddenly risen from 2.6 to 8.2 percent of U. S. consumption. The lion's share of U. S. imports, as in the case of telecommunications equipment, comes from Japan and East Asia. The U.S. share of OECD computer exports was 46 percent in 1982. For computers and office machines (such as typewriters and word processors) combined, the U. S. export share has remained fairly constant for the last decade at about 35 percent.[6]

Interestingly, while the United States and Japan have the largest shares of OECD computer exports, the three largest European producers (France, West Germany, and Britain) are all more export-intensive than either of the leading countries, with West Germany and Britain exporting well over 50 percent of their production. On the other hand, these three European countries are also leading importers, and each has a negative trade balance in computer equipment.

Electronic Components. Electronic components industries (SIC 367) provide many of the key ingredients of telecommunications and computing equipment. As in the equipment industries, imports are growing faster than exports. Since 1977, exports have remained relatively stable at 18-20 percent of total production, while imports have increased from 15 to 20 percent of consumption. The U. S. share of OECD electronic components exports has decreased from about 40 percent in 1970 to 27 or 28 percent in 1980. A key indicator of declining U. S. competitiveness in these industries is our trade balance with Japan in integrated circuits, which in 1978 moved from surplus to deficit. In 1982, it is estimated that United States imports from Japan were almost three times as large as our exports from that country. In 1983, for the first time, the United States is expected to have a slight deficit with the rest of the world in the electronic components sector as a whole.

In summary, the U. S. telecommunications equipment industry is only beginning to become a major export sector for the United States, mainly because of Western Electric's voluntary exile from export markets and the difficulties of

159

exporting to monopsonistic markets. Although exports in this sector are growing rapidly, imports are growing even faster. In the computing equipment industry, on the other hand, the United States has long held a dominant share of the world export market, but is beginning to face strong challenges from Japan and other countries. Finally, the decline in relative competitiveness that is feared by U.S. computer makers has apparently arrived for at least part of the electronic components industry. The Japanese, and increasingly other manufacturers in the Far East and Latin America, have eroded the U.S. position in that sector.

The discussion below presents issues and options in four general categories of trade policy:

o    elimination of foreign barriers to U.S. exports and extension of trade agreements;

o    protection of U.S. suppliers from unfair foreign competition;

o    improvement of export promotion and removal of U.S. export barriers; and

o    treatment of telecommunications and information services under trade policy.

## Reduction of Trade Barriers

One aspect of the trade dilemma that the United States faces in telecommunications and information is the reduction of barriers to free trade and investment in the equipment industries. Among the barriers that have been erected or maintained by countries throughout the world are the following:

o    Traditional trade barriers such as quotas and tariffs are still used, especially in developing countries, but have been replaced in many countries by non-tariff barriers such as those listed below.

o    Government procurement policies may constitute the most serious trade barriers in the telecommunications industry, and also provide significant protection for data-processing and other information industries. A majority of telecommunications equipment is purchased by government agencies. In some countries, government procurement is subject to explicit "buy-national" policies. In others, discrimination against foreign suppliers occurs informally, often through failure to adequately publicize bidding opportunities or unexplained delays for approval of products offered.

160

o   Technical Standards have also functioned as significant trade
    barriers, inasmuch as even terminal equipment must be approved by a
    PTT before it can be sold. Standards of other countries are often
    different from those in the United States, and have arguably been
    applied to discriminate against U.S. firms.   In addition, the
    equipment approval process often results in long and unnecessary
    delays. Technical standards appear to pose a greater obstacle in the
    telecommunications than in the information equipment sector.

o   Industry-targeting practices aimed at promoting a country's domestic
    telecommunications and information industries, through subsidies,
    loans, tax breaks, government-business joint ventures, and market
    segmentation, can create major barriers to importation.

o   Performance requirements, including local content or employment
    quotas and technology transfer requirements, are imposed on
    subsidiaries of foreign manufacturers in order to support local
    production. These import substitution policies are most commonly
    used by developing countries, but in the telecommunications and
    information sectors, they are also being practiced by industrialized
    countries.

Trade Agreements.   In negotiating for a reduction of such barriers, the
United States suffers from a lack of bargaining chips -- trade restrictions of our
own that can be exchanged for the reduction of trade barriers in other countries.
In the telecommunications sector, the United States was the first country to decide
that its government-regulated monopoly should give way to a more competitive
industry structure.  Moreover, the United States has until recently perceived little
need to intervene to protect or promote our computer and electronics industries.
Trade barriers are more likely to be found in declining U.S. industry sectors than
in growing ones.

As a result, other countries have good reason to believe that they can freely
enter the U.S. market without opening their own markets in return.  It is not
particularly surprising, therefore, that U.S. efforts to negotiate for more liberal
government procurement practices and technical standards requirements, limits on
government-subsidized R&D, and a floor on export financing terms have met with
limited success.

161

A major negotiating setback for the United States was the refusal of European countries to allow coverage of PTT (i.e., telecommunications) purchasing under the GATT Government Procurement Code. Although the United States has concluded a separate telecommunications procurement agreement with Japan, further success in reducing barriers will not come easily. The Government Procurement Code is scheduled for review in 1984.

Even after agreements have been reached, there is the further problem of their implementation and enforcement. Identifying violations is not at all easy, because they often take the form of subtle discouragement rather than explicit rejection of imports. For example, the U.S.-Japan telecommunications procurement agreement has so far produced little in the way of NTT orders from U.S. suppliers. Since the time of this agreement, Japanese exports of telecommunications equipment have increased by over 60 percent, from about $400 million to about $660 million in 1981. The Electronics Industry Association estimates that in 1982, telecommunications equipment imports from Japan were approximately $1 billion, while U.S. exports to Japan were about $40 million.

In view of the difficulties encountered in making agreements and enforcing them, there has been growing sentiment in favor of a more aggressive U.S. stance. For example, in 1981-82 there was considerable Congressional support for adoption of a "reciprocity" policy, in which U.S. equipment imports from a given country would be conditioned on the hospitality of the latter to U.S. exports, regardless of any agreement. Such proposals were included in various bills. A "sectoral" approach to reciprocity, however, has been strongly opposed by the Administration.

Options

o    Continue negotiating for extended GATT coverage of telecommunications procurement policies and other import barriers.

The advantages of negotiating in the GATT are that it reinforces the post-war trading system, in which world trade and economic interdependence have achieved unprecedented progress, and there is also a common framework of principles to serve as the basis for agreements. Moreover, agreements made in the

162

GATT cover a majority of countries. The main disadvantage is that the negotiation and enforcement of GATT agreements take a long time. In addition, there is some doubt as to whether other countries would be willing to enter a multilateral agreement on telecommunications and computing equipment, and as to how the U.S. might induce the unwilling to participate.

o <u>Pursue bilateral agreements</u> with key countries in the telecommunications and information equipment sector.

This approach may be particularly effective in addressing the problems posed by a country such as Japan, which not only maintains an effective array of import barriers, but also poses a significant competitive threat to the U.S. in the high-technology sector.

o <u>Develop "linkage"</u> between the telecommunications and information sectors and other industries, in order to increase negotiating leverage and define issues.

For "linkage" to be used effectively, the United States must be willing to trade-off barriers in its declining industries. Unfortunately, domestic pressure for continuing protection of such typically labor-intensive industries may often outweigh any incentives to exchange them for export opportunities in thriving sectors.

o <u>Enact sectoral reciprocity legislation</u> for the telecommunications and information equipment industries.

Under sectoral reciprocity legislation, foreign suppliers' access to U.S. markets would be conditional on "equivalent" access of U.S. firms to the corresponding foreign markets. One appeal of such a policy is its conceptual simplicity. A major disadvantage is that it would almost certainly lead to violation of U.S. treaty obligations, triggering a chain reaction of protectionist counter-measures. Sectoral legislation operates automatically: it is triggered by a finding that U.S. products have been excluded, and there is only limited discretion to withhold sanctions for foreign policy reasons. Such an automatically triggered sanction could violate the GATT in two ways: (1) by bypassing the established

163

GATT complaint procedure, and (2) by erecting trade barriers which are illegal under the GATT. Thus, sectoral legislation would provide other countries with a legal excuse for retaliation against the United States in other sectors.

In addition, sectoral reciprocity legislation would accomplish little unless the offending country valued access to the U. S. market as much as or more than we value access to theirs. In the computer industry, for example, only a few countries are in a position to benefit from open U. S. markets to the same extent as we stand to benefit from access to their markets. Where a sectoral approach is likely to be successful, it should be pursued under a more flexible statutory structure.

Sectoral legislation has been strongly opposed by the Reagan Administration and could lead to serious disruption of the GATT system.[7] Nevertheless, there is likely to be further Congressional pressure for such legislation if current economic conditions persist.

o    Strengthen the Executive branch's authority to retaliate against the most harmful foreign trade barriers.

Under this option the U. S. would retaliate against closed foreign markets, where appropriate, but the occasions for retaliation and the means chosen would remain within the Executive branch's discretion. If credibly exercised, such a policy could be more effective than sectoral legislation, and would involve less risk of violating treaty obligations.

Statutory authority for such retaliation exists, under section 301 of the Trade Act of 1974. Section 301 could be particularly effective as a response to foreign actions that impair the United States' obligations under the GATT and other agreements, but which are not easily provable under other trade laws (see below). However, the section 301 process as currently practiced works extremely slowly. Additionally, section 103 of the Revenue Act of 1971 (26 U.S.C. Sec. 48(a)(7)(d)) delegates to the President authority to suspend eligibility of foreign-made products for the investment tax credit when he determines that a foreign government has unjustifiably restricted U.S. commerce by its "tolerance of international cartels." Petitions urging the exercise of such authority have been

164

filed with the U.S. Trade Representative. The value of this potential remedy has not yet been established, however.

Unfair Foreign Competition

The telecommunications and information industries have been "targeted" for government-promoted growth by increasing numbers of both industrialized and developing countries. The result of this "targeting" phenomenon, it is widely believed, is to render obsolete the United States' traditional mechanisms for preventing unfair foreign competition in its domestic telecommunications and information markets. Although these domestic industries remain generally strong, specific sectors within them have been successfully challenged by foreign imports.

The following are the basic kinds of "targeting" practices that have been identified by the Department of Commerce with respect to high-technology industries:

o    Financial assistance and fiscal incentives are used by many countries to "target" the telecommunications and information industries by means of direct subsidies, loans, or tax incentives. Assistance for R&D is particularly commonplace, because the telecommunications and information industries are R&D-intensive and because R&D investment entails considerable risk.

o    Government participation in the economic development of domestic telecommunications and information industries often can result in unfair export practices. Such participation may take the form of authorization for intercorporate cooperation and market segmentation activity, government-industry joint ventures in R&D, and government direction of capital or credit to specific sectors.

o    Import barriers such as those described in the preceding subsection have an indirect export-promotion effect when they are applied to "targeted" industries.

Existing Unfair Trade Practice Laws. Industry-targeting practices are not easily addressed by existing U.S. trade laws. Violations take a long time to prosecute, and are often difficult to prove under the present anti-dumping and countervailing-duty statutes. When a case can eventually be proved, the unfair practice may have changed the competitive situation to an extent that cannot be

165

compensated by provable damages. There is growing sentiment that these statutes should be revised to streamline procedures and ease the burden of proof. Such revision would be particulary useful in the high-technology industries involved here, because the lapse of time and the difficulty of proof make prosecutions especially problematic for those industries.

Options

o      Streamline existing laws by tightening deadlines, providing for interim relief, and for permitting "fast-track" treatment of the most serious cases.

o      Enact new legislation that widens the coverage of existing unfair-competition laws, and eases the burden of proof for industry-targeting practices in high-technology industries.

o      Conduct aggressive bilateral negotiations with those countries in which targeting practices pose a serious threat to fair competition in U. S. telecommunications and information markets.

o      Consider use of 1971 Revenue Act sanctions in appropriate circumstances, as discussed above.

Export Promotion and Self-Imposed Barriers

In the telecommunications and information equipment sector, export promotion has assumed greater importance for a number of reasons. First, this export sector is viewed as a prime growth sector of the world economy that is increasingly important to the U.S. trade balance. Second, the sector is characterized by a variety of non-tariff barriers and diverse business practices in different parts of the world; Government assistance can be crucial in helping U.S. firms to circumvent barriers and understand business practices. Third, the sector has seen a proliferation of small suppliers of terminal equipment, computers, and electronic components, who are particularly in need of trade development assistance. Fourth, especially in the telecommunications equipment sector, many companies -- even large ones -- are only recently exploring export markets, or are seeking markets in countries that have just begun to modernize their telecommunications networks. For all these reasons, the Department of

166

Commerce's export promotion programs could play a key role over the next two decades in establishing or maintaining a healthy export sector.

In addition to traditional export promotion activities, the Government can also affect the health of the export sector by removing or moderating the impact of laws and regulations that act as a disincentive to exports. Such disincentives are created by a variety of U. S. laws, including tax, regulatory, patent, antitrust, and export control statutes. In addition, U. S. policies on research and development and the availability of export credit may act as export incentives or disincentives.

Trade Development Programs. Traditional export promotion (or trade development) activity is carried out primarily by the Commerce Department's International Trade Administration (ITA), particularly the Office of the Assistant Secretary for Trade Development. In addition, ITA's Foreign Commercial Service and other embassy officials provide on-the-spot information and assistance for exporters to particular countries. Key aspects of trade development include (1) the provision of information to exporters about market opportunities, business practices, and government policies in particular countries, (2) the arrangement of contacts between U.S. suppliers and foreign buyers or distributors, and (3) the coordination of U.S. participation in trade shows and other promotional events to increase the visibility of U.S. products.

Unfortunately, many exporters in these sectors are small businesses without the resources to handle the complexities of world markets on their own. If exporting to more than one country, they face a wide variety of market conditions and opportunities, as well as idiosyncratic distribution systems. Even in one country, the U.S. exporter confronts a bewildering array of non-tariff barriers, many of them subtle and ill-defined, that hinder effective trading by outsiders. Finally, exporters may face considerable difficulties in simply getting their goods out of the United States, due to the self-imposed barriers described below. In coping with these manifold problems, exporters may need more help than they are currently receiving from the U.S. Government.

167

Export Financing. Telecommunications equipment is frequently bought in bulk, as part of a package deal for large-scale improvement of the national network. This is particularly true in the developing countries, where many telecommunications networks remain in poor shape, but where there is a growing recognition of the importance of a sound telecommunications infrastructure to the whole industrial base. Because of the capital-intensive nature of telecommunications projects, the terms of financing often determine who gets the contract. Other developed countries are willing to offer government-subsidized credit arrangements that undercut anything now available from the United States. In this regard, it should be noted that the Reagan Administration has proposed increases in Export-Import Bank financing authorities.

Regulatory Disincentives. It has long been recognized that aspects of U. S. tax, antitrust, and other domestic policies create unnecessary disincentives to exporting, which cause the greatest harm in strong industrial sectors such as computers and telecommunications. Some steps have already been taken to remove such disincentives—e.g., the Export Trading Company Act of 1981 and the depreciation provisions of the Tax Recovery Act of 1981. Others should be explored—including a revision of the regulations and procedures for granting export licenses under the Export Administration Act.

Attitudinal Problems. The Government's past uneven record in trade development and its maintenance of self-imposed barriers to export may suggest a more fundamental underlying problem in export promotion. Partly because of our experience in an earlier era when U.S. high-technology products "sold themselves," partly because of our strong commitment to free markets and free trade, and partly because of concern about too close cooperation between Government and business, there may be a lingering attitude in many quarters that Government efforts to promote international trade are inappropriate, because they inevitably favor certain industries or certain companies and by implication disfavor others. Concerns have also been voiced that any expansion of Federal efforts in these key

168

"high-tech" sectors may lead to the unwise instituting of various protectionist schemes. Nonetheless, there is growing recognition that export promotion in these sectors must receive greater attention. Examples of increasing interest in export promotion include the enactment of the Export Trading Company Act of 1981 and the recent formation of an R&D consortium among several U.S. computer firms. This is an area where despite obvious potential downside risks, there are also very substantial upside gains. It is also an area where the risks of inaction to the long-term performance of our economy are great. Moreover, the steps that the Government takes or fails to take have direct implications for the ability of U.S. firms effectively to compete abroad. This is because such steps signal the importance that the U.S. Government attaches to these industries and its willingness and ability effectively to counteract foreign actions to ensure our firms a full and fair opportunity to compete.

Options

o    Leave export promotion primarily to the private sector.

o    Enact legislation to remove the most serious self-imposed barriers. The Cabinet Council on Commerce and Trade is currently seeking to identify such barriers in the high-technology sector.

o    Authorize a concentrated government effort to support telecommunications and information exports with financial assistance, tax benefits, antitrust exemptions, and export credit.

Trade Issues in Telecommunications and Information Services

With the development of high-speed data communications, and the convergence of data processing and telecommunications technology, the importance of telecommunications and related services to world trade has increased dramatically. For many industries, telecommunications and data processing services have become key factors of production, in which innovations can radically decrease operating costs. International data communications have become crucial to the operation of U.S. multinational companies.

169

Telecommunications and data processing services are also major growth industries in themselves. Mature countries such as the United States increasingly rely on these industries to offset the decline of low-technology sectors, and it has become virtually a requirement of U.S. economic health for such industries to expand abroad.

As U S. trade policy has turned to the problems of trade in services and foreign investment, the importance of telecommunications and information services in the overall trade picture has begun to be appreciated. Barriers to the supply and use of such services can have a serious impact on U.S. trade in services and foreign investment activities.

Barriers to Trade and Investment. Three types of service-related barriers to trade and investment have become evident in the new telecommunications and information environment.

First, there are the barriers arising from the application of traditional regulatory policies in a new technological setting. In every industrialized country, technological advances have posed a dilemma between the preservation of a regulated monopoly or cartel providing uniform, universal service, and the pressure for greater economic efficiency and more open competition. The United States, however, has moved much faster than other countries toward the adoption of pro-competitive policies. As a result, there is a clash of expectations between U.S. multinational firms, who wish greater freedom to experiment with new applications of technology, and foreign telecommunications administrations, who perceive traditional regulatory objectives to be threatened by such freedom.

Second, there are barriers that arise from socio-political concerns about the impact of new technology. Such concerns include privacy, cultural integrity, and national security; the policies to which they may give rise are discussed in more detail in other parts of this report.

Finally, some countries have begun to use the traditional tools of telecommunications regulation as an instrument of trade policy, in order to promote infant industries and limit foreign competition in information-intensive

170

sectors. The most vocal proponent of such an approach is Brazil, but the same tendency is visible in other countries. One serious challenge to U. S. trade policy is to develop an appropriate response in such cases, where trade considerations form the dominant motive for maintaining a barrier, and where there is no standard international process for resolving grievances.

Non-Tariff Barriers. What follows is a partial list of regulations that can be regarded as non-tariff trade barriers. No distinction is drawn between those barriers that are explicitly "trade-oriented" and those that are merely the product of traditional regulatory policies, or socio-political concerns.

- o   Restrictions on the Use of Leased Private Lines. Private-line policy in other developed countries is far more stringent than in the United States. A variety of restrictions in these countries limit resale and shared use of private lines, as well as interconnection between private lines and the public switched network. Such restrictions pose significant problems for multinational users and particularly for companies providing data processing and other information-based services. (see, e.g., the KDD-Control Data controversy in Japan.)

- o   Unreasonable High Rates for International Services. Transatlantic tariffs for both private lines and public switched circuits are substantially higher than in the United States. International rates that are unreasonably high in comparison with domestic rates would arguably constitute an unfair barrier to foreign investment. However, the appropriate standard of comparison is not easy to find.

- o   Restrictions on the Connection of Terminal Equipment. Although terminal equipment has been almost completely deregulated in the United States, most other countries still require government approval of such equipment and require that it be obtained from or through the government-owned telecommunications monopoly. Limitations on the type of equipment that may be connected can be applied in a discriminatory manner or severely limit the international user's network options.

- o   Discriminatory Technical Standards for Data Communication Services. Standards for protocols in data communications can be used to discriminate against foreign users by limiting the compatibility of U.S. and foreign equipment or software.

171

o     Restrictions on the Use of Foreign Data Processing Facilities. In Canada and West Germany, bank records may not be transferred to other countries for data processing without the approval of bank regulatory authorities. In addition, leased line restrictions in many countries may have the intended or unintended effect of assuring that data processing takes place within the borders. Finally, Brazil pursues an explicit policy that makes multinationals' access to international communications links conditional on the use of domestic labor and machinery for their data processing requirements.

o     Vulnerability and National Security. Increasingly, governments are asserting the right to determine that certain sensitive data and data processing functions remain within their borders, on the grounds that it is too risky to allow them to leave the country.

o     Cultural and Other Information Restrictions. Broadcasting, advertising, and data-base transactions by foreign firms are subject to restrictions in many countries for a combination of economic and cultural reasons. The most well-known example is the Canadian statute imposing special tax burdens on Canadian firms for advertising on U.S. television stations received by Canadians. See also, however, the recent UN declaration on direct satellite broadcasting.

o     National Assertions of Data Ownership. Increasingly, countries are asserting the right to protect data pertaining to them from exploitation by other countries, on the grounds that information is a national resource subject to government control. This right has been asserted, for example, in order to oppose "remote sensing" of geographic data by satellites.

o     Privacy. Laws in many European countries authorize limits on transborder transmission of computer-stored personal data in order to protect the privacy of their citizens. Licenses to transport such data can be denied if the privacy laws of the receiving country are not equivalent to those of the originating country. In a few countries, this restrictive authority covers data about "legal persons," such as corporations and unions, as well as private individuals.

Problems in Negotiation. The resulting challenge to U.S. trade policy is substantial. First, many other countries are not ready to address these issues in existing forums. On the one hand, the members of the GATT have only recently begun to consider coverage of investment and trade-in-service issues. On the other hand, international telecommunications and data processing organizations such as the ITU have traditionally maintained a technical focus.

172

Second, it is not easy to separate objectionable barriers from legitimate ones. As pointed out earlier, not all the barriers listed above are motivated wholly or even in part by trade considerations. Discrimination against foreign companies generally, or U.S. firms in particular, is not always easy to prove. Furthermore, the application of the "national treatment" principle to telecommunications is not yet accepted by many countries. It is also necessary to devise reasonable "ground rules" for international telecommunications, given the growing interdependence of nations and their mutual need for maintaining high-volume communications links.

Finally, there is the reluctance of injured parties to make complaints to the U.S. Government. The typical victim of the barriers described above is a multinational company, with a strong interest in maintaining good relations with the country in question. Given the lack of tested forums for resolving disputes, the ambiguity of U.S. policy on most of the issues involved, and the well-known problems of U.S. Government coordination in these sectors, it is understandable that many multinationals prefer to reach their own accommodations with regulatory authorities. Such reluctance, however, may contribute to some of the difficulties encountered in finding a place for these issues on the U.S. trade policy agenda.

Options

o     Status Quo: continue to seek multilateral and bilateral negotiations on services, while withholding (in most cases) the application of strong trade sanctions.

The existing policy toward trade barriers in services is flexible but largely ad hoc. Problems brought to the Government's attention are addressed in the forum and in the fashion that seems most appropriate. Over the long term, the GATT is being encouraged to examine services and investment issues on a more systematic basis, and to develop new work programs in these areas. Although the GATT was not originally designed to cover services, member countries recently agreed to begin studying services issues. The short-term results of current policy have not been entirely unsatisfactory: negotiation of OECD guidelines on the

173

privacy issue, bilateral exchanges on specific problems in which the "trade" element seems dominant; partial resolution of primarily technical and regulatory problems in traditional forums, such as the ITU Committees. Building on these initial efforts, the United States and other like-minded countries may eventually develop a more cohesive multilateral approach to the long-term problems of a sector that is increasingly important to the world economy.

o  Sectoral Reciprocity: impose "reciprocal" conditions on the entry of specific foreign technologies and service suppliers into U.S. markets.

Under this option, which the Reagan Administration has strongly opposed, the conditions under which foreign firms can enter U.S. markets as suppliers (or users) of telecommunications and information services would be adjusted to "mirror" the treatment of U.S. firms in the corresponding foreign countries. Since there is no GATT coverage of services, sectoral reciprocity legislation in the services sector would be less likely to violate U.S. treaty obligations than would similar legislation in the equipment sector. However, it is open to other objections. A major disadvantage of sectoral reciprocity is its inflexibility. A "mirror-image" matchup takes no account of whether firms from country X are actually in a position to enter the corresponding U.S. market. Even in the one recent case where a mirror-image policy has received widespread approval -- the Canadian border broadcasting case — it is considered questionable whether the proposed legislation will inflict enough injury to cause a change in Canadian policy. An even more serious disadvantage of sectoral reciprocity is that it may be impossible to apply while preserving the cooperative aspects of international telecommunications. Its unthinking application could jeopardize the existing operations of U. S. multinationals.

o  Selective Sanctions: extend the Executive branch's discretion to exert leverage on unfair trade practices in cases where it is clearly warranted and is likely to have a beneficial effect.

This approach has been suggested or used on a number of occasions: (1) the Canadian broadcasting dispute, where the withholding of U.S. approval for Canadian Telidon technology has been suggested as an effective, if unrelated, bargaining chip, and (2) the KDD-Control Data problem, where the attachment of conditions to approval of a new transpacific facility desired by the Japanese was urged in vain upon the FCC. A selective policy is more difficult to implement than rigid, sectoral reciprocity, but could ultimately prove more effective.

174

It is likely that leverage is applied more often than is generally believed outside the government, but in a subtle fashion that rarely comes to the attention of the public. However, the subtle and flexible application of leverage is a strategy best practiced by the Executive branch, whose authority over foreign entry in the communications sector is limited. Effective diplomacy in this area may require greater Executive control over the available policy levers in those sectors.

Regardless of the option chosen, it will be necessary for the U.S. Government to gain more experience in the economics and politics of international telecommunications and information services sector. Policymaking in this amorphous area requires far more knowledge than we now have about the impact of service-related trade barriers on the affected industries, the significance of various multinational operations to the U.S. economy, and the likelihood of change in the telecommunications and information policies of other countries.

### NOTES TO CHAPTER SEVEN

[1] A comprehensive list of telecommunications and information equipment would include such categories as radio and television sets and other consumer electronics gear; photographic, photocopying, filmmaking and tape recording equipment; engineering, scientific, and other measurement instruments.

[2] The abbreviation "SIC" refers to the Standard Industrial Classification system used by Federal statistical agencies. Unless otherwise indicated, all statistics in this chapter are derived from U. S. Industrial Outlook, ch. 27-29 (U. S. Department of Commerce, January 1983).

[3] Industrial Outlook, p. xxi.

[4] Industrial Outlook, p. xxiv.

[5] The utility of SIC 3662 for trade analysis is significantly diminished by the inclusion of vast mounts of equipment with primarily military applications. The largest subclassification, "search and detection and navigation and guidance systems," accounts for 58 percent of SIC 3662 shipments. If shipments and exports in this subclassification are subtracted from SIC 3662 shipments and exports, a somewhat more realistic trade picture emerges.

[6] OECD, Foreign Trade, Series C.

[7] President Reagan has stated that "America must be an unrelenting advocate of free trade. As some nations are tempted to turn to protectionism, our strategy cannot be to follow them but to lead the way toward freer trade." State-of-the-Union Message, January 25, 1983.

Chapter Eight

INFORMATION

International concern over information per se -- its creation, dissemination, and content -- as distinguished from transmission facilities and services,[1] raises a variety of policy issues, including:

o     mass media and press freedom, development of communications capacities;

o     direct broadcast by satellite and claims of national sovereignty in determining content of information broadcast into a country;

o     transborder data flows of personal information and privacy protection;

o     economic aspects of transborder data flow;

o     valuation and taxation of information;

o     encryption; and,

o     intellectual property rights.

BACKGROUND

Some of these information policy issues have been the subject of international debate for generations; others are just emerging as a result of recent technological developments. Growth in the use of computers and in the capacity and efficiency of transmission facilities permit the rapid movement of large amounts of information from one country to another. As governments have come to perceive the growing significance of information to their economic, social, and political interests, they have begun to devise policies for promoting or controlling its creation, processing, storage, and transmission. Examples include calls for licensing of journalists, privacy protection laws, requirements for in-country computer processing, information "gateways" that funnel all computer data leaving

176

and entering a country through a single network node, and attempts to devise methods of taxing information based on the value of its content. Thus, at a time when technology is increasing the capacity to create and disseminate information internationally, too many governments are moving to increase their control over information flows. Such actions are already creating problems for U.S. interests. If these kinds of policies should increase in number and frequency, as seems likely, they will have serious effects on free expression and on U.S. economic interests.

## MASS MEDIA AND DEVELOPMENT OF COMMUNICATIONS CAPACITIES

In mass media, particularly print and broadcast journalism, there have been serious efforts by individual governments and international organizations, in particular, the United Nations Educational, Scientific, and Cultural Organization (UNESCO), to impose restrictions on the activities of journalists. This issue has arisen as part of the debate on a "new world information order," a phrase used by some representatives of developing countries for a reduction of Western influence in mass media and redressing of what they view as an "imbalance" of flows of information.

### Press Freedom

In 1972, the Soviet Union prepared for the UNESCO General Conference a "Draft Declaration on the Use of the Mass Media" which supported state control of the media. This set in motion a series of debates and draft declarations in UNESCO on control and responsibility of the press, licensing of correspondents, establishment of codes of ethics, the setting of state-imposed standards for journalists, limiting access to information, and the invocation of sanctions against those who violate the codes.

Current Policy. The United States has consistently provided uncompromised support for a free press, and has strongly opposed any attempts by nations or international organizations to control mass media for political purposes. The issue

177

is taken so seriously that a recent law -- Sections 108-109 of the 1983 State Department Authorization Act (Public Law 97-241) referred to as the "Beard Amendment" -- requires withholding of U.S. funding for UNESCO if that organization "implements any policy or procedures the effect of which is to license journalists or their publications, to censor or otherwise restrict the free flows of information within or among countries, or to impose mandatory codes of journalistic practice or ethics."

Options. One respondent to the NTIA Notice of Inquiry stated that "a way must be found to develop principles to regulate program content on an international basis. Such principles will have to respect national sovereignty and national cultures." In contrast, another commented that "the concept of a New World Information and Communications Order involves the regulation of content of information flowing among nations. . . . [The respondent] urge[s] NTIA to include in its report a statement expressing strong opposition to such threats to worldwide press freedom." Most of those who commented on this issue generally supported this latter view.

Recommendations. U.S. policy will continue uncompromised support for a free press and free international flows of information. Actions that work to counter movements that seek to control content or restrict the activity of journalists should be strengthened and reemphasized at every opportunity. Through positive actions, policy should work toward attaining and upholding the objectives of Article 19 of the United Nations Universal Declaration of Human Rights (1948) which states, "Everyone has the right to freedom of opinion and expression: this right includes freedom to hold opinions without interferences and to seek, receive and impart information and ideas through any media regardless of frontiers."

## The Role of Communications in Development

In recent years there has been increased attention given to the role of communications in economic and social development. A simultaneous recognition

178

of this importance of communications to development on the one hand, and of the discrepancies that exist between developed and developing countries in communications infrastructures, access to technology and know-how, and the availability of information on the other, has raised a contentious international issue requiring attention in years to come: namely, what is the most effective means of closing the gap between countries with well developed communications sectors and those with poorly developed communications sectors?

Current Policy. U.S. policy on this issue supports the view that the most effective way to reduce the current imbalance is not by attempting to control or inhibit the existing communications capacity of developed countries, but by increasing the communications capacity of the developing countries. In support of this view, the United States proposed in 1978 the creation of the International Program for the Development of Communication (IPDC) under the auspices of UNESCO, and in 1982 the creation of the U.S. Telecommunications Training Institute (USTTI).

International Program for the Development of Communications. The concept of the IPDC was formally established at the UNESCO General Conference in Belgrade in 1980. The original U.S. proposal was for an "aid clearinghouse" sponsored jointly by UNESCO, the Universal Postal Union, and the International Telecommunication Union. Because the developing countries regard UNESCO as the organization over which they exercise the greatest influence and because the UNESCO secretariat was especially enthusiastic, IPDC eventually evolved into a totally UNESCO-sponsored organization.

Established as an autonomous body, IPDC is coordinated by an Intergovernmental Council of 35 member states of which the United States is a member. It first met in Paris in June 1981 to discuss practical communications and information needs of the developing countries and to consider the criteria for presentation, selection, and financing of specific projects. At its second meeting in Acapulco in January 1982, IPDC became operational when it adopted a budget of

179

$910,000 and approved and funded 15 regional and intra-regional projects. Its third and most recent meeting, held in Paris in December 1982, brought the approval of a $1,662,000 budget and several new projects.

The function of the IPDC is still evolving. At the second meeting, there were still major disputes over whether the IPDC would serve only as an aid clearinghouse or as a donor agency. A "Special Account" was established for general donations to be allocated to projects chosen by the IPDC. Bilateral assistance to projects proposed through the IPDC was also found acceptable, although several developing countries urged an "administrative fee" to be paid to the IPDC to handle money not given directly to the Special Account. The United States successfully argued against such a fee at the Acapulco meeting.

The United States has consistently pressed at all stages of the development of IPDC for the private sector to be considered both a legitimate recipient and a legitimate donor of aid. This was agreed to at the Acapulco meeting. Through private initiative, a U.S. Alliance for Communications Development Abroad is being created to mobilize private sector resources and expertise. It is to serve as the link between major elements of the information industry — mass media, telecommunications, information processing, and business users of information -- and UNESCO's IPDC. Its purposes are to heighten the communications industry's awareness of the issues and of opportunities in this aspect of international communications, and to mobilize the private sector for expanded participation in the development of overseas communications.

United States Telecommunications Training Institute.   At the ITU Plenipotentiary Conference held in Nairobi in 1982, the United States announced creation of the United States Telecommunications Training Institute. Its purpose is to promote the planning and operations of sound telecommunications and information systems as part of national development in developing countries. The initial curriculum includes courses such as switching systems, basic telegraphy, satellite communications management, broadcast management, and spectrum management. The Institute will provide advanced training to senior management

180

and technical personnel from developing countries at training sites throughout the United States. Private firms will provide the training, equipment, and funding.

Recommendation. On the question of communication development, U.S. policy is evolving in conformance with the basic principles of free flow and free markets discussed in other chapters of this report. Private initiative is providing an important component of the expertise and guidance needed for the development of indigenous telecommunications and information sectors of developing countries. Greater efforts by the private sector in this kind of activity will be mutually beneficial. Such activities will serve as a spur to the growth of the developing countries and their markets and thus increase opportunities for two-way trade and exchanges.

Because of the importance with which developing countries view the evolution of their telecommunications and information sectors, and because of U.S. interests in their countries in coming years, it would be desirable for the agencies in Government responsible for the granting of foreign aid to review the position of assistance for communications development. A signal from Government could spur further private-sector support.

### Direct Broadcast by Satellite (DBS)

By the early 1970's, it was clear that it would ultimately be technically feasible to broadcast directly from a geostationary satellite to a home receiving set. In time, with the development of larger and more powerful satellites and new techniques that increased satellite power (such as the focusing of a satellite's beam), it would become possible to transmit a signal powerful enough to be picked up by a small receiving antenna -- one that would cost no more than several hundred dollars. Broadcasting by satellite directly to the home might then become a reality.

The problem, as most observers then saw it, was whether the development of DBS was economically feasible. The developed nations already had extensive terrestrial facilities for national broadcasting; and for them, the development of

181

DBS did not seem to make economic sense. It is true that some developed countries -- Canada and Australia, for example -- have remote areas that are sparsely populated and poorly served (if served at all) by their national television systems. The direct broadcast satellite -- which can span large geographical distances and obviate the need for terrestrial facilities -- offered the promise that adequate service could be provided these areas for the first time. But even here, DBS would be less a matter of economic logic and more a matter of social policy.

For the developing world, however, DBS did seem to make economic sense. The developing nations have limited television facilities, which are typically confined to their largest cities. For them, the creation of national television systems using terrestrial facilities would never be economically feasible. But the direct broadcast satellite is another matter. It could make it economical to establish national systems, particularly if the developed nations provided technical and financial assistance. It would also make it possible for nations sharing a common language and a common culture to establish regional networks. With a national or regional system in place, there would be an enlarged opportunity to serve the people of the nation or region beneficially. The satellite could be used to educate, to disseminate information for the improvement of health and economic well-being, and to provide a stream of cultural and entertainment programs.

But nations perceived serious risk as well as potential benefits in the direct broadcast satellite. The risk arises because the beam of a direct broadcast satellite cannot be confined within the borders of a nation or group of nations. The signals will inevitably spill over into neighboring countries. They will do so unintentionally. They may also do so deliberately -- because one nation or group of nations has aimed its satellite beam so that it can broadcast directly to the peoples of other nations. And it is this potential for spillover -- both unavoidable and intentional -- that has dominated the international discussion of DBS for the past ten years.

The international concern about spillover reflects the nature of television. Governments recognize that it is the most powerful mass medium created by man.

182

It has an immediacy and an impact that no other medium has. Some governments are concerned that the direct broadcast satellite can be used for political propaganda -- to broadcast programs that are deliberately designed to change or influence people's views. But it is not only overt propaganda that is of concern. For some governments, ordinary news programs and foreign cultural programs are equally anathema, because they can bring in unwelcome information, be hostile in tone, or invite unfavorable comparisons. They fear a break in the walls surrounding their closed societies.

But even among governments that are not worried about propaganda and do not maintain a closed society, there is widespread concern. It may be characterized as a concern for national sovereignty. One aspect is cultural -- a fear that a national culture may be submerged, or at least deeply affected, by a foreign direct broadcast satellite. The fear is that the foreign broadcast will inculcate alien values. Another aspect is institutional -- that a foreign direct broadcast satellite will seriously affect a nation's arrangements for the form of its national television system and the kinds of services the system provides. Each nation (including the United States) believes strongly that it should determine for itself the essential character of its national television system, and satellite broadcasting across borders poses a threat to the interest of a nation in determining its own television destiny.

The Soviet view is that direct satellite broadcasting should be placed under a regime of strict control. In August 1972, the Soviet Union submitted a draft convention on international satellite broadcasting to the General Assembly of the United Nations. The convention combined a code of broadcasting conduct with a requirement that the country receiving a satellite broadcast consent to the broadcast when it is deliberate and be consulted when it is unintentional.

In the following months, this proposal was debated heatedly; and, in November 1972, the General Assembly voted to refer the matter to its Committee on the Peaceful Uses of Outer Space. The resolution recited both the potential benefits of satellite broadcasting and the need to respect the sovereignty of States in its use, and it requested the Outer Space Committee "to elaborate principles

183

governing the use by States of artificial earth satellites for direct television broadcasting with a view to concluding an international agreement or agreements." The United States cast the only vote against this resolution.

Concurrently, UNESCO issued a "Declaration of Guiding Principles on the Use of Satellite Broadcasting for the Free Flow of Information, the Spread of Education and Greater Cultural Exchange." Article IX stated that "it is necessary that States, taking into account the principle of freedom of information, reach or promote agreements concerning direct satellite broadcasting to the population of countries other than the country of origin of the transmission."

The Outer Space Committee established a special Working Group on Direct Broadcast Satellites to pursue this matter. The work of the Group continued over the years. In 1974, the Soviet Union submitted to the Working Group a draft declaration of principles in substitution for its 1972 draft convention. The draft contained a shortened but equally rigid code of broadcasting conduct. Article IV stated:

> States undertake to exclude from television programs transmitted by means of artificial earth satellites any material which is detrimental to the maintenance of international peace and security, which publicizes ideas of war, militarism, national and racial hatred and enmity between peoples, which is aimed at interfering in the internal domestic affairs of other States, or which undermines the foundation of the local civilization, culture, way of life, traditions or language.

The Soviet declaration retained the requirement that there be prior consent for deliberate satellite broadcasts and consultations when there is a potential for interference or when signals may spill over unintentionally.

For the United States, there were several objections to the Soviet declaration. First, the code of conduct is expressed so broadly and in so general a way as to be meaningless as a foundation of international legal obligation. The proscriptions of the code have no precise meaning and do not embody clear-cut legal concepts. Second, the United States felt that the Soviet declaration was premature. It was the American view that the nations of the world should first experiment with DBS -- to develop its potential and the spirit and methods of

184

international cooperation in this field. The United States felt that in time cooperative relationships could be developed that might well do the work of an agreement. Finally, and most importantly, the United States opposed the Soviet position because it ran directly counter to the cherished American principle that information and ideas should be allowed to flow freely throughout the world. The Soviet proposal for a regime of strict control over international DBS offended the American tradition of free speech, and enforcement by the United States Government of any such regime would clearly violate the First Amendment of the United States Constitution.

In 1974, the United States set forth its own position in a declaration of principles that it proposed for adoption. The declaration was short and couched in general terms. While it placed no express restrictions on the conduct of international satellite broadcasting, it stated that it "should be carried out in a manner compatible with the maintenance of international peace and security with a view to enhancing co-operation, mutual understanding and friendly relations among all States and peoples." The declaration then reiterated the American view that international satellite broadcasting "should . . . be conducted in a manner which will encourage and expand the free and open exchange of information and ideas." At the same time, the declaration recognized that differences among cultures must be taken into account, and that the ultimate good was to maximize the beneficial use of this new space communications technology. The declaration also contained several articles on international cooperation in the field of satellite broadcasting.

Canada and Sweden introduced a fresh declaration of principles to govern international direct satellite broadcasting in the hope that they could mediate the differences between the Soviet and American proposals. Unlike the Soviet proposal, the Canada/Sweden declaration did not seek to proscribe any specific program content. But there was a primary requirement that "direct television broadcasting by satellite to any foreign State shall be undertaken only with the consent of that State." Canada and Sweden maintained, however, that consent could best be made a reality if nations worked together. And so the declaration went on to say that a consenting State "shall have the right to participate in

185

activities which involve coverage of territory under its jurisdiction and control" and that "participation shall be governed by appropriate international arrangements between the States involved." The Canada/Sweden declaration looked to international cooperation to smooth much of the way for satellite broadcasting, and it called explicitly for extensive cooperation.

For the United States, the Canada/Sweden declaration, while less restrictive than the Soviet proposal, would still constitute an undue barrier to the free flow of information and ideas. It contained no limitation on the power of a State to withhold consent, and that power could be exercised arbitrarily without reference to any international standard or obligation. The right of consent conferred on a recipient nation would be absolute. The United States was thus firmly opposed to the Canada/Sweden declaration.

By 1976, experimentation with DBS had begun. Canada was first with its Hermes satellite and was soon followed by the United States (the ATS-6 satellite). Shortly afterwards, Japan (the Yuri system) and the Soviet Union (the Gorisant satellite) began to experiment with DBS. These experiments have now given way to a broad range of operational plans -- by the United States, Canada, the Soviet Union, Japan, Austrialia, and several Western European countries. The Western European plans are both national and regional. Japan will deploy a DBS "starter" system this spring. If these nations stay the course, DBS will be a fairly widespread reality by 1986 -- only a few years hence.

These plans have varying motivations. Some are designed so that outlying or remote areas that now have poor television service may be served. Others are designed to add new channel capacity to an existing national system so that new services may be introduced. And intermingled is the motive of industrial development. In a study prepared in 1981 for the British Home Office, it was estimated that the worldwide market for satellites capable of direct broadcasting was of the order of two billion British pounds (or more than $3.5 billion). While some of this market would lie in the developed world and be the captive of domestic manufacturers within a particular country, a substantial portion would lie outside, notably in the developing world, and be open to international competition.

186

The earliest attempt to deal with the issue of spillover was undertaken by the ITU. In 1971, the ITU held a World Administrative Radio Conference for Space Telecommunications and much of its attention was devoted to establishing the technical rules that should govern the use of the geostationary orbit. The rules that were adopted have the status of treaties under international law.

The rules set forth procedures to provide advance information on the establishment of a satellite system, the coordination of new space facilities with space and terrestrial communications of other nations, and consultations and negotiations to resolve technical problems in advance of the emplacement of a new satellite system. The 1971 Conference also adopted an important new regulation dealing with satellite radiation of foreign territory. Number 428A of the new Radio Regulations provided:

> In devising the characteristics of a space station in the Broadcasting-Satellite Service, all technical means available shall be used to reduce, to the maximum extent practicable, the radiation over the territory of other countries unless an agreement has been previously reached with such countries.

The precise meaning of this provision is not clear. For one thing, there is obviously considerable room for interpretation and differences of opinion concerning what technical means are "available" and what constitutes "the maximum extent practicable." But more important is the question of the regulation's reach. The regulation itself makes no explicit reference to program content, but speaks only of reducing radiation. A large number of countries have taken the position that since it is impossible as a practical matter to distinguish between a signal and its content, Number 428A means that a broadcaster may not establish a system that transmits beyond the range of unavoidable spillover without the recipient nation's consent, which may be withheld for any reason, including program content. (Where spillover is unavoidable, that is, where it is not technically practicable to reduce it further, spillover is not prohibited by the regulation.) The United States has always disagreed with this position. In its view, Number 428A is a technical regulation confined to technical matters and does not authorize a regime of prior consent concerning program.

187

Subsequently, the forum of international discussion became the Working Group on Direct Broadcast Satellites established by the United Nations Outer Space Committee. Its discussions continued throughout the 1970's without any final result. In the meantime, UNESCO continued to follow the issue. In 1978, it adopted a second "Declaration of Guiding Principles on the Use of Satellite Broadcasting for the Free Flow of Information, the Spread of Education and Greater Cultural Exchange." The declaration stated that "satellite broadcasting shall respect the sovereignty and equality of all States"; and it called upon states, while taking into account the principle of freedom of information, to reach or promote prior agreements concerning direct satellite broadcasting within countries other than the country of origin of the transmission. This declaration, however, is not a binding document and created no international legal obligations.

As the pace of DBS development has quickened in recent years, the international discussion of the problem of spillover has acquired a new urgency. For the nations of the Soviet bloc, the issue remains the same: how to prevent satellite broadcasts from reaching its citizenry. For the developing world, the issue is still that of cultural imperialism. As the representative of a Latin American nation stated recently before the General Assembly of the United Nations, DBS "implies the greatest danger of exporting culture which one could imagine."

The United States, however, remains dedicated to the principle of the free flow of information and ideas. For the United States, the problem may not always be an academic one. A British consortium -- United Satellites -- plans to establish a system for DBS in 1986. The British satellite -- to be called Unisat -- will radiate the eastern portion of the United States because of the orbital slot it has been assigned. It is estimated that Unisat will be capable of reaching as much as 40 percent of the American population (if one assumes that the necessary receiving equipment is in place).

The development of DBS has now led to action in the General Assembly of the United Nations. In December 1982, the General Assembly adopted a resolution

188

on DBS. One hundred and eight nations voted for adoption. Thirteen nations, including the United States, were opposed, and another 13 abstained from voting. The crucial portion of the resolution is Section J, entitled "Consultations and Agreements between States." It reads as follows:

> 13. A state which intends to establish or authorize the establishment of an international direct television broadcasting satellite service shall without delay notify the proposed receiving state or states of such intention and shall promptly enter into consultation with any of those states which so requests.

> 14. An international direct television broadcasting satellite service shall only be established after the conditions set forth in Paragraph 13 above have been met and on the basis of agreements and/or arrangements in conformity with the relevant instruments of the International Telecommunication Union and in accordance with these principles.

> 15. With respect to the unavoidable overspill of the radiation of the satellite signal, the relevant instruments of the International Telecommunication Union shall be exclusively applicable.

Section J no longer speaks of prior consent for deliberate direct satellite broadcasts. Instead, it requires that all such broadcasts be made on the basis of "agreements and /or arrangements" with the recipient country. The effect is the same -- to give the recipient country an absolute right to bar satellite broadcasts where spillover can be avoided. Admittedly, where spillover is unavoidable, a direct satellite broadcast would not be barred. But here, too, there may be controversy. There will surely be instances in which the issue of what is unavoidable and what is not would itself become a matter of dispute.

The resolution of the General Assembly is not a binding legal instrument. It does not itself create new law, and for the moment the principle of free flow is still the prevailing rule of international law. But the December 1982 resolution is clearly only a first step, and there will undoubtedly be an attempt to enshrine its principles in a new treaty that will modify the present rule. The major battle in defense of the principle of free flow is thus yet to be fought, and the United States will be called upon to defend the principle with all its vigor.

189

In June 1983, the nations of the Western Hemisphere (ITU Region 2) will be meeting in RARC-83 to determine what kind of DBS planning (rigid, flexible, etc.) will be appropriate for them. The potential for future international TV DBS in this hemisphere cannot be determined until this conference has been concluded. However, since the Latin Americans were the leaders in bringing about the UN vote on restrictive DBS principles, there is little cause for optimism. The U.S. preparations for the RARC are well along but the UN vote on DBS should signal an increased concentration on the political aspects of our groundwork.

Recently, stimulated in part by Congressional questioning, several U.S. Government agencies involved in international broadcasting have been investigating the potential for direct broadcasting from satellites. This activity should be continued with appropriate safeguards and notification to our allies.

## TRANSBORDER DATA FLOW

Growing capacity to store and process large amounts of data in computers and rapidly to transmit the data among computers located in different countries has given rise to concerns over privacy protection, and the economic aspects of international data and information.

### Privacy Protection

Practices followed by financial and insurance institutions, retailers, employers, and governments regarding the kinds of information collected on individuals and the way it is stored and used have been the subject of attention by many governments.

To protect personal data stored in automated systems, several European countries including Austria, Denmark, the Federal Republic of Germany, Norway, France, Sweden, and Luxembourg have enacted comprehensive or "omnibus" privacy laws uniformly covering all sectors of the economy. Comparable legislation is being considered in the United Kingdom and Italy.

190

While governments can work to improve privacy protection for their citizens through their domestic laws, they have far less control over the treatment of information held in computers outside of their own territories. The communications and information technologies that permit large volumes of information to flow rapidly from computers in one country to computers in another, potentially compromise the effectiveness of national data protection laws unless the receiving countries have comparable safeguards. Judging what constitutes "comparable" safeguards among countries with different legal traditions has been the subject of international debate.

To avoid the erection of barriers to flows of personal data among countries in the name of privacy protection, there have been international efforts to establish commonly accepted standards for the protection of individual privacy. The "Guidelines Governing the Protection of Privacy and Transborder Flow of Personal Data," a voluntary agreement adopted by the Organization for Economic Cooperation and Development (OECD) in September of 1980, and signed by the United States is the result of one of these efforts.

The Guidelines outline minimum standards of privacy protection, including:

o    limitations on the collection of personal data;

o    requirements that what is obtained be relevant, accurate, complete, and up-to-date;

o    specification of the purposes for which the data will be used;

o    limitations on disclosure without the subject's consent or by authority of law;

o    safeguards against unauthorized access;

o    openness about developments, practicies, and policies with respect to personal data; and

o    the right of subjects to see information about them and to challenge, correct, or amend it.

The OECD Guidelines have provided a basis for voluntary agreement among countries with varying national approaches to the protection of privacy.

191

In October 1980, the Council of Europe with 21 member nations adopted a "Convention for the Protection of Individuals with Regard to Automatic Processing of Personal Data." When ratified by five member nations, it will be a treaty, legally binding on the countries that have ratified it. The terms of the Convention are such that the United States, even if so disposed, could not ratify the Convention without unprecedented legislative changes in the present approach to privacy protection. These changes would include the enactment of an all-encompassing statute covering computerized personal data held privately or by the Government, as well as the requirement that data bases be registered with a central authority. The United States does not approach privacy protection this way.

In most instances, laws and practices regarding privacy protection pertain exclusively to individuals, or "natural persons." The data protection laws of Austria, Denmark, Luxembourg, and Norway, however, extend the same protections to corporations and institutions, or "legal persons." Such laws increase the burden of compliance for international firms and may thus inhibit flows of many kinds of data necessary to conduct business internationally.

Current Policy. The United States has a long-established tradition of laws and case law protecting personal information. Privacy law in the United States is characterized by unusual diversity derived from a variety of sources, including the Constitution, the common law, and statutes and regulations at both Federal and state levels. This tradition is in sharp contrast to the unitary schemes of regulation adopted by many countries of continental Europe.

An international problem arises when personal information flows among countries that take these different approaches to privacy protection. Whose standards should apply? Will the standard of protection offered in one country be met in others? If not, are the purposes of the laws compromised? Should this justify restrictions on flows of personal data to keep them in-country where protection is enforceable?

192

The United States supports the position that individual countries should seek to promote the protection of privacy within their own national legal structure and traditions. It is signatory to the OECD Guidelines, which seek to harmonize disparate approaches to privacy protection in member countries through voluntary compliance with basic, generally accepted privacy principles. The United States instituted a successful program to inform private sector firms about the Guidelines and to seek their support through voluntary adoption of policies that adhere to the principles set down. To date, approximately 180 major corporations and trade associations have publicly endorsed the Guidelines.

Options. Short of making the dramatic changes in U.S. law that would be necessary to bring our approach to privacy protection into precise conformance with approaches taken by other countries -- a development that is neither likely nor desirable -- there are few alternatives to current policy.

Recommendations. U.S. efforts to obtain support for the OECD Guidelines have been successful, both in raising the awareness of U.S. corporations to privacy as an international issue and in obtaining their voluntary compliance with the principles involved. Policymakers in international telecommunications and information should continue to recognize the need for adequate privacy protection, and support efforts made by individual countries to implement privacy safeguards according to their own legal traditions. We believe the U.S. legal structure provides adequate safeguards for protection of personal privacy. It also necessitates a reliance on international agreements that support recognition of varying legal traditions. Unnecessary barriers to international flows of information erected in the name of privacy protection could have serious effects on commerce. Any such developments should receive swift attention with immediate resolution sought through high-diplomatic channels.

193

Economic Aspects of Transborder Data Flow

The growing significance of information as a component of gross national product in industralized countries is well-documented. Increasingly, telecommunications and information technologies facilitate international commerce. Large-scale networks routinely transmit computerized data among subsidiaries of multinational corporations located in different countries. These capabilities are helping to shape the structure of international commerce -- the geographic distribution of subsidiaries, the types of industries that operate internationally, the kinds of goods and services that will be provided, and the overall efficiency with which productive resources will be consumed.

Individual governments and several international organizations have turned their attention to the issue of transborder data flow. There are indications that this attention will result in restrictions of various kinds on flows of information as a means of achieving commercial or economic objectives. These developments, when projected into the future, will have serious consequences for U.S. direct foreign investment and for the operations of U.S. multinationals in coming years. Many of the issues raised with regard to policy fall under the heading "trade in services" and are treated elsewhere in this report. The issues relevant to information per se include economic consequences of attempts to value and tax flows of information and the risks this kind of activity would entail for control of content.

Valuation and Taxation of Information. Under certain limited circumstances, information can be packaged and sold just as any other "commodity," with its market value established by transactions between sellers and purchasers. The market value is determined essentially by prevailing competitive and technological conditions that affect supply of information, and by what the purchasers believe the information will be worth in their use of it. Their assessment of its value is expressed by what they are willing to forego to have the information, which is indicated by their spending a particular amount of money on the information instead of on something else. If they have the authority to do so,

194

tax agencies may assess some sort of excise tax on the basis of the transaction, just as might be done with any other commodity.

A vast majority of information, however, while certainly of great value to its user, never has an "objective" market value established for it. Information that serves some "valuable" intermediate function in the production process of a firm by contributing to the ultimate value of its final product has no "market" value as described above, and hence no objective basis upon which to assess a tax.

The international aspect of the value of information comes into play when information as an intermediate good is transferred among the geographically dispersed subsidiaries of a multinational firm. Officials of a particular country may consider that something of value is crossing the border, and that it ought to be subject to the same tariff procedures or customs duties as other objects of value crossing the border.

There seems to be a growing concern that an increasing proportion of the value of economic activity in the future will emanate from the production, processing, and dissemination of information, and that the provision of information-intensive "services" will gradually overtake production of physical merchandise as proportions of total output in developed economies.

If the economies of the future are information-based, governments will have to ascertain how they can maintain an adequate tax base. In the case of countries that rely on the value-added tax, the methods of assessing taxes will require attention. When an increasing proportion of value added comes from information with no objective market value, how can the taxing authorities efficiently distribute the tax burden?

A second motivation for attempting to place a value on information, which then becomes taxable, arises from a perceived increase in the volume and significance of international information flows, primarily in the form of computer-to-computer communications among dispersed subsidiaries of transnational corporations. With information entering and leaving countries in this manner, a great deal of "value" is crossing borders. Some governments would argue that the information ought to be subject to the same tariff principles that apply to physical goods that have value and cross borders.

195

Recommendations. The majority of information used in industrial and services activities, commerce and trade, is an "intermediate" product whose economic value cannot be determined in isolation. All that can be known with certainty is that some unknown portion of the value of a final product exchanged on the market can be accounted for by the information "embodied" in it. Attempting to value this intermediate product would be an arbitrary and capricious exercise, entailing unnecessary and costly disruptions in the production process. Alternative means of regulating and taxing productive activities are available.

The U.S. position on this matter, consistent with the long-range goals of promoting the role of telecommunications and information technology as a contributor to the efficient utilization of resources, would be to strongly oppose any actions that would interfere with the ability of producers and users to make optimum use of information as a productive resource. This will lead to a more efficient utilization of resources. It will also lead to greater revenues for both private entities and, ultimately, for taxing authorities.

A second argument against trying to value information as an "intermediate" good used in productive activity is perhaps more compelling than the first: the obvious need for surveillance of content in the process of evaluation. This could lead to dangerous abuses of personal and proprietary information. One can imagine the dilemma posed by communications networks that carry all forms of information -- voice, video, record -- on all subject matters -- news, personal, corporate, research, educational -- in an indistinguishable stream of bits. Surveillance of specific kinds of information for economic reasons could too easily become surveillance of all information for political reasons.

These same arguments also militate against unnecessary regulation of information sold as a final product. Information as a final product that has an established market price may seem to solve the problem of valuation because an exchange takes place at an agreed upon price. Government involvement in such transactions for purposes of taxation or other reasons may seem less burdensome or dangerous than in the case of the mass media or when information is an intermediate commodity. Nevertheless, the basic view that Government should not manipulate information as a tool of policy should apply there too.

196

Encryption

Concern over unauthorized surveillance of personal or nonpersonal information or other forms of disruption of communications have accompanied an increase in the volume and types of flow of information -- electronic funds transfer, electronic mail, and proprietary corporate data of all sorts. There is a growing demand for new or improved techniques of assuring the security of communications. Cryptography, the use of codes to render messages or data unintelligible to unauthorized parties, is one technique.

Cryptographic methods are generally used to prevent two kinds of tampering. The first is "passive" surveillance, through which the unauthorized party gains access to the signals or messages of other parties (with or without their knowing it), obtaining knowledge of the content, which may then be used to some commercial or political advantage. The second kind of tampering is the "active" variety, when the unauthorized party not only gains access to the message of other parties, but may then change the content, moving a decimal point a few places in a financial transaction, or changing a word or meaning in other communications.

Until recently, cryptography had been an issue of interest largely to agencies of Government responsible for national security that have to send secure messages and that seek to break codes. A growing demand for secure communications in commercial activities, however, is engendering a transfer of cryptographic technology to nongovernment users.

Issues. Two related aspects of the cryptographic issue have emerged as issues of policy. One concerns the national security implications of research on cryptography, and the broad dissemination of new cryptographic techniques. The other concerns the encryption of everyday communications.

> The U.S. Government's primary concern regarding the first aspects
> is that open research and publication in cryptography jeopardize
> national security by making available to foreign governments
> encryption techniques that (the National Security Agency) would
> have difficulty breaking, calling to the attention of foreign
> governments the vulnerability of their current encryption methods,
> and revealing knowledge that might endanger the inviolability of
> codes used by the U.S. Government.[2]

197

Controversial efforts have been made by governments to inhibit the transfer of technology on cryptography.

The issues regarding the potential demand for an application of cryptographic techniques in international communications include the availability of cryptographic services altogether and the question of standards. Tariffed encryption services are not now available from either domestic or foreign international communications carriers. In developing such services, there will always be at least two telecommunications entities involved, and they will have to come to agreement on procedures to be followed and equipment to be used. In addition, the wide adoption of tariffed encryption techniques could require an elaborate international standards-setting procedure. Encryption services available to the users of private dedicated leased-line networks may be less cumbersome to develop, and may provide additional incentive for resisting actions of communications administrations seeking to encourage the use of public networks.

Recommendations. Currently there is no clear U.S. policy on encryption. It is a difficult issue to resolve because of the role encryption plays in national security. Nevertheless, methods of protecting proprietary data from surveillance will likely experience growing demand in coming years as a consequence of growth in information flows. Efforts should be undertaken to formulate a policy that will accommodate both the concerns raised by national security and the needs of users of international facilities and networks.

Intellectual Property Rights

Incentives to create new information such as contents of data bases, computer software programs, novel "firmware" programs with algorithms permanently etched on microchips, are provided in part by the expectation of financial returns from selling such properties. Some of the peculiar attributes of these new kinds of property, however, complicate the recognition and enforcement of property rights in these intangible "commodities" through traditonal patent and copyright concepts. Recent revisions to U.S. copyright law have attempted to address some of these issues.

198

Factors which make the enforcement of property rights a problem include the following: information does not come in well-defined units, it is not "used up" in consumption, the creation of information can be costly, but the incremental cost of reproducing it very low, and excluding nonpaying beneficiaries is very difficult. While computer and communications technologies have created new opportunities for creating and disseminating information, they have simultaneously complicated the methods of establishing and enforcing property rights in it.

The issue is further complicated by national policies in some countries which require registration of imported software or data bases while at the same time denying copyright protection.

Society has not reached a consensus on the most appropriate balance between the right to use and the right to exclude use of these new kinds of property. Problems inherent in conventional technologies, such as print, are magnified by evolving computer and telecommunications technology. Among the questions that will require the attention of policymakers in coming years are: How will technological developments and the accompanying difficulties in establishing and enforcing property rights affect incentives to produce new information? What inhibitions on international flows of information will result from the system society eventually chooses for production of these property interests? What international agreements or procedures should be used to protect property rights in information?

The U.S. is signatory to two major international conventions on intellectual property rights, the Universal Copyright Convention, and the Paris Convention on Industrial Property. The principle international organizatons in this issue are the World Intellectual Property Organization (WIPO), a U.N. specialized agency, and UNESCO.

WIPO addresses several issues raised by new technologies, such as piracy of sound and audiovisual recordings and piracy of broadcasts. UNESCO has not been as valuable a forum for protection of the interests of intellectual property holders but it has recently taken on some useful work in the piracy area.

The United States should also aggressively pursue unauthorized reproduction and dissemination of recordings and broadcasts on a bilateral basis by urging

199

passage and enforcement of stricter national copyright laws in the countries where the offences occur. Additionally, the Senate should promptly consider ratification of the 1976 Brussels Convention. This international agreement obligates signatories to take adequate steps to curtail the unauthorized reception and commercial exploitation of copyrighted and proprietary information transmitted via satellite. Trade in film, television programs, and similar "software" constitutes an important component of our overall export portfolio, and steps necessary to safeguard this trade and commerce should thus be accorded prompt and favorable consideration.

The United States should maintain close contact and cooperation with other countries to ensure development of mutually acceptable forms of protection for these new kinds of property, and continue within the bounds of existing arrangements to protect the interests of U.S. businesses in this area.

### NOTES FOR CHAPTER EIGHT

[1]This is not to suggest that a sharp distinction can be made between policy on facilities and policy on what flows over the facilities. Indeed, conditions placed on the use of facilities can affect the way information flows internationally, and rules imposed on information flow will influence the development of facilities and networks.

[2]Stephen H. Unger, "The Growing Threat of Government Secrecy," Technology Review, February/March, 1982, p. 32.

Chapter Nine

RESEARCH AND DEVELOPMENT IN TELECOMMUNICATIONS
AND INFORMATION INDUSTRIES

Longstanding U.S. leadership in telecommunications and information technology is being challenged by increasingly strong and concentrated foreign competition. Further erosion of the U.S. position has serious implications for the long-term competitiveness of the U.S. telecommunications and information industries and would also adversely affect the entire U.S. industrial sector. A thorough review is thus needed of current U.S. policy in research and development (R&D) as it relates to telecommunications and information.

This chapter discusses some of the factors that require attention. The material reviewed does not indicate the United States has neglected R&D funding, or that U.S. research and development no longer generates patentable inventions or advanced products. The evidence does indicate, however, that the United States no longer enjoys an overwhelmingly dominant position in "high-technology" industries.

## BACKGROUND

For decades the United States enjoyed a position as a world leader in technology. Underlying U.S. technological leadership was its ability to generate new scientific knowledge and innovations, and to continually transform them into useful products and services in ways superior to foreign competitors. Investments in research and development have contributed importantly to exports,[1] job creation,[2] new products, productivity improvements[3], enhanced the quality of life, and accelerated advancements in science.

Projections for the 1980s indicate very rapid growth in high technology American industries. Projected growth rates include: for robotics (25 percent), computers (18 percent), semiconductors (12 percent), guided missiles and space vehicles (16 percent), and communications equipment (5 percent).[4] Each of these

202

"sunrise" industries is highly dependent on telecommunications and information technology. Technological advances in these industries have brought improvements in productivity to all sectors of the economy, through such innovations as digital communications, electronic funds transfer, electronic mail, automated office equipment, factory assembly operations, and smaller, more affordable, computers for home, business, and scientific purposes.

Recent foreign technological advances create concern that the U.S. leadership position in high technology is eroding. U.S. trade deficits (especially with Japan), declining world market shares, increased competition for the U.S. domestic and international markets, and the rapid appearance of sophisticated foreign products, such as semiconductors, satellite communications, lasers, computers, consumer products, and robotics, are cited as evidence of a deteriorating U.S. position. The ability of other nations to select technologies for concentrated R&D focus, to provide government subsidies, to encourage joint government-industry cooperation, to devote resources to nonmilitary enterprise, and to protect indigenous enterprises from competition through tariff and nontariff barriers, are seen as factors contributing to foreign advantages.

A review of U.S. R&D in telecommunications and information technology has particular importance because technological leadership in these and related areas is widely seen as the cornerstone of economic advancement in the decade of the 1980s.[5] Nations having outstanding capabilities for generating and applying advanced technologies are likely to flourish.

This chapter reviews U.S. R&D in telecommunications and information technologies from a number of vantage points, and recommends improvements. Although substantial progress has already been made, continued efforts are needed to improve incentives for making the best use of U.S. genius for innovation and commercialization of new products. Aggressive foreign competition for world leadership and in telecommunications and information technology, as well as in other technological fields, is likely to be permanent. In this environment, the United States will have to use every possible means of maintaining a strong position capable of countering foreign policies.

203

R&D Perspective: Current Strengths,
Trends and Problems

Government Role in R&D

Federal Government support for R&D activities falls into three categories: first, backing those activities which meet needs in which the Government is the sole or primary user (such as national defense); second, backing those activities which assure the strength of the economy and the welfare of its citizens (such as agriculture, energy, and health); and third, funding basic research. The 1983 Budget of the United States helps clarify the distinction between Government and private sector responsibilities for R&D. The Government views its role as follows:

o     providing a climate for technological innovation which encourages private sector R&D investment;

o     focusing its direct R&D support in areas where there is likely to be significant economic gain to the nation, but where the private sector is unlikely to invest adequately because of long-term risks;

o     maintaining a growing technological base in categories where government and industry must cooperate fully; and

o     promoting basic science and engineering research.

Federal Support for R&D

The Government supports R&D in many ways -- by sponsoring Federal laboratories; by providing over $40 billion annually for R&D; by contracting for R&D with research universities, colleges, and businesses; by allowing tax credits for industry-conducted R&D; and by encouraging entrepreneurs. The United States spent $4.6 billion for R&D in telecommunications in 1980 -- $2.8 billion in private sector investment, and $1.8 billion in Federal Government expenditures -- mostly through the Department of Defense (DOD).[6] DOD will increase funding for R&D in intelligence and communications[7] from $1.13 billion in 1981 to $2.77 billion in 1983.[8]

204

About one-half the total Federal obligations for all basic research are made to support researchers in universities and colleges, who account for about one-half of all basic research conducted in the U.S.[9] The key questions here are:

o      are we investing enough in the proper areas and through the most suitable institutions?

o      how can we measure and project U.S. progress in contrast with our most aggressive international competitors?

o      should we discount some DOD-funded research as a generally inadequate substitute for civil agency-funded research, in terms of contributing to the U.S. technological position?

o      where can improvements be made (in terms of removing obstacles to private sector investment, in transferring technology to the private sector, in providing incentives to private sector investment)?

o      what are the most promising opportunities for advancement of technologies, and are we positioning ourselves properly?

Federal Laboratories

Continued efforts to improve the role of Federal laboratories will ensure that appropriate types of R&D are undertaken, that long-term, high-risk programs with significant potential commercial pay-off are funded, that suitable industry collaboration is involved, and that research results are promptly transferred to the private sector. NASA's Advanced Communications Technology Satellite program is an example of a Federal laboratory targeting high-risk, long-term research based on industry advice, and contracting out a substantial portion of the research, thereby rapidly transferring research findings.

Planned budget reductions in the Space Shuttle program between now and 1994 -- and termination of NASA production of Atlas and Delta-Centaur rockets, the main launching vehicle for communications and other commercial satellites -- are prompting the private sector to consider increasing its investment in these activities.[10] Partly as a consequence of the shift in NASA involvement, delays in the Space Shuttle program, and the $1 billion investment of the European Space Agency for development of the Arianne rocket, strong foreign competition for the commercial space launch market is expected within a few years.[11]

## Industry Support for R&D

Despite economic recession, industrial research and development spending surged in 1981. In particular, companies producing computer peripheral equipment and providing data processing services in the information processing industry led other industries with a 34.2 percent increase in R&D spending (to $344 million). Office equipment manufacturers in the information processing field increased R&D expenditures by 24.8 percent, and telecommunications firms' expenditures increased by 20.1 percent.[12]

The Semiconductor Industry Association has established a Semiconductor Research Cooperative which will channel $40 million into university laboratories by 1986.[13] Advances in telecommunications and information technology, as well as in applications, have continued to progress in areas ranging from large-scale computer and personal microcomputers (now a $6 billion market, with continued rapid growth projected), to subscriber loops, earth sensing from space, and office automation and medical electronics.[14] Foreign countries, such as Japan, West Germany, and the United Kingdom, however, are also very active in R&D in many of these areas -- especially in integrated circuits, in fiber optics and opto-electronic components, in portions of the satellite communications components field, and in office automation. While it is unclear whether there is a shortage of industry support for R&D, a comprehensive summary of R&D investments among the world's leading competitors -- including amounts, rate of change, areas of focus -- would be helpful in assessing the comparative U.S. position.

## U.S. Patents and Licensing Trends

*Trends in U.S. Patents.* The number of U.S. patent grants (U.S. origin plus foreign origin) in telecommunications increased from an average of 174 in the 1969-70 period to 420 in 1981-82, a growth of over 140 percent. The proportion of foreign-origin patents to U.S.-origin patents has risen from 30 percent to 36 percent for these periods.[15] Japan's share of U.S. foreign-origin patents has risen to slightly more than 50 percent in the 1981-82 period from 34 percent for the 1969-70 period.[16]

206

During the 1978-80 period, the actual growth of U.S. patent awards in semiconductors and circuits improved by 48 percent, indicating substantial activity in solid state technology.[17] The General Purpose Programmable Digital Computer Systems and the Miscellaneous Digital Data Processing Systems subclasses commanded a major share of patent activity.

Trends in Foreign-Owned U.S. Patents. An area worthy of further investigation is the changing role of foreign multinational corporations (FMNCs) in the United States. A recent study by the U.S. Patent and Trademark Office[18] notes that foreign direct investment in the U.S. has been growing at an average rate of 20 percent since 1973. Part of the study focused on the largest FMNCs -- five European and five Japanese -- and sought to gain insights into questions including how much U.S. technology the FMNCs control, how much of their R&D is performed in this country, what technologies they patent, and what the trends are in their patent activities?

The study scope was not limited to particular technologies (although four Japanese and one European FMNCs are in the electronics and appliance industry group). It indicated that:

o    one out of eight U.S. patents of foreign origin was owned or controlled by only 10 FMNCs during the time frame of the study, an indication of their strong position in the international technology marketplace.

o    foreign-origin patents, as a whole, increased from 20 percent of all U.S. patents in 1963-66 to 40 percent in 1980.

o    ten FMNCs own or control, on average, 4.7 percent of all U.S. patents granted each year.

o    while the five European FMNCs had an average of about 10 percent of their patents filed as being of U.S.-origin[19], during 1976-80 the five Japanese FMNCs averaged about 0.4 percent.

o    the percentage growth[20] of the five Japanese FMNCs patents compared to the average[21] was especially high in the Computers and Data Processing Systems class (71.6 percent versus 49.8 percent) and in Static Information Storage and Retrieval (67.6 percent versus 47.1

207

percent), but slightly below the average for telecommunications (44.4 percent versus 47.2 percent).

Licensing of Technology to Overseas Companies. A recent survey of 161 companies' attitudes, based on prior experience with licensing technology to overseas companies,[22] indicates that the predominent result of the overseas licensing was long-term damage to the licensors. The consensus conclusion, based on comments of 107 of the companies, is that U.S. technology manufactured abroad by foreign firms finds its way into the U.S. domestic market.

Industry sources also note that Comsat -- and formerly AT&T -- are required to license their technology to other companies. Foreign firms that establish U.S. subsidiaries have made use of this regulation to acquire U.S. technology. Reciprocal licensing arrangements are not prevalent in foreign countries.

U.S. Restrictions on Technology Transfer

The central issue of technology transfer is balancing national security goals with other national goals, such as preserving First Amendment rights and the tradition of open academic exchange, while at the same time encouraging invention, commercialization, and exports.

National security interests sometimes require restrictions of technology transfer in the form of products, industrial processes, designs, and technical data that might aid current or potential foreign adversaries in a direct military way, or indirectly, by providing them with resources that otherwise would be allocated from military endeavors. The range of technologies that can be restricted includes telecommunications and information technology.[23] The mechanisms for effecting restrictions include: the Export Administration Act and the Inventions Secrecy Act, both administered by the Commerce Department; the International Traffic in Arms Regulations, administered by the State Department; and the national security classification system.

208

Studies have been ordered by Congress through the Department of Defense. Some of these studies recommended that restrictions on technology transfer affecting "cornerstone" technologies, processes, and designs be minimized and clarified. In the most recent effort toward clarification, the Commerce and Defense Departments were to prepare a joint Militarily Critical Technology List in 1982. There have been difficulties in implementing such recommendations, however, and some public confusion still exists.

The United States has the most stringent restrictions on technology transfer in the Western World. While there is little doubt that national security interests justify restrictions on transferring critical technology overseas, there is also a pressing need to streamline these restrictions as much as possible, while balancing them with overall U.S. policy goals. With clarified guidelines to protect national security goals, the private sector will be able to compete more effectively in the international marketplace through rapid technological advancement.

## U.S. Entrepreneurs

Entrepreneurs play an important role in the United States in advancing technology, in providing employment opportunities, and in sustaining the competitive position of the United States. Collectively, American entrepreneurs represent a critical component of the nation's vitality, contribute to U.S. exports and have created approximately 70 percent of all new private sector jobs during the last decade. California's Silicon Valley alone adds over 25,000 new jobs annually, and Massachusetts' small and mid-sized high-tech firms have sparked an industrial renewal that now accounts for over 250,000 manufacturing jobs.

Associations of entrepreneurs (e.g., National Association of Small Business Investment Companies, American Electronics Association, American Business Conference), generally claim that the U.S. Government does not understand their needs, and favors big business in tax legislation. Entrepreneurs recognize "protectionism" policies as anathema to innovation and a process that leads to higher consumer prices. A recent GAO survey of 72 young "high-tech" companies started with venture capital shows that more than 15 percent of their total sales ($900 million) were to overseas customers.

209

A substantial amount of U.S. innovation is provided by small businesses and independent inventors. Federal support for innovative research by small businesses can be found in recent legislation, which requires Federal agencies to increase their R&D activities with small businesses, and which creates a new Small Business Administration information service to keep small businesses alert to opportunities for participation.[24]

Small, high-technology businesses are extremely sensitive to tax laws and policies, such as capital gains taxes, accelerated depreciation, R&D tax credits, and borrowing capabilities.[25] All of these affect the ability to generate investment capital to finance expansion. If tax policies encourage entrepreneurs, the long term benefits to the United States could be significant.

Foreign Strength in Key Technological Areas

Although the levels of U.S. R&D expenditures and growth in U.S. patents give the appearance of well-being, other factors suggest significant risks in some key areas. One such factor is the rising cost of continuing technological advancement, coupled with an uncertain pay-off in the distant future. An example of the problem of rising cost and questionable long term compensation is in the field of supercomputer technology, where there has been an erosion of the U.S. leadership position over the past 20 years.

Supercomputers. Many U.S. companies once were active in supercomputer development. The high expense and risks for this low volume market, however, have reduced their number to two -- Cray Research, Inc. and Control Data Corp.[26] As of June 1982, as few as 50 U.S. supercomputers were in operation worldwide -- 38 in the United States, 10 in Europe, and two in Japan. U.S. Government laboratories have 25, while a few private companies use the remainder, thus accounting for the absence of national support for supercomputer development.[27]

Japanese industry recognizes the importance of supercomputer research and has instituted an ambitious joint government-industry program to advance the state

210

of the art in this and other selected technologies. One large program, the National Superspeed Computer Project, is aimed at developing a computer more powerful than any now available. This $200 million program is jointly funded by the government and six major Japanese companies, with 85 percent of the research contracted among the companies. Another large project is aimed at developing fifth generation computer technology with new capabilities in problem-solving, man-machine interfaces, and cognitive processes. A number of U.S. scientists who recently visited Japan and were briefed on these programs were generally confident of their success, while others expressed some doubt.[28]

A major recent report[29] on the U.S. position in supercomputers in relationship to the positions of West Germany, France, Great Britain, and especially Japan, concludes that the United States is rapidly losing its leadership. The report observes that the United States retreated from its support of large scale computing in universities and elsewhere during the 1970s when other countries' support grew substantially. An expert panel concluded that "there is little likelihood that the United States will lead in the development and application of this new generation of machines." The final report provides well considered recommendations for improving the U.S. position.

Integrated Circuits. During 1982, U.S. leadership in semiconductor or chip technology was shocked by Japanese companies' early market entry with a highly reliable 64K byte memory chip, the first time a foreign country posed a serious threat to U.S. leadership in this area. This was quickly followed by development of a prototype Japanese 256K byte chip. In the mid-1970s, the Japanese committed $350 million to a joint government-industry research project for very large scale integrated circuits. Japanese companies spent nearly 20 times as much during this program, which resulted in Japan's leadership in world markets for the 64K byte random access memory chip,[30] and perhaps for the next generation, the 256K byte chip as well.

These examples illustrate how concentrated efforts by a foreign country can drastically increase its technological leadership in a relatively short time. Loss of

211

technological leadership has a number of serious consequences ranging from loss of access to the most advanced machinery for conducting research and forfeiture of technology spinoff opportunities, to inability to undertake new applications available through more sophisticated technology. In addition, there is the possibility that advanced U.S. scientific and military research could become dependent on access to supercomputers of foreign manufacture.

### Other Nations' Support of R&D

The United States lags most industrialized nations in providing government incentives for invention and innovation, such as cost-sharing, salary grants, or interest free loans to strengthen the industrial technological base. Cost-sharing of high-risk efforts and more advantageous tax treatment is commonplace in other countries. For example, West Germany's accelerated depreciation for buildings and general purpose equipment devoted to R&D is tending to shift an increasing amount of U.S. R&D abroad.[31]

Canada's Industrial Research and Development Incentives Act, and the Program for the Advancement of Industrial Technology, provide tax free grants-in-aid up to 50 percent of R&D operating costs and 50 percent of the cost of new facilities, excluding land. In addition, Canada reimburses private firms for the salaries of their technical personnel assigned to government-approved research projects and allows all research costs, undiluted by grants, to be deducted from earnings for tax purposes.[32]

Japan provides even more incentives, including outright subsidies, cash grants repayable out of successful projects, and long-term, low-interest rate loans from development banks. Tax benefits include a 20 percent tax credit for increases in industrial research over expenditures during a base period (limited to a maximum of ten percent of the corporations' tax liability). Excluded from taxable income are 70 percent of royalties received from the export of technology.[33] In the computer area the Japanese government, acting jointly with leading Japanese computer firms, spent over $1 billion on computer R&D programs between 1972 and 1982 to catch up with the United States.[34]

212

Israel provides R&D grants that cover 50 percent of costs where the product to be developed is intended primarily for export.[35]

## Current Activities to Improve the U.S. R&D Position, and Continuing Problems

### Improvements in Federal Policies

There is widespread awareness that the U.S. position in the commercial marketplace and in technological leadership is increasingly threatened by strong, aggressive foreign competitors. To bolster the U.S. position, a variety of steps are being considered or have been taken, which include those based on Congressional or Administration initiatives, or on recommendations from trade associations and the academic and scientific communities. Few of these efforts focus primarily on telecommunications and information technologies, however, with some notable exceptions, such as NASA's space shuttle, DOD's Very High Speed Integrated Circuits program, and part of NSF's program to establish technical centers jointly supported by universities and industry, all of which are Federally supported programs.

There is a need for continued efforts to bolster the ability of the U.S. telecommunications and information industries to remain competitive technologically. Such efforts include:

o  removal of unnecessary Federal disincentives to private sector research investment (in the form of antitrust laws and procurement regulations);

o  creation of new incentives (such as improved tax deductions for R&D expenses and promotion of joint research projects); and,

o  Congressional attention to improve the nation's education system (e.g., to upgrade science and mathematics education in elementary and high schools, to facilitate universities' ability to upgrade obsolete laboratory equipment and to retain competent faculty, as well as to retrain the work force).

Efforts already under way to improve the U.S. technological position include:

213

o       added incentives for R&D investments through the Economic
        Recovery Tax Act of 1981;

o       broader use of limited partnerships;

o       changes in patent and technology transfer policies; and,

o       better alignment of Federal laboratory programs with industry
        needs.[36]

Some areas identified for further review, which are discussed below include
tax policies, Federal funding of research, and support for industry research
consortia.

Tax Policies.  A study performed by Data Resources, Inc. (DRI) for Texas
Instruments, Inc., indicates that a 25 percent credit on R&D spending starting in
1966 would have added 0.2 percentage point per year to annual productivity during
1966-77, 0.3 percentage point per year in 1978-87, and 0.4 percentage point per
year in 1988-97.  DRI estimated that a 50 percent tax credit would have the effect
of returning R&D expenditures to their (1964) peak of 2.15 percent of GNP within
eight years, and that it would take about 35 years to achieve the same level of
productivity improvement with a 25 percent R&D tax credit.[37]

Incentives for Investments in Research.  Federal tax laws[38] provide a credit
for investments for certain qualifying R&D of 25 percent of the   maximum
incremental increase over the base period investment.  This may be an overly
restrictive ceiling that discourages additional investment.  Similarly, many types of
R&D are not tax deductible, such as research and development for quality control
and testing.  Firms that are new or starting up receive no initial inducement to
invest in research, while limited partnerships receive no deduction incentives at
all.

A review of existing tax policies is warranted to determine whether a more
favorable investment environment can be structured[39] which would be more
sensitive to the needs and special characteristics of high-tech firms.  These firms
are different from others in a number of ways:

214

o   They must make substantial, continual investment in R&D, which in turn necessitates rapid replacement of existing plant and equipment. Therefore, favorable tax policies relating to the treatment of R&D expenditures and short-lived equipment are important.

o   These companies often have rapid growth in sales -- between 15 and 30 percent -- and retained earnings that are generally insufficient to meet capital needs. Typically, new equity investment must be obtained as the primary means of meeting these needs. Tax policies that favor debt financing thus may not be especially useful in promoting U.S. high technology firms.

o   They often must have significant international sales and operations. To stay ahead of foreign competition, they must be competitive in world markets, and therefore, are especially sensitive to U.S. tax policies relating to foreign operations and to U.S. exports.

Federal Funding of Research. Federally funded research will increasingly focus on longer-term, higher-risk, basic research, such as the NASA Advanced Communications Technology Satellite program, in which the private sector is unlikely to invest adequately. There is also increased Government funding emphasis on contracting through research universities, as well as encouraging joint industry-university cooperation. Over the years, the National Science Foundation (NSF) established seven centers for research which are eventually to become self-sufficient. The most recently established center is for research in communications and signal processing at North Carolina State University, which will include both basic and applied research leading to industrial products and services. The NSF grant is $650,000 over five years, with each participating private company contributing approximately $50,000. Nine companies are taking part in this cooperative effort. MIT (in polymer processing) and Rensselaer Polytechnic Institute (in computer graphics) are among other universities participating.[40]

Cooperation between Federal laboratories and industry is also being encouraged. The Department of Commerce has begun working closely with the Federal Laboratory Consortium to encourage technology transfer from the hundreds of U.S. Government laboratories to state and local governments and to industry. Small companies, independent inventors, and universities at the periphery of an industry, have also accounted for many of the major inventions in the

215

twentieth century.[41] Under NSF's Small Business Innovation Research Program, approximately 52 percent of the grants have gone to firms with 10 or fewer employees, and several new firms have been started as a result of these grants. Annual funding is expected to reach $150 million in grants through NSF and other agencies.

Support for Industry Research Consortia. Some high technology industries faced with very high R&D costs and intensely subsidized foreign competition, have proposed joint R&D consortia that would be immune from some conventional antitrust restrictions. Recently the Justice Department approved establishment of the Microelectronics and Computer Technology Corporation, a consortium of several major computer firms. Similar consortia may also be accorded freedom from any threats of Government antitrust prosecution. The position the Justice Department has taken may encourage improved U.S. leadership in selected technologies, such as computers and microelectronics.[42]

## Continuing Problems

Education-Related Problems. In order to maintain a viable position in technology and international trade, it is essential to ensure adequate talent is available to perform the research necessary to develop new concepts and new products. America's strength in these fields has long been a functon of its engineering and scientific human resources. In 1981, approximately 18,000 students graduated with Bachelor's, Master's, and Doctoral degrees in high technology fields in the United States. Since 1979, however, there has been a declining number of students in these important fields.[43] The problem that began with inadequate elementary and secondary school student preparation in science and mathematics in the Sixties and the Seventies is now being reflected in the shortage of college engineering graduates. With a shortage of U.S. engineers, U.S. companies currently confront an additional problem in the form of proposed restrictions that would prohibit foreign nationals from being hired immediately after graduating from U.S. universities.

There are thus three problems contributing to the present engineering conundrum:

(1)    Students entering higher–level education in science and engineering too often are inadequately prepared. This problem begins at the primary and secondary education level, where there is a lack of adequate teaching proficiency in mathematics and science.

(2)    Competent high school and university instructors are leaving teaching careers, often to double their salaries in industry, producing a 40 to 50 percent shortage of engineering faculty.

(3)    Much of the laboratory equipment in the academic environment has become obsolete. The 97th Congress considered several bills to provide tax incentives to industry to provide more modern equipment to higher level institutions. The same opportunities are not yet available for secondary school education.

President Reagan spoke concerning these educational deficiencies at a May, 1982, National Academy of Science Conference. He noted that elementary and secondary school science and mathematics had deteriorated to the point that they threatened "to compromise the nation's future ability to develop and advance our traditional industrial base and to compete in the international marketplace." He called remedial action "long overdue," and invited private industry to do more to help schools.[44] Two recently created organizations, the National Commission on Excellence in Education under the Department of Education, and the National Science Board's Commission on Pre–college Education in Mathematics, Science and Technology are seeking remedies for these educational inadequacies,[45] and Congress may soon consider proposals to provide assistance to improve elementary, secondary, and post secondary education in mathematics and science.

Education at the secondary level provides the basis for those pursuing higher education needed for development and innovation of products instrumental in determining the advancement of U.S. society and its standing in international trade. Even more importantly, the quality of technical and scientific secondary education is reflected in the majority of the population entering the labor force. The success of this country will depend upon how well prepared our children are to face the information oriented world that is emerging due to massive technological advancements today.   From the standpoint of the needs of research and development, with little additional training these students will be the technicians who create and apply R&D products.[46]

One effort to modernize primary and secondary education is through introduction of computers at this level.  Proposals have been made to allow tax incentives for industry to contribute computer equipment to primary and secondary schools, as well as to provide grants to states for electronic and computer technician vocational education programs.[47]

In regard to the issue of foreign national graduates, immigration policies also are relevant as a number of qualified potential research employees educated at U.S. universities are not U.S. citizens.[48]  The basic problem is, of course, not the retention of foreign students, but rectifying educational deficiencies that lead to this lack of American engineering talent.  These educational deficiencies could cause profound, long-term damage to the U.S. technological and international trade positions, as well as to national security.  Twenty-four measures were proposed during the 97th Congress to deal with these issues.[49]  Continued intensive attention is warranted until suitable remedies are found.


Bell Telephone Laboratories.  Bell Telephone Laboratories (BTL), AT&T's research arm, has produced a remarkable number of technological advances for more than 50 years.  BTL is recognized as an undisputed world leader, at the forefront of technologies such as semiconductors, computers, and lasers.

With a 1982 budget of $2 billion, of which $156 million was spent for basic research, funding for research has been generous as well as consistent.  BTL has almost 20,000 patents in effect, and currently receives new ones at the rate of one per day.[50]  Under the 1956 Western Electric antitrust consent decree, AT&T was required to license these patents to other companies.  Consequently, it has 400 licensing agreements with U.S. companies and nearly 200 more with overseas corporations today.[51]  Some of these licenses have spawned entire new industries, perhaps years sooner than they might otherwise have been launched.

218

In August 1982, the Justice Department ended its 1974 antitrust suit against AT&T. A major reorganization of AT&T was required. The terms of the consent decree may affect future BTL research and development in a number of potentially significant ways.

First, under the new consent decree, AT&T will no longer be required to license its patents. Second, BTL is less likely to continue its traditional pattern of publishing hundreds of scientific and technical papers annually without concern for commercial value or patentability. Third, the new consent decree would also limit the operating companies and the Long Lines Department to funding specific, directed research through BTL. Previously, BTL basic research was funded by all parts of the Bell System through payment of a general license fee.[52] Pressures on the unregulated portions of AT&T to be competitive in the marketplace are likely to result in more product-oriented research by BTL at the expense of basic research.[53]

The AT&T settlement does permit the retention of BTL as a single entity. The long-term consequences of the divestiture on BTL's continued ability to generate technological advances, however, are not predictable.

Recommendations for Stimulating U.S. R&D

Our review of the U.S. international position in R&D in telecommunications and information technologies shows significant shortcomings, and obstacles affecting continued advances by U.S. industry. The main observation is that foreign competition for leadership in these technologies is exceptionally aggressive, and has grown rapidly over the past few decades. The single most important conclusion drawn is that continued U.S. success will be very much dependent both on Federal funding for R&D as well as on policies that create an environment conducive to continued vigorous private sector investment in R&D.

Option: Declare R&D A National Priority

Over the past few decades achievement in scientific and technological fields has varied as a priority in the United States. Administrations have at times actively sought scientific and technological advice from the private sector and at other times avoided it. Government funding of nondefense R&D has generally risen between 1953 and 1982, with some exceptions, but frequently at a rate below that of inflation. Between 1981 and 1983, total Government nondefense R&D will decrease by $1 billion to $17.3 billion, a 5.7 percent drop before adjusting for inflation.[54] At the same time, the Administration's overall economic recovery program has restored needed stability and predictability with the result that the private sector has stepped up its support of basic research.

If the U.S. becomes determined to make every feasible effort to maintain a position of technological leadership, then this effort should become a national priority. Maintaining technological leadership will require reinforcing current activities to remove investment disincentives, as well as providing additional incentives for the private sector. As noted earlier, investment incentives may be achieved by:

o    partial relaxation of some actual or perceived antitrust constraints on joint research activities (now underway);

o    revision of procurement regulations that deny contractors full rights to patents developed under Federal programs (already accomplished for nonprofit companies and for universities,[55] but not for larger companies);

o    improved tax credits for R&D expenses; and

o    promotion of joint research projects.

Option: A New Federal Policy on Funding of R&D

The need to "[C]reate the incentives and the supply of technological innovation" is applicable to the telecommunications and information technologies as well as to others.[56]

Given the long term interests of the nation, aggressive Federal funding of R&D in telecommunications and information technology may be warranted. Ideally, funding for this research and development would be consistent, generally increasing at least as fast as the inflation rate, and sufficiently flexible to counter foreign activities.

220

Most agree that projects in which Federal resources are allocated to assist private industry and universities build long-range cooperative research capabilities should be encouraged and strengthened. A review should be made to determine whether sufficient Federal grants and contracts for R&D in telecommunications and information technologies are targeted toward small businesses, independent inventors, and universities. Ongoing U.S. Government activities that stimulate innovation include:

o    focusing Federal policy to support basic research in R&D;

o    improving technology transfers from Federal laboratories;

o    finding incentives for industry support of innovation; and

o    steps toward establishing joint university-industry centers of technology.

Demand for innovation, competition, and economic reward are three factors that stimulate innovation. Federal policies can positively influence the last two factors by establishing a suitable environment with tax advantages, minimal regulatory impediments, and direct Federal funding of R&D. Methods should also be sought, however, to encourage business and industry to transform research results into commercial products as soon as practical. It has been estimated, for example, that a considerable amount of research never leaves government laboratories. Efforts should be continued to use tax credits, improved Federal procurement regulations and patent policy, and consortiums with industry to motivate increased innovation. The long-term benefits to the nation should appear in the form of increased exports, employment, tax revenues, and decreased dependence on foreign technology.

## Option: Create a Government Structure to Obtain Industry Advice

The Office of Science and Technology Policy is charged with advising the President on the nation's science and technology needs, and currently obtains private sector advice through the White House Science Council. Additionally, a White House Conference on Productivity was mandated through legislation at the

221

end of the 97th Congress,[57] and the creation of a White House Council on Industrial Competitiveness is under consideration. Outside advice to the U.S. Government for Federal funding of R&D is strongly encouraged in order:

o    to identify the best emphasis for Federal funding;

o    to obtain expert views for decisionmaking concerning targeted versus generic research;

o    to provide guidance on the best balance of support for research conducted by universities and by private industry;

o    to improve commercial exploitation of government funded R&D; and,

o    to evaluate the merits of joint industry and joint government-industry research projects.

Option: Increase Use of R&D Limited Partnerships (RDLP)

U.S. industry could make far broader use of limited partnerships in research and development as a major means of funding technological advances. Because of the current trend toward lower interest rates, coupled with the effect of recently enacted reductions in Federal taxes, the volume of funds available for venture capital is growing substantially.

As a first step toward forming an RDLP, private businesses could identify individual R&D projects which, when commercialized, would make substantial contributions to U.S. competitiveness. The criteria for undertaking these projects should be that they:

(a)    require more than simply the financial or technical competence of one firm acting alone, and

(b)    have good prospects for being commercialized within a short period, such as four years.

Subsequent to project identification, market and technical data should be assembled to prepare a "commercial opportunity package," showing market segments, expected domestic and foreign demand, linkages into user industries, patent needs, etc.   Private business (with Government encouragement, and technical and organization assistance, as needed) should develop a research and development limited partnership to fund the chosen venture, and to manage the R&D. The RDLP can provide tens of millions, even hundreds of millions of dollars of off-balance sheet funding without any obligation of repayment if the R&D is unsuccessful. Depending on the structure, the General Partner (the key player in any RDLP) can exercise management control. If structured properly, major antitrust problems can be avoided. The limited partners benefit from liberal tax shelter provisions, and the expectation of royalties which can be taxed at long term capital gain rates. A sponsoring company can retain control of proprietary rights. Equity participation is also possible.

The Department of Commerce's Office of Productivity, Technology, and Innovation can provide assistance in the RDLP area.

Recommendations:

Appropriate Level for R&D Funding. The appropriate amount of U.S. Government funding for R&D might be determined through indirect measures, such as a comparison of the U.S. position with that of other nations in terms of technical advances, patents, and innovative product development, plus amounts expended for R&D, both in dollars and as a percentage of GNP, etc.[58] A comprehensive analysis would be useful for developing periodic projections of U.S. R&D funding in comparison with that of major competitors over the long term.

U.S. Patent Position versus that of Foreign Multinational Corporations. The U.S. Patent and Trademark Office initiated a major statistical effort in the mid-1970s to develop a comprehensive data base with which to examine trends in U.S. patents both by technology and by country of origin. A recent study cited previously[59] notes that very few foreign multinational firms (FMNCs) control a significant proportion of all foreign origin patents (one out of eight, in fact, for the ten FMNCs for the time frame studied). These USPTO patent analysis studies should be encouraged and expanded -- along with earlier warning methods -- to develop insights into areas of potential foreign penetration into U.S. and world markets.

223

Licensing of Patents Rights. A study cited earlier notes a survey of 161 companies' attitudes based on experience with licensing technology to foreign firms. The survey was primarily negative in tone, reflecting the companies' view that the licensees too often become competitors for U.S. or foreign markets. Further study is suggested to expand these findings, to target similar studies on selected areas of high technology in the future, and to advise U.S. industry of the results.

Trade Practices. Many studies have been undertaken that concentrate on the ability of foreign competitors to subsidize sales, marketing, and R&D for new products. Their ability to "dump" (sell below cost) products on the U.S. market; and their practice of providing low-cost, long-term loans for procurement has also been reviewed. Nevertheless, we recommend that further study be initiated to determine how our major foreign competitors fund or subsidize R&D in telecommunications and information technologies. The results of this type of study should be useful for projecting the future U.S. technological position in regard to that of foreign competition and for planning U.S. strategies.

Bell Telephone Laboratories

In view of the singular importance associated with the BTL's historically large production of innovative technology, future BTL progress should be monitored for indications of decline, and, if needed, alternatives to restore overall U.S. innovations should be explored.

U.S. Restrictions on Technology Transfer

We recommend that restrictions on the export of telecommunications and information technology for national security purposes be

o    limited to that which is essential,

o    clarified for the public, and

o    orchestrated in a way that substantially narrows the negative influence on invention and exports, and retains an atmosphere of open academic exchange.

Implementation of the above recommendations will assist the U.S. telecommunications and information industry to remain competitive and competent technologically in an increasingly aggressive world market. In addition, periodic assessments of the position of the U.S. industrial sector in relation to foreign competitors would serve to point out when further adjustments are needed.

224

NOTES TO CHAPTER NINE

[1]In 1981, over 40 percent of U.S. exports were represented by high technology products, according to U.N. Series D Trade Data from ITA in the Department of Commerce.

[2]The growth in employment in high technology and its supporting industries is approximately 50 percent higher than the growth in all U.S. business employment, according to U.N. Series D Trade Data from ITA in the Department of Commerce.

[3]At the Conference on U.S. Competitiveness at Harvard University, John W. Kendrick's calculations noted that a full 40 percent of U.S. growth in productivity over the last 50 years must be attributable to technological innovation. Research Management, July 1982, p. 40.

[4]1983 U.S. Industrial Outlook, U.S. Commerce Department.

[5]In his news conference of January 5, 1982, President Reagan recognized this shift in the nation's economy. He stated, "I think in this restructuring of our workforce we're going to find that there are industries that have traditionally been at a certain level in our country, and we're going to find that we have switched to other lines of industry; to service types of industry rather than being a 'smokestack' industry-type. . . . We're going to have to prepare for them."

[6]Electronic Industry Association, "Electronic Market Data Book 1982," p. 121, Table 5-10, 1980 data.

[7]More detailed data are not available. It is likely, however, that much of the DOD funding includes non-telecommunications technology.

[8]American Association for the Advancement of Science, "Research and Development, AAAS Report VII, Federal Budget -- FY 1983 Impact and Challenge 4," p. 27, Table 2-2.

[9]Special Analysis K, Research and Development, The Budget of the U.S. Government, 1983, OMB, February 1982, pp. 2-3.

[10]IEEE Spectrum, January 1983.

[11]"We Mean Business," Forbes, January 1983, pp. 76-78

[12]These figures are based on data provided by companies surveyed by Business Week. See "R&D Scoreboard 1981," Business Week, 5 July 1982, p. 54. See also Research Management, September 1982, p. 2.

[13]Research Management, September 1982, p. 3.

225

[14] Institute of Electrical and Electronics Engineers (IEEE), Spectrum. Special Issue on Technology '83, January 1983.

[15] The data on patent grants are based on statistics for the first half of 1981 provided by the U.S. Patent and Trademark Office and adjusted for the full year. Foreign patents in communications equipment and electronics components increased from 16 percent in 1963 to 27.9 percent in 1973. Also, see "Patent Activity and International Competitiveness," Research Management, Vol. 21, #6, pp. 34-37, November 1978.

[16] Japan's patents as a proportion of U.S.-origin patents rose from 10 percent to 37 percent during the same periods.

[17] USPTO, Technology Assessment and Forecast (10th Report), November 1981, Section I, Active Technologies, p. 16.

[18] USPTO, Technology Assessment and Forecast (10th Report), November 1981, Section II, Patent Trends.

[19] An application is of U.S.-origin if the first inventor listed on the patent has a U.S. residence.

[20] Percentage growth is defined by the USPTO as the number of patents granted in the three-year period (1978-80) divided by the number of patents granted in the six-year period (1975-80) taken as a percentage.

[21] Average percent growth is calculated from all patents in the class.

[22] Forbes, 1 August 1982. Also see Research Management, November 1982, pp. 2-3.

[23] All exports are restricted except those which are specifically exempted.

[24] Small Business Research Act of 1981, Pub. L. No. 97-219 (22 July 1982).

[25] "Why Entrepreneurs Trust No Politician," Washington Post, 16 January 1983 p. B1.

[26] J.E.E. (Japan) Progress on IC Technology and Full Scale Development of Overseas Local Production, July 1982, p. 88.

[27] "Japanese Supercomputer Technology," Science 218, 17 December 1982, pp. 1189-1193.

[28] Id. at pp. 1189-1193.

[29] U.S. Department of Defense in coordination with the National Science Foundation, Large Scale Computing in Science and Engineering, report prepared by a panel of experts, 26 December 1982. The report is available from NSF.

226

[30]"Japan's High Technology Challenge," News Week, 9 August 1982, pp. 48-54.

[31]"Technological Innovation – Key to Productivity," Research Management, pp. 33-41, July 1982.

[32]Ibid, pp. 33-41.

[33]Ibid, pp 33-41.

[34]U.S. Industrial Outlook, 1983, pp. 27-28.

[35]Research Management, pp. 33-41, July 1982.

[36]White House, Office of Science and Technology Policy in cooperation with the National Science Foundation, Annual Science and Technology Report to the Congress, Report No. NSF 82-9, 1981.

[37]Research Management, July 1982, pp. 33-41.

[38]As modified by the Economic Recovery Tax Act of 1981.

[39]"High Technology Industries and Tax Policy in the 1980's," National Journal, 1 January 1983, pp. 46-49. See also "Why Entrepreneurs Trust No Politician," Washington Post, 16 January 1983, pp. Bl-2.

[40]Research Management, p. 3, November 1982.

[41]"Technological Innovation – Key to Productivity," Research Management, July 1982, p. 34.

[42]Washington Post, 28 December 1982.

[43]Research Management, November 1982, reports a declining number of qualified science and engineering students, with peaks for Bachelor, Master, and Doctors degrees occurring in 1973, 1974, and 1979 respectively.

[44]Speech to National Academy of Science Conference, May 1982.

[45]Research Management, Industrial Research at Universities, July 1982, p. 6.

[46]The significance of the educational problem is pointed out in a recent GPO publication (P-95 No. 76), which observed that the total number of Soviet scientists and engineers engaged in R&D during 1979 was 57 percent more than the number in the United States.

[47]U.S. Congressional Record, 98th Cong., 1st Sess., 6 January 1982, Vol. 129, pp. H 97, E 83.

227

[48]Intel, one of the leading U.S. semiconductor manufacturers recruits about 30 percent of its employees as foreign nationals.

[49]See Appendix C on legislation relating to R&D in telecommunications and information.

[50]U.S. Congress, Hearings Before the House Committee on Science and Technology, Subcommittee on Investigations and Oversight and Subcommittee on Science, Research and Technology on AT&T, 97th Congress, 2d Session, 8 December 1982 Statement of C. Kumar N. Patel.

[51]Business Week, 5 July 1982, pp. 46-52.

[52]Id. at pp. 46-52.

[53]Contrary to this analysis, an AT&T spokesman notes that the corporation is committed to sustaining BTL's basic research vitality, and does not anticipate any precipitous decline in BTL's focus or funding in the near term.

[54]"Science Advice Through the Years," National Journal, 25 September 1982, p. 1635.

[55]See Patent and Trademark Laws Amendments, 1980, Pub. L. No. 96-517. H.R. 4564 and S. 1657, introduced in the 97th Congress, were aimed at establishing and maintaining a uniform Federal policy for Federally sponsored R&D for all government contractors.

[56]"Technological Innovation - Key to Productivity, Research Management, July 1982, pp. 33-41.

[57]See Pub. L. No. 97-367 (October 1982), pertaining to The White House Conference on Productivity.

[58]Some of these measures are compiled periodically by the NSF, AAAS, EIA, Business Week, and other services.

[59]USPTO, Technology Assessment and Forecast (10th Report), November 1981, Section II, Patent Trends.

Chapter Ten

NATIONAL SECURITY

Analyses of international telecommunications and information policymaking must include consideration of the impact of any actions on the Nation's security. This includes not only the immediate tactical and strategic communications needs of the military. Also included are the facilities and services necessary for the United States to conduct its foreign relations and ensure the economic vitality of the country. The strength of the domestic industries providing telecommunications and information services and equipment is vital to our national security. The communications necessary to deal with natural or man-made disasters and other crises or emergency situations are also a critical dimension.

Effective and reliable worldwide communications have served as a pivotal component of our national defense since World War II. Indeed it was the wartime demands of the military and the technological response to their needs that first established a worldwide communications network, which in turn provided significant benefits to commerce, aviation, and many other civilian enterprises. From 1945 through 1947, the Congress held hearings focusing on the concern that the communications networks necessary during the war might be too readily abandoned in peacetime, to the Nation's detriment.[1]  The significance of telecommunications to both national defense, defined narrowly, and national security, defined more broadly, has since grown dramatically.[2] Telecommunications systems and their actual and perceived robustness have a direct impact, moreover, on the credibility of our nuclear deterrent and ability to safeguard world peace.

Military Command, Control, Communications and Intelligence ($C^3I$) Systems. The growing need by the military for command, control, communications,

(229)

and intelligence ($C^3I$) systems has produced substantial Department of Defense (DOD) demand for commercial as well as military international communications facilities and services. DOD operates various military satellite systems, such as the Defense Satellite Communications System with six operating communications satellites of its own, and U.S. government-owned terrestrial communications equipment, in order to communicate both between and within numerous countries.[3] Yet the Department is still the largest single U.S. user of commercial leased international telecommunications services, expending more than $50 million per year for private line channels alone.[4] The Armed Forces now use approximately 290 submarine cable circuits and 225 commercial satellite channels.[5] While it no longer follows an official policy of dividing equally its use of military systems, commercial cable systems, and commercial satellite systems, nonetheless DOD mixes its use of media to enhance survivability and redundancy.[6] The Department also uses approximately 106,000 radio frequency spectrum allocations internationally.[7]

DOD has all of the legitimate concerns of other major U.S. users of international communications facilities, such as costs, availability, and standards. DOD also has significant concerns unique to its critically important mission. It thus has been actively involved in U.S. regulatory and legislative forums, international organizations, and in direct consultations and negotiations with foreign entities.

Other National Security Related International Communications. In addition to U.S. Armed Forces international communications needs, DOD has arrangements whereby it provides point-to-point or mobile telecommunications services to government entities of other countries (e.g., Canada, United Kingdom, Federal Republic of Germany) and to multilateral international organizations (e.g., NATO).[8] Other U.S. Government agencies also make "significant use" of DOD international communications facilities.[9]

In order to fulfill its foreign affairs mission, the Department of State has a continuing need to communicate with its Chiefs of Mission and posts abroad. It

231

must also meet the telecommunications requirements of those agencies which have representatives overseas or are responsible for conducting negotiations on behalf of the United States. The Secretary of State must communicate with representatives of foreign governments and international organizations. The Department of State thus has in operation a worldwide telecommunications system to meet both the normal and crisis needs of Federal entities.[10]

The National Communications System. The National Communications System (NCS) was established by the President in 1963 "to provide necessary communications for the Federal Government under all conditions ranging from a normal situation to national emergencies and international crises, including nuclear attack."[11] Initial emphasis was to be on "meeting the most critical needs for communications in national security programs, particularly to overseas areas."[12] Policy direction responsibilities were retained in the Executive Office of the President, while the Secretary of Defense was named Executive Agent for the NCS. The Secretary of Defense in turn designated the Director of the Defense Communications Agency (DCA) to also serve as the day-to-day manager of the NCS. The NCS looks not only to DOD, but also to the international communications assets of the Department of State and other agencies to meet its challenge. In 1979 Presidential Directive/NSC-53 (PD 53) emphasized:

> It is essential to the security of the United States to have telecommunications facilities adequate to satisfy the needs of the nation during and after any national emergency. This is required in order to gather intelligence, conduct diplomacy, command and control military forces, provide continuity of essential functions of government, and to reconstitute the political, economic, and social structure of the nation.[13]

## ISSUES

The national defense and security community seeks to ensure secure, reliable, restorable, and survivable means of carrying out all necessary communications. Many telecommunications policy issues affect their ability to succeed. Two issues commonly labelled "security" are nonetheless distinct: 1) message security, or the protection from interception or tampering of the information being transmitted; and 2) the protection of the physical facilities being used to communicate, their survivability and the availability of alternative facilities.

Message Security and Encryption. Communications via cable are considered more secure from interception and tampering than satellite or microwave transmissions, and fiber optics are more secure than traditional cable.[14] These preferences are tempered not only by cost and availability, but also by the need for a mix of media to enhance survivability, as discussed below. In each case, encryption is commonplace. Use of encryption requires close coordination and cooperation among NATO and other combined military forces and our allies. It also requires protection of encryption technology from our potential adversaries. The debate over private cryptographic research for use by banks or other commercial entities with their own security needs, as well as the debate over technology transfer, both focus in part on the potential damage to the ability of the U.S. military, foreign affairs, and intelligence agencies, to maintain adequate message security.

Facilities Protection and Survivability of Networks. Many actions are taken to protect vital communications systems from accidental disruption, natural disaster or military attack. These include physical hardening of transmission media through use of underground relay and terminal points, burying of cables, protection of radio relay antennas, etc. A key aspect of survivability, however, is redundant routing of circuits by various paths. It is for this reason DOD distributes its communications among a mix of media — commercial cable, commercial satellite, as well as Government-owned and operated facilities. It is also why DOD has strong interest in maintaining the quality and viability of both international cable and satellite transmission media and the health of the U.S. firms providing those services.[15]

233

Ensuring sound defense communications requires application of accepted standards and ongoing international negotiations to assure interoperability of equipment and required interconnection of systems. Military systems must interchange with commercial systems, commercial systems must be able to substitute for each other, domestic systems must link to international systems, and there must be a great deal of cooperation among various foreign and international systems as well. Achieving this level of effectiveness is far from simple; pre-planning and cooperation are crucial. As DOD spokesmen have stated:

> to facilitate military deployment or overseas sale of equipment without costly modification. . . .[DOD] must be able to conduct its telecommunications operations both in the United States and abroad with the same equipment and under regulations which are as consistent as possible.[16]

Private Lines, Volume Sensitive Pricing, and the FCC's Resale and Shared Use Proceedings. The FCC's consideration of proposals to permit unrestricted resale and shared use of private international leased lines causes some concern in the defense community. National security interest in this issue was summarized in recent testimony to the Congress where the DOD expressed concern about "serious adverse repercussions" from any "unilateral attempt" by the FCC to bring about unlimited resale and sharing:

> First, without prior bilateral international agreements between the entities involved, providing reasonable assurance that unlimited resale and sharing will not result in the demise of international private line services, there is substantial risk of significant adverse operational impact upon our ability to provide secure international communications for Defense and non-defense users (e.g., limitations upon the use of U.S. secure communications equipment). Second, unilateral FCC action could generate actions by foreign telecommunications entities to remove current "flat-rate" pricing techniques applicable to international private line services, thereby substantially increasing the costs of DOD's voluminous and vital international telecommunications needs.[17]

DOD concern about the costs of being forced onto the public switched networks of foreign countries extends not only to the increased costs of volume sensitive pricing, but also to the costs of converting protocols to function on these networks.

234

Service Initiation, Circuit Restoration, and Preemption Priorities. Over its own facilities, DOD can determine priorities for initiating service among users, set restoration priorities for circuits rendered inoperable by enemy action or natural disaster, and preempt use of its networks for higher priority messages. Domestically, assuring that the capability exists to accomplish this in the case of commercial facilities may require legislation. Internationally, however, the U.S. Government cannot unilaterally exercise such control over foreign-owned or jointly-owned facilities. Pre-planning and the negotiation with PTT's and foreign governments of specific agreements establishing such plans are thus essential.

Research and Development, Technology Transfer, and Domestic Sources of Supply. Policy issues surrounding telecommunications research and development and technology transfer have been discussed elsewhere in this report. The Department of Defense maintains that:

> this Nation's domestic and international telecommunications resources are critical to our national defense and security and emergency preparedness. From this perspective, therefore, the maintenance of U.S. technological leadership in telecommunications and related technology, through a technologically advanced and internationally competitive United States telecommunications industry is vital.[18]

Translating the broad goal of maintaining technological leadership into specific workable strategies, however, is difficult. Concern over the flow of U.S. technology overseas is not limited to losses to hostile nations. U.S. industry often finds itself in head-to-head competition with foreign firms from friendly nations which have capitalized on U.S. research efforts. DOD is legitimately concerned that the U.S. not become dependent upon foreign firms to provide vital telecommunications equipment or services nor upon foreign dominated technology. Prior to the Second World War, the United States found itself almost exclusively dependent on Germany for critical high-grade optics, and heavily dependent on foreign sources for other necessary defense materials (e.g., rubber, strategic minerals). Our mobilization base was inadequate to meet the challenges of that

235

conflict. The needs of today's far more complex defense establishment are even greater and include products such as silicon chips and related microcircuitry which constitute fundamentally important building blocks essential to build and maintain advanced weapons systems.

In recognition of the strategic importance of domestic supplies of critical high technology, and for related purposes, DOD supported AT&T's selection of the lowest cost domestic bidder to provide fiber optic cable in the Northeast Corridor, despite competing bids from foreign suppliers. This construction was viewed as a unique opportunity to begin decreasing the vulnerability of U.S. telecommunications from disruption. DOD focused on the need to limit unnecessary foreign firm involvement in classified analyses and discussions of improving the survivability of the nation's long-haul telecommunications infrastructure. Also stressed was the need to encourage domestic fiber optics research and development to ensure the ready availability of domestic technology and sources of supply should emergency reconstruction ever become necessary.[19] In short, and despite the benefits of free trade and openly competitive markets,[20] national security requires appreciation of the defense implications of foreign competition and the export of telecommunications technology. As DOD has stated, there is a strong national interest in a telecommunications industry predominantly owned and controlled by Americans to ensure national defense, security, emergency preparedness, and related economic needs.

Policymaking and Operational Responsibilities. As previously discussed, the DOD and other Government entities constitute large users of U.S. international telecommunications facilities and services. They also lease substantial amounts of communications services directly from foreign commercial entities. As described by DOD:

> In leasing or operating the Department's international telecommunications services and facilities, many of the Department's international telecommunications activities are governed by provisions of Status of Forces Agreements. The Department. . .is heavily involved in the Allied Radio Frequency

236

Agency of the North Atlantic Treaty Organization. Furthermore, the Department of Defense's lease of commercial international services requires extensive dealings with foreign communications entities, and it is common for the Department to order, pay for, use and terminate international communications services within relatively short time periods (e.g., 7-30 days).[21]

These governmental activities require continuing consultation and negotiation, contractual or otherwise, with foreign entities. DOD and the State Department also frequently negotiate memorandums of understanding or other arrangements with foreign governments. This has led DOD to believe that any telecommunications policymaking structure which might be established should not be directly involved in the many day-to-day planning, programmatic, and operational decisions affecting their international systems and operations.

Telecommunications Policymaking. Many telecommunications policymaking issues raising serious national security concerns are discussed elsewhere in this report. These include:

1)  explicit inclusion of national defense, national security, and emergency preparedness in legislatively-mandated standards for telecommunications policymaking and specifying the weight to be accorded such interests by regulators;

2)  participation of national defense and national security agencies in the coordinated development of unified Executive branch positions on telecommunications policy issues;

3)  having national defense and national security policy determinations made within the Executive branch rather than by an independent regulatory agency;

4)  establishing a Presidential veto power over FCC actions on national defense or national security grounds;

5)  streamlining the international telecommunications facility authorization and licensing process to avoid unnecessary delays in obtaining necessary commercial communications internationally; and,

6)  assuring effective representation of U.S. interests in international negotiations and conferences.

237

NOTES TO CHAPTER TEN

[1]See Senate Comm. on Interstate and Foreign Commerce, Investigation of International Communications by Wire and Radio, S. Rep. No. 19, 80th Cong., 1st Sess. 2-5 (1947).

[2]See, e.g., Statement of Richard D. DeLauer, Under Secretary of Defense, in Hearings on S. 898, before the Senate Comm. on Commerce, Science, and Transportation, 97th Cong., 1st Sess. 145-146 (1981); Statement of Lt. Gen. William J. Hilsman, Director, Defense Communications Agency, in hearings on S. 2469 before the Senate Comm. on Commerce, Science, and Transportation, 97th Cong., 2d Sess. 93-94 (1982) (hereinafter cited as "DCA Hearings").

[3]Statement of Lt. Gen. William J. Hilsman, DCA Hearings at 89, 93.

[4]Id. at 93.

[5]Response of J. Randolph MacPherson, Department of Defense, DCA Hearings at 91.

[6]Ibid.

[7]DCA Hearings at 97.

[8]Id. at 93.

[9]Letter from William H. Taft, IV, General Counsel of the Department of Defense, to Hon. Jack Brooks, Chairman, House Comm. on Government Operations reprinted in Hearings on H.R. 1957, 97th Cong., 1st Sess. 270 (1981) (hereinafter cited as "Brooks Hearings").

[10]Letter from Thomas J. Ramsey, Director, Interagency Affairs, A/OC, Department of State to NTIA (Dec. 20, 1982).

[11]Memorandum from the President to the Heads of All Executive Departments and Agencies, Establishment of the National Communications System at 1 (August 21, 1963).

[12]Ibid.

[13]President Directive/NSC-53, National Security Telecommunications Policy at 1 (November 15, 1979).

[14]See Petition for Reconsideration of the Department of Defense, In the Matter of Policy to Be Followed in Future Licensing of Facilities for Overseas Communications, FCC Docket No. 18875 at 3 (1978).

238

[15]Statement of Lt. Gen. William J. Hilsman, DCA Hearings at 94.

[16]See Brooks Hearings at 271.

[17]Id. at 95.

[18]Id. at 96.

[19]See Comments of the Department of Defense in Re AT&T (Northeast Corridor Light Guide System), 51 P.& F. Radio Reg. 2d 717, 725 (1982).

[20]DCA Hearings at 96.

[21]Brooks Hearings at 270.

APPENDIX A

Notice of Inquiry

List of Respondents

49694          Federal Register / Vol. 47, No. 212 / Tuesday, November 2, 1982 / Notices

**SUMMARY:** Pursuant to Title II of the Communications Amendments Act of 1982 (Pub. L. 97–259), the National Telecommunications and Information Administration (NTIA) will conduct a comprehensive study of the long-range international telecommunications and information goals of the United States, the specific international telecommunications and information policies necessary to promote those goals, and the strategies that will ensure that the United States achieves them. As part of the study, NTIA will also conduct a review of the structures, procedures, and mechanisms which are utilized by the United States to develop international telecommunications and information policy.

To assist in this effort, NTIA is soliciting comments from interested parties on any or all of the issues involved. Additional information on the proposed scope of the study and examples of specific questions that will be addressed are provided below under Supplementary Information.

**PROPRIETARY INFORMATION:** Information and comments submitted in response to this notice that are designated proprietary will be held in confidence and protected to the fullest extent of the law.

**DATES:** The study will be completed for submission to Congress early in calendar year 1983. Therefore, comments in response to this notice must be received by December 2, 1982.

**ADDRESS:** Send comments to: Bernard J. Wunder, Jr., Assistant Secretary of Commerce for Communications and Information, Special Project on Long-range Goals, National Telecommunications and Information Administration, U.S. Department of Commerce, Washington, DC 20230.

**FOR FURTHER INFORMATION CONTACT:** Kenneth Leeson, Acting Director, Office of International Affairs, National Telecommunications and Information Administration, U.S. Department of Commerce, Washington, DC 20230, (202) 377–1866.

**SUPPLEMENTARY INFORMATION:**

**Scope of NTIA Inquiry**

A comprehensive assessment of long-range goals, policies, and strategies in international telecommunications and information will require that attention be given to the following areas:

(1) Research and development in telecommunications and information technology transfer;

(2) Trade in telecommunications and information equipment; market access; non-tariff trade barriers;

(3) International telecommunications facilities and networks, their structure, technological characteristics, and the international institutions and organization that affect their development;

(4) Telecommunications and information services provided by the networks; trade in services; international flows of information; terms of access to facilities by users; and cost of use;

(5) Mass media; broadcast and other electronic media; free flow of information; and

(6) National defense, security, and emergency preparedness requirements and concerns.

For each of these areas, consideration will be given to issues including:

(a) The appropriate role, if any, of the U.S. government in influencing and directing developments in each area;

(b) The public interest;

(c) Economic interests of the United States; interests of users of telecommunications and information goods and services; market access,

(239)

Federal Register / Vol. 47, No. 212 / Tuesday, November 2, 1982 / Notices 49695

market share; commercial trade and investment;

(d) Orderly mechanisms for establishing international agreements on technical standards;

(e) Selection of and support for appropriate international forums for discussion and negotiation;

(f) Procedures for effective preparation of U.S. delegations to international meetings;

(g) Effectively addressing social and political concerns raised by developments in international telecommunications and information, especially with regard to the problems and needs of developing countries; and

(h) Effective U.S. government organizational structures to formulate and execute policy.

### Specific Questions

Questions of particular relevance to the study include those provided as examples under the seven headings that follow.

1. *Research and Development; Technological Base*—Any erosion in the technological lead of the United States would have serious implications for long-term competitiveness of the entire telecommunications and information sector and would adversely affect other commercial activities that rely heavily on efficient telecommunications and information services.

• *What policies will ensure the technological lead of the United States in telecommunications and information industries?*

• *What policies will promote greater efficiency in the commercial exploitation of basic research and the existing knowledge base?*

• *Under what conditions is technology in telecommunications and information to be sold, tranferred to, or shared with other countries?*

2. *Trade in Telecommunications and Information Equipment*—Equipment producers rely on access to foreign markets for sales.

• *When access to foreign markets is threatened by the trade and investment policies of other countries, what is the appropriate response?*

• *What actions, if any, should be taken to develop and promote access to emerging markets, particularly those of developing countries?*

• *Can self-imposed barriers to U.S. exports in this area be identified? If so, what steps should be taken to reduce or remove them?*

3. *International Telecommunications Facilities and Networks*—Establishing and maintaining the international networks that provide

telecommunications and information services is a cooperative venture carried out by private companies, quasi-government entities, and governments through bilateral agreements, and through international organizations that set technical standards and operating procedures. International and regional organizations and institutions that currently serve as forums of cooperative efforts of this kind include, among others, INTELSAT, the International Telecommunication Union (Consultative Committee on International Telegraph and Telephone, Consultative Committee on International Radio, the International Frequency Registration Board, and the Administrative Council), INMARSAT, and the Inter-American Telecommunications Conference (CITEL).

• *Should U.S. support for or participation in these organizations be modified: strengthened or weakened?*

• *Should alternative organizations be developed to foster more effective cooperation among countries?*

A number of recent international conferences including those involving telecommunications and information have seen disputes arise between developed and developing countries. Examples include the 1979 World Administrative Radio Conference, the 1982 UNISPACE Conference, the 1982 ITU Plenipotentiary meeting, and the UNESCO Belgrade Conference in 1980.

• *What steps should be taken by the United States to address these developments in order to ensure the attainment of U.S. objectives while simultaneously addressing the legitimate concerns of developing countries?*

• *Should we consider the feasibility and desirability of alternatives to the ITU and, if so, what alternatives are reasonably available?*

The subject of preparation by the United States for the 1979 World Administrative Radio Conference and the 1982 ITU Plenipotentiary Conference have received much attention. There has been public and congressional comment and testimony that the United States is not effectively preparing for such conferences.

• *What are the deficiencies in U.S. preparation for international conferences, and what measures should be taken to improve such preparation?*

The U.S. commitment to INTELSAT as the sole provider of international communications via satellite has contributed to the establishment of a

highly successful international satellite system.

• *What are the consequences to the INTELSAT organization and U.S. interests of the establishment of regional satellite systems?*

• *Are there aspects of the 1962 Communications Satellite Act that require revision?*

4. *Telecommunications and Information Services provided by the Networks*—Though not clearly separable from issues concerning the structure of facilities and networks, the issues of the services offered and terms and conditions of use of the facilities raise somewhat different questions. The issues center on access rather than on technological configuration and capacity, and focus more on the interests of users rather than on the interests of facilities providers.

• *To what extent is the international provision of telecommunications and information services and of information flow primarily a matter of trade policy and foreign direct investment?*

• *Should strategies be adopted to reduce non-tariff barriers to the international provision of telecommunications and information services? What role should reciprocal agreements play? Which are the appropriate forums or vehicles for carrying out the strategies?*

The use of telecommunications and information technologies, particularly satellite technologies and the combination of computers and telecommunications, have raised a number of social and political concerns among nations.

• *Are U.S. policies and positions adequate regarding issues such as national sovereignty, privacy, and external influences on regional or national culture?*

• *How can the principle of free flow of information be clarified to reflect the diversity of meaning of the concept?*

5. *Mass Media*—The United States is committed to the concept of freedom of the press, both domestically and internationally.

• *What threats to press freedom are posed by heightened political attention to international telecommunications and information activities? What policies and strategies should the U.S. pursue to preserve free flows of information?*

6. *Organization of the Executive Branch*—The issues raised in international telecommunications and information policy are diverse and affect domestic telecommunications and

49696    Federal Register / Vol. 47, No. 212 / Tuesday, November 2, 1982 / Notices

information policy, employment and economic policy, trade policy, monetary policy, foreign policy, and national security policy. Currently there are cabinet level and other major groups set up with primary responsibility for each.

- *Given the variety of areas and interests affected by international telecommunications and information issues, is the Executive Branch organized to formulate and execute consistent, effective policy? If not, what organizational adjustments are required to improve performance in this area?*
- *Are there more fundamental structural problems surrounding federal agencies that have to be addressed in order to formulate and execute effective, consistent policy?*
  7. *General*—Questions relevant to all of the areas above include:
- *Among all issues raised in this notice or other issues that should be considered in a comprehensive study of long-range goals and strategies, which require the most urgent attention?*
- *How best can competition, deregulation, and other policies applied in the U.S. domestic setting serve as the basis for international policy?*

**Bernard J. Wunder, Jr.,**
*Assistant Secretary of Commerce for Communications and Information.*

October 28, 1982.

[FR Doc. 82-30044 Filed 11-1-82; 8:45 am]
**BILLING CODE 3510-60-M**

List of Respondents to the Notice of Inquiry

Aeronautical Radio, Inc.
American Institute of Aeronautics and Astronautics
American Library Association
American Newspaper Publishers Association
American Satellite Company
American Telephone and Telegraph Company
Association of Data Processing Service Organizations
CBS
Dr. George Codding, University of Colorado, Boulder
Communications Industries Association of Japan
  by Anderson, Hibey, Nauheim, and Blair
Communications Satellite Corporation
Computer and Business Equipment Manufacturers Assn.
Freedom House
Honorable Michael R. Gardner, Akin, Gump, Strauss, Hauer, and Feld
Georgetown Center for Strategic and International Studies
Information Industry Association
International Business Machines Corp.
Kessler Marketing Intelligence
Morality in Media, Inc.
Motorola, Inc.
National Academy of Sciences
National Association of Broadcasters
National Association of Manufacturers
National Commission of Libraries and Information Science
National Public Radio
National Science Foundation
RCA Corporation
RCA Global Communications, Inc.
Satellite Business Systems
Scientific-Atlanta, Inc.
Simplex Wire and Cable Company
Southern Pacific Communications
The Washington Post
.Toward Freedom
Transnational Data Reporting Service, Inc.
TRT Telecommunications Corporation
United States Department of State
United States Information Agency
United States Telecommunications Suppliers Assn.
U.S. Telephone and Telegraph Corporation
Weinschel Engineering
Western Union International, Inc.
Wometco Enterprises by Cohn and Marks
Xerox Corporation

APPENDIX B

INTERNATIONAL ORGANIZATIONS IN COMMUNICATIONS

This appendix presents brief descriptions, in alphabetical order, of 20 international organizations in the telecommunications and information field. Some of the organizations profiled have an impact on only a few of the issues covered in this report. Others, such as the International Telecommunication Union, have a major role in many aspects of the subject. Involvement of the United States in the forums described here ranges from heavy to little or none. (In some of the organizations, the United States is not a member, and any U.S. participation is limited to observation). As discussed in this report, the United States should review the nature and extent of participation in each of these international forums.

Allied Radio Frequency Organizations (ARFA)
Conference of European Postal and Telecommunications Administrations (CEPT)
Conference of Inter-American Telecommunications (CITEL)
Council of Europe (CoE)
Intergovernmental Bureau of Informatics (IBI)
International Civil Aviation Organization (ICAO)
International Maritime Organization (IMO)
International Maritime Satellite Organization (INMARSAT)
International Program for Development of Communication (IPDC)
International Standard Organization (ISO)
International Telecommunications Satellite Organization (INTELSAT)
International Telecommunication Union (ITU)
Organization for Economic Cooperation and Development (OECD)
United Nations Centre on Transnational Corporations (UNCTC)
United Nations Committee on Information
United Nations Committee on Peaceful Uses of Outer Space (UNCOPUOS)
United Nations Development Program (UNDP)
United Nations Educational, Scientific and Cultural Organizations (UNESCO)
Universal Postal Union (UPU)
World Intellectual Property Organization (WIPO)

243

## ALLIED RADIO FREQUENCY AGENCY (ARFA)

Affiliation: NATO agency formed to serve NATO.

Membership: Members of the NATO Alliance: Belgium, Canada, Denmark, France, Germany, Greece, Italy, The Netherlands, Norway, Portugal, Turkey, United Kingdom, and the United States.

Function: Conducts radio frequency planning in support of allied war plans and frequency coordination for day-to-day operations of the member administrations.

Background, History: The forerunner of ARFA was the European Radio Frequency Agency (ERFA), formed in 1950-1951, with headquarters in London. In the early 1960's the name was changed to ARFA, the headquarters moved to Brussels, and was located in the building housing NATO with 30 full-time staff members. The chairmanship has been rotated among different administrations with the U.S. having provided approximately 75 percent of the chairmen. The current chairman is Col. J. H. Weiss, U.S. Army, and the U.S. member is stationed at the Headquarters of the U.S. European Command in Germany.

Issues Addressed: The basic issues addressed are: (1) development of long range radio frequency plans in support of NATO war and peacetime operations; and (2) basic frequency coordination and assignment functions required for daily military operations of the member administrations such as the resolution of interference, planning for different frequency bands, channelization, determination of policy issues, and consideration of the impact of ITU Conferences on ARFA activities.

U.S. Involvement: Since the chairman of ARFA is from the U.S. and the U.S. was instrumental in the formation of ERFA in the early 1950's, many of our European allies consider the U.S. to be the most involved of all the NATO administrations. The Military Communications Electronics Board (MCEB) of the Department of Defense is in constant liaison with ARFA, and examines all ARFA documentation to provide guidance to the U.S member.

244

## CONFERENCE OF EUROPEAN POSTAL AND TELECOMMUNICATIONS ADMINISTRATIONS (CEPT)

Affiliation: Independent; closed regional organization.

Membership: Austria, Belgium, Denmark, Finland, France, West Germany, Greece, Iceland, Ireland, Italy, Luxembourg, the Netherlands, Norway, Portugal, Spain, Sweden, Switzerland, Turkey and the United Kingdom, plus every other Western European state. The Montreaux Agreement requires that only the European PTTs of member countries of UPU, or ITU members, can be members of the Conference.

Function: To maintain and extend international cooperation for the use of telecommunications among European nations; and to coordinate national policies, practices, and standards in telecommunications and postal services.

Background, History: Agreement was signed on June 26, 1959, by representatives of certain administrations. Ratification followed, and the Agreement went into effect under Article 11, officially establishing CEPT.

Issues Addressed: CEPT has established a Special Group on Integrated Services Digital Network (ISDN) and there are several organizational units within CEPT dealing with CEPT problems to provide a means of European cooperation on studies of digital local networks. CEPT representatives have been involved in the North Atlantic Consultative Process (NACP) for the last seven years to improve the planning of cable transmission facilities across the North Atlantic. There is also an established CEPT standard on videotex.

U. S. Involvement: U. S. is not a member of CEPT, but monitors its involvement with issues described above.

**CONFERENCE ON INTER-AMERICAN TELECOMMUNICATIONS (CITEL)**

Affiliation: Regional organization, Organization of American States (OAS)

Membership: Permanent Secretary: Mr. Mario Pachajoa Burbano; United States, Canada, Cuba, all of Central America, and South America.

Function: Serves as the center of consultation and cooperation for the member states to facilitate the orderly development of telecommunications in the Western Hemisphere. Assists in developing telecommunications on a regional level.

Background, History: The first International Conference of American States (Washington, DC, 1889-1890) established the International Union of American Republics, forerunner of the Pan American Union and present day OAS. Government subsidies for a submarine telegraph cable to link Pacific Ocean ports to Chile were discussed. In 1924, the first inter-American conference devoted to telecommunications matters was held in Mexico City. Four Inter-American Radio Conferences were held between 1937-1949 to address radio spectrum and broadcasting matters in the American Hemisphere. In 1963, a predecessor body to the present CITEL (Inter-American Telecommunications Commission) was set up as a special committee of the Inter-American Economic and Social Council of the OAS. The earlier CITEL met annually from 1965-1970. The organizational structure of CITEL was elevated to that of a specialized conference in 1971. The full CITEL, in accordance with its organization plan, convenes once every four years, while its executive organ, COM/CITEL, meets once a year. The Citel headquarters is in the OAS Secretariat in Washington, DC.

Issues Addressed: Coordinates and prepares regional views and positions for conferences and activities of the ITU. CITEL has three permanent technical committees dealing with the following subjects:

Committee I — Inter-American Telecommunications System — is concerned with three principal areas of activity: planning and development, technical standards, and tariffs and operations.

Committee II — Radio Broadcasting — deals with technical standards on broadcasting, conducts studies on the use of the broadcast frequency spectrum, assists member countries with national broadcasting plans and their implementation, and promotes the establishment of bilateral and multilateral agreements in the broadcasting field.

Committee III — Radio Communications — deals primarily with aeronautical, maritime, and meteorological telecommunications, radio spectrum matters, and educational television.

The 12th meeting of the Executive Committee of CITEL was held May-June, 1982, in Buenos Aires. Permanent Secretary Pachajoa presented a document, COM/CITEL 256, on the activities of the General Secretariat in development of information networks, related to the following: the study of the use of existing telecommunication networks for promotion of education, science and culture, and use of data networks for an exchange of information at the inter-American level. Reference was also made to the Inter-American University Organization (IUO) with headquarters in Canada as an educational and cultural project to be used by the inter-American telecommunications network.

U. S. Involvement: The U. S. has been an active participant in planning sessions under the auspices of CITEL. The second CITEL elected the U. S. as a member of COM/CITEL along with Argentina, Brazil, Costa Rica, Guatemala, Mexico, Paraguay, Peru and Venezuela. CITEL is the most important regional organization in which U.S. deals on communication.

Other Coordination/Involvement: CITEL negotiates before the ITU, OAS, and UNDP on "Regional Integration of Telecommunications" with UNDP/ITU project and LAR/77/010 to be maintained before the end of 1983.

246

## COUNCIL OF EUROPE (CoE)

Affiliation: Independent.

Membership: 21 European nations: Austria, Belgium, Cyprus, Denmark, France, West Germany, Greece, Iceland, Ireland, Italy, Liechtenstein, Luxembourg, Malta, the Netherlands, Norway, Portugal, Spain, Sweden, Switzerland, Turkey, United Kingdom.

Function: To implement and enforce the European Convention on Human Rights of 1950. Its aims are to work for greater European unity, improve living conditions and develop human values in Europe, and uphold the principles of parliamentary democracy and human rights.

Background, History: The Council of Europe was the first West European political organization to be created and is still the one with the largest membership. Its statute, endowing it with two organs -- a committee of Ministers and Parliamentary Assembly, was signed in London on May 5, 1949. Its headquarters were established in Strasbourg the same year.

Issues Addressed: To coincide with its mandate, the Council has drafted a "Convention for the Protection of Individuals with Regard to Automatic Data Processing of Personal Data." It will be legally binding and will come into effect when ratified by five member countries at the end of 1983. CoE's committees include, inter alia, those on: Political Affairs, Economic Affairs and Development, Social and Health Questions, Legal Affairs, Culture and Education, Science and Technology, Regional Planning and Local Authorities, Agriculture Relations with European Nonmember Countries and Migration, Refugees, and Demography.

The CoE attaches great importance to international communications and is particularly concerned with the mass media and the recent growth of data processing in industrialized societies and its impact on the computer industry. The Committee of Ministers established a steering committee to follow the development of the mass media as a whole. It will analyze all aspects (legal, economic, technical and soci-political) of the press, radio and television.

U.S. Involvement: The U.S. is not a member of CoE but remains interested in issues which the organization addresses.

Other Coordination/Involvement: Due to a large number of intergovernmental organizations with competence in matters of economic cooperation between European countries -- such as European Economic Community (EEC), United Nations (UN) and the Organization for Economic Cooperation and Development (OECD), the Committee of Ministers under CoE's statute, now deals with matters in this field.

Once a year, the Assembly devotes a day's debate to OECD activities. The Committee on Economic Affairs and Development prepares the main report on the subject accompanied by opinions from other committees concerned. The Parliamentary Assembly has thus become an unofficial parliamentary body for OECD.

The Parliamentary Assembly also takes a close interest in the European Free Trade Assocation (EFTA), and the concerted actions of multinational corporations and multilateral trade negotiations in the GATT.

The Committee on Science and Technology deals with Europe's needs regarding remote-sensing, the space techniques in the management of natural resources, and periodically organizes discussions of European space policy.

247

## INTERGOVERNMENTAL BUREAU FOR INFORMATICS (IBI)

Affiliation: Independent, outside UN.

Membership: 40 nations composed predominantly of developing countries. France, Italy, Ireland and Spain are the only developed member countries with France providing most of its budget.

Function: Provides forum to aid countries in understanding broad policy and legal questions related to transborder data flow (TBDF) and related electronic information issues. IBI is most influential among less developed countries,and its resolutions have major impact. Its goal is to have these countries sensitized to impact of informatics on society and discover potential of informatics capabilities. IBI has been successful in causing less developed countries to understand the issues behind and the impact of information flows. Its major objectives are the promotion of applications of information technology in developing countries; as well as advising, promoting, and recommending adoption of national and international policies for informatics.

Background, History: IBI, formerly the International Computation Center (ICC) established in Rome in 1961, was created under the auspices of the UN and UNESCO by general resolutions dating back to 1946. A decision was made in 1969 to modify the organization's objectives, and in 1974 the name was officially changed. The headquarters is in Rome.

Issues Addressed: International Working Party on "Data Protection and International Law" first met May 25-26, and country case studies were proposed on economic and commercial aspects of TBDF. Other issues are described above. In addition, IBI conducts a large number of specialized activities, such as an experts group on standardization in informatics and a user's group on informatics applications in the field of public health.

U. S. Involvement: The U. S. is not a member of IBI, but has official observer status as do several other developed countries. It has participated in several IBI sponsored international conferences. The first was its Intergovernmental Conference on Strategies and Policies for Informatics (SPIN I) held in 1978 in Spain. It provided main publicity for the IBI with 78 countries in attendance. The next major conference was the World Conference on Transborder Data Flows held in June, 1980. Three working groups on TBDFs were formed, each of which has met once. They are:

(1)    International Working Group for the Analysis of Economic and Commercial Aspects of Transborder Data Flows;

(2)    International Working Group on Data Protection and International Law; and

(3)    International Working Group on the International Contact of Transborder Data Flows.

Other Coordination/Involvement: Interacts with UNESCO. The MacBride Commission suggested UNESCO and other organizations take a closer look at informatics and telecommunications. IBI received official observer status at the ITU five days before the World Conference on Transborder Data Flow Policies in Rome in 1980. IBI's major activity will be SPIN II (the Second Intergovernmental Conference on Strategies and Policies for Informatics) in Havana, Cuba, in September, 1984. It plans to sponsor SPIN II without the co-sponsorship of UNESCO.

248

## INTERNATIONAL CIVIL AVIATION ORGANIZATION (ICAO)

Affiliation: Specialized agency of the United Nations; intergovernmental.

Membership: 150 nations.

Function: To develop the principles and techniques of international air navigation; to foster the planning and development of international civil aviation, including promoting safety of flight.

Background, History: ICAO was established under the convention on International Civil Aviation concluded at Chicago on December 7, 1944, and the U. S. became a member in 1945. It became a specialized agency of the UN system on May 13, 1947.

Issues Addressed: As part of its responsibility in ensuring safety of flight, ICAO's focus is to develop Standards and Recommended Practices (SARPS) pertaining to the orderly uses of telecommunications used for aviation applications. Within the allotment for civil aviation, ICAO apportions specific bands for various aviation uses and the frequency assignment to specific services.

ICAO's primary value is in standardizing technicial evaluations and procedures. The organization has done work recently in replacing current instrument landing systems.

U. S. Involvement: The U. S. recognizes ICAO as the technical forum for adopting international standards and recommended practices (SARPs) to ensure the regularity of international air navigation. The U. S. is a member of ICAO's council and maintains a permanent mission in Montreal. We also participate in the various committees, commissions, and working groups of ICAO.

The U. S. is supportive of ICAO's work in establishing standards and practices in technical areas affecting the safety and orderly flight of civil aviation. The U.S. however, is in opposition to the majority view that ICAO should play a larger role in the economic sphere as, in activities such as establishing airline fares, rates, and regulation of air transport services, and collection of statistics. These ICAO goals are contrary to the U.S. interest in achieving greater deregulation of and competition in civil air services.

Other Coordination/Involvement: ICAO works closely with the ITU in those aspects of frequency management associated with the radio spectrum allotted to the aeronautical services. The two organizations have been coordinating positions for the 1983 Mobile WARC. ICAO provides the technical inputs to ensure that the uses and assignment of frequencies allocated are consistent and applicable with ITU radio regulations.

249

## INTERNATIONAL MARITIME ORGANIZATION (IMO)

Affiliation: Specialized Agency of the United Nations.

Membership: 122 countries.

Function: IMO is charged with establishing technical standards for maritime safety and preventing marine pollution.

Background, History: The convention establishing the International Maritime Convention (IMCO) was negotiated in 1948. It came into being in 1958 following its acceptance by the required number of states. The title of the convention and the organization name was changed to its present form in May, 1982.

Issues Addressed: IMO's focus is primarily to facilitate international cooperation on technical matters affecting shipping, particularly as it relates to the safety of life at sea. The organization operates through an assembly which meets biennially, the Council, which meets semi-annually, and the principal committees concerning maritime safety, marine environment protection, legal and technical cooperation, and facilitation.

IMO had originally interpreted its role in maritime communications to be restricted to matters related to distress and safety.

U.S. Involvement: U.S. is preparing for the 1983 Mobile Radio Conference in February in Geneva.

Other Coordination/Involvement: IMO has a Subcommittee on Radio Communication which sets carriage requirements for vessels on international voyages. In addition, IMO has a Maritime Safety Committee and coordinates with CCIR of ITU on radio communication.

250

### INTERNATIONAL MARITIME SATELLITE ORGANIZATION (INMARSAT)

Affiliation: Independent. Set up in a parallel manner to INTELSAT of which Comsat is also a signatory.

Membership: 37 major maritime nations and associated operating entities.

Purpose: To develop and operate the space segment (satellites and ground equipment) of the global satellite system to serve maritime, commercial, and safety needs.

Background, History: INMARSAT was formed based on international agreements on July 16, 1979. The Radio Subcommittee of the International Maritime Convention (IMCO) began a long process stimulated by the success of MARISAT. It operates under two international agreements: the convention, signed by the government of each participating nation (party), and the Operating Agreement, signed by the government or designated public or private telecommunication entity (signatory). INMARSAT consists of an Assembly comprised of representatives of Parties, and a Council, now consisting of 24 representatives of signatories. The headquarters is in London. Service began February, 1982.

Issues Addressed: The major issue for INMARSAT is its financial viability. The issues of interest to U.S. are the joint Aeronautical/Maritime Satellite, its use in ports and harbors, and the second generation space segment.

U. S. Satellite Involvement: COMSAT is the U. S. signatory of INMARSAT, based upon the 1978 Act. It has a financial interest in INMARSAT facilities, and shares the revenues and expenses.

251

## INTERNATIONAL PROGRAM FOR THE DEVELOPMENT
## OF COMMUNICATION (IPDC)

Affiliation: Autonomous body of UNESCO.

Membership: Member states of UNESCO.

Function: To help meet the practical communication needs of developing countries.

Background, History: The U.S. initiated the IPDC concept to offer UNESCO an alternative to unproductive, political debates on the New World Information and Communication Order (NWICO), an off-shoot of the New International Economic Order. NWICO proposals, which the U.S. strenuously opposes, include international codes of journalistic ethics, restrictions on commercial news agencies and advertising, licensing of journalists, and endorsement of government "use" of the media for political purposes.

The IPDC was established in 1980. The first meeting in Paris, June 1980, was primarily concerned with organizational business. At the second meeting in Acapulco in January, 1982, IPDC became operational when it adopted a budget of $910,000 and approved a number of regional and inter-regional projects. A budget of $1,662,000 and several new projects were approved at the third IPDC meeting (Paris, December, 1982).

Issues Addressed: Developing project proposals for training, procurement of equipment, and other practical needs of Third World media, soliciting voluntary financial and technical assistance from donors in order to meet these needs, and helping to raise communications as a priority issue among development planners, donors, and the general public.

U. S. Involvement: At the second IPDC meeting, the U. S. announced that $100,000 in AID funds was being reprogrammed for bilateral assistance to IPDC-approved projects. A second $100,000 was earmarked by AID at the third IPDC meeting, together with a $350,000 grant from USIA for educational exchanges. The U.S. has not contributed to the IPDC Special Account.

The U. S. sits on the 35-member Intergovernmental Council, which sets policy for IPDC at yearly meetings, and the eight-member bureau, which guides the IPDC between Council meetings.

Other Coordination/Involvement: IPDC coordinates with other communication programs in UNESCO and other agencies in the U.N. system, such as ITU and UNDP. There is a standing inter-agency committee of participating U.N. specialized agencies. It also coordinates with regional and international organizations, such as INTELSAT, the Arab Gulf Program, the African Development Bank, as well as bilateral aid donors, and numerous other public and private organizations that have an interest in communications development. Among these are several in the U. S., such as the World Press Freedom Committee, and the American Newspaper Publishers Association, an affiliate of the International Federation of Newspaper Publishers (FIEJ), both of which have observer status with UNESCO.

252

## INTERNATIONAL STANDARDS ORGANIZATION (ISO)

Affiliation: Independent, non-treaty organization.

Membership: 89 national standards bodies.

Function: Develops, coordinates and promulgates international standards that cover all fields except electrical and electronics engineering, which is the responsibility of the International Electrotechnical Commission (IEC).

Background, History: ISO was founded in 1946 in London. Its headquarters are now located in Geneva. The General Assembly meets every three years which elects the President of the organization. The Council acts as the organization's Board of Directors and is responsible for accepting publication of International Standards developed by its technical committees. There are 163 technical committees and 200 subcommittees and working groups reporting to the technical committees.

Issues Addressed: ISO fulfills the need for international standards for use by all countries. One of the issues it is currently concerned with are the challenges posed by GATT standards codes. It sees a need to develop more product-oriented standards than in the past.

U.S. Involvement: The U.S. is represented at ISO by the American National Standards Institute (ANSI). It coordinates U.S. participation in ISO technical work and also has a voice in its administration in being a member of the governing body (Council). As the participating member of many ISO technical committees, it determines the interests of industry, government, and other groups. It forms a U.S. Technical Advisory Group (TAG) which also represents these groups. For example, ANSI is a participating member of the technical committee on photography.

Other Coordination/Involvement: More than 400 international organizations have liaison status with ISO. This includes all U.N. specialized agencies working in similar fields. ISO has consultative status with the U.N. Economic and Social Council and equal status with nearly all bodies and specialized agencies of the U.N. system.

253

## INTERNATIONAL TELECOMMUNICATIONS SATELLITE ORGANIZATION (INTELSAT)

Affiliation: Independent.

Membership: 108 countries and associated operating entities. Several other nations use the system although not members.

Background, History: INTELSAT was formed on August 20, 1964, when representatives from 19 nations signed "interim" agreements establishing the International Telecommunications Satellite Consortium. During the following years, the global satellite communications system was established and many more countries joined the consortium.

Interim agreements called for a series of conferences to be held in Washington, DC, to negotiate "permanent" agreements during the 1969-1971 period to establish a permanent structure. Two agreements (Intergovernmental Agreement and Operating Agreement) resulted and went into effect in 1973. These agreements established the International Telecommunications Satellite Organization with a four-tier organizational structure, which is described below.

(1) Assembly of Parties -- meeting of the governments that are Parties to the Agreement . The Assembly considers those aspects primarily of interest to the Parties as sovereign states, as well as resolutions, recommendations or views from the Meeting of Signatories or the Board of Governors. It meets biennially as called for in the Agreements, unless there is an extraordinary basis for a special meeting.

(2) Meeting of Signatories -- composed of representatives of all governments or designated telecommunications entities to Operating Agreement. The Meeting of Signatories considers matters put to it by either the Assembly of Parties or Board of Governors and matters relating to financial, technical and operational aspects of the system.

(3) Board of Governors -- composed of Signatories whose investment shares, either individually or groups, are no less than a specified amount. Responsible for all decisions related to the design, development, construction, operation, and maintenance of INTELSAT satellites and all other activities. Assisted by Advisory Committees on Technical Matters and Planning and a Budget and Accounts Review Committee. The votes of the Signatories are weighted according to their investment shares.

(4) Executive Organ -- staff of 400, headquartered in Washington, DC, headed by Director-General Santiago Astrain, responsible to Board of Governors for its management and operation.

254

Issues Addressed:   As an international organization responsible for global communications for two-thirds of the world, the INTELSAT system provides global service, and is concerned with research and development activity on satellites for its space segment.  Other issues include the leasing of INTELSAT satellite capacity for domestic communications, earth station standards, regional satellite systems, allocation of satellite orbital slots, and maritime services to INMARSAT.

U. S. Involvement:   COMSAT, the Communications Satellite Corporation, is the U. S. signatory to the INTELSAT system.   Under the Satellite Act, it is the only entity eligible to participate in INTELSAT.  Through its World Systems Division, it provides communications satellite services, using INTELSAT facilities, among the U. S. and other countries, as well as (although on a limited basis) between the continental United States   and offshore U. S. points.   To date, COMSAT is primarily a carriers carrier.   It should be noted, that based on the 1962 Communications Act, INTELSAT is a U.S. originated organization.

Other Coordination/Involvement:   INTELSAT has and maintains a working agreement with the ITU (a U.N. entity); its agreements are in accordance with UN General Assembly Resolution 1721, and it sends a report of its activities annually to the U.N. General Secretary.

255

## INTERNATIONAL TELECOMMUNICATION UNION (ITU)

Affiliation: Specialized agency of the United Nations for telecommunications.

Membership: 157 nations.

Function: To achieve agreement and cooperation among nations on the rational use of all telecommunications.

Background, Structure: The ITU was created in 1932 by the merger of two existing organizations, the International Telegraph Union (founded in 1865) and the signatories of the International Radio Telegraph Convention. ITU consists of four major elements: (1) the Plenipotentiary Conference; (2) the Administrative Conferences; (3) the Administrative Council, and (4) the Permanent Organs: General Secretariat; International Frequency Registration Board; and the International Consultative Committees for Radio (CCIR), and for Telephone and Telegraph (CCITT). The Plenipotentiary Conference is its supreme body and meets every five to nine years. Between Plenipotentiary Conferences, the Administrative Council acts yearly on behalf of the entire membership to formulate policy. Administrative Conferences, either worldwide or regional, convene when need arises to consider specific telecommunications matters.

Issues Addressed: The ITU works to effect the efficient allocation of the radio frequency spectrum and to register radio frequency assignments (through the International Frequency Registration Board) to avoid harmful interference between radio stations of different countries. In addition, the ITU addresses issues such as the development of telecommunications facilities and networks; the creation, development, and improvement of telecommunications equipment and networks in developing countries, participating in appropriate programs of the United Nations. Other duties include the establishment of the lowest possible rates consistent with efficient service and taking into account the need to maintain independent financial administration of telecommunications; establishment of telecommunications standards through the CCITT and CCIR; communications development assistance to LDCs for expanding and building communications infrastructure; as well as undertaking studies, making regulations, adopting resolutions, and collecting and publishing information concerning telecommunications matters.

Other Coordination/Involvement: The ITU interacts with UNESCO, UPU, and UNDP on technical cooperation and assistance projects to less developed countries.

256

## ORGANIZATION FOR ECONOMIC COOPERATION AND DEVELOPMENT (OECD)

Affiliation: Independent.

Membership: 24 industrialized countries: U. S., Canada, Japan, Australia, New Zealand, 19 Western European countries.

Function: The OECD provides a high-level forum for discussion of economic, trade, and industrial policy issues. Most actions of the OECD are non-binding on signatories, such as the Guidelines on the Protection of Privacy or the Declaration on Trade Policy.

Background, History: The OECD was formed in 1948 as the Organization for European Economic Cooperation (OEEC) as a means for the European countries to cooperate in administering the Marshall Plan. In 1960, recognizing their economic interdependence, the Marshall Plan countries, plus the United States and Canada signed the OECD Convention. Australia, New Zealand and Japan later became members.

A Working Party on Information, Computer and Communications Policy (ICCP) was created in the Directorate for Science, Technology and Industry in 1977. An Experts Group on Transborder Data Flows was created under this Working Party in 1978. In 1982, the ICCP Working Party was elevated to a full committee, and the Experts Group became the Working Party on Transborder Data Flows.

Issues Addressed: The Working Party on Transborder Data Flows drafted the Guidelines governing the Protection of Privacy and Transborder Flows of Personal Data in 1979, and has since been engaged in an examination of the legal aspects of transborder data flow, and the economic aspects of transborder data flow of non-personal data. The OECD Committee on Information, Computer and Communications Policy has addressed issues in the last five years such as the impact of microelectronics on productivity and employment, the vulnerability of computerized society, information technology statistics, opportunities for energy saving through microelectronics, the transfer of technological information to developing countries, and most recently, the international implications of changing market structures in telecommunications services. Current projects include studies on the use of information technology in manufacturing and on software.

U. S. Involvement: The U. S. has been a full and active participant in OECD activities. Other OECD Committees have addressed the telecommunications equipment industry (Industry Committee), science and technology policy (Committee on Scientific and Technological Policy), trade in telecommunications services (Trade Committee), and the impact of computer technologies on consumer information (Committee on Consumer Policy). The OECD is also involved in high technology trade discussions agreed to by heads of state at the June, 1982, Versailles Summit.

Other Coordination/Involvement: The Committee on ICCP has cooperated where appropriate with the ITU, and has recently been informed about the activities of the United Nations Center on Transnational Corporations and the Intergovernmental Bureau for Informatics by representatives of those organizations.

257

## UNITED NATIONS CENTRE ON
## TRANSNATIONAL CORPORATIONS (UNCTC)

Affiliation: United Nations Commission on Transnational Corporations

Membership: 48 countries.

Function: To do the staff work for the U. N. Commission on Transnational Corporations. Transborder Data Flow (TBDF) has been placed on its agenda as a permanent item. Specifically, UNCTC is to aid in strengthening the negotiating capability of developing countries vis-a-vis multinational corporations.

Background, History: Established in 1974 through a resolution of the U. N. General Assembly. UNCTC and the U.N. Commission on Transnational Corporations serve as focal points of the U. N. system on all matters relating to Transnational Corporations (TNC's). In 1981, the Commission and the Center began examining questions relating to the role of transnational corporations in transborder data flows. Since then, the work program has focused on country case studies of the developmental impact of transborder data flows and the role of TNCs in these flows, issues pertaining to the international market and remote-sensing data. The headquarters are in New York.

Issues Addressed: UNCTC is in the first year of a five-year work program on transborder data flows. The programs consists of a study on less developed countries' access to the international on-line data base market; country case studies on the role, impact of, and policy responses to TBDF; and a study on TNCs and remote-sensing data.

U. S. Involvement: The U. S. recently became an active participant in UNCTC activities. At its 1982 Commission meeting, Brazil submitted an extensive case study of its telecommunications and computer policies. The U. S. considered this an appropriate forum and good opportunity to present the free-market approach, and has decided to submit a U. S. case study, at the next Commission meeting in June, 1983.

258

### U.N. COMMITTEE ON INFORMATION

Affiliation: Standing Committee of the U. N. General Assembly

Membership: 67 members representing a regional cross-section of the General Assembly.

Function: The Committee has a three-fold mandate:

(1)     To continue to examine United Nations public information policies and activities in the light of the evolution of international relations, particularly during the past two decades, and in regard to the evolution of the imperatives of the New International Economic Order (NIEO), and of a New World Information and Communication Order (NWICO);

(2)     To evaluate and follow up the efforts made and the progress achieved by the United Nations system in the field of information and communications; and

(3)     To promote the establishment of a new, more just and more effective world information and communications order intended to strengthen peace and international understanding, based on the free circulation and wider and better balanced dissemination of information, and to make recommendations thereon in the General Assembly.

Background, History: The Committee was established in its present form in 1978. It meets for several weeks in the summer to examine U.N. information activities, coordination and planning, and to produce a report of its work for the fall meeting of the Special Political Committee (SPC) of the General Assembly. This report becomes the basis of a draft resolution in the SPC on "Questions Relating to Information." The U. S. had joined the consensus in adopting Committee reports, but on two occasions (1981 and 1982) voted against SPC resolutions which, in our view, departed from the consensus reports.

Issues Addressed: The Committee primarily examines ongoing public information programs of the UN Department of Public Information, such as the proposal to lease a satellite television channel, commence international shortwave radio broadcasts on UN activities, continue publication of Development Forum and publish the UN Chronicle in all official languages, strengthen U.N. Information Centers, regionalize its Arabic radio and visual services, strengthen cooperation with the Pool of Non-Aligned News Agencies and with regional news agencies of developing countries, and promote the establishment of a New World Information and Communications Order.

U. S. Involvement: The U. S., as a member of the 67-member Committee on Information since 1978, participates actively in Committee meetings and in the Special Political Committee of the U.N. General Assembly.

Other Coordination/Involvement: The Committee is represented in the Joint United Nations Information Committee (JUNIC), the U.N. system-wide public information coordinating body. Representatives of UNESCO, the ITU and other U.N. specialized and international agencies participate in Committee sessions, speaking for their organizations and supplying information as requested.

259

## UNITED NATIONS COMMITTEE ON THE PEACEFUL
## USES OF OUTER SPACE (COPUOS)

Affiliation: United Nations General Assembly (Standing Committee)

Membership: 47 nations.

Function: To study the legal problems arising from the use of outer space.

Background: COPUOS was established in 1959. Through its subcommittees, whose deliberations are based on consensus rather than voting, COPUOS has become the focal point in the formulation of international law governing the use of outer space. The Outer Space Treaty of 1967 is considered to be the basis of space law embodying the principles of: (1) equal access by all nations; (2) use in the interest of peace, security, cooperation, and understanding in accordance with international law; and (3) strictly nonmilitary purposes.

Issues Addressed: The Scientific and Technical Committee of the COPUOS recommended in 1964 that intensive study of DBS be undertaken. Its Working Group on Direct Broadcast Satellite (DBS) was formed in 1968 as a direct response to this suggestion. The increasing possiblity of direct television broadcasting, remote-sensing satellite, and the expansion of membership to accommodate the wishes of developing countries has led to a hardening of ideological positions. The Working Group has been trying to reach consensus on legal instruments and principles to govern DBS. The debate centers around the conflict of free flow versus national sovereignty (prior consent). In addition, COPUOS has been examining the physical, technical, and legal attributes of the geostationary orbit, including claims by the equatorial countries that orbital positions and slots above them are a natual resource and belong exclusively to them.

U. S. Involvement: The U.S. has been an active participant in COPUOS and the prior consent debate for ten years. Significant departure from consensus principle in outer space activities occurred in November, 1982. The U. N. Special Political Committee approved a resolution barring DBS across international boundaries without the prior consent of the government of the receiving country. Vote was 88 to 15 with 11 abstentions, backed by 18 Asian, African, and Latin American countries. U. S. feels it violates freedom of expression, and considers it an obstacle to the Western Hemisphere Conference on DBS service in Geneva, in the summer of 1983.

Other Coordination/Involvement: The issues under consideration are directly relevant to and have serious consequences for actions taken by the ITU in the planning of the geostationary orbit for DBS and other use. Reference is continually made to the applicability of international law and to the technical procedures of ITU.

260

## UNITED NATIONS DEVELOPMENT PROGRAM (UNDP)

Affiliation: United Nations.

Membership: State members of the United Nations or any specialized agency.

Function: To provide developing countries with technical cooperation and assistance for economic development. Is the central organization in the U.N. system for technical cooperation between developed and developing countries.

Background, History: Following a consolidation by the U.N. General Assembly of the Expanded Program of Technical Assistance (created in 1949) and the U.N. Special Fund (established 1958), the UNDP was established in 1966. The main role in planning and programming UNDP assistance is played by less developed countries themselves.

Issues Addressed: UNDP has been a dominant source of communications development assistance to less developed countries with various training institutions established -- i.e., for broadcast engineering with the National Broadcasting Academy at Bangkok -- and other regional projects based on its course development in telecommunication (CODEVTEL) funded by UNDP.

Other Coordination/Involvement: The ITU is annually allocated approximately $30 million (3-5 percent of UNDP funds) for technical assistance in telecommunications to less developed countries. (Within the UNDP and less devloped countries, telecommunications assistance has a lower priority than programs in agriculture, food, health, literacy, transportation or construction.) The bulk of the Union's technical cooperation activities are carried out as an Executing Agency of the UNDP. The ITU is involved in a wide variety of educational and training programs many of which are funded by ITU. UNDP also coordinates with UNESCO, ESCAP (Economic and Social Council for Asia and the Pacific), as well as 27 other international agencies to aid in supporting many development projects in less developed countries.

261

## UNITED NATIONS EDUCATIONAL, SCIENTIFIC AND CULTURAL ORGANIZATION (UNESCO)

Affiliation: One of 14 UN specialized agencies.

Membership: 158 nations.

Function: Promotes exchanges and collaboration among nations in the field of education, natural sciences, social sciences, culture and communications. UNESCO headquarters are located in Paris.

Background, History: UNESCO was created in London in 1945 by 44 nations including the United States. UNESCO is recognized in the U.N. system as having a central role in the field of information, including media issues and communications development. With the adoption of the 20th UNESCO General Conference in 1978 information issues in UNESCO were put into sharp focus with a major document, known informally as the "Mass Media Declaration," which called for the promotion of the establishment of a New World Information and Communication Order (NWICO). Several unacceptable NWICO concepts, particularly the endorsement of goverment "use" of the media for political purposes, were included in original drafts of the Declaration, but were negotiated out of the version which was finally adopted.

To turn UNESCO away from unproductive and political debate on NWICO issues, the U. S. proposed creating the International Program for the Development of Communication (IPDC), an autonomous body of UNESCO which was formed to help meet the practical communications needs of developing countries. (See profile on IPDC.)

Apart from IPDC projects, the Communication Sector of UNESCO, which was established as an equal sector with the Educational, Scientific, and Cultural Sectors on December 1, 1981, also carries out communication projects. These basic projects include theoretical programs, such as seminars, studies, analyses, meetings of "experts," and some training programs.

UNESCO's Second Medium-Term Plan (1984-1989), the six-year planning document governing the regular programs in communications, contains many improvements initiated by the U. S., and should strengthen the trend away from unacceptable NWICO initiatives.

Issues Addressed: In the communications sphere, UNESCO covers the range of issues from journalistic ethics to the development of communication facilities in the Third World. The U. S. strenuously opposes all initiatives within UNESCO to limit free press practices, such as international codes of journalistic ethics, restrictions on commercial news agencies and advertising, licensing of journalists,

262

and endorsement of government "use" of the media for political purposes. In addition, the U.S. supports constructive non-ideological initiatives to help developing countries improve their communications facilities.

U. S. Involvement: Ongoing UNESCO affairs are monitored by the U. S. Mission to UNESCO in Paris in consultation with the Department of State. The U. S. contributes 25 percent of UNESCO's budget under a long-standing formula.

The Beard Amendment to the Department of State appropriation authorization for FY 1982 and FY 1983 is a key element in U. S. strategy regarding communication issues, because it demonstrates U. S. resolve against anti-free press initiatives. The measure calls for withholding all funds from UNESCO if the Organization implements anti-free press measures.

Other Coordination/Involvement: UNESCO coordinates with other communication programs in the ITU, UNDP, and regional and international organizations, bilateral aid donors, and numerous public and private organizations that have an interest in communcations and research and development.

263

## UNIVERSAL POSTAL UNION (UPU)

Affiliation: Specialized agency of the United Nations.

Membership: 163 countries.

Purpose: To secure the organization and improvements of postal services, and to promote international cooperation in that sphere.

Background, History: The UPU's predecessor agency — the General Postal Union — was founded in 1874 to facilitate the reciprocal exchange of letters and postal items. The U. S. was an original member representing the first participation of the U. S. in an international organization. The union became a specialized agency of the U.N. on July 1, 1948 — six months prior to the ITU attaining the same status.

Issues Addressed: The UPU's focus is to establish standards and operating procedures for the international exchange of mail. Its technical responsibility includes the setting of postal rates and fees, determining air conveyance dues, and transit charges. Due to the rapid evolution of electronic information and communications systems — including "electronic mail" — UPU has, by virtue of its responsibilities, become involved in communications issues. It is also involved in the controversial issue of the subsidization of costly mail delivery systems through high tariffs on electronic communications systems. This cross-subsidization is common among countries with integrated government administration of postal, telephone, and telegraph systems and, therefore, has an impact on the dependence of multinational firms on such international communications.

The UPU has established a Working Party of the Consultative Council for Postal Studies (CCPS) to examine electronic mail as part of its ongoing review of the future of the Postal Service.

U. S. Involvement: The lead agency is the U. S. Postal Service. The U. S. is a member of the UPU Executive Council until 1989 and participates as a member of the CCPS.

Other Coordination/Involvement: The UPU is considered to be ITU's sister organization. In much of the world, the same ministries of Posts and Telecommunications (PTTs) have both the postal and telecommunications responsibilities. These members have interests in maintaining their monopoly against U. S. moves to deregulate and create competition in the marketplace. The UPU and ITU continue to have consultations on electronic mail and the future of the Postal Service.

264

**WORLD INTELLECTUAL PROPERTY ORGANIZATION (WIPO)**

Affiliation: United Nations Specialized Agency, intergovernmental.

Membership: 97 countries.

Function: To promote the protection of intellectual property through cooperation among nations and administer the various "unions," each founded on a multilateral treaty and dealing with the legal and administrative aspects of intellectual property.

Background, Structure: Although the origins of what is now WIPO go back to 1883, WIPO was established in 1967 in Stockholm by "The Convention Establishing the WIPO." It entered into force in 1970. WIPO is divided into two parts:

(1)     Governing bodies consisting of representatives of states who decide matters on treaties and states; and

(2)     A secretariat or international bureau which ensures cooperation and coordination among the intellectual property unions created by the treaties which WIPO adminsters.

The two principles unions are:

(1)     Paris Union of Countries -- signatories to Paris Convention of Industrial Property of 1883; and

(2)     Berne Union of Countries -- signatories to Berne Convention of 1886 for the Protection of Literary and Artistic Works.

A country doesn't have to belong to either to be a member. Its headquarters is in Geneva, Switzerland.

Issues Addressed: WIPO assists in explaining its treaties to member countries, helps draft domestic legislation for member countries and gives legal and technical assistance to less developing countries in modernizing their industrial property and copyright systems. The Geneva Convention for the Protection of Producers of Phonograms Against Unauthorized Duplication of their Phonograms signed October 29, 1971, is an example of a convention where WIPO cooperated with interested groups to prepare and provide protection for the text of an instrument that would accord protection for their creative work. WIPO continues to do studies and provide services designed to facilitate protection provided in the Convention. It also follows new technological developments -- i.e., cable television and computers -- and assists member states in adapting the protection of the convention to the new technologies. A recent event held to highlight a problem that has become particularly acute is the Worldwide Forum on Piracy of Sound and Audiovisual Recordings, held in Geneva, March, 1982.

U.S. Involvement: The U.S. is a member of WIPO. It is one of the organizations of main interest due to its involvement with trademarks and copyright, industrial designs, unfair competition, international protection and patents. The Paris Convention is fundamental to the protection of ownership rights of U.S. businesses engaged in foreign investment and technology transfer.

Other Coordination/Involvement: Many of the programs in the copyright area are sponsored in cooperation with UNESCO and the International Labor Organization (ILO) in the communications area. The important event was the Convention relating to the Distribution of Program E-Carrying Signals transmitted by satellite in May, 1974. This was also established due to coordination between WIPO and UNESCO. All three organizations provide Secretariat services for the International Convention for the Protection of Performers, Producers of Phonograms and Broadcasting Organizations (Rome Convention), October, 1961.

**APPENDIX C**

**BILLS AND PUBLIC LAWS RELATING TO INTERNATIONAL TELECOMMUNICATIONS AND INFORMATION POLICY IN THE 96TH AND 97TH CONGRESSES (1979 - 1982)**

A compilation of the significant bills and public laws pertaining to international telecommunications and information policy appears below, listed according to a subject index and numerically by bill and public law number. This listing is intended to supplement the report with a substantive representation of bills introduced and laws passed in the last four years; it is not, however, all-inclusive in scope.

(266)

267

## Subject Index

I. BILLS CONCERNING RESEARCH AND DEVELOPMENT

To Stimulate the Use of Computers
 H.R. 5573
 H.R. 6397
 S. 240
 S. 2281
The Federal Role in Technology Transfer
 H.R. 4564
 S. 881 (Public Law 97-219)
 S. 1657
 S. 2272
Educational Initiatives in New Technology
 H.R. 4242 (Public Law 97-34)
 H.J.R. 266 (Public Law 97-34)
 H.R. 4326
 H.R. 5573
 H.R. 5742
 H.R. 5820
 H.R. 6093
 S. 2421
 S. 2475
Employment and Training of Skilled Workers
in New Technology
 H.R. 5254
 H.R. 5812
 H.R. 5820
 H.R. 6950
 S. 2224
 S. 2476
To Encourage Joint Government-Industry-University Research and
Development
 H.R. 3137
 H.R. 4242
 H.R. 4672 (Public Law 96-480)
 H.R. 5890 (Public Law 97-324)
 H.R. 6262
 H.R. 6933 (Public Law 96-517)
 S.414 (Public Law 96-517)
 S. 1250 (Public Law 96-480)

II. BILLS CONCERNING FACILITIES AND NETWORKS
 H.R. 4927 (Public Law 97-130)
 S. 271 (Public Law 97-130)
 S. 2469

268

III. BILLS CONCERNING INTERNATIONAL TELECOMMUNICATIONS AND INFORMATION SERVICES

    To Deregulate Certain Types of Carriers and Services
        H.R. 4927 (Public Law 97-130)
        H.R. 5158
        S. 271
        S. 611
        S. 2469
        S. 2827
    Foreign Entry into U.S. Service Markets
        H.R. 4225
    To Regulate Foreign Ownership of Cable Television Franchises
        H.R. 4225
        S. 2172

IV. BILLS CONCERNING TRADE IN SERVICES AND EQUIPMENT

    To Promote Service Sector Trade
        H.R. 5383
        H.R. 5519
        H.R. 5690
        H.R. 6093
        H.R. 6773
        S. 1233
        S. 2058
    To Promote Export Trade
        H.R. 4612 (Public Law 96-481)
        S. 734 (Public Law 97-290)
    To Reduce Trade Barriers
        H.R. 5205
        H.R. 6433
        H.R. 6436
        S. 2283
        S. 2356
    To Promote Reciprocity
        H.R. 4177
        H.R. 5205
        S. 2051
        S. 2067
        S. 2094
        S. 2223
    To Promote International Negotiations
        H.R. 5579
        H.R. 5596
        S. 2058

269

IV. <u>BILLS CONCERNING TRADE IN SERVICE AND EQUIPMENT</u> (Continued)

To Deny Preferential Treatment to Countries with Substantial
Exports to the U.S.
    H.R. 6623
To Centralize Trade Functions in an Independent Office
    H.R. 7015
    S. 970
    S. 2837

V. <u>BILLS CONCERNING NATIONAL SECURITY AND EMERGENCY
PREPAREDNESS</u>

To Ensure National Security Controls and the Free Flow
of Scientific Information
    H.R. 109
    H.R. 513
    H.R. 3567 (Public Law 97-145)
    H.R. 4590
    H.R. 4934
    H.R. 7015
    S. 1860
    S. 2837

VI. <u>BILLS CONCERNING GOVERNMENT ORGANIZATION AND INTERNATIONAL
ACTIVITIES</u>

To Reorganize U.S. National and International Activities
    H.R. 1957
    H.R. 3137
    H.R. 8443
    S. 611
    S. 2469
    S. 2827
    S. 2837
To Improve Domestic Competition
    H.R. 4801
    H.R. 4927
    H.R. 5158
    H.R. 7292 (Public Law 97-367)
    S. 270
    S. 271
    S. 898
    S. 1159
To Authorize NTIA
    H.R. 3239
    S. 2181
To Authorize the Department of State
    H.R. 4814 (Public Law 97-241)
    S. 1193 (Public Law 97-241)

270

VII. BILLS CONCERNING PARTICIPATION IN INTERNATIONAL ORGANIZATIONS

To Prepare for International Conferences
H.J.R. 36
H.J.R. 515
H.J.R. 108
To Control Efforts of International Organizations to Restrain Freedom of Expression
H.R. 4814 (Public Law 97-241) (Beard Amendment)
S. 1193 (Public Law 97-241) (Beard Amendment)

VIII. BILLS CONCERNING MASS MEDIA AND INFORMATION ISSUES

To Promote Patent and Copyright Protection
H.R. 1805
H.R. 2007 (Public Law 97-366)
H.R. 2108 (Public Law 97-366)
H.R. 4242
H.R. 4441 (Public Law 97-366)
H.R. 4564
H.R. 6168 (Public Law 97-215)
H.R. 6260 (Public Law 97-247)
H.R. 6933 (Public Law 96-517)
S. 414 (Public Law 96-517)
S. 603 (Public Law 97-366)
To Promote Privacy Issues
H.R. 3486 (Public Law 96-440)
H.R. 5935
S. 503
S. 865
S. 1790 (Public Law 96-440)
To Facilitate Public Broadcasting
S. 270

IX. PUBLIC LAWS CONCERNING INTERNATIONAL TELECOMMUNICATIONS AND INFORMATION

To Promote Research and Development
Public Law 96-480
Public Law 97-34
Public Law 97-219
Public Law 97-247
Public Law 97-324
Public Law 97-367
To Promote Trade in Equipment
Public Law 96-481
Public Law 97-145
Public Law 97-290

IX. PUBLIC LAWS CONCERNING INTERNATIONAL TELECOMMUNICATIONS AND INFORMATION (Continued)

International Copyright Legislation
Public Law 96-517
Public Law 97-215
Public Law 97-366
To Promote Trade in Services
Public Law 97-130
To Control the Efforts of International Organizations to Restrain Freedom of Expression
Public Law 97-241
Mandate to Study U.S. Long Range International Telecommunications and Information Goals
Public Law 97-259

271

## House Bills on International Telecommunications and Information Issues*
### (1979-1982)

H.R. 109    To amend the Arms Export Control Act. Authorizes Secretary of Defense to regulate information pertaining to items on the Munitions List. Publication of such information is prohibited in order to preclude its unauthorized export. Opposed by the Association for Computing Machinery on the ground that it will inhibit research and development of computing technologies, and "treats the publication of ideas in the same category as the export of hardware." The bill has created quite a stir in the academic community and high technology industries. Bennett (R-FLA), 1/5/81. To Foreign Affairs Committee.

H.R. 513    To amend the Export Administration Act of 1969 by assigning to Secretary of Defense the primary responsibility for identifying the types of technologies and goods that should be controlled for national security purposes. Provides for stiffer export controls for critical technologies. Roe (R-NJ), 1/5/81. To Foreign Affairs and Armed Services Committees.

H.R. 1805   Commercial Use of Sound Recordings Amendment, also known as the "Pay-For-Play Bill." To give copyright owners of sound recordings (usually performers or record companies) public performance rights in these works. Currently, copyright owners of songs and music (song and music writers) have public performance rights in their works. Bill distinguishes these two sets of rights (rights in "sound recordings" and rights in "literary, musical, or dramatic works") as separate and independent. Bill would require broadcasters (and others) to pay a royalty fee to performers/producers of records whenever they play these records over the air (through the mechanism of a compulsory license). Currently, broadcasters pay such a fee to copyright owners of songs through BMI and ASCAP. The new fees would be in addition to these. One of the arguments given in favor of this bill was that 65 foreign countries have established such rights, and that other nations will not pay royalties to our performers unless we give their performers similar rights. Hearing 5/20/81.

H.R. 1957   International Communications Reorganization Act of 1981. A bill to reorganize the international communications activities of the Federal Government. English (D-OK), 2/19/81. To Government Operations Committee; hearings 3/31/81 and 4/2/81. To Committee of the Whole, 7/16/81.

* Asterisks indicate bills which have become Public Law.

*H.R. 2007    Public Law 97-366. Copyright Office Fees, Performance Rights, and Commissioner of Patents and Trademarks. See under listing for Public Laws.

*H.R. 2108    Public Law 97-366. Copyright Office Fees, Performance Rights, and Commissioner of Patents and Trademarks. See under listing for Public Laws.

H.R. 3137    Information Science and Technology Act of 1981. To maintain and enhance U.S. leadership in information science and technology by establishing an Institute for Information Policy and Research to address national information policy issues; to provide a forum for the interaction of government, industry, and commerce, and educational issues in the formulation of national information policy options; to provide a focus and mechanism for planning and coordinating Federal research and development activities related to information science and technology; and to amend the National Science and Technology Policy, Organization, and Priorities Act of 1976 to create a new position of Special Assistant for Information Technology and Science Information. Brown (D-CA), 4/8/81. To Science and Technology Committee. Hearings by Science, Research, and Technology Subcommittee 5/27, 5/28, and 6/9/81.

*H.R. 3239    Public Law 97-259. Communications Act of 1934, Amendment. See listing under Public Laws.

*H.R. 3486    Public Law 96-440. First Amendment Privacy Protection Act of 1979. A bill to limit governmental search and seizure of privately-owned documentary materials. Kastenmeier (D-WI), 4/5/79. To Judiciary Committee. Hearings held by Courts, Civil Liberties, and the Administration of Justice Subcommittee, 4/24, 4/25, and 4/31/79. Reported out of Subcommittee as amended 2/26/80. Reported as amended by Judiciary Committee 4/17/80. H.Rept. No. 96-1064 filed by Judiciary Committee and referred to Committee of Whole House. Bill passed as amended, and was incorporated into S. 1790, 9/22/80.

*H.R. 3567    Public Law 97-145. Export Administration Amendments Act of 1981. See listing under Public Laws.

H.R. 4177    Communications Act of 1923, Amendment. A bill to amend the Act to authorize the Federal Communications Commission to regulate the entry of foreign telecommunications carriers into domestic U.S. telecommunications markets upon terms which are reciprocal with terms under which U.S. telecommunications carriers are permitted entry into the foreign markets involved. English (D-OK), 7/16/81. To Energy and Commerce Committee.

273

H.R. 4225   Communications Act of 1934, Amendment. A bill to amend the Act to establish certain limitations relating to the ownership of cable television franchises by certain foreign entities. Walgren (D-PA), 7/21/81. To Energy and Commerce Committee.

*H.R. 4242   Public Law 97-34. Economic Recovery Act of 1934. See listing under Public Laws.

H.R. 4326   A bill to establish a National Commission to study the scientific and technological implications of information technology in education. Scheuer (D-NY), 6/5/79. To Education and Labor, and Science and Technology Committees. Hearing by Science, Research, and Technology Subcommittee, 10/9/79.

*H.R. 4441   Public Law 97-366. Copyright Office Fees, Performance Rights, and Commissioner of Patents and Trademarks. See listing under Public Laws.

H.R. 4564   Uniform Federal Research and Development Utilization Act of 1981. To promote patent protection and the commercial use of new technologies resulting from federally-sponsored research. Requires the Office of Science and Technology Policy (OSTP) to upgrade planning and administration of federal programs pertaining to inventions, patents, trademarks, copyrights, and rights in technical data. Specifies conditions under which government or contractor will own the invention, and conditions for licensing of federally-owned patents. Ertel (D-PA), 9/23/81. To Judiciary and Science and Technology Committees. Hearing, 9/30/81. Reported out of committee, 12/10/81 (H.Rept. No. 97-379, Pt.1).

H.R. 4590   To amend the Export Administration Act of 1969. Provides stiffer export controls for critical technologies. Similar to H.R. 513. Dornan (R-CA), 9/24/81. To Foreign Affairs Committee.

*H.R. 4672   Public Law 96-480. Stevenson-Wydler Technology Innovation Act. See listing under Public Laws.

H.R. 4801   Communications Act of 1934, Amendment.Record Carrier Competition Act of 1981. A bill to amend the Communications Act to eliminate certain provisions relating to consolidations or mergers of telegraph and record carriers, and to create a fully competitive marketplace in record carriage, and for other purposes. Wirth (D-CO), 10/22/81. Ordered reported, as amended, by Telecommunications, Consumer Protection, and Finance Subcommittee, 10/22/81. This bill was changed to H.R. 4927 by House Energy and Commerce Committee.

*H.R. 4814   Public Law 97-241. Department of State Authorization for FY 1982 and 1983. See listing under Public Laws.

274

*H.R. 4927    Public Law 97-130. Record Carrier Competition Act of 1981. A bill to amend the Communications Act of 1934 to eliminate certain provisions relating to consolidations or mergers of telegraph and record carriers and to create a fully competitive marketplace in record carriage, and for other purposes. Wirth (D-CO), 12/08/81. To Energy and Commerce Committee. This measure was incorporated into S.271, which passed in lieu of H.R. 4927, 12/8/81.

H.R. 4934    To amend the Export Administration Act of 1969. Similar to H.R. 513. Introduced by Dornan (R-CA), 11/10/81. To Foreign Affairs Committee.

H.R. 5158    Telecommunications Act of 1981. A bill to amend the Communications Act of 1934 to revise provisions of the Act relating to deregulation of certain types of telecommunications carriers and services, and for other purposes. Wirth (D-CO), 7/20/82. Markup by Committee on Energy and Commerce, 7/13-15, 20/82. Wirth abandoned efforts to pass the bill on 7/20/82, citing AT&T's campaign of fear and distortion.

H.R. 5205    Would amend 1954 IRS Code to deny the deduction for amounts paid for advertisements carried by foreign broadcast undertakings. Prohibition of deductions would only be directed against advertisements appearing in countries which deny similar deductions for advertisements placed with a U.S. broadcaster. Conable (R-NY), 12/14/81. Similar to S. 2051. To Ways and Means Committee.

H.R. 5254    National Engineering and Science Manpower Act of 1982. Federal Agencies required to establish training programs for technical and engineering personnel, and to cooperate on this same issue with State and local governments. Establishes coordinating council on engineering and scientific manpower and education in NSF. Authorizes funds. Fuqua (D-FL), 12/16/81. To Science and Technology Committee. Hearing 4/27/82.

H.R. 5383    Gives trade negotiating priority to service sector issues and changes trade laws to deal more efficiently with service sector problems. Bill claims that 75 percent of non-farm labor and 54 percent of GNP is in services. Also that productivity in services grew 20 percent from 1967-1979, far more than in goods-producing sector. Also claims a $36 billion trade surplus in services compared to a $25 billion trade deficit in merchandise trade. Claims that trade barriers have hurt U.S. exports in this area and requires the U.S. Trade Representative and the Secretary of Commerce to take service sector issues more seriously. Commerce is required to develop a data base of service sector statistics and trade, analyze U.S. regulatory and tax policy concerning the service sector, and ten or more other projects. Trade sanctions are provided for those foreign countries which restrict our export of services. Gibbons (D-FL), 1/27/82. To Ways and Means, Energy and Commerce, Foreign Affairs, and Judiciary Committees.

H.R. 5519    Bill is concerned with interstate trade as well as foreign trade. It requires the Department of Commerce to establish a Service Industries Development Program, and requires the Secretary to establish a comprehensive national policy on service sector issues. Requires foreign firms to register and provide data on their activities before they can provide services in U.S. The Secretary of Commerce must then give an opinion on whether or not the foreign country represented by the foreign service firm includes international data flow restrictions. Sanctions are provided when foreign service firms are subsidized by their government to the extent that they sell in this country below cost, and when this hurts a U.S. service firms. Dingell (D-MI), Florio (D-NJ), 3/10/82. Similar to H.R. 5383. To Ways and Means, Energy and Commerce, and Foreign Affairs Committees. Hearing 3/11/82. Reported out of Energy and Commerce Committee 8/19/82 (H.Rept. 97-766 Pt. 1).

H.R. 5573    Computer Equipment Contribution Act of 1982 ("Apple Bill"). Tax encouragement for charitable contributions of computers and other technical equipment to elementary and secondary schools (not for higher education). The equipment can be at most two years old and this incentive will last for one year only. Stark (D- CA), Shannon (D-MA), and Edwards (D-CA), 2/23/82. To Ways and Means Committee. Hearing 7/12/82; reported out of committee (9/17/82 (H. Rept. 97-836). Passed House, sent to Senate Finance Committee 9/27/82. Reported out of committee 10/1/82 (S.Rept. 97-647).

H.R. 5579    High Technology Trade Act of 1982. To authorize negotiations directed toward opening foreign markets to U.S. exports of high technology products. Authorizes the President to reduce or eliminate restrictions on U.S. trade and investment by entering into bilateral or multilateral agreements. Gibbons (D-FL), 3/23/82. Similar to H.R. 5383, H.R. 5596, H.R. 6433, and H.R. 6773. Joint referral to Judiciary, Foreign Affairs, Energy and Commerce, Ways and Means Committees. Trade Subcommittee hearing 7/26/82.

H.R. 5596    Trade and Investment Equity Act of 1982. Authorizes the President to propose legislation to restrict goods or services from countries that do not provide equivalent commercial opportunities, and to negotiate bilateral or multilateral agreements to eliminate barriers to restrictions in trade. Frenzel (D-MN), 2/24/82. Similar to H.R. 5383, H.R. 5579, H.R. 6433, and H.R. 6773. To Ways and Means Committee.

*H.R. 5612    Public Law 96-481. Small Business Programs and Federal Litigation Assistance. See listing under Public Laws.

H.R. 5690    Service Industries Development Act. Establishes a service industry development program in the U.S. Trade Representative's office (not in Commerce like S. 1233). In other ways similar to S. 1233 and H.R. 5383.    Stark (D-CA), 3/2/82.    To Ways and Means and Foreign Affairs Committees.

H.R. 5742    Establishes a National Commission on Science, Engineering, and Technology Education. Purpose is to coordinate a national effort to study the status of such education in the U.S.  Claims we have a national crisis because we train too few people in these areas.  Will bring together private sector, government and education concerns, and issue a report no later than two and one-half years.  Skelton (D-MO), 3/4/82.    To Education and Labor, and Armed Services Committees.

H.R. 5812    Critical Industries Reindustrialization Tax Act.  To provide tax incentives for training skilled labor in labor-short industries.  Amends IRS code to increase tax incentives for those industries where there are more available skilled jobs than skilled workers as defined by Secretaries of Labor and Defense. Duncan (R-TN), 3/11/82. To Ways and Means Committee.

H.R. 5820    The Electronic and Computer Technical Vocational Education Act. Involves grants to states for electronic and computer technical vocational education programs.    Industry's participation in both financing and program development is encouraged.  Bill provides $50 million a year.   Miller (D-CA) and Edwards (D-CA), 3/11/82.    To Education and Labor Committee.

*H.R. 5890    Public Law 97-324. NASA Authorization for Fiscal Year 1983. See under listing for Public Laws.

H.R. 5935    Federal Privacy of Medical Information Act. A bill to protect the privacy of medical information maintained by medical care facilities. Preyer (D-NC), 11/16/79. To Governmental Operations, Interstate and Foreign Commerce, and Ways and Means Committees.  Hearings held by Government Information and Individual Rights Subcommittee, 12/11 and 12/19/79. Reported as amended by Government Operations Committee, 3/4/80.  (H. Rept. No. 96-832)  Hearing held by Health and Environment Subcommittee 4/17/80.  Reported out of Health and Environment Subcommittee 6/18/80.  Reported out of Interstate and Foreign Commerce Committee 6/26/80 (H. Rept. No. 96-832, Pt. 2). Record vote demanded; House consideration postponed pursuant to ruling by the Chair (Motion failed to receive necessary two-third majority), 12/1/80.

277

H.R. 6093    Educational, Scientific, and Cultural Materials Importation Act of 1982. Would treat as duty-free import of certain books, documents, visual and auditory materials, and tools for scientific instruments, provided these have no significant adverse impact on competing domestic industries. Included is duty-free treatment of (1) catalogues of educational, scientific, or cultural visual and auditory materials, (2) architectural or engineering drawings or plans, (3) developed photographic film, motion pictures, and video tapes, (4) sound recordings, (5) certain tools used for scientific instruments. Gibbons (D-Fla), 4/6/82. To Ways and Means Committee.

*H.R. 6168   Public Law 97-215. Extension of the manufacturing clause of the Copyright Act. Kastenmeier (D-WI), 4/28/82. See listing under Public Laws.

*H.R. 6260   Public Law 97-247. Patent and Trademark Office Appropriations FY 1983 - 1985. See listing under Public Laws.

H.R. 6262    Joint Research Act of 1982 (R&D Consortium Program). Purpose is to encourage business to undertake joint research and development with the goal of increasing efficiency and competitiveness. Directs the Attorney General to issue "certificates of review" to joint research and development ventures when and if such ventures do not violate antitrust laws. Edwards (D-CA) and Hyde (R-IL), 5/4/82. H.R. 6262 was rendered ineffective by the passage and enactment of S. 734 (The Export Trading Company Act) on 10/8/82. This bill is also aimed at improving the U.S. export position, and loosens antitrust laws for export trading companies. H.R. 1321, H.R. 1399, H.R. 1648, H.R. 2123, H.R. 2851, H.R. 3066, H.R. 5235, and S. 144, S. 795, S. 871, S. 969, and S. 1068 all aim at goals similar to those in S. 734. Enactment of S. 734 has, therefore, ended further consideration of these bills.

H.R. 6397    Income tax credits for educational, professional, and other non-recreation uses of computers in the home. Gingrich (R-GA), Wolf (R-VA), Hiler (R-Ind), 5/18/82. To Ways and Means Committee.

H.R. 6433    High Technology Trade Act of 1982. Identical to S. 2283. Directs the President to liberalize trade in high technology categories by ending both U.S. and foreign trade restrictions in this area. Shannon (D-MA), Edwards (D-CA), 5/19/82. To Ways and Means, and Foreign Affairs Committees.

H.R. 6436    High Technology Trade Act of 1982. Identical to S. 2283. Directs the President to liberalize trade in high technology categories by ending U.S. and foreign trade restrictions in this area. Stark (D-CA), 5/19/82. To Ways and Means, and Foreign Affairs Committees.

278

H.R. 6623    To amend the Trade Act of 1974 to establish certain limitations with respect to the generalized system of preferences. Whenever the President determines that the U.S. has imported from any country during a calendar year a quantity of articles (in a standard industrial classification) in excess of a certain value, the country shall no longer be treated as a beneficiary developing country, and shall be denied general system of preference treatment. Bailey (D-PA), 5/17/82. To Ways and Means Committee.

H.R. 6773    Reciprocal Trade and Investment Act of 1983. To ensure the continued expansion of reciprocal market opportunities in trade, trade in services, and investment for the United States. The U.S. Trade Representative along with a newly-established trade organization (described in the Trade Expansion Act of 1962) must identify and analyze acts, policies, or practices which create barriers to U.S. exports of goods and services, and direct foreign investment by U.S. citizens, estimating the impact on U.S. commerce. The report must be sent to the Senate Finance Committee and the House Ways and Means Committee. Frenzel (R-MN), 7/15/82. Similar to H.R. 5383, H.R. 5579, H.R. 5596, and H.R. 6433. Joint referral to Banking, Finance, and Urban Affairs, Foreign Affairs, Judiciary, Rules, Energy and Commerce, and Ways and Means Committees. Markup by House International Economic Policy and Trade Subcommittee (Foreign Affairs Committee) 9/21 and 9/22/82.

*H.R. 6933    Public Law 96-517. Patent and Trademark Laws Amendments. See listing under Public Laws.

H.R. 6950    Establishes a National High-Technology Technical Training Program, utilizing the resources of the nation's two-year community colleges to contribute to U.S. economic strength by creating a pool of skilled technicians in strategic high-technology fields, to increase national productivity, to improve U.S. competitiveness in international trade, etc. Walgren (D-PA), 9/30/82. To Elementary, Secondary, and Vocational Education Subcommittee. Hearings adjourned.

H.R. 7015    Office of Strategic Trade Act of 1982. Identical to S. 2837 -- would centralize export administration functions of the Federal Government in an independent Office of Strategic Trade. Introduced by Beard (R-TN), 8/17/82. To Foreign Affairs Committee.

*H.R. 7292    Public Law 97-367. White House Council on Productivity. See listing under Public Laws.

H.R. 8443    International Communications Reorganization Act of 1980. A bill to reorganize the international communications activities of the Federal Government. Preyer (D-NC), 12/05/80. To Foreign Affairs Committee.

H.J.R. 36    A Joint Resolution to Provide for the Convening of an International Conference on Communication and Information, and for Other Purposes. Goldwater (R-CA), 1/15/79. To International Operations Subcommittee.

H.J.R. 515    Joint Resolution to Provide for the Convening of an International Conference on Communication and Information, and for other purposes. Goldwater (R-CA), 3/19/80. To Foreign Affairs Committee.

H.J.R. 108    International Conference on Communication and Information -- Provision. Joint resolution to provide for the convening of an International Conference on Communication and Information. Goldwater (R-CA), 1/22/81. To Foreign Affairs Committee.

279

## Senate Bills On International Telecommunications and Information Issues*
### (1979 - 1982)

*S. 2181    Public Law 97-259. Communications Amendments Act of 1982. See listing under Public Laws.

S. 240    Federal Computer Systems Protection Act of 1979. A bill to make the fraudulent or illegal use of any computer owned or operated by the U.S. Government, certain financial institutions, or firms affecting interstate commerce, a crime. Ribicoff (D-CT), 1/25/79. To Judiciary Committee. Hearings adjourned by Judiciary Committee 2/28/80.

*S. 271    Public Law 97-130. International Record Carrier Competition Act of 1981. A bill to amend the Communications Act of 1934 to eliminate certain provisions relating to consolidations or mergers of telegraph and record carriers, and to create a fully competitive marketplace in record carriage. Goldwater (R-AZ), 1/27/81. To Commerce, Science, and Transportation Committee. Passed in the Senate, 6/22/81. Referred to House Energy and Commerce Committee, 6/24/81. Signed in the Senate and House, 12/22/81. Signed by the President 12/29/81.

*S. 414    Public Law 96-517. Patent and Trademark Laws Amendments. See listing under Public Laws.

S. 503    Privacy Act Amendments of 1980. To protect the privacy of medical records. Javits (R-NY), 3/1/79. To Constitution Subcommittee, Governmental Affairs Committee, and Judiciary Committee. Hearings by the Governmental Affairs Committee 6/27, 8/3, and 11/13/79. S. Rept. No. 96-935, 9/10/80.

*S. 603    Public Law 97-366. Copyright Office Fees, Performance Rights, and Commissioner of Patents and Trademarks. See listing under Public Laws.

S. 611    Communications Act Amendments of 1979. A bill to amend the Act to provide for improved domestic telecommunications and international telecommunications, rural telecommunications development, and to establish a National Commission on Spectrum Management. Hollings (D-SC), 7/13/79. Ordered printing of amendment(s), by Packwood (R-OR) (Amendment 323).

*Asterisks indicate bills which have become Public Law.

280

S. 720    Public Telecommunications Act of 1981. States that the Corporation
          for Public Broadcasting is the appropriate entity to facilitate the
          development of public audio and video programs. The Corporation
          shall consist of a President and six members appointed by the
          President and confirmed by the Senate. Quarterly disbursements of
          funds shall be made to the Corporation by the Secretary of the
          Treasury. Goldwater (R-AZ), 3/17/81. To Commerce, Science, and
          Transportation Committee.    Hearings by the Communications
          Subcommittee 4/6, 4/8. 1981. S. Rept. No. 97-98, 5/15/81.

*S. 734   Public Law 97-290. Export Trading Company and Association Act of
          1982.  Similar to a dozen or so other bills in this area, this bill
          promotes export trade in a number of ways including the following:
          (1) Directs Commerce to provide information to facilitate contacts
          between producers of exportable goods and export trading companies;
          (2) Loosens the restrictions on banking organization investment in
          export trading companies; (3) Provides loan guarantees to exporting
          organizations; and (4) Exempts certified export trading companies
          and associations from antitrust laws. Heinz (R-PA), 3/18/81. Passed
          Senate 4/8/81. Passed House (H. Rept. No. 97-924). (Conference
          Rept. No. 97-644). Signed by President 10/8/82.

S. 865    Privacy of Medical Information Act.  To protect the privacy of
          medical records.    Ribicoff (D-CT), 4/4/79.    To Constitution
          Subcommittee, Judiciary, and Governmental Affairs Committees.
          Hearings by the Governmental Affairs Committee 6/27, 8/3, and
          11/13/79. S. Rept. No. 96-935.

*S. 881   Public Law 97-219. Small Business Innovation Research Act of 1981.
          Federal support for small business innovative research. Directs Small
          Business Administration (SBA) to "maintain an information program
          which provides small businesses an opportunity to participate in
          Federal Small Business Innovation Research programs." Requires
          Federal agencies to increase their R&D activities with small
          business.   Directs the Office of Science and Technology Policy
          (OSTP) to review Federal progress in this area.   Introduced by
          Rudman (R-NH), 4/7/81.   Sent to Committee on Small Business.
          Reported 9/25/81 (S. Rept. 97-194).   Passed Senate as amended
          12/8/81.  Passed House in lieu of H. R. 4326, 6/23/82. Signed by
          President, 7/22/82.

S. 898    Telecommunications Competition and Deregulation Act of 1981. A
          bill to amend the Communications Act of 1934 to provide for
          improved domestic telecommunications. Packwood (R-OR), 4/7/81.
          Measure passed Senate as amended, 10/7/81. Referred to House
          Energy and Commerce Committee, 10/20/81.

281

| | |
|---|---|
| S. 970 | International Trade and Investment Reorganization Act of 1981. A bill to establish as an Executive Department of the U.S. Government a Department of International Trade and Investment. Roth (R-DE), 4/9/81. To Governmental Affairs Committee. Hearing held 6/4/81. |
| S. 1159 | Clayton Act, Amendment. A bill to amend Section 10 of the Clayton Act to ensure effective application of antitrust principles to prevent anticompetitive action by monopoly common carriers. Thurmond (R-SC), 5/11/81. To Senate Judiciary Committee. |
| *S. 1193 | Public Law 97-241. Department of State Authorization for FY 1982 and 1983. See listing under Public Laws. |
| S. 1233 | Service Industries Development Act. Authorizes Commerce Department to establish statistical and policy analysis programs to promote service industry development, including export market expansion. Aimed at making the services industries more internationally competitive. Similar to H.R. 5383 and H.R. 5690. Packwood (R-OR), Inouye (D-HAWAII), and Pressler (R-SD), 5/20/81. To Commerce, Science, and Transportation Committee. S. Rept. No. 97-324, 3/22/82. Amended on Senate floor and passed Senate as amended, 4/22/82. Received in the House, 4/26/82. |
| *S. 1250 | Public Law 96-480. Stevenson-Wydler Technology Innovation Act. See listing under Public Laws. |
| S. 1657 | Uniform Science and Technology Research and Development Utilization Act. Similar to H.R. 4564. Introduced by Schmitt (R-NM), 9/23/81. To Commerce, Science, and Transportation. Hearings on 7/28/81 and 9/23/81. Reported 5/5/82 (S. Rept. 97-381). |
| *S. 1790 | Public Law 96-440. Privacy Protection Act of 1980. A bill to limit governmental search and seizure of privately-owned documentary materials. Bayh (D-IN), 9/21/79. To Judiciary Committee. Hearing held by Judiciary Committee 6/28/80, and reported out (S. Rept. No. 96-874). Passed Senate 8/4/80. Received in the House 8/18/80. Provisions of H.R. 3486 incorporated into S. 1790, replacing all after enacting clause. S. 1790 passed as amended 9/22/80. Conference Report filed by House (H. Rept. No. 96-1411), 9/26/80. Conference Report filed in Senate (S. Rept. No. 96-1003), 9/29/80. Signed in the House and Senate; sent to President, 10/2/80. Signed by President, 10/13/80. |
| S. 1860 | Foreign Surveillance Prevention Act of 1981. A bill to protect U.S. domestic communications from interception by foreign governments. Moynihan (D-NY), 11/18/81. To Senate Committee on Foreign Relations. |

282

S. 2051    To amend the Internal Revenue Code of 1954 to deny the deduction
           for amounts paid or incurred for certain advertisements carried by
           certain foreign broadcast undertakings.    Danforth (R-MO), 2/2/82.
           Similar to H.R. 5205.    To Finance Committee.    Joint hearing by
           International   Trade   and   Taxation   Subcommittee   and   Debt
           Management Subcommittee 5/14/82.

S. 2058    Trade   in   Services   Act   of   1982.     Authorizes   the   U.S.   Trade
           Representative to negotiate the reduction of barriers to U.S. trade
           and   investment   in   services,   and   authorizes   the   Secretary   of
           Commerce to establish an export promotion program for services.
           Roth (R-DE), 2/3/82.   Similar to H.R. 5383, H.R. 5519, and S. 2094.
           To Finance Committee. Joint hearing by Senate International Trade
           and  Taxation  Subcommittee  and  Debt  Management  Subcommittee
           5/15/82.

S. 2067    Authorizes   the   President   to   respond   to   foreign   practices   which
           unfairly discriminate against U.S. investment abroad.  Symms (R-ID),
           1/25/82.  Similar to S. 2094.  To Finance Committee.

S. 2094    Reciprocal Trade and Investment Act of 1981.   Requires the U.S.
           Trade Representative to report to Congress annually on the proposed
           U.S. response to major foreign trade barriers and non-reciprocal
           treatment of U.S. suppliers. Danforth (R-MO), 2/10/81. Similar to S.
           2067.  To Finance Committee.  Reported out of Finance Committee
           with an  amendment (S. Rept. No. 97-483) 6/16/82.    International
           Trade Subcommittee hearing 7/21/82.

S. 2172    Cable Telecommunications Act of 1982.   To permit the FCC to
           regulate foreign ownership of cable under certain circumstances.
           Goldwater   (R-AZ),   3/4/82.      To   Commerce,   Science,   and
           Transportation Committee.    Hearings 4/26-28, 1982.    Goldwater
           Amendment in the nature of a substitute marked up 7/22/82.  S.
           Rept. No. 97-518 filed 8/10/82. NTIA supported S. 2172's attempt to
           provide   a   competitive   marketplace   for   cable   systems   in   the
           telecommunications industry. However, areas not supported by NTIA
           included sections dealing with municipal ownership of cable systems,
           leased channel access for small cable systems, and the sports
           provisions, which call for a regulatory approach to a copyright
           problem.

*S.2181    Public Law 97-259.  Communications Act of 1934, Amendment.  A
           bill relating to the National Telecommunications and Information
           Administration.   Authorization of appropriation of $12,417,000 for
           FY 1983 for the administration of NTIA. The Secretary of State will
           select   delegations   to   conferences   involving   international
           telecommunications matters from representative U.S. agencies

283

*S.2181    (Continued)

involved in such matters, as well as from the private sector. Goldwater (R-AZ), 3/9/82. To Commerce, Science, and Transportation Committee. Measure passed the Senate as amended, 6/9/82. Received in the House 6/14/82. Incorporated with provisions of H.R. 3239 in joint House-Senate Conference Report on 8/19/81. (H. Rept. No. 97-765). H.R. 3239 was signed by the President 9/18/81. See listing under Public Laws.

S. 2223    Multilateral Trade Agreements Enforcement Act. To improve and augment the ability of the President to enforce multinational trade agreements, as well as his ability to retaliate in cases arising under multilateral international agreements. Bentsen (D-TX), 3/17/82. To Finance Committee.

S.2224    Tax credits for business charitable contributions for job training. Twenty percent of cost up to a maximum $250,000 can be used as a tax credit when training handicapped, economically disadvantaged (on welfare or income under poverty level), or displaced workers (because of change in technology). Specter (R-PA), 3/16/82. To Finance Committee. Hearing 7/15/82.

S.2272    Technical Information Clearinghouse Fund Act of 1982. Sets up a Technical Information Clearinghouse Fund to enhance transfer of technical information to industry, business, and the public. Establishes a $5 million revolving fund in NTIS -- basically a line of credit for NTIS during low cash flow periods. It was an administration proposal, approved by the Secretary of Commerce, and sponsored by Packwood to help make NTIS self-supporting. The fund allows NTIS to keep excess cash (unlike the current trust fund) in order to spend it on future capital expenditures, and might increase NTIS's competition with the private information industry. Packwood (R-OR) and Schmitt (R-NM), 3/24/82. To Commerce, Science, and Transportation Committee. S. Rept. No. 97-335. Passed Senate as reported 4/29/82, and sent to House Energy and Commerce Committee 5/3/82.

S. 2281    Computer Equipment Contribution Act of 1982 ("Apple Bill"). Identical to H.R. 5573. Danforth (R-MO), 3/25/82. To Finance Committee. Hearing 5/10/82.

S. 2283    High Technology Trade Act. Identical to H.R. 6433, H.R. 6436, and S. 2356. Negotiations toward liberalizing trade and investment in high technology goods and services. Directs the President to liberalize trade in high technology categories by ending both U.S. and foreign trade restrictions in this area. Directs the Secretary of

284

Commerce to monitor, evaluate, and report to the President on the openness of international trade and investment in high technology goods and services. Glenn (D-OH), 3/24/82. To Finance Committee.

S. 2356     High Technology Trade Act. Bill is identical to S. 2283. Hart (D-CO), Heinz (R-PA), Cranston (D-CA), 4/1/82. To Finance Committee.

S. 2421     Establishes a National Coordinating Council on Technical, Engineering, and Science Manpower and Education. Provides matching funds for over four years to stimulate scientific and math education. Glenn (D-OH) and Cannon (D-NE), 4/22/82. To Governmental Affairs Committee.

S. 2469     International Telecommunications Deregulation Act of 1982. A bill to amend the Communications Act of 1934 to provide for improved international telecommunications. Goldwater (R-AZ), 11/30/82. Would empower the FCC to "classify or reclassify" as regulated any international services or facilities that it deems are "not subject to effective competition." All regulated firms would have to file tariffs. The FCC ordered to reduce regulation as competition develops. Domestic and international carriers would be required to interconnect "with any carrier, facility, equipment, or private system upon reasonable request." Report filed by Senate Committee on Commerce, Science, and Transportation 10/1/82 (S. Rept. 97-669). Placed on Senate Calendar 11/30/82.

S. 2475     Tax credits for charitable contributions of research equipment and services to universities. (Public Law No. 97-34, the Economic Recovery Tax Act of 1981, allows companies to take larger deductions for charitable contributions of equipment used in scientific research, as well as giving companies a 25 percent tax credit of 65 percent of all payments they make to universities to perform basis research.) Bentsen (D-TX), 5/4/82. To Finance Committee.

S.2476     Skilled Labor Training Act. Changes IRS code to allow tax credits for training skilled labor. Skilled Labor is labor that equires 6 months training and no college degree. Credit can be taken only when training workers in areas where there is a divergence of 80 percent or greater between number of trainees and future job openings in the area. Credit consists in 50 percent of first $6,000 of wages in the first year, and 25 percent of the first $6,000 wages in the second year. Bentsen (D-TX), 5/4/82. To Finance Committee.

S. 2827     Communications Act Amendments of 1980. A bill to amend the Communications Act of 1934 to provide for improved domestic and international telecommunications. Hollings (D-SC), 12/10/80. To Commerce, Science, and Transportation Committee.

S. 2837     Office of Strategic Trade Act of 1982. Identical to H.R. 7015. Would centralize export administration functions of the Federal Government in an independent Office of Strategic Trade. Attempts to improve the efficiency and strategic effectiveness of export regulation, without unduly harming U.S. exports. Introduced by Garn (R-VT), 8/13/82. To Banking, Housing, and Urban Affairs Committee.

285

### Recent Public Laws Concerning International Telecommunications and Information Subjects (as of December 1982)

P. L. 96-440   From H.R. 3486 and S. 1790. Privacy Protection Act of 1980. Provision to limit governmental search and seizure of privately-owned documentary materials. Was incorporated into S. 1790 and passed 9/22/80. Signed by President 10/13/80.

P.L. 96-480   From S. 1250 and related bill H.R. 4672. Stevenson-Wydler Technology Innovation Act. Aims to promote industrial innovation by establishing Centers for Industrial Technology (for cooperative industry and university research), and by establishing Offices of Research and Technology in government labs. Includes efforts to transfer technology from federal laboratories to state and local governments and to the private sector, and also includes an exchange program among these institutions for scientific and technical personnel. Budget cuts may have prevented the implementation of many of these provisions for technology transfer. Passed House 9/8/80 and passed Senate 9/26/80. Signed 10/21/80.

P.L. 96-481   From H.R. 5612. Small Business Programs and Federal Litigation Assistance. The relevant section is Title III, which establishes two export promotion centers to coordinate federal information on export assistance and financing, and authorizes FY 81-83 appropriations for Commerce Department grants for development of a small business international marketing program. Passed House 6/10/80 and Senate 9/26/80, (amendments agreed to in both houses 10/1/80). Signed 10/21/80.

P.L. 96-517   From H.R. 6933 and S. 414. Patent and Trademark Laws Amendments. Establishes uniform federal patent procedures for small business and non-profit organizations, including universities. Allows non-profit industries and small businesses to retain title to inventions resulting from federally funded R&D. Contains provision allowing owners of a copyrighted computer program to make a single copy of their own for archival purposes. Bill was virtually passed unanimously in both houses (on 11/17/80 in House and on 11/20/80 in Senate) and was signed on 12/12/80. The 97th Congress introduced bills aimed at establishing such a uniform policy concerning use of federally sponsored R&D for all Government contractors (for example, S. 1657 and H.R. 4564).

P.L. 97-34   From H.R. 4242 and H.J.Res. 266. Economic Recovery Act of 1981. This comprehensive piece of legislation allows companies to take larger deductions for charitable contributions of equipment used in scientific research, as well as giving companies a 25 percent tax credit of 65 percent of all payments they make to universities to perform basic research. Tax credits are also given for 25 percent of all qualified research expenditures. Passed House 7/29/81 and Senate 7/31/81. Signed 8/13/81. (See S. Rept. 97-176 and H. Rept. 97-215.)

286

P.L. 97-130    From H.R. 4927 and S. 271. Record Carrier Competition Act of
1981. Aims "to amend the Communications Act of 1934 to eliminate
certain provisions relating to consolidations or mergers of telegraph
and record carriers, and to create a fully competitive marketplace in
record carriage, and for other purposes." This law amends Section
222 of the Act to allow Western Union participation in the
international record communications market. It also allows
International Record Carriers to compete in domestic
telecommunications. Passed Senate 6/22/81, House 12/8/81. Signed
12/29/81.

P.L. 97-145    From H.R. 3567. Export Administration Amendments Act of 1981.
Included in this Act are provisions which increase the criminal fine
for failing to report that goods exported under a validated export
license are being used by the importing country for military or
intelligence purposes contrary to conditions of the license. Relevant
to trade in computer and communications equipment and services,
this Act exhibits the continued tension between national security
concerns and promoting a favorable balance of trade (as well as
avoiding restrictions on the high technology industries). Passed
House 6/8/81, Senate 11/12/81, passed both houses as amended 12/81.
Signed 12/29/81.

P.L. 97-215    From H.R. 6168. Extension of the Manufacturing Clause of the
Copyright Act. This law extends the requirement that books must be
printed in the United States in order to get full U.S. copyright
protection. Passed House 6/15/82 and Senate 6/30/82, vetoed by
President 7/8/82, veto overridden 7/13/82 (Senate 84-9, House
324-86).

P.L. 97-219    From S. 881. Small Business Innovation Research Act of 1981. This
law provides federal support for small business innovative research.
Directs Small Business Administration (SBA) to "maintain an
information program which provides small businesses an opportunity
to participate in Federal Small Business Innovation Research
programs." Requires federal agencies to increase their R&D
activities with small business. Directs the Office of Science and
Technology Policy (OSTP) to review federal progress in this area.
Introduced by Rudman (R-NH), 4/7/81. Sent to Committee on Small
Business. Reported 9/25/81 (S. Rept. 97-194). Passed Senate as
amended 90 to 0, 12/8/81. Passed House in lieu of H. 4326, 6/23/82.
Signed by President 7/22/82.

P.L. 97-241   From S. 1193 and H.R. 4814. Department of State Authorization for FY 1982 & 1983. The Beard Amendment contains provisions opposing UNESCO's attempt to regulate news content and the activities of the world press.   Prohibits U.S. funds from being used to support UNESCO if that organization establishes policies to (1) license journalists or their publications; (2) restrict the free flow of information; or (3) impose mandatory journalistic standards or ethics. The Beard Amendment directs the Secretary of State to report to Congress annually about whether UNESCO has implemented any such policies. An affirmative report would trigger an automatic cut-off of U.S. financial support for UNESCO.   A separate section of the same Act requests a companion Presidential report on the current relevance of UNESCO programs to American interests, and on the "quality" of U.S. participation in the organization.   Also exempts certain private parties representing the U.S. in international telecommunications conferences from criminal sanctions which apply to federal employees. In addition, this law includes regulations and restrictions on Scientific and Technological Exchange Agreements with the USSR.   Introduced 5/15/81.   Passed Senate 6/18/81 and House 10/29/81; after being amended passed both houses on 8/9-11/81. Signed 8/24/82.

P.L. 97-247   From H.R. 6260.   Patent and Trademark Office Appropriations FY 83-85. Included in other provisions is one which requires a 50 percent reduction in fees paid by independent inventors, non-profit organizations, and small business, thus providing support for small innovators. Introduced by Kastenmeier, (D-WI) 5/4/82. Passed House 6/8/82. Signed into law 8/27/82.

P.L. 97-259   From S. 2181 and H.R. 3239.   Communications Amendments Act of 1982.   FY 1982 authorization for NTIA.   Contains the Schmitt amendment requiring NTIA to study the long range international telecommunications and information goals of the U.S.   Also requires NTIA to study how the U.S. develops these policies. Introduced as an amendment to S. 2181. Signed into law 9/13/82.

P.L. 97-290   From S. 734.   Export Trading Company and Association Act of 1982. A result of a dozen or so bills in this area, this Act promotes export trade in a number of ways including the following: (1) directs Commerce to provide information to facilitate contacts between producers of exportable goods and export trading companies; (2) loosens the restrictions on banking organization investment in export trading companies; (3) provides loan guarantees to exporting organizations; and (4) exempts certified export trading companies and associations from antitrust laws.   Introduced by Heinz (R-PA) on 3/18/81. Passed Senate 4/8/81, vote was 93 to 0. Passed House (See H. Rept. 97-924, and Conference Rept. S. 97-644).   Approved and signed by President 10/8/81.

288

P.L. 97-324   From H.R. 5890. NASA Authorization for FY 1983. Permits R&D funds to be used for purchase of research facilities and capital equipment by universities (and other non-profit organizations if they are primarily engaged in scientific research). Gives NASA Administrator greater discretion to use funds for the above purposes. Introduced by Fuqua (D-FL), 3/18/82. Passed House 5/13/82, and Senate 6/9/82. Signed into law 10/15/82.

P.L. 97-366   From H.R. 4441 and H.R. 2108, H.R. 2007, and S. 603. Copyright Office Fees, Performance Rights, and Commissioner of Patents and Trademarks. Originally duplicating a bill which would allow the Copyright Office to retain only the application fees (of $10) when registration was not successful (H.R. 4441), this law contains several more significant provisions. Besides the application fee provision, the law upgrades the position of the Commissioner of Patents and Trademarks to the level of an Assistant Secretary of Commerce. The reason given for this change was that the Commissioner is an important U.S. spokesman on intellectual property issues. The law also deals with substantive copyright issues by exempting the performance of nondramatic literary and musical works by veteran and fraternal organizations from royalty payments when the proceeds are used solely for charitable purposes. (This exemption was contained in H.R. 2108, H.R. 2007, and S. 603.) Introduced by Rodino (D-NJ) as H.R. 4441 on 9/9/81. After various reports (See H. Rept. 97-930) and amendments, it passed both houses 10/1/82. Signed 10/25/82.

P.L. 97-367   From H.R. 7292. White House Conference on Productivity. Establishment of such a conference. Passed both houses on 10/1/82. Signed 10/25/82.

○

# Abbreviations
## and
## Acronyms

**AID:** Agency for International Development (U.S. Department of State)
**ANPA:** American Newspaper Publishers Association
**ANSI:** American National Standards Institute
**AT&T:** American Telephone and Telegraph Company
**AUTODIN:** data network of the U.S. Department of Defense
**AUTOVON:** voice network of the U.S. Department of Defense

**Benelux:** Belgium, the Netherlands, and Luxembourg
**BOC:** Bell Operating Company
**BT:** British Telecom
**BTL:** Bell Telephone Laboratories (AT&T)

**CAB:** Civil Aeronautics Board
**C³I:** command, control, communication, and intelligence (defense)
**CBEMA:** Computer & Business Equipment Manufacturers Association
**CCIR:** International Consultative Committee on Radio (ITU)
**CCITT:** International Consultative Committee on Telegraph and Telephone (ITU)
**CEPT:** Conference on European Postal and Telecommunications Administrations
**CIA:** Central Intelligence Agency
**COG:** continuity of government (in national security)
**Computer II:** FCC decision of 1980 deregulating "enhanced" data communication services
**COMSAT:** Communications Satellite Corporation
**CPE:** consumer premises equipment

**DBS:** direct broadcast satellite
**DCA:** Defense Communications Agency
**DCS:** Defense Communications System
**DOD:** Department of Defense

**EC:** European Community
**ECS:** European Communications Satellite
**EOP:** Executive Office of the President
**EPA:** Environmental Protection Agency
**ESOC:** Earth Station Ownership Committee

**FAA:** Federal Aviation Administration (Department of Transportation)
**FCC:** Federal Communications Commission
**FEMA:** Federal Emergency Management Agency
**FMNC:** Foreign multinational corporation
**FTTC:** an international record carrier

**GAO:** General Accounting Office (U.S. Congress)
**GATT:** General Agreement on Tariffs and Trade
**GHz:** gigahertz (a unit of frequency)
**GSA:** General Services Administration
**GSO:** geostationary orbit (for satellites)

**HF:** high frequency (range of electromagnetic spectrum)

**IBI:** Intergovernmental Bureau for Informatics
**ICA:** International Communications Association (U.S. trade group of large telecommunication user firms) *or* International Communications Agency (name of USIA in 1979-1982 period)
**IDN:** integrated digital network
**IFRB:** International Frequency Registration Board (ITU)
**INMARSAT:** International Maritime Satellite Organization
**INTELSAT:** International Telecommunications Satellite Organization
**IPDC:** International Program for the Development of Communications (UNESCO)
**IPTC:** International Press Telecommunication Council
**IRAC:** Interdepartmental Radio Advisory Committee (NTIA, Department of Commerce)
**IRC:** international record carrier
**ISDN:** integrated services digital network
**ITA:** International Trade Administration (Department of Commerce)
**ITT:** an international record carrier
**ITU:** International Telecommunication Union
**IWP 41:** Interim Working Party 41 (CCIR)

**JCS:** Joint Chiefs of Staff (U.S. Department of Defense)
**JCSAN:** Joint Chiefs of Staff Alerting Network

**KDD:** Japan's international telephone and telegraph corporation (Kokusai Denshin Denwa Kabushikigaisha)

**LDC:** lesser developed country

**MCC:** Microelectronic and Computer Technology Corporation
**MCI:** a specialized common carrier
**MITI:** Ministry of International Trade and Industry (Japan)
**MNC:** multinational corporation
**MTS:** message telephone service

**NASA:** National Aeronautics and Space Administration
**NCS:** National Communications System
**NORDTEL:** made of PTTs from Norway, Sweden, Finland, Denmark and Iceland
**NSC:** National Security Council
**NS/EP:** national security and emergency preparedness
**NSF:** National Science Foundation
**NSTAC:** National Security Telecommunication Advisory Committee
**NTIA:** National Telecommunications and Information Administration (Deptartment of Commerce)
**NTT:** Nippon Telegraph and Telephone (Japan)

**OECD:** Organization for Economic Cooperation and Development
**OMB:** Office of Management and Budget (Executive Office of the President)
**ORB:** orbit (refers to "ORB-85," an upcoming ITU meeting)
**OSTP:** Office of Science and Technology Policy (Executive Office of the President)
**OTA:** Office of Technology Assessment (U.S. Congress)

**PD:** Presidential Directive
**PTT:** Ministry of post, telegraph, and telephone
**PUC:** public utility commission

**R&D:** research and development
**RAM:** random access memory (computer)
**RARC:** Regional Administrative Radio Conference (ITU)
**RCA:** an international record carrier
**RCCA:** Record Carrier Competition Act of 1981
**RDLP:** research and development limited partnership
**RPOA:** recognized private operating agency

**S. 999:** Senate Bill 999 (98th Congress, 1st Session), "The International Telecommunications Act of 1983"
**SAC:** Strategic Air Command (U.S. Air Force)
**SBS:** Satellite Business Systems
**SIO:** Scientific and Industrial Organization
**SLAC:** Stanford Linear Accelerator Center

**TAT:** transatlantic telephone (cable—always followed by a number)
**TBDF:** transborder data flow
**TDMA:** time-division multiple access
**TRT:** an international record carrier

**UNCTC:** United Nations Committee on Transnational Corporations
**UNESCO:** United Nations Educational Scientific and Cultural Organization
**USIA:** U.S. Information Agency
**USPTR:** U.S. Patent and Trademark Office
**USTR:** U.S. Trade Representative

**VLSI:** very large scale integration (microchips)

**WARC:** World Administrative Radio Conference (ITU)
**WATS:** wide area telephone service
**WEOGS:** Western Europeans and other governments
**WUI:** Western Union International (an IRC)